The Burden of White Supremacy

DAVID C. ATKINSON

The Burden of White Supremacy

Containing Asian Migration in the
British Empire and the United States

The University of North Carolina Press *Chapel Hill*

Set in Arno Pro by Westchester Publishing Services
Manufactured in the United States of America

The University of North Carolina Press has been a member
of the Green Press Initiative since 2003.

Library of Congress Cataloging-in-Publication Data
Names: Atkinson, David C., 1975–
Title: The burden of white supremacy : containing Asian migration in the
    British Empire and the United States / David C. Atkinson.
Description: Chapel Hill : University of North Carolina Press, 2017. |
    Includes bibliographical references and index.
Identifiers: LCCN 2016012016| ISBN 9781469630267 (cloth : alk. paper) |
    ISBN 9781469630274 (pbk : alk. paper) | ISBN 9781469630281 (ebook)
Subjects: LCSH: Asians—Migrations. | Immigrants—Great Britain—Social
    conditions. | Immigrants—United States—Social conditions. | White
    nationalism—Great Britain. | Asia—Emigration and immigration. | Great
    Britain—Emigration and immigration. | United States—Emigration and
    immigration. | White nationalism—United States.
Classification: LCC JV8490 .A9 2017 | DDC 325/.250941—dc23
    LC record available at https://lccn.loc.gov/2016012016

Cover illustration: Cartoon by N. H. Hawkins on Chinese immigration from *Saturday Sunset*,
August 24, 1907 (courtesy of the Vancouver Public Library, image #39046).

Portions of this book were previously published in a different form as "Out of One Borderland, Many:
The 1907 Anti-Asian Riots and the Spatial Dimensions of Race and Migration in the Canadian-U.S.
Pacific Borderlands," in *Entangling Migration History: Borderlands and Transnationalism in the United
States and Canada*, ed. Benjamin Bryce and Alexander Freund (Gainesville: University Press of
Florida, 2015), 120–40, and "The White Australia Policy, the British Empire, and the World," *Britain
and the World* 8, no. 2 (2015): 204–24. Both are used here with permission.

To Charity,
who was there from the beginning,
& Josephine,
who so sublimely punctuated the end.

Contents

Acknowledgments

The process of researching and writing a book is an invigorating and exciting one. At times it is also exhausting and fretful. Like every author, I am therefore grateful to the many people who have supported or dragged me through this experience. I have been fortunate to benefit from outstanding mentorship and would never have attempted to tackle a project of this scope without the wisdom, expertise, and example of William Keylor at Boston University. He continues to be a model for both my scholarship and my teaching. Likewise Brooke Blower is the best kind of critic; funny, fair-minded, and always incisive. Nina Silber also played an important role in helping me envision this book, and her commentary was always perceptive and highly valued. Bruce Schulman's support for my work and the work of so many others over the years is inestimable. Arianne Chernock, Charles Delheim, Lou Ferleger, Fred Leventhal, David Mayers, Brendan McConville, Cathal Nolan, Sarah Phillips, Jon Roberts, Diana Wylie, and Jonathan Zatlin all provided important insights during the early phases, and I am grateful to them for their help.

Conducting research in five countries on three continents was expensive, and I am indebted to numerous grants and fellowships. The Boston University Graduate School of Arts and Sciences provided a Research Abroad Fellowship, which funded my research in Australia and New Zealand. This was supplemented by the Angela J. and James J. Rallis Memorial Award from the Boston University Humanities Foundation. Bruce Schulman and Julian Zelizer enabled my research in Great Britain by sending me to Cambridge University as an American History Fellow, under the auspices of the Boston University American Political History Institute. The Boston University History Department also funded my research in Canada through an Engelbourg Travel Fellowship and provided invaluable support for a year of uninterrupted writing with a John Gagliardo Fellowship. I am especially grateful to the anonymous donor(s) who fund this award. I also benefited from a Summer Faculty Grant from the Purdue Research Foundation during the project's latter stages.

I profited from the considerable knowledge and expertise of archivists and librarians during my research in the United States and abroad, and I would like to acknowledge and thank the staff of the following archives: the National Archives of Australia, the Australian National Library, the Australian War Memorial, the National Archives of New Zealand, the National Library of New Zealand, the Wellington City Library, the National Archives of the United Kingdom, the British Library, the Churchill Archives Centre, the Archives of the University of Cambridge, Library and Archives Canada, the United States National Archives and Records Administration (at both College Park and in D.C.), and the Library of Congress. Those who curate the invaluable collections at these repositories do incredible work, sometimes under unpredictable conditions, and their efforts are always greatly appreciated. Research time in England also meant the opportunity to catch up with family and friends in Leeds and London, and I would like to thank them for their support. Although she will not see the final product, I know that Delia Naughton is proud and glad that I listened. I would also like to express my gratitude to Greg Hughes, Jane Larkin, and Emily Hodgson, who provided an especially hospitable place to stay in London on more occasions than they probably care to remember. I hope that Greg enjoys "our book." Anthony Birchley and Dominic Bishop deserve special thanks as well for offering great company and a comfortable place to sleep.

Generous friends and colleagues who read some or all of the manuscript during its various iterations have made this a much better book than it would have been under my sole custody. The Purdue University History Department is an unusually welcoming and productive place to work, and I am grateful for my companions in University Hall. Will Gray read the entire manuscript and offered characteristically trenchant critiques. Carrie Janney has been an indefatigable mentor and guide throughout my time at Purdue, and I am thankful for her support and friendship. Katie Brownell has suffered with this book for as long as I have, first in Boston and now in West Lafayette. I doubt either of us could have guessed that I would still be able to pester her in person for readings, advice, snacks, and tea, but I am fortunate that I can. Similarly Darren Dochuk, Jennifer Foray, Stacy Holden, Doug Hurt, Rebekah Klein-Pejšová, Wendy Kline, John Larson, Dawn Marsh, Silvia Mitchell, Nancy Gabin, Yvonne Pitts, Randy Roberts, Margaret Tillman, and Whitney Walton provided perceptive readings, good counsel, and plenty of laughs along the way. Debra Dochuk, Brian Kelly, Jennifer Lindemer Gray, Spencer Lucas, and Mike and Janet Vuolo have made West Lafayette an enjoyable place to call home and therefore a productive place to work.

Beyond Purdue I have benefited from the wisdom of many exceptional scholars over the years. They may or may not recognize their imprint on the final product, but their intercessions were nevertheless instrumental. I am of course especially grateful to the manuscript's anonymous reviewers, whose astute and thoughtful commentaries radically improved this book. Paul Kramer rescued me from repeated interpretive whirlpools, and this book owes much to his extraordinary eye for the big picture. Kristin Hoganson and Andrew Preston provided similarly sagacious and greatly appreciated readings of key parts of this book. I would also like to thank Stephen Arguetta, Eric Arnesen, Ben Bryce, Anne Blaschke, D. J. Cash, Mauricio Castro, Kornel Chang, Sam Deese, Zach Fredman, Lily Geismer, Akira Iriye, Kate Jewell, Francois Lalonde, Erika Lee, Erez Manela, Scott Marr, Adam McKeown, Alex Noonan, Meredith Oyen, and Matthew Schownir for their help at various stages in this process. I appreciate the many panelists, commentators, chairs, and members of the audience who shared their thoughts on my work at numerous conferences, workshops, and seminars. Whatever errors might remain are, of course, all mine. The editorial and production staff at the University of North Carolina Press have been a pleasure to work with from the beginning, and I am grateful to them for taking such good care of this book. I sincerely appreciate Chuck Grench's stewardship of the manuscript, ably assisted by Jad Adkins and Iza Wojciechowska.

Finally, I would like to thank Charity Tabol. Charity has sacrificed a lot for this book and for my career, and she has been a constant source of support throughout the past decade. She supported my absence during a long year of research abroad, and she has tolerated my disappearances on far too many evenings and weekends. Not having to endure my "humor" and my apparently "uncanny" ability to find annoying but canonical movies on obscure cable channels is one thing, but earning a PhD while working a demanding full-time job and being the best mother our daughter could hope for requires an entirely different level of fortitude. I hope, in some small way, it was worth it. And to our daughter, Josephine: I'm glad this book is finished because I don't want to miss any more of your beautiful smiles.

The Burden of White Supremacy

Introduction

The Politics of Asian Mobility in the British Empire and the United States

Empires thrive on mobility. The British and American empires of the late nineteenth century were no exception. In both cases the circulation of people, goods, money, and ideas connected imperial cores to distant colonial outposts, compelling diffuse communities into new and existing networks of trade, labor, and capital. Like others before them, British and American administrators depended upon the mobility of settlers and bureaucrats, evangelists and adventurers, free laborers and indentured coolies to sustain imperial ventures over space and time. In ways neither benevolent nor benign, representatives of British and American imperial power cajoled disparate populations into new webs of interaction, transcending boundaries in search of power, profit, and strategic advantage.[1] Recent historical scholarship reproduces these dynamic notions of empire. Inspired by what Thomas Bender has called a "transnational sensibility," examples of circuits and conjunctures are now everywhere we look, supported by similarly abundant evidence of flows, transfers, and exchange.[2]

This book examines a potent countervailing tendency. In the following chapters I analyze efforts to restrict Asian labor mobility in the British dominions and the United States during the late nineteenth and early twentieth centuries. Rather than focusing on the ways in which empires, states, corporations, and migrants carved new circuits of mobility—as much of the recent literature does—I focus instead on the efforts of white settler societies to stanch and restrict those networks. In contrast to the imperial preference for maintaining global flows and apertures, I examine the predisposition of settler societies toward occlusion and sclerosis, particularly with regard to the migration of specific groups of people. Instead of illuminating how global "nodes" and "hubs" facilitated transnational mobility, I examine how white settlers established nodes of immobility to impede the movement of nonwhite migrants across newly regulated borders. Ultimately this is a study of the ways immobility, disconnection, and disjuncture remained salient in the context of transnational, imperial, and international formations that were predicated upon mobility and exchange.[3]

I pursue three interrelated arguments throughout this book. First, I argue that racial militants across the British Empire and throughout the American West enacted regimes of immobility and enclosure in response to the real and imagined mobility of Asian migrants. The networks engendered by imperial agents across the globe allowed the movement of British manufactures, Australasian wool, and Californian gold in the nineteenth century. Those same circuits of trade and capital also enabled—and often demanded—the mobility of Chinese, Japanese, and South Asian migrants.[4] Whether as free laborers seeking higher wages in British Columbian canneries or as coolie miners indentured to the Witwatersrand gold mines, Asian migrants traveled throughout the Pacific and beyond in search of the same economic opportunities that impelled migrants out of the British Isles or away from the eastern seaboard of the United States.[5] Many white residents in these communities nevertheless believed that Asian migrants constituted an existential racial and economic threat whose mobility required urgent suppression.

Second, and in contrast to much of the recent literature, I argue that the resultant restriction movements were largely analogous rather than affiliative, contemporaneous but not usually collaborative. Agitators in Australasia, North America, and southern Africa certainly drew upon a similar cluster of antipathies and stereotypes, which were derived from contemporary European and American discourses on social Darwinism, racial Anglo-Saxonism, whiteness, and yellow peril.[6] Although infatuated by the same exclusionary impulses, local campaigns nevertheless developed independently and idiosyncratically, and collaboration among activists across and between empires was actually quite limited. In each case a distinct combination of political, economic, geographic, international, and imperial considerations conditioned anti-Asian protests, and those dynamics in turn engendered distinctive strategies of restriction. I therefore contend that local, imperial, and international contingencies were often more determinative than current scholarship suggests.

Third, this does not mean that the politics of Asian exclusion were narrowly confined within Australasian, North American, and southern African borders. On the contrary, I also explore the responses of British, American, Japanese, South Asian, and Chinese administrators and diplomats who worked to mitigate the worst excesses of the settler impulse to erect borders against the mobility of nonwhite labor migrants. I argue that these tensions constituted the most conspicuous shared characteristic of colonial and American restriction campaigns. In the imagination of white colonial and American activists, Asian restriction represented a constructive posture that guaranteed the racial integrity and economic prosperity of their communities. In practice these policies inflamed domestic, imperial, and international tensions that undermined the very ties they were designed to strengthen. The friction engendered by Asian immigration restriction therefore highlights the conflict between British, American, and Japanese imperial and international policies that favored a larger measure of mobility and openness, and the aspirations of white settler communities in Australia, New Zealand, Canada, South Africa, and the western United States that preferred stasis and containment.

The causes and consequences of the white settler impulse to restrict Asian migration have received considerable attention in recent years. The literature generally resolves into two broad and often overlapping categories, both of which stress the mobility and circulation of people and ideas. On one hand, much of the latest work comes from scholars of migrants and migration. These studies are especially attuned to migration's transnational dimensions and typically emphasize the circuits of migrant mobility. Metaphors of movement and interconnection suffuse much of this work, which has greatly enriched our understanding of the migrant experience.[7] One study of Chinese migration to California, for example, exemplifies the discursive terms in which Asian mobility is typically described: "The flow of people with different interests and desires was accompanied by the flow of goods, money (as capital and remittances), communication, information, and the bones and coffins of deceased emigrants. These flows—intricately intertwined, multi-directional, and often circular—created all kinds of networks that in turn facilitated further movements and transactions across the Pacific."[8] Thanks to this kind of work we now know a great deal about the lives, encounters, and connections of individual migrants across the Pacific.

This book focuses less on the movements and struggles of individual migrants and more on the international and imperial implications of their mobility and on the repeated attempts of white activists to curtail that mobility. I examine the activities of a diffuse coalition that came together around a shared resentment and anxiety toward Asian migrants. For example, I highlight the colonial, state, provincial, and national legislators and bureaucrats from across the political spectrum who typically agreed upon the urgent need to inhibit Asian labor mobility, even as they disagreed on the appropriate strategy to achieve those restrictions. The newspaper publishers, editorialists, journalists, and intellectuals who both inspired and channeled public antipathy toward Asian migrants also feature prominently throughout this story, along with the labor campaigners who lobbied to cauterize the conduits that permitted migrant movement. This focus on predominantly white, male restriction advocates might seem outmoded given recent conceptual and methodological innovations, but they played an essential role in resisting the globalizing imperatives of empire: theirs was a politics of immobility and abruption that both paralleled and contested the transnational currents that dominate much of the recent historiography.

The second historiographical trend focuses on the motives, strategies, and consequences of Asian immigration restriction in the British dominions and the United States. This literature has an older genealogy that has long recognized the importance of Asian exclusion movements in specific cities, colonies, countries, or regions.[9] The most recent scholarship on restriction practices has adopted an even more capacious framework in common with innovative new work on migrants and migration. Rachel Bright, Kornel Chang, and Adam McKeown, for example, have all documented the transnational dimensions of specific Asian restriction efforts and their implications for imperialism and globalization.[10] Similarly, in their book *Drawing the Global Colour Line*, Marilyn Lake and Henry Reynolds trace the networks through which conceptions of Asian inferiority and exclusion traveled, ideas that, they argue, connected white settlers in a "larger frame of transnational solidarities."[11]

Yet this transnational frame tempts us to overstate the extent to which anti-Asian initiatives and campaigns were characterized by solidarity, empathy, and cooperation among white militants across North America, Australasia, and southern Africa. Strategies of Asian immigration restriction were often less mobile than these scholars contend. As the following chapters demonstrate, the transnational white solidarity and collusion flaunted by contemporaries such as the American eugenicist Lothrop Stoddard and emphasized by scholars like Lake and Reynolds was often more aspirational than real: an ambition that floundered before the dictates of local politics, British imperial responsibilities, and international realpolitik.[12] Indeed the enactment of legislative restriction was just as often characterized by autonomy and disagreement as by coordination and cooperation. Sometimes such solidarities were in fact actively curbed and resisted, even by ardent advocates of restriction. Moreover this transnational framework still largely portrays Asian immigration restriction as a globally inflected story of interchange and connection. Instead of emphasizing the mobility of migrants, it underscores the mobility of racial stereotypes, anxieties, and exclusion strategies. Extensive archival research in Australia, Great Britain, Canada, and New Zealand leads me to conclude that white restriction regimes were often much less collaborative and much more autochthonous than recent scholarship suggests. Each campaign against Asian mobility did, however, share one thing in common: they all provoked imperial and international discord and antagonism. Disharmony was therefore the one constant, underlying commonality that united these otherwise distinct restriction regimes.

Studies that accentuate transnationalism and global connectivity certainly admit the many limits on integration that characterized the period. Scholars of this period also acknowledge that catastrophic events could violently decelerate or even reverse the pace of global integration—none more viciously than the First World War—and that powerful countercurrents like protectionism, nationalism, and racism routinely inhibited transnational flows. Yet the discursive core of these studies still usually pivots around a context of increasing globalization and transnationalism, albeit one sometimes limited in scope and buffeted by resistance. As Tony Ballantyne and Antoinette Burton insist, "we must be careful not to ascribe the outcome of every event, idea, practice, or policy to an inevitably imperial global hegemony without attention to the kind of contingencies and ruptures to which we understand all histories to be subject."[13] The "contingencies and ruptures" that characterized anti-immigration politics across the British Empire and the American West constitute the core of this book.

I do not deny the existence of a "world connecting," to borrow the title of an important collaborative global history of the period.[14] Instead I recast Asian immigration restriction as one of the most significant and divisive corollaries to that interconnectedness in the early twentieth century. By placing immobility and enclosure at the interpretive and historiographical center of the discussion, *The Burden of White Supremacy* complements rather than repudiates much of the recent literature on migration, empire, and international relations history. In that regard this study goes against the grain of current historical scholarship in the same way that its subjects—militant white laborers, legislators, intellectuals, and newspaper editors—defied the tendency toward global interdependence that animated many of their contemporaries.

The Politics of Japanese and South Asian Restriction

My book emphasizes efforts to restrict migrants from Japan and India rather than those from China. When earlier efforts to exclude Chinese migrants are separated from later campaigns to restrict Japanese and South Asians, the differences in both the rationales and strategies of restriction across white settler communities become much clearer. The politics of Chinese exclusion surfaced in the 1850s following the arrival of Chinese immigrants on the goldfields of California, British Columbia, Australia, and New Zealand and crested in the 1880s with the widespread adoption of restrictive legislation across these white enclaves in the Pacific. In response to perceived Chinese influxes, colonial, state, and provincial governments in the Australasian colonies, Canada, and the western United States imposed a host of regulations that significantly curtailed Chinese labor migration. Tonnage ratios restricted interoceanic mobility, head taxes inflicted prohibitive costs on individual immigrants, and exorbitant license fees priced Chinese laborers out of lucrative labor markets.[15] By the end of the 1880s colonial and American legislatures had effectively neutralized legal Chinese immigration networks in their communities using these overt exclusion strategies. Diplomatically weak and rent by internal turmoil, the slowly decaying Qing regime rarely prevailed in its efforts to moderate these discriminatory impositions upon its subjects, although determined individual migrants continually challenged these obstacles for years to come.[16]

While earlier colonial and American strategies of explicit Chinese labor containment bore many resemblances to one another, later struggles to restrict Japanese and South Asians were characterized by a greater degree of variation. This was due in large part to a more complex interplay of local, imperial, and international considerations. British diplomacy vis-à-vis the emerging Meiji Empire—exemplified by the 1902 Anglo-Japanese Alliance—limited the possibilities available to advocates of Japanese restriction in the settler colonies. This unprecedented pact recognized Japan's regional power, entangled British and Japanese policy in East Asia, and diminished the Royal Navy's role in the Pacific, leaving many white Australasians bereft at Great Britain's apparent abandonment of their interests and physical safety to the Japanese.[17] Given the complex racial politics of the empire, British authorities were also intolerant toward colonial restrictions on South Asian immigration. Similarly the rhetorical and legislative embarrassments propounded by western restrictionists exacerbated the American government's increasingly strained relationship with Japan, just as Americans were projecting their commercial and naval power into the central and western Pacific. These factors ensured that state and colonial prescriptions against Japanese and South Asian migration were subject to greater scrutiny and resistance than earlier assaults on Chinese migrants. White activists throughout the Pacific therefore deployed a much wider range of devices in their efforts to restrain Japanese and South Asian mobility, and they differed in each community. Alternatively brazen and stealthy, these included employment controls, literacy tests, bilateral and multilateral agreements, administrative procedures, judicial regulations, and even violence.

Japanese authorities proved especially resistant to restriction as the strength and reach of their empire grew in the late nineteenth century. Keen to avoid the fate that befell so many of their neighbors, Meiji officials pursued expansionist policies that culminated in decisive military victories against China and Russia in 1895 and 1905, respectively. These successful campaigns ensured Japanese suzerainty over the Korean peninsula and established a formidable military and colonial presence on the East Asian mainland and the island of Formosa. At once both defensive and aggrandizing, Japanese imperialism contained the same ironies that have bedeviled empires throughout history. Regional expansionism strengthened the Meiji state and prevented the foreign colonization of the Japanese islands, but it also exacerbated competition with rival European and American imperial projects in East, South, and Southeast Asia.[18]

Japanese expansionism—bolstered by both indigenous and imported conceptions of empire and civilization—also propelled Japanese settlers, laborers, manufacturers, merchants, and diplomats into a deeper engagement with the world in the late nineteenth century.[19] Successful restrictions on Chinese mobility further stimulated the movement of Japanese migrants, as labor-intensive industries that had previously contracted Chinese workers turned toward alternatives sources of Asian labor after the Meiji government eliminated emigration constraints in 1885.[20] Campaigns to restrict Japanese migrant mobility intensified throughout the Pacific's white communities as the pace of Meiji military and economic assertiveness quickened in the first years of the new century. Motivated by overlapping calculations of power, prosperity, and prestige Japanese officials assiduously defended the rights of their emigrants to expect respectful treatment abroad as subjects of a civilized emergent power.

As part of this broader effort to project Japanese influence overseas, the Meiji government also labored to expunge the indignities inflicted by four decades of unequal treatment by Western powers. In the 1890s the Japanese sought revisions of the asymmetrical treaties imposed by the United States, Great Britain, Russia, France, and the Netherlands during the 1850s (and later by Prussia). Japanese diplomats successfully negotiated new treaties of commerce and navigation with Great Britain and the United States in July and November 1894, respectively. These agreements began the process of abolishing extraterritoriality for Britons and Americans in Japan and established conditions whereby the Meiji government would eventually regain control of its tariffs.[21]

The first provision of each treaty also guaranteed Japanese freedom of movement throughout the British and American empires. Japanese officials therefore based their future protests against restriction upon the protections afforded by these agreements. Article I of the Anglo-Japanese Treaty stated, in language mirrored in its Japanese-American analogue, "The subjects of each of the two high contracting parties shall have full liberty to enter, travel or reside in any part of the dominions and possessions of the other contracting party, and shall enjoy full and perfect protection for their persons and property."[22]

Japanese mobility rights were in fact circumscribed from the outset. In the British case the self-governing colonies refused to join when invited by the British and Japanese governments in 1895 because they would not concede Japanese rights of admission, domicile, and employment in their communities. Colonial reluctance persisted even after Japan and Britain modified the treaty and the Japanese Foreign Ministry assured the colonies that their adherence would not result in "the immigration of countless Japanese subjects."[23] In fact the modified treaty exempted British colonies from the right of entry provisions, and Queensland, New South Wales, and Victoria finally adhered on this basis in 1896. Nevertheless New Zealand, Canada, and the remaining Australian colonies refused to accept even these generous new terms.[24] In the American case discussions between the State Department and the Japanese Foreign Ministry culminated in an amendment to the Japanese-American treaty in October 1894. The modified agreement included a new provision stating that nothing in the treaty "in any way affects the laws, ordinances and regulations with regard to . . . the immigration of laborers . . . which are in force or which may hereafter be enacted in either of the two countries."[25] These concessions engraved a painful contradiction onto Anglo-Japanese and Japanese-American relations.

The British government also resented restrictions on South Asian migrants, who were at least nominally entitled to all the rights of domicile and employment accorded other British subjects throughout the empire. From the perspective of white residents in the British settler colonies, however, imperial citizenship excluded nonwhites. During debates in the first federal Parliament in 1901 one Australian legislator contended that South Asians were merely subjects of the British Empire, while white Australians were also citizens.[26] Many South Asians and British imperial theorists begged to differ.[27] If they wished to retain the commercial and strategic advantages of empire,

British imperial administrators were also bound to refuse the urge of white settlers to humiliate South Asian subjects. This contest over the ambiguous scope and inclusiveness of imperial citizenship underlay much of the struggle over South Asian mobility in the British colonies of settlement and even the United States during the early twentieth century. Despite the ostensible success of Chinese exclusion, then, Asian immigration restriction remained an extraordinarily difficult imperial and diplomatic problem, with profound implications for the British Empire, the United States, and international relations in general.

My emphasis on Japanese and South Asian migration also explains why this book begins in 1896, after the fait accompli of Chinese exclusion and just as campaigns against Japanese and South Asian immigration reached a sustained and critical point in Britain's self-governing dominions, necessitating the imperial government's intervention the following year. That is also why this book ends in 1924, when the legislative architecture of Japanese and South Asian restriction finally stabilized throughout the British Empire's white dominions and in the United States.[28] The years in between were marked by almost constant domestic, imperial, and international disputes, as the struggle over exactly how to enact the white supremacist yearnings of far-flung British colonists and agitated western Americans waxed and waned in the face of British imperial liabilities, the imperatives of American foreign relations, and Japanese and South Asian mobility and resistance. These quarrels permeated the formative deliberations over Australian nationhood in 1901; they conditioned Theodore Roosevelt's efforts to project American power in the early twentieth century; they festered during the Great War's calamitous bloodletting; and they pervaded postwar discussions at every level, from the halls of Versailles to the committee chambers of national legislatures.

The Motives and Scope of Asian Immigration Restriction

The question remains: Why did Asian mobility engender such profound anxiety among the Pacific's white settlers? The objectives and rationales espoused by those who preached restriction were multifaceted but generally settled into a combination of racial, economic, and strategic apprehensions. Those anxieties were inextricably entangled, steeped in contradiction, and embedded in the politics and culture of white settler societies. Racial concerns informed economic arguments against Asian immigration and vice versa, and assumptions of racial difference and fear of economic competition always permeated strategic concerns. Taken together these compulsions inspired the white settler predisposition toward Asian immobility and containment.

A commitment to white mobility and nonwhite immobility was in fact central to the logic of settler colonialism as practiced throughout the British and American empires: populating the earth's "empty spaces" with white bodies necessitated expunging or prohibiting the movement and settlement of nonwhite bodies.[29] Having secured these lands, white immigrants had to become white settlers, as James Belich argues in his wide-ranging study of this process. Belich contends that a loose ideology of formal and informal "settlerism" facilitated this "settler transition."[30] In this respect, then, the white settler's alleged permanence on newly annexed colonial and frontier landscapes around the Pacific's temperate fringes stood in contrast to the Asian migrant's purported transience. The former demonstrated commitment to the political, cultural, and economic cultivation of these territories, while the latter's mobility and ethnicity marked them as sojourners who expatriated wealth that belonged in white coffers and communities. As Lorenzo Veracini contends, migrants in settler societies typically do not "enjoy inherent rights and are characterized by a defining lack of sovereign entitlement."[31] Contrary to the acquired nativity and rootedness of white settlers, Asian migrants were depicted as irrevocably foreign usurpers.[32]

In this context race was not simply synonymous with color, although color was certainly a significant and dependable marker of difference. The nineteenth-century racial lexicon encompassed everything from the quality of a nation's civic and political institutions to an individual's capacity for morality. Race in this sense was seen as a reliable indicator of political, cultural, social, and economic dynamism, the raw material of an individual's and a nation's potential vigor and "fitness." Whites were uniquely moral, civilized, and capable of self-government, whereas *nonwhites* were depraved, uncivilized, and predisposed toward authoritarian rule. The surest path to racial degeneration was simple proximity to supposedly inferior races. Allowing Asia's multitudes to settle in "white men's countries" was tantamount to racial suicide.[33]

But here was one of white supremacy's abiding contradictions. At its core, white supremacy on the periphery of European and American settlement was fragile, apprehensive, and insecure. These anxieties were inherent in the logic of scientific racism, which promised all the glory of conquest and domination while simultaneously warning of racial decline. Racial supremacy was an ongoing and often tenuous process that required perpetual vigilance, continual reinforcement, and vigorous preservation. For this reason a sense of impending racial disaster pervaded the rhetoric of Asian restriction through-out Britain's self-governing dominions and the American West by the turn of the twentieth century, even as white militants celebrated the fortunate cir-cumstances of their birth.

Economic concerns were embedded in these racial fears. In order to pre-vent the alleged degradations of race pollution, the white working man's wage had to be protected against the incursion of inferior races and their detrimen-tal impact on colonial living standards. Fearful of cheap Asian labor, many white racial activists supposed the white man's livelihood would suffer if Chinese, Japanese, and South Asian workers gained a foothold in their communities. Asian immigrants, they argued, worked for impossibly low wages, thereby undermining the white man's living standards and enfeebling his racial virility.[34] This economic rationale for restriction ascribed absolute racial characteristics to Asian laborers, essentializing them as immutably de-based, hyperactive, and cheap.

Here too, however, was a fundamental contradiction. The British high commissioner in South Africa, Sir Alfred Milner, addressed this paradoxical argument against Asian immigration in 1904. At the time Milner faced intense criticism throughout southern Africa and the broader empire for his deci-sion to temporarily indenture over 60,000 Chinese laborers into the Trans-vaal to revive the new British colony's underperforming gold mines. He wrote to Britain's new secretary of state for the colonies, Alfred Lyttelton, in March 1904, "The opponents of Asiatic immigration must make up their minds which of the two self-contradictory arguments they are going to rely upon. The Asiatics cannot both be so bad, intellectually low and morally worse, that their presence will corrupt the native community, and so good, so clever, so thrifty, so frugal and so industrious that even the white man, to say nothing of the poor native, will have a bad chance against them."[35] The opponents of Asian immigration could never reconcile these two arguments, but to them the inconsistency was immaterial. Both arguments coexisted in the rhetoric of anti-immigration activists not only in southern Africa but also in the United States, Canada, and Australasia.

Strategic concerns also impelled efforts to stem Asian mobility. The Brit-ish dominions in particular saw themselves as flourishing beacons of civili-zation in an otherwise benighted sea of barbarism. Nevertheless they were far from the imperial center—and often far from the Royal Navy's protective embrace. This strategic insecurity was especially acute in Australia and New Zealand since those dominions were at the farthest reaches of the British Empire. Proximity to Asia and its millions of "Asiatics" caused particular apprehension, especially when Japan claimed its place among the Great Powers. The more exposed white racial militants felt, the more vociferous their commitment to Asian restriction. In August 1908, for example, as the American battle fleet approached Auckland on its epic circumnavigation of the globe, the *New Zealand Herald* proudly declared, "The English-speaking States of the Pacific are to stay European, and not Asiatic. Whether Japan likes it or not; however China may dissent; whatever Cochin-China or Hindustan, or any other part of Asia, may attempt; the White Man's lands are for the White Man, and for none other."[36]

Despite the *Herald*'s flippant disregard for Asian national sensitivities, some restrictionists recognized the paradoxical nature of their position. Many white Australians in particular understood the tremendous political, strategic, and economic challenges inherent in defending their claim to an entire continent. This was exacerbated by their relatively small numbers—some five million whites in 1901. In the words of one Australian legislator before the Victorian Parliament in 1899, "We have a territory with a suitable climate, but with a sparse population, while on the other hand, we have quite adjacent to our shores hundreds of millions of a very undesirable class of people." How could Australians justify their exclusionary policies over a thinly populated continent while at the same time bemoaning the supposed urges of Chinese, Japanese, and South Asians to escape their apparently densely populated borders? For this Australian these conditions suggested only one solution: "It should be one of our ideals to maintain, if possible, a pure Australian blood, or a pure British blood, or a pure British and European blood, within the shores of Australia."[37] Many of his white contemporaries across the British Empire and the American West concurred. Similar strategic concerns prevailed in Canada, principally in the western province of British Columbia. Far from the federal government in Ottawa, British Columbia's location on the Pacific coast engendered a powerful sensitivity toward non-European immigrants among much of its white population, a concern they shared with Americans in the western United States. Ultimately, as white Australians, New Zealanders, British Columbians, South Africans, and Californians contemplated their respective racial futures in the late nineteenth and early twentieth centuries, they were just as likely to reflect on the fragility of their precarious position as to revel in their roles as colonial masters and pioneers.[38]

Unraveling the Imperial and International
Politics of Immobility

In the first three chapters I analyze the establishment and consequences of new Asian restriction regimes in Australasia, southern Africa, and North America from 1896 to 1908. Activists in each of these sites strove to limit the Japanese, Chinese, and South Asian labor mobility that purportedly threatened their borders. These largely separate campaigns were each inspired by a lattice of diverse motivations and relationships that resulted in distinct politics and policies. Australasians employed literacy tests to preemptively stanch potential networks of Japanese and South Asian migration in their colonies before they could establish a foothold. In southern Africa local, regional, and imperial activists tried to prevent the imposition of Asian migration by fiat when colonial administrators and mine owners imported Chinese indentured labor to stimulate development in the Transvaal. In North America, British Columbian legislators thwarted new conduits of Japanese and South Asian labor mobility by limiting access to occupations and livelihoods; Californians tried to immobilize existing Asian migrant communities through segregation; and protestors on both sides of the Canadian-U.S. border adopted extralegal strategies of violence and intimidation. Despite these different rationales, tactics, and implications, these cases nevertheless shared one thing in common; they agitated imperial relationships and inflamed international tensions across the Pacific and the Atlantic oceans. The first half of the book ends by exploring the failure of efforts to foster colonial, American, and British collusion against Asian mobility in 1907 and 1908.

In chapter 1 I analyze the architecture and implications of Japanese and South Asian restriction in Australia and New Zealand from 1896 to 1901. The explicit legislative controls on Asian mobility imposed by these colonies in the late nineteenth century troubled the British, Japanese, and Indian governments, all of which sought to moderate the impolitic expression of white colonial anxieties. To this end the secretary of state for the colonies, Joseph Chamberlain, prevailed upon the Australasian premiers to accept the "Natal formula" at the 1897 Conference of Colonial Premiers in London. This measure—first implemented in the South African colony of Natal—subjected prospective Asian migrants to a manipulated literacy test and represented a compromise that Chamberlain hoped would limit the toxic imperial and international consequences of Asian restriction. New Zealanders and Australians begrudgingly incorporated variations of the Natal formula into their expanded restriction regimes in 1899 and 1901, respectively. They did so only after passionate debates during which some legislators in both colonies adjudged that explicit curbs on Japanese and South Asian mobility were preferable to the Natal formula's ambiguity, regardless of the possible imperial and international repercussions.

In the second chapter I examine debates over indentured Chinese labor importation in the Transvaal gold mines from 1903 to 1904, the circumstances and implications of which derived from an entirely different matrix of local, imperial, and international concerns. Supporters of Chinese indenture believed that tightly controlled labor importation would stimulate the mobility of gold, capital, recalcitrant black labor, and redemptive British migration after the South African War. Opponents argued the opposite, that Chinese miners would breach the confines of their indenture, rendering the new British colony unsuitable for large-scale white immigration. In an ironic inversion of prevailing racial and economic orthodoxy, High Commissioner Milner dismissed the critics' claims. Instead he insisted that Chinese labor would resuscitate the Rand gold mines, which would in turn foster prosperity and attract desirable British migrants, thus ensuring the success of white supremacy in the Transvaal. Put differently, Milner believed that indentured Chinese would unclog lucrative circuits of imperial trade, labor, and migration that would entrench British rule in southern Africa.

In chapter 3 I analyze the resurgence of anti-Asian agitation in North America, where Japanese and South Asian mobility once again inspired anxiety. Efforts to restrain Asian migration in Canada and the United States were modulated by a range of distinctive local, regional, imperial, and international considerations. British Columbia was a vital Pacific transit point in the Canadian West—an essential node of globalization that linked oceans and continents. Provincial white activists worked tirelessly to stop the circulation of Asian migrants through that imperial and international hub after 1897, often against the diplomatic and imperial interests of the British, Japanese, and Canadian governments. A similar campaign transpired in California, when the San Francisco school board resorted to school segregation in 1906, precipitating an international crisis designed to induce federal controls on Japanese mobility. The Roosevelt administration struggled to find a resolution that would placate both the Japanese government and anti-Asian sentiment in the American West. The situation grew increasingly complex in September 1907, when anti-Asian riots broke out within days of each other in Bellingham, Washington, and Vancouver, British Columbia. As these events unfolded, American and Canadian diplomats negotiated separate "gentleman's agreements" with Japan that suspended Japanese migrant mobility and collapsed existing circuits of Asian labor in the transpacific. At the same time, the federal government in Ottawa inhibited South Asian migration to North America by instituting a "continuous journey" requirement on immigrants entering Canada. Since direct commercial travel from India to Canada was impossible, this regulation effectively arrested South Asian migration to the dominion.

Having established the coterminous but largely distinct origins of Japanese and South Asian restriction in the British colonies of settlement and the United States, in chapter 4 I examine a number of unsuccessful attempts to cultivate collaboration against Asian labor mobility in the aftermath of the Bellingham and Vancouver riots. Allegations of American influence in the Vancouver disturbances led to investigations, denunciations, and estrangements within the North American restriction community. More dramatically, in 1908 President Roosevelt attempted to foster explicit Anglo-American cooperation against transpacific Asian mobility. The British and Canadian governments immediately demurred: diplomatic considerations precluded participation in Roosevelt's proposed alliance against Japanese migration. Across the Pacific some Australians and New Zealanders optimistically sought a similar alliance with the United States when the U.S. Fleet visited Auckland, Sydney, and Melbourne in 1908. Others vehemently rejected that notion and chided their colleagues for disregarding Britain's Pacific interests. The response in New Zealand was particularly intriguing. Disturbed by American racial attitudes, some leaders of that dominion's indigenous Maori population resented the welcome extended by New Zealand's Parliament and press.

While the first half of the book considers how colonial and American efforts to curtail Japanese and South Asian labor mobility unfolded largely independently between 1896 and 1908, the second part shifts to a more integrative and international framework. Here I focus on the damage to international politics provoked by these restriction regimes during the tumultuous years before and after the First World War. The imperatives of global war accentuated the tensions fostered by Japanese and South Asian restriction, as evidenced by the *Komagata Maru*'s challenge to Canadian restriction in 1914 and by the deterioration of Australian-Japanese relations between 1914 and 1918. Peacetime offered no relief, and the implications of restrictions on Japanese and South Asian mobility undermined imperial and international conferences designed to impose new structures of peace after four years of unremitting warfare. The immediate postwar years saw the implementation of final renovations to existing structures of Asian immobility in the Pacific.

These experiences before and during the Great War demonstrate the deleterious effects of racial prejudice on the British Empire's integrity and the negative consequences of racially motivated immigration policies for twentieth-century international relations.

Chapter 5 explores the imperial and diplomatic implications of Asian restriction during the First World War. South Asian nationalists challenged Canadian immigration regulations just months before the war's outbreak when they attempted to establish a direct conduit of South Asian mobility to British Columbia. The *Komagata Maru* sparked an imperial crisis when it arrived in British Columbia carrying 376 prospective South Asian immigrants who directly challenged Canada's continuous journey directive. The war itself saw Japan join forces with its British—and, by extension, Australian—ally against the Triple Alliance. During the war Australians' commitment to continental white supremacy generated friction between Great Britain and Japan and also between Japan and Australia. Great Britain and its empire depended on Japanese naval support in the Pacific, yet many Australian leaders still imagined that a resentful and devious Japan coveted the Commonwealth's land and resources. Aware of British strategic constraints, the Japanese press—and the Japanese government—expressed exasperation with Australian immigration policies and derided Britain's tacit connivance in its colony's restrictive policies. Mutual distrust and their respective seizure of Germany's Pacific colonies eroded an uneasy rapprochement between Australia and Japan in the early years of the conflict. Tensions increased as the war progressed, and the fragile alliance was constantly challenged by Australian apprehensions and Japanese resentment.

In chapter 6 I describe the ongoing divisiveness of restrictions on Asian mobility at the Imperial War Conferences of 1917 and 1918, the 1919 Paris Peace Conference, and the 1921–22 Washington Naval Conference. The colonial premiers and the India Office approved a new reciprocity formula at the imperial conferences that tried to efface the underlying racial antipathy behind dominion restriction. At the Paris Peace Conference, Prime Minister William Morris "Billy" Hughes of Australia waged a successful campaign against the Japanese delegation's proposed racial equality amendment, which he believed threatened to resuscitate Asian migration networks. Hughes exacerbated tensions by insisting upon the White Australia Policy's application to the Commonwealth's new League of Nations mandates in the Pacific. Two years later British, Australian, and American diplomats feared that Japan would revive its failed racial equality amendment at the Washington Naval Conference. They were relieved when Japan did not pursue its grievances. Nevertheless the Australian and New Zealand premiers actually defended the previously maligned Anglo-Japanese Alliance during the Washington Conference. They concluded it was safer to have Japan in alliance with Great Britain, lest the former pursue a potentially aggressive independent foreign policy in the Pacific. Ultimately these conferences demonstrate that colonial and American commitments to Asian labor immobility continued to encumber imperial and international diplomacy during the Great War and beyond.

The seventh chapter traces the intensification and final culmination of Asian restriction in the British dominions and the United States after the First World War. The years 1920–24 witnessed the apex of anti-Asian nativism in Australia, Canada, New Zealand, and the United States, as the most ardent advocates of restriction finally prevailed in the decades-long struggle to enclose remaining apertures. Once again each site pursued distinct and independent strategies of restriction that further aggravated existing imperial and international tensions. New Zealanders instituted a remote application procedure designed to ensure that "unsuitable" immigrants were denied entry before they even left their home. Canadians tightened their regulations in 1923 by simply prohibiting all Chinese immigration and somewhat more diplomatically negotiated lower quotas with Japan. In 1924 the U.S. Congress imposed de facto Japanese exclusion through the concept of "aliens ineligible for citizenship." Japan unsuccessfully sought redress for this insult. If Asian labor mobility was a function of globalization and empire at the end of the nineteenth century, then regimes of Asian immobility were a marker of sovereignty and nationalism for white settler societies by the third decade of the twentieth century. Indeed sovereignty emerged as the primary justification for exclusion following this overhaul of colonial and American restrictions in the early 1920s.

Taken together these chapters demonstrate that white militants in the British dominions and the United States spent two decades assiduously constructing restrictive immigration regimes in response to an almost entirely imaginary deluge of color. In the white colonial and American imagination, Asian migrants coveted their vast and underdeveloped territorial expanses and craved their abundant natural resources. According to their most extreme racial delusions, an incalculable horde bristled behind every successful Chinese, Japanese, and South Asian immigrant, poised to breach the opening created by their compatriots. In the view of white activists, only absolute exclusion could avert the racial catastrophe that would accompany even the slightest Asian immigration. Otherwise their white enclaves would eventually yield to the Asian immigrant's supposedly voracious appetite for land, and white supremacy would be fatally compromised by unremitting economic competition, miscegenation, and overwhelming volume. This book unravels the disruptive consequences of that fantasy and reveals the distress it wrought upon international and imperial relations in the first decades of the twentieth century.

CHAPTER ONE

The Language of Immobility in Australasia

A surge of global migration arose during the second half of the nineteenth century. For the tens of millions engaged in this astonishing transfer of people, migration variously represented an attempt to escape the privations of poverty and war, the wrenching theft of personhood that characterized enslavement and indenture, or a chance to pursue new opportunities and experiences. Whatever the inspiration, this immense outflow of human beings forged new communities throughout the southern and western hemispheres, even as it violently dislocated surviving indigenous societies and transformed the African, Asian, and European polities from which multitudes of men, women, and children departed. The mass migrations of this period often reflected the expansive imperatives of both old and emerging empires, the administrators of which sought increased commercial and strategic influence or the alleviation of domestic social and economic problems. This ongoing swell continued to define the colonies established to achieve those ends as the nineteenth century drew to a close.[1]

In this chapter I examine one particular aspect of this world-historical paroxysm of mobility: the supposed threat posed by large-scale Asian labor migration to Australia and New Zealand. Though these colonies were themselves sustained by migration, their governments carefully managed migrant inflows, privileging British immigrants almost exclusively and erecting barriers against non-British—and particularly nonwhite—entry. Many white Australasians especially dreaded the unbridled movement of racially debilitating and economically competitive Asian workers, who circulated through imperial networks of trade and labor with increasing frequency as the nineteenth century progressed. So while the conduits of mobility in the British South Pacific generously expanded for those Britons deemed suitable settlers, they tightly contracted when prospective Asian immigrants approached Australasian ports.

While Canadian, American, and South African agitators promoted analogous restriction policies during these years, the Australasian case is distinct for reasons that existing studies often overlook, either because they emphasize congruities in the character of Asian restriction across the British Empire and the United States or because they focus on Chinese rather than

Japanese or South Asian migration.[2] First of all, a particular blend of anxieties and concerns motivated Australasian activists. Proximity to Asia—and relative remoteness from British naval protection and other centers of white population—motivated the governments of both New Zealand and Australia to enact nationwide systems of restriction that were broadly popular colonywide. Australians in particular agonized about the enormous size and relative emptiness of their continental colony: fewer than four million white Australians clustered along some 16,000 miles of coastline in 1901. These numbers provoked a pervasive sense of demographic, geographic, and racial crisis, especially when compared to the hundreds of millions of potential migrants that purportedly strained against overcrowding in Asia. Conversely the most visceral outbreaks of anti-Asian politics in North America were at least initially confined to western regions of Canada and the United States, where Asian migrants typically settled and worked. Similarly white settlers in southern Africa's four pre-union colonies encountered Asian migrants differently depending on their experience with South Asian or Chinese indentured labor.

In addition the governments of New Zealand and Australia ultimately based their immigration controls upon language literacy tests. They did so after experimenting with more direct forms of racial exclusion and only following pressure from the British and Japanese governments. The debate over the enactment of these educational tests incited controversy in both colonies. As those legislators who preferred explicit racial exclusion complained, indirect restriction via such examinations at least theoretically left open the possibility that some racially undesirable applicants might legitimately gain entry. Australasians were obliged to accept the literacy test as a mode of exclusion in part due to the timing of the pivotal restriction drives described in this chapter. These campaigns crested between two seminal events in British foreign relations: the negotiation of the Anglo-Japanese Treaty of Commerce and Navigation in 1894 and the ratification of the Anglo-Japanese Alliance in 1902. This vital imperial and international context exerted significant pressure on Australasian legislators as they contemplated checks on Japanese immigration in particular during this period. The deployment of literacy tests in Australasia therefore contrasted with remote systems of restriction in Canada and the United States, which eventually either limited migrant mobility at the source or elsewhere beyond the border.

The New Zealand restriction campaign also differed from its contemporaries because very few Japanese and South Asian migrants actually settled there. Instead the impassioned intracolonial and interimperial discussions I examine derived mostly from anxieties about the simple possibility of unrestrained Japanese and South Asian movement across New Zealand's borders. The government depicted new immigration curbs as an urgent countermeasure against an upsurge of Asian mobility that was almost entirely imaginary. New Zealand's immigration controls were therefore prophylactic rather than reactive, preventative measures designed to paralyze circuits of Japanese and South Asian labor in the South Pacific before they inundated the colony. This once again contrasted with the situation in southern Africa, North America, and even Australia, where South Asian and Japanese migrants settled or sojourned in larger numbers in the prerestriction years, thanks to more extensive transpacific commercial relationships, imperial systems of indenture, established migration networks, or the existence of older, more established immigrant communities.

As elsewhere, however, the Australasian restriction battles of the late nineteenth and early twentieth centuries aggravated tensions inside the British Empire and complicated international politics in the Pacific. Left to their own devices, the governments of New Zealand and the six prefederation colonies of Australia would have enacted racially explicit border controls to prohibit all nonwhite immigration in the late nineteenth century. But they were compelled to restrain their exclusionary urges. As subjects of an extensive British Empire that administered considerable nonwhite populations, Australasian colonists were expected to respect Great Britain's manifold imperial commitments. Similarly Britain's deepening relationship with the emergent Meiji Empire—demonstrated first by the 1894 Anglo-Japanese Treaty of Commerce and Navigation and later by the 1902 Anglo-Japanese Alliance—forced white Australians and New Zealanders to defer their basest legislative instincts, much to the irritation of those who advocated categorical racial exclusion.

This dilemma pitted British imperial prerogatives that favored a greater degree of labor mobility and commercial openness against the colonial preference for racial homogeneity and wage protectionism. Sydney's *Bulletin*, an avowedly nationalistic and racist weekly publication, encapsulated the Australasian position in May 1897. Anticipating London's agenda at the forthcoming Conference of Colonial Premiers, the *Bulletin* insisted, "Britain is too remote from Asia to suffer by Asiatic immigration . . . therefore it doesn't care in the least about Asiatic exclusion itself." The periodical's exasperated editorialists concluded that the secretary of state for the colonies, Joseph Chamberlain, would protect British commercial interests in Asia at the expense of Australasians' racial aspirations: "[Britain] can get valuable trade privileges from Asiatic states if it gives their subjects, in return, free access to British territories. And, as the only important British territory that is within easy reach of Asiatic immigration is Australasia, this means that J. Bull would get the commercial advantages for himself, while Australasia would pay for them by being eaten up with the swarming brown and black and yellow millions."[3] At the same time, a Colonial Office official succinctly summarized the imperial government's predicament: "The Colonies wish to exclude the Indians from spreading themselves all over the Empire. If we agree, we are liable to forfeit the loyalty of the Indians. If we do not agree we forfeit the loyalty of the Colonists."[4] The Foreign Office might have issued a similar warning by simply substituting Japan for India. Determined to maintain white supremacy in their distant settlements, white colonists had created an intractable problem that would perturb British imperial and foreign relations for decades to come.

In the first section I examine the New Zealand Parliament's attempt to attenuate inbound Asian migration flows in 1896. The politics surrounding this episode exemplify the tenor and substance of broader Australasian restriction efforts prior to Great Britain's intercession the following year. Despite claims to the contrary, New Zealand's proposed legislation was a preventative measure that divided even its supporters into those who demanded total and explicit Asian exclusion and those who counseled caution and conceded the imperial and international complications that approach would cause. In the second section I analyze the imperial government's response to that bill and others like it throughout the Australian colonies. Chamberlain was cognizant of the prevailing mood and recognized the inevitability of restriction. He nevertheless strove to moderate the toxicity of Australasian laws during the 1897 Colonial Conference in London by insisting upon adoption of the Natal formula, a language examination that disbarred Asian immigrants on educational rather than racial grounds. Australians were reluctant to implement that device. The Natal formula became the cornerstone of the infamous White Australia Policy following federation in 1901, enshrined in the Immigration Restriction Act that supported that policy for the next seven decades. But many Australian legislators initially resented this approach because it did not actually prevent Asian mobility and instead required enforcement either at the border or, in some cases, within the Commonwealth itself. The debate over Australia's formative restriction measure was therefore deeply contentious and dominated by arguments over the appropriate form of exclusion in the midst of a particularly sensitive imperial and international context. The future prime minister of Australia, William Morris Hughes, captured that core issue when he declared during the debates, "We want a white Australia, and are we to be denied it because we shall offend the Japanese or embarrass His Majesty's Ministers? I think not."[5]

Limiting Asian Mobility before the Natal Formula: The New Zealand Case, 1896

On the evening of November 25, 1896, the British foreign secretary received an agitated visit from Katō Takaaki, the Japanese envoy in London. The Marquis of Salisbury reported the Japanese diplomat's exasperation with recently passed discriminatory legislation in Britain's Australasian colonies. Having enacted prohibitions against Chinese immigrants in the previous decade, legislators in the six Australian colonies and New Zealand had recently turned their attention toward Japanese and South Asian exclusion. Katō quite reasonably insisted that restrictions on his country's migrants in New Zealand and New South Wales were both unconscionable and unwarranted given the almost complete absence of Japanese immigrants in New Zealand and the negligible number then residing in New South Wales. Such legislation violated the spirit of the recently concluded Anglo-Japanese Treaty of Commerce and Navigation and served only to distress Japanese relations with the two British colonies. Katō therefore urged the Foreign Office to disallow the offensive statutes.[6] After conferring with his counterpart in the Colonial Office, the foreign secretary promised to veto the Australasian legislation pending further discussion with colonial representatives at the following summer's Conference of Colonial Premiers in London.[7]

Katō's protest came amid a deluge of anti-Asian immigration laws in Britain's Australasian colonies. The previous summer, for example, the government of New South Wales had attempted to expand the colony's existing restrictions, which since 1881 were directed against only Chinese immigrants. The colony's newly proposed bill went much further, explicitly prohibiting the entry of "all persons belonging to any coloured race inhabiting the Continent of Asia or the Continent of Africa."[8] Legislators were candid about the intent of their new statutes. In language that characterized the tone of the debate, Representative John Haynes enjoined his colleagues to "bring the matter forward for final settlement on behalf of the white races of Australia and declare that there will be no divergence whatever from the complete exclusion of the inferior races of the globe from this country."[9] Similarly indelicate legislation was under consideration in the other Australasian parliaments. In each case legislators fully expected the British government to begrudge the insensitivity of their bills toward imperial subjects—especially South Asians—as well as new strategic partners and customers in East Asia. And yet they persisted, convinced that the danger posed by Asian immigration demanded action regardless of British and Japanese sensibilities.

In addition to revealing the intensity, architecture, and implications of Asian restriction in Australasia at the close of the nineteenth century, New Zealand's 1896 measure also exposes three interrelated characteristics of all antipodean restriction efforts before Chamberlain's intervention at the Colonial Conference the following year. First, this case reveals the transition from targeted controls on Chinese immigrants to broader and more diplomatically awkward attempts to preemptively curtail South Asian and Japanese mobility. Officials in both the Foreign Office and the Colonial Office had long tolerated legislative slights against Chinese subjects, who suffered under near-colonial domination with British complicity. They would not, however, countenance affronts by white governments against South Asian and Japanese subjects, especially ones so boldly and emphatically enshrined in law. Second, these discussions uncover the conflicted domestic politics of Australasian restriction. There was widespread support for restriction, but the bluntness of the proposed legislation nevertheless alienated some legislators who correctly predicted that the British government would not condone unconcealed racial discrimination. Others nonetheless believed that only explicitly enumerated restriction clauses could definitively achieve the widely held goal of Asian exclusion. These arguments over the forthrightness of Asian restriction characterized contemporaneous debates throughout the Australasian colonies during this period. Third, this example demonstrates the divisive and far-reaching imperial and international tensions engendered by white Australasians' commitment to limiting the movement of Asian migrants, along with the efforts of British imperial authorities to ameliorate the potentially damaging consequences of colonial racism.

New Zealand's 1896 bill was just the latest in a series of restrictive immigration laws introduced by that colony's government during the late nineteenth century. Parliament first passed the Chinese Immigrants Act in 1881, following two decades of anti-Chinese agitation. That regulation imposed tonnage ratio restrictions on arriving vessels along with a £10 tax on every Chinese immigrant, echoing analogous legislation in the Australian colonies.[10] Richard Seddon, a future prime minister, was instrumental in this campaign, and his fervent opposition to Asian immigration was almost unsurpassed. From his perspective—a perspective he shared with a majority of his colleagues—Chinese immigrants constituted a racial, social, and economic scourge upon New Zealand that threatened to undermine the Pacific colony's predominantly British character and retard its national development.[11]

After assuming the premiership in 1893, Seddon annually introduced bills that aggressively expanded these earlier controls by explicitly prohibiting all Asian immigration, and each time the British government disallowed them.[12] Undaunted by London's intransigence, Seddon once again introduced a restrictive act in 1896. Like earlier incarnations, the new measure correlated Asian mobility with white racial degeneration and colonial economic devitalization. The bill's preamble declared, "It is expedient to safeguard the race-purity of the people of New Zealand by preventing the influx into the colony of persons of alien race."[13] This latest bill proposed further restraints on the ability of Asian migrants to cross New Zealand's border. It called for an increased head tax of £100 on all Asian immigrants, including South Asians and Japanese subjects, and increased the tonnage limitations on vessels carrying Asian migrants from one immigrant per 100 tons to one per 200 tons.[14]

The growing Asian menace threatening New Zealand in 1896 was an invention that rested upon a number of false allegations. The prime minister and his allies portrayed an unfolding crisis instigated by the uninhibited geographic, social, and economic mobility of Chinese migrants in and around New Zealand. Seddon claimed that New Zealand's existing Chinese residents, most of whom had arrived during the midcentury gold rushes, were infiltrating the colony's major cities, where they aggressively competed with white traders and debauched colonial morality through intermarriage, gambling, and unsanitary living conditions. He conjured images of diverted steamers bearing thwarted Chinese migrants across the Tasman Sea following the imposition of new restrictions in the Australian colonies. The prime minister intimated that Chinese settlement was a disease propagated by roving Chinese migrants that required containment. When presented with evidence proving this influx was a figment of his imagination, Seddon summarily questioned the veracity of census statistics and emphasized the Chinese immigrant's guile in subverting New Zealand's regulations.[15] He and his supporters reiterated these fabrications throughout the debate, and his notion of an imminent crisis kept the measure alive despite his dubious statistics.

Yet there was little evidence of significantly increased Asian itinerancy either within the colony or at the border: the apparent rampancy of Asian migrants was a fiction. As the prime minister's critics in opposition complained, the enterprise was partly a political ruse, designed to enthuse the working-class supporters of Seddon's Liberal Party against the specter of wage competition and racial contamination before the looming general election.[16] At the same time, however, supporters on both sides of the aisle sincerely considered restriction a precautionary measure that would mitigate the need for more challenging legislation in the future. For example, one of Seddon's harshest political opponents, Walter Clarke Buchanan, chided the prime minister for his unsubstantiated claims about the rising population of Chinese in the colony, yet he supported the government's proposed legislation, claiming, "It is better to take time by the forelock and prevent them coming, prevention being always so much better than the cure."[17]

In fact this manufactured crisis over Chinese mobility was designed to camouflage the real intention of the bill. Many advocates of the new regulations believed that Japanese and South Asian migrants posed an even greater threat than those from China. The 1896 census had revealed that only forty-six South Asians and fifteen Japanese actually resided in the colony, but in common with legislators throughout Australasia, New Zealand lawmakers aspired to curtail the mobility of Japanese and South Asian migrants before they inundated the southwest Pacific.[18] The bill was therefore designed not only to retard the growth of New Zealand's existing Chinese communities but also to eliminate future immigration from Japan and South Asia. Speaking before the colony's Legislative Council, New Zealand's immigration minister, William Campbell Walker, highlighted the peril posed by Japanese migrants in the region: "They may be upon us one day, and if we do not protect ourselves, of course this colony will be the dumping-ground to which they will first come."[19]

As Seddon, Walker, and others cast their gaze across the region, they visualized the burgeoning migration networks that interlaced the Pacific. They feared those webs would soon ensnare their own colony, exposing it to the putative depredations of large-scale Asian labor immigration. They were particularly concerned about the proximity of Japanese migrant labor hubs that coalesced around the plantation economies of Hawaii and Queensland. The bill's supporters conceived those locations as transmigration nodes from which Asian labor could disseminate throughout the Pacific, depending on the needs of local and transpacific economies. They also regarded these racially mixed communities as portents of the fate that awaited New Zealanders in the absence of strict immigration controls. Seddon claimed that previously imported Japanese workers in Hawaii had almost completely ousted both native and American labor, commerce, and capital. Based on that experience he maintained, "We should profit by it and take every step to prevent the Japanese coming here to New Zealand."[20] To counter that possibility New Zealand would have to become a node of Asian immobility or risk becoming another juncture in the globalizing labor economy of the Pacific.

A dedicated core of the legislation's supporters therefore wanted strict, clearly enumerated controls that would leave no doubt as to the intended targets of New Zealanders' expanded restriction regime.[21] Others counseled restraint. Their moderation did not signal tolerance—most were in fact strong proponents of Asian exclusion—but they understood that such candid restriction threatened the entire enterprise. Two interrelated issues framed the discussion moving forward, the bigger of which concerned the international implications of Japanese restriction. There was broad consensus that large-scale Japanese immigration was both undesirable and dangerous, yet many legislators recognized Japan's growing importance to British foreign policy, and they therefore tempered their public disdain. A second problem concerned the imperial dimensions of South Asian restriction. While some representatives worried that South Asian migrants would soon descend upon New Zealand, brandishing their status as imperial subjects, most recognized that explicit South Asian exclusion would founder upon the British government's commitment to equality and color blindness—not to mention the strategic and economic importance of the Raj—however flawed and rhetorical that commitment was in practice. For the rest of the debate, then, legislators fretted over whom to exclude and how to exclude them, all while trying to avoid British censure and Japanese antipathy.

Seddon's proposal to enact South Asian restriction was doomed to failure from the outset. It was promoted by uncompromising Liberal Party exclusionists like William Earnshaw, who felt that comprehensive exclusion was "in the best and highest interests of our Anglo-Saxon race," and William Bolt, who thought it was absurd that Parliament would consider tightening restrictions on Chinese immigrants without imposing similar constraints on South Asian and Japanese migrants, since "the racial and economic aspects of the question come up in regard to these people just the same as they do to the Chinese."[22] But Seddon had clearly overreached. A majority in the upper house correctly surmised that any explicit attempt to limit South Asian immigration practically guaranteed British disallowance of the whole bill. Appointed to seven-year terms by the governor-general, members of the Legislative Council were not subject to the vagaries of popular opinion, and on this question most were sensitive to the imperial government's wishes.[23] Dr. Morgan Grace encapsulated the Council's opposition. While he accepted that further restrictions ought to be imposed on Chinese immigrants, he also recognized that New Zealanders could not treat Britain's nonwhite subjects so disdainfully. He criticized Seddon's statute as "a Bill which assumes the portentous proportions of dictating to the Empire a whole policy." It was "a monstrous proposition," he scolded, to assume that New Zealand could prescribe terms to the imperial government in this way.[24] Cognizant of London's certain aversion to such unabashed controls, the Legislative Council exempted British subjects from the provisions of the legislation, and Seddon reluctantly relented.

Exempting Britain's South Asian subjects promised to mollify the India Office, but the Foreign Office was unlikely to accept the bill's exclusion of Japanese subjects, and this proved to be the most difficult issue facing proponents of expanded restrictions. Almost every speaker shuddered at the thought of significant Japanese immigration, but many doubted the necessity or wisdom of explicitly prohibiting their entry under this act. It became clear that a schism was emerging between those who favored direct Japanese exclusion and those who preferred a more sagacious approach. As the independent Dr. Alfred Newman (himself born in India) pointed out to his colleagues, the recently concluded Anglo-Japanese Treaty of Commerce and Navigation had significantly complicated their task, and despite his firm opposition to all Asian immigration he cautioned the House against tactlessly antagonizing Britain and Japan. Thomas Mackenzie, another future prime minister, agreed with Newman, warning, "Japan is becoming a power sufficiently strong to cause us to respect them."[25] One of the colony's foremost military figures, Major General George Stoddart Whitmore, similarly warned that New Zealand was still "an insignificant community in the world," especially when "compared to a nation of forty millions that has already proved its power at sea, its power on land, and it has shown that it knows all that can be known in strategy."[26]

At this point Seddon nevertheless tried to resuscitate the broader bill. He informed his colleagues that his government would not accede to the recently concluded Anglo-Japanese Commercial Treaty. He insisted that they were therefore free to exclude Japanese immigrants. With that the bill was read for a second time and debate was adjourned. The bill emerged from committee the following month, wherein Seddon had sponsored a new clause denying naturalization to any Chinese immigrant not already naturalized.[27] On August 27 Whitmore submitted a last-minute revision to replace "Asiatic" with simply "Chinese," but the measure was narrowly defeated.[28] The final version exempted British subjects, but Japanese migrants remained subject to restriction. The bill was finally passed by the New Zealand Parliament in Wellington, only to be predictably disallowed in November 1897 by the imperial government in London.

The demise of this legislation demonstrates the domestic, imperial, and international resistance to such explicit and overt Asian exclusion. Domestically defeat was assured when eleven councilors protested directly to the Colonial Office.[29] Internationally the Japanese Foreign Ministry protested the act through their minister in London, complaining that New Zealand's actions were "wholly gratuitous so far at least as Japanese are concerned, because there are practically no Japanese in New Zealand."[30] Katō was especially offended that "Japan should be spoken of in formal documents . . . as if the Japanese were on the same level of morality and civilization as Chinese or other less advanced populations of Asia."[31] Nevertheless the actions of New Zealand legislators contributed to the Japanese government's later decision to offer the British colonies exemption from the immigration provisions of the Anglo-Japanese Commercial Treaty.[32] Despite its failure, however, the legislative debates of 1896 amply demonstrated the many tensions evident in Australasians' dedication to a national policy of white supremacy through immigration restriction. By the time the colonial premiers convened in London in the summer of 1897, Chamberlain was eager to find a resolution that could accommodate both colonial racial anxieties and the British government's imperial and international obligations.

The 1897 Colonial Conference and the Natal Formula

On June 22, 1897, throngs of British subjects crowded London's meandering streets. That day marked Queen Victoria's Diamond Jubilee, commemorating the sixtieth anniversary of her ascension to the throne. She celebrated the occasion with a procession through the capital's storied thoroughfares. The queen naturally commanded the crowd's attention, although her customary mourning attire contrasted sharply with the exuberance of the occasion, evidenced by the fervent cheers and colorful decorations that festooned every awning, lamppost, and windowpane. According to official sources, the Jubilee was a tribute to the glory and munificence of Victoria's long reign, reflecting "a natural impulse in the hearts of the people of the British Empire to do honour to their beloved sovereign."[33] Reflecting upon that "never-to-be-forgotten-day," Victoria herself marveled at the enthusiasm of her assembled subjects and reveled in their adulation, recalling, "No one ever, I believe, has met with such an ovation as was given to me, passing through those six miles of streets."[34] It was imperial theater at its most lavish and magnificent.

Yet this carefully managed exhibition of imperial unity belied the tensions that simmered beneath the empire's confident façade. Perhaps nobody in the British government understood those tensions better than Chamberlain. Chamberlain in fact played a major role in planning the Jubilee, envisaging an opportunity to bind the empire's increasingly autonomous white self-governing colonies to his vision of an interdependent, mutually beneficial commercial and political union. To this end he extended invitations to the premiers of Canada, the six Australian colonies, New Zealand, the Cape Colony, and Natal, all of whom accepted.[35] In addition to granting them pride of place among the visiting dignitaries, he also convened the Conference of Colonial Premiers to address the challenges that bedeviled the late Victorian empire.

The issue of Asian migration within the empire was the most stubborn problem that chafed beneath the harmonious pretense of the Jubilee, and the proceedings of the 1897 Colonial Conference illustrate how caustic the politics of restricting Asian mobility had become. Keen to assuage the potential harm engendered by Australasian colonists' restrictive compulsions, Chamberlain proposed the adoption of Natal's literacy test as an alternative to the more openly racial regulations previously enacted by colonial legislatures. He believed that this approach would spare British embarrassment vis-à-vis both Japan and India, while still insulating Australasian colonists against the alleged miseries of indiscriminate Asian immigration. The Australasian premiers contested his proposal, repeatedly arguing that nothing less than total explicit exclusion could stanch a rush of Asian migrants. They wanted to sequester themselves from that menace and from the political, economic, and diplomatic arrangements that made it possible.

The secretary of state for the colonies nevertheless called for more openness, not less, when he convened the colonial premiers on June 24, 1897. In his introductory remarks Chamberlain envisioned folding the self-governing colonies into a rejuvenated imperial system, designed to ensure greater cooperation and cohesion. That system would be supported by integrated communication and transportation networks, a secure Pacific cable line, an empirewide penny postage program, and uniform commercial and shipping codes. The creation of a commercial union would further enmesh the colonial economies in a lucrative imperial trading combine, while political federation and increased military cooperation would reinforce the centripetal bonds of empire. It was a bold proposal that sought to concentrate the energies of a diffuse and haphazard global empire across space and time.[36]

However, the colonial premiers harbored a very different array of impulses. They rejected Chamberlain's federative vision and instead turned inward. In addition to resisting calls for greater imperial integration, they also defended their right to immobilize the global flows that facilitated Asian labor migration. As the recent epidemic of legislation in the Australasian colonies had demonstrated, the exclusionary instinct coursed throughout Britain's white settler colonies, and the colonial premiers who traveled to fete Victoria came determined to defend the racial integrity of their respective outposts of Greater Britain, however illusory the objective and however imaginary the threat. On the eve of the Jubilee celebrations, then, Asian restriction threatened to fray the bonds of empire and disrupt imperial foreign relations as white colonial racism collided with Britain's global interests.

Chamberlain resolved to diminish the escalating tensions over Asian immigration restriction, and the proceedings began on a conciliatory note. The colonial secretary assured the premiers that imperial authorities sympathized with their underlying apprehensions. He acknowledged "the determination of the white inhabitants of these Colonies which are in comparatively close proximity to millions and hundreds of millions of Asiatics that there shall not be an influx of people alien in civilization, alien in religion, alien in customs," and he conceded that large-scale Asian immigration would undermine white labor in the colonies. At the same time, however, he gently chided the premiers over the imperial and diplomatic callousness of their recent restriction acts. He reminded them that they were participants in a broader imperial enterprise, one that (at least rhetorically) valued equality and eschewed racial discrimination. India especially had earned the empire's respect and secured a place for its subjects in the self-governing colonies. It was unconscionable, he felt, "to put upon those men a slight which . . . is absolutely unnecessary for your purpose, and which would be calculated to provoke ill-feeling, [and] discontent." Chamberlain then tried to unilaterally moderate colonial rhetoric by reorienting the debate away from race and toward class and social status. He interpreted the white colonial desire to restrict Asian migrants in socioeconomic terms and elided the recent colonial exclusion acts' racial foundations, suggesting, "It is not because a man is of a different colour from ourselves that he is necessarily an undesirable immigrant, it is because he is dirty, or he is immoral, or he is a pauper." There were legitimate sanitary and moral reasons to prohibit prospective immigrants, he accepted, but the imperial government could not sanction white colonists' explicitly racial discriminatory practices given the multiethnic composition of the empire.[37]

Intent upon moderating the worst excesses of colonial immigration policies, Chamberlain offered the premiers a compromise measure known as the Natal formula. This measure represented the modus vivendi by which

colonial racism could discreetly coexist with the British government's imperial and diplomatic obligations. It originated in southern Africa the previous
year, when Natal's legislature had attempted to prohibit free Asian immigration in the same forthright manner as New Zealand and the Australasian
colonies.[38] When the Colonial Office rejected Natal's explicit exclusion of
South Asian and other Asian immigrants as it did similar Australasian laws,
the colony's government swiftly engineered a way to circumvent imperial
objections: the Natal formula imposed a dictation test in lieu of overt racial
restriction. Potential immigrants were required to transcribe a brief application form before an immigration officer, affirming their name, address,
employment details, and date of birth in "the characters of any language of
Europe."[39] Since the immigration officer administering the test was the sole
arbiter of the prospective immigrant's language ability, the result could be
manipulated to ensure exclusion on the grounds of literacy and education
rather than race. Chamberlain believed that this subterfuge would appease
Asian sentiment and ameliorate the imperial and international tensions engendered by outright and explicit exclusion.

The colonial premiers were skeptical; their concerns derived from their
fear of unfettered Asian mobility. George Reid of New South Wales was the
most outspoken. He agreed that colonial legislators should be responsive to
the imperial government's concerns but felt that Australian public opinion
was overwhelmingly in favor of direct action. He refuted Chamberlain's claim
that Asian ignorance or social conditions were the motivating factor behind
restrictive legislation. "We cannot veil the issue that way," he insisted. Reid
instead volunteered that proximity, race, and sheer volume were the true
foundations of Australasian anxiety toward Asian immigration: "Situated as
we are so near these hundreds of millions of coloured people . . . we must set
up at once a clear barrier against the invasion of coloured labour." This purported invasion had already established beachheads in the various colonies.
It was fundamentally a question of national survival, and he invoked a
metaphor of irresistible Asian movement to illustrate his point: "Here is the
coloured flood coming in upon us, and we feel that we cannot have any
holes in the dyke; we feel that we must present a solid front to this danger,
and under those circumstances we feel that the course taken in Natal would
not be one we could follow." Outright exclusion was therefore preferable to
the Natal formula's deceptions.[40]

Reid also addressed the diplomatic implications of Japanese and Chinese
restriction, although Chamberlain had wisely confined his comments to the
imperial ramifications of prohibitions against South Asians. Reid felt confi-

dent that Japan would not object since New South Wales's recent restriction act did not specify particular countries or people. Not without merit, as Katō's later remonstrance against New Zealand's legislation revealed, Reid hypothesized that Japanese antipathy would be assuaged "so long as we do not couple them with the Chinese." Rather more implausibly he also reasoned that if the British government assented to legislation that excluded South Asians it would "remove much of the sting" felt by the Japanese. Reid further pointed out that the Japanese government had accepted the Australian colonies' right to regulate their own immigration policies under the 1896 amendment to the Anglo-Japanese Treaty of Commerce and Navigation. Under these circumstances Reid took exception to the British government's unwillingness to allow South Asian exclusion. "It would be a great disappointment to Australia," he remarked, "if we found Her Majesty's Government as regards her coloured subjects less disposed to meet our wishes than the Japanese Government."[41]

The other Australasian premiers were united on the ultimate objective of immobilizing Asian labor migration networks in order to guarantee total exclusion. Charles Kingston, the premier of South Australia, was unequivocal. His colony also craved "a white Australia, and the exclusion . . . of anything in the shape of servile races."[42] Sir George Turner of Victoria echoed these sentiments, and he too preferred a direct approach. Only explicit restrictions could protect his colony's racial vigor; anything less would permit ambiguity and denude the effectiveness of Australian legislation.[43] Although absent from the July 8 gathering, Prime Minister Seddon had made New Zealand's position clear earlier in the conference. "We claim to have the right to speak for our race, and to express the feelings of our race," he announced, "and we take the action we have taken with no desire to be offensive to the people of any other country."[44]

The conference disbanded without firm resolution, but both sides had clearly outlined their positions. From an imperial perspective, the British government sought judicious legislation—preferably some variation on the Natal formula—while at the same time accepting that the settler colonies would never countenance large-scale South Asian or Japanese mobility in their vicinity.[45] Struck by the potency of the colonial premiers' anti-Asian sentiment, Chamberlain was persuaded that white colonial opposition to Asian immigration constituted a major challenge for British imperial and foreign policy, especially vis-à-vis Japan. Following the conference's conclusion he informed the Foreign Office that without some form of restriction "it would be impossible in communities so democratic as those of Australia to avoid such popular outbreaks against a coloured element, as have been experienced in the United States." Such violence, he warned, would be more detrimental to Anglo-Japanese relations than the actual act of exclusion.[46] The Japanese government itself proved amenable to the Natal formula, and Katō was especially convinced of its efficacy. From his perspective Japanese prestige remained unsullied, providing the colonial governments avoided explicit, racially inflected exclusion laws and as long as they refrained from aggregating his people together with other Asian populations.[47] The colonial legislatures would nevertheless continue to test Japanese patience in the coming years.

The Natal Formula and the White Australia Policy

Chamberlain's compromise promised to mitigate antipodean legislators' most tactless insensitivities, but the actual implementation of the Natal formula proved extremely contentious. Australian legislators in particular engaged in passionate and candid debates when the time came to enact a centralized immigration policy following federation of the six Australian colonies on January 1, 1901. While some members of the new Parliament were willing to soothe the British government's disquiet by moderating their insistence on absolute exclusion, others remained wedded to their racial and economic jealousies and demanded direct exclusions based on race and nativity. The Australian debate was never about *whether* to implement a restrictive immigration regime; it was about *how* to implement those controls. That question pivoted around the imperial and international implications of either embracing or rejecting the Natal formula.

Two *Sydney Morning Herald* editorials published in the months following federation captured the essential dilemma. During the Australian Commonwealth's first federal election in March 1901, *Herald* editorialists expressed strong support for the legislative exclusion of Chinese, "Hindoos," and "men of other Eastern races" from the new dominion. Preventing large-scale Asian immigration constituted one of the chief motivations for federation, after all, and inaction augured only misery and ruin. "The experience of all countries shows the danger of unrestricted coloured immigration," the *Herald*'s editorialists opined, "and if we are to have 'a white Australia,' the Federal Parliament must devote its attention to the matter at an early stage."[48] At the same time, however, the editorialists recognized the complex imperial and international sensitivities inherent in Australian attempts to explicitly restrict Asian migrants. The key point, expressed in a June 1901 editorial, was this: "While we remain integral parts of the Empire we cannot expect to be able to legislate freely against our fellow subjects or the subjects of powerful and sensitive states."[49] As the *Herald's* conflicting—and indeed conflicted—editorials illustrate, the implementation of Asian restriction in Australia entailed a practically intractable impasse. On one hand, federation afforded the opportunity to finally enact a consistent and well-defined system of Asian exclusion and white citizenship across the entire Australian continent. On the other hand, Australians remained constitutionally obliged to respect the priorities of British foreign and imperial policy, which necessitated a restrained immigration policy.[50]

Prime Minister Edmund Barton attempted to resolve this dilemma when he introduced the Immigration Restriction Bill on August 7, 1901. Barton was candid about its purpose. It was necessary to harmonize the immigration policies of the six prefederation colonies into one central act for both practical and constitutional reasons. Just as important, Barton expressed concern about the perceived racial threat that unrestricted Asian migration posed to the newly federated Commonwealth. Quoting from Charles H. Pearson's 1893 book, *National Life and Character*, Barton proclaimed, "We are guarding the last part of the world in which the higher races can live and increase freely for the higher civilization." According to Pearson, the dominant white races would eventually face an unassailable racial, economic, and diplomatic challenge from nonwhites across the globe. This was the challenge of overwhelming Asian mobility that white Australians were destined to meet, not only on behalf of the Commonwealth's future generations but also for the welfare of the world's white races.[51]

Barton nevertheless committed his government to the Natal formula despite these unambiguous principles, and he did so in deference to British interests. Despite their recent federation, Australians still occupied a tentative political space between colony and nation, self-governing in domestic matters but beholden to British authority in imperial and foreign affairs. The new Commonwealth remained enmeshed in an international and imperial system directed by Great Britain and subject to the imperatives of British foreign and imperial policy. Chamberlain's admonition from four years earlier therefore continued to resonate, and Barton was honest about the British government's likely rejection of the bill if an alternative method of proscription prevailed. International and imperial opposition was assured, he affirmed, "the moment we begin to say that every one of a certain nationality or colour shall be restricted." In his view Australians should not "make discriminations which will complicate the foreign relations of the Empire." Barton reassured his colleagues that his government would reinforce the act if the literacy test proved ineffective.[52]

Not every Australian representative felt so compelled to respect the British government's call for restraint. When debate got under way on Barton's bill the following month, the Labour Party leader John Watson immediately introduced an amendment that rejected the Natal formula and expressly excluded "any person who is an aboriginal native of Asia, Africa, or of the islands thereof." Watson offered familiar justifications for his proposal. Fear of aggressive commercial and industrial competition, compounded by the potentially devastating consequences of "racial contamination," convinced him that total and explicit restriction represented the only solution to the problem of Asian labor mobility. He also believed the Natal formula did not actually exclude, because the first iteration of the government's bill mandated only English as the basis of the literacy test, a requirement that many educated Japanese and South Asian migrants would theoretically be able to satisfy. He further dismissed Barton's assumption that Britain would veto legislation containing explicitly exclusionary provisions. Australians had to assert their rights of self-government as citizens of the empire, Watson contended: South Asians possessed no such rights as mere imperial subjects who were denied the privilege of self-rule.[53]

Opposing the Natal Formula

The rest of this chapter examines the contours of this debate during the Australian Commonwealth's first Parliament in 1901. I illuminate how opponents and supporters of the Natal formula interpreted and negotiated the international and imperial implications of their actions. Most Australian lawmakers supported the effort to immobilize Asian labor migrants, but they remained deeply divided over how exactly to achieve that goal. Support for Watson's amendment cut across party lines, uniting Protectionists, Free Traders, and Labourites in support of outright exclusion. The question of whether to risk embarrassing the British, Japanese, and Chinese governments by enacting open and explicit restriction (as advocated by proponents of the Watson amendment) or to disguise the legislation's intent and spare Britain's sensibilities along with the prestige of its friends, colonies, and partners (as preferred by Barton's Protectionist ministry and the Colonial and Foreign Offices in London) therefore guided the discussion. Existing studies tend to either overlook the centrality of that question or assert rather than analyze the fundamental importance of imperial and international politics to these debates.[54] Yet the Barton government's use of the Natal formula was vigorously contested, and the central deception at the core of the White Australia Policy—the literacy test—was never a foregone conclusion.

Proponents of Watson's amendment invoked a variety of interrelated arguments to repudiate the Natal formula in defiance of the Australian and British governments. They blended predictable racial, economic, and strategic concerns with notions of geographic vulnerability, fears of Asian labor encroachment, and barely concealed resentment of Australians' continued obligation to respect British foreign relations. A keen sense of Australian exceptionalism also underlay many of their arguments. The extraordinary demands of populating a remote continent with appropriate white settlers—all while being stalked by jealous Asian governments—required determination from Australia's founding Parliament and the forbearance of British authorities. Barton's bill tolerated too many breaches in the Commonwealth's new borders at the behest of distant imperial bureaucrats, whose interest lay primarily in securing commercial and strategic advantages for Great Britain.

Australia's proximity to an imagined mass of potential Asian migrants convinced many supporters of explicit restriction to reject the Natal formula. In the first speech of the debate, for example, the deputy leader of the opposition Free Trade Party, Sir William McMillan, denounced the Barton government's strategy as "an absolute fraud." The unique realities of Australian geography distinguished the Commonwealth from other British dominions, according to McMillan, and required the imperial government's indulgence regardless of the implications. The sparsely populated island continent neighbored "millions and millions of people of an alien and servile character," many of whom lived under British suzerainty. Australians could not evade that reality, nor could they rely on the Natal deception to safeguard against an eventual influx. The continent's immense coastline compounded the danger. Australia's inaugural legislators could not afford to prevaricate when policing such extensive borders, especially since the Natal formula relied on the fortitude and ingenuity of future civil servants. This commonly held anxiety created unlikely alliances. Samuel Mauger of Barton's own Protectionist Party also supported the Watson amendment, citing the same concern as McMillan. "We have something like 800,000,000 Chinese and Japanese, within easy distance of Australia, from whom we have to fear contamination," Mauger observed.[55] Indeed this exhortation was axiomatic among defenders of the White Australia Policy before, during, and after these founding debates.

Drawing upon similar arguments other supporters of Watson's amendment also worried about the propinquity of migrant labor economies that might overflow their boundaries and contaminate continental Australia. In his own appeal for direct exclusion Watson expressed concern that Japanese, Filipino, Javanese, and Malay immigrants were already imbedded in the pearl and plantation economies of North Queensland and neighboring territories. From there they could—and did—infiltrate the rest of the Australian mainland. Watson's Labour colleague from Queensland, James Page, attested to such an incursion occurring even as they spoke. "The Japanese are practically acquiring the ownership of the whole of Northern Queensland," Page claimed, and they would extend their reach "inch by inch" until they had ousted white labor from the region entirely.[56] Despite aligning with Parliament's free traders, McMillan shared these Labour Party members' queasiness about the closeness of populations that supposedly thrived in the blistering heat of northern Australia. McMillan eyed the neighboring colonial conglomerate of British Malaya with particular trepidation. He imagined that the possibility of colonizing Australia's tropical North seduced Malaya's most enterprising Asian residents, who could easily insinuate themselves under a cloak of British sovereignty.[57]

As these arguments suggest, climate and environment represented other unique features of Australian geography that necessitated specific prohibitions on Asian mobility. The northern reaches of the continent were bathed in an oppressive tropical heat. Many colonial and imperial theorists believed that white labor was physiologically incapable of arduous work in such conditions and proclaimed that only degeneration, disease, and indolence awaited white men in the tropics.[58] Eager to exploit the economic potential of the region, some observers therefore advocated nonwhite labor importation as a remedy to the stresses of this sweltering environment. Writing just months before deliberations began, for example, the veteran imperial traveler and novelist Gilbert Parker publicly doubted the northern third of the Australian continent could be preserved solely for white settlement: "The world over, sugar, cotton, rice, and coffee can be satisfactorily cultivated only by the employment of black labour. . . . White labour has its physical limitations, and the tropical sun obdurately imposes one of them."[59] Inside Parliament the Free Trade Party's William Knox offered the same assessment of the tropical climate's deleterious effect on white laborers. Citing medical experts and his own observations, Knox concluded that when a white man labors in Queensland's cane fields, "he does irreparable harm not only to him-

self but to the race, because his children degenerate, so that in the third generation they will not reproduce at all."[60]

Notwithstanding these arguments James Ronald articulated the sentiments of those who favored Watson's amendment despite possible commercial injury to the Commonwealth: "There is something higher and greater
than the making of money to be considered, and that is the character, the
morals, and the health of our children." Parliament had a responsibility to
"keep before us the noble ideal of a white Australia—a snow-white Australia
if you will." He concluded, "Let it be pure and spotless." One future High
Court justice, H. B. Higgins, agreed: "I would sooner see northern Australia
unused and undeveloped for a generation or two than have it peopled with
Asiatics."[61] Like Seddon and his allies in New Zealand, Australian restrictionists observed such proximate migrant labor nodes with suspicion; like
their compatriots across the Tasman Sea, they endeavored to thwart the expansion of those hubs and the Asian labor upon which they thrived.

White Australians were of course complicit in the construction and exploitation of the very plantation and contract systems that Watson, McMillan, Page, Ronald, and Higgins now denounced. The 1901 restriction debate
was in fact partly a response to earlier economies of indenture that Australians themselves had participated in creating.[62] Some colonial landowners, in-
vestors, administrators, and especially plantation operators had embraced
nonwhite contract labor in the wake of the transportation system's demise
in the 1830s. Queensland plantation owners were particularly eager, successfully indenturing workers from the neighboring South Sea Islands by
midcentury.[63] Approximately 60,000 "Kanakas" came to Australia, often
unwillingly, until the practice was outlawed in 1904. Most of those who remained were eventually deported under the 1901 Pacific Island Labourers
Act.[64] They were subjected to a harrowing existence when first introduced
on a large scale in 1862.[65] Throughout these debates the Commonwealth's
new representatives also obstinately ignored the continent's indigenous
population as they agonized over defending their racial integrity. Indeed
many assumed that Aboriginal Australians would soon vanish from the
Commonwealth. Attorney General Alfred Deakin reflected in what must be
one of the most tragic statements ever uttered in the Australian Parliament,
"There is that single exception of a dying race; and if they be a dying race, let
us hope that in their last hours they will be able to recognise not simply the
justice, but the generosity of the treatment which the white race, who are dis-
possessing them and entering into their heritage, are according them." That

attitude allowed legislators like Higgins to declare that Parliament must "state outright that we do not want yellow and black faces in Australia."[66]

If some opponents of the Natal formula bemoaned the negative features of their continent's geography, others drew inspiration from an affirmative conviction in Australian distinctiveness. They relished the opportunities that fashioning a new society on a new continent provided, and they imbued that mission with a sense of Australian exceptionalism that required the frank exclusion of nonwhites. Tasmania's King O'Malley added God's imprimatur to the Commonwealth's national mission. A staunch Labourite and evangelical Christian, O'Malley grandly proclaimed, "We are here upon a continent set apart by the Creator exclusively for a Southern empire—for a Southern nation—and it is our duty to preserve this island continent for all eternity to the white race, irrespective of where they may come from." O'Malley's parable of Australian racial destiny assumed that Britain would never again interfere with the inalienable rights of autonomous white colonists as they had unsuccessfully done a century earlier in the American colonies. Belief in such principles also crossed party lines. James Hume Cook of Barton's Protectionist Party shared O'Malley's concern for Australia's national and racial future. "For the safety of the Australian nation, for the good of her national life, we require that Australia shall be white," he asserted, reiterating O'Malley's confidence that Britain would not jeopardize that birthright—or Australia's future value to the empire—just to spare the feelings of "alien coloured labour." Hume Cook's fellow party member George Cruickshank shared that vision. "I should like to see the Australian people constitute the noblest and ablest race upon this sphere," he professed, and they could not safely allow any Asian migrants to make their home in the Commonwealth without "vitiating that future national greatness which is the very foundation of every patriotic Australian's day dream."[67]

American by birth, O'Malley illuminates yet another important argument put forward by advocates of Watson's amendment. While recounting his belief in Australian predestinarianism, he drew an analogy between Australians' potential racial future and Americans' actual racial past: "If the Australian people had only lived in the Southern states of America—as I have—and had seen the dire results of the present mingling of the Africans with the whites, they would put their feet down and say—'We are going to profit by the terrible mistake of the American people, and we are not going to leave it to posterity to solve such an unholy problem.'" Despite lacking his direct experience, several of O'Malley's colleagues drew upon their own often distorted notions about the United States to validate Watson's total exclusion approach.

They did not turn to Americans for solutions; rather they invoked American society as a cautionary tale that provided urgent lessons in race pollution. Watson's defenders deemed Americans' racial experience so dreadful that nonwhites must never be allowed to immigrate and prosper in Australia. For example, Higgins surmised that the black minority in the United States had destabilized the republic and diluted its racial purity. Australians now had the chance to learn from that folly, for the sake of both white Australians and the British Empire. Higgins contended, "We have only to look at the great difficulty which is being experienced in America in connexion with the greatest racial trouble ever known in the history of the world, in order to take warning and guard ourselves against similar complications."[68]

Others saw a direct parallel between African Americans in the United States and the hordes of Asian migrants they imagined were desperate to deluge the Australia continent. William Henry Wilks shared this interpretation of American race relations and all it portended for Australia. According to Wilks, "the black people [in the United States] have increased to such an extent, and have gained such power, that the jurists and statesmen there pause and look with fear upon them." While his assessment of black power and influence in the American South bore no resemblance to reality, he nevertheless felt assured that "a repetition of the trouble will occur in this country if these servile and objectionable races are allowed to continue to invade our shores."[69] Race pollution on this scale could not be permitted in Australia, and here was an opportunity to guarantee the Australian Commonwealth's whiteness from the outset.

While many who contested the Natal formula tried to justify their opposition judiciously and with regard for Britain's diplomatic liabilities, others were much less circumspect and flatly rejected the imperial government's right to intervene. They bridled against British control over the new Commonwealth's foreign relations, and they derided the imperial government's blandishment of the upstart Japanese Empire. The irascible William Hughes was especially blunt. Without acknowledging Australians' own military dependence on the home government, Hughes mocked British antagonism toward explicit racial exclusion as selfishly strategic: "It is notorious that to-day Great Britain stands almost without an ally. She is now driven into a corner, and she is dependent upon the support, tardy and reluctant, of Japan." Australians should not sacrifice their recently earned—albeit still circumscribed—autonomy because of British strategic concerns. "We object to these people because of their vices, and of their immorality, and because of a hundred things which we can only hint at," Hughes pronounced, "and our objections are not to be met by the declaration that the Imperial Government will be embarrassed by them." O'Malley proved similarly disposed to dispense with diplomatic niceties. "Is it proper," he asked, "that the rights of the Australian people should be sacrificed on the altar of foreign compromise?" The issue was simple: "The Asiatic immigrant is nothing more or less than a coffee-coloured, copper-headed viper in the bosom of the Commonwealth, and if we do not kill that viper, that viper will kill us." Like many others, O'Malley declared that he would vote for the Watson amendment regardless of the international and imperial consequences.[70]

Defending the Natal Formula

Those who defended Barton's adoption of the Natal formula almost universally harbored the same array of racial, economic, and strategic apprehensions that enthused its opponents. Bruce Smith of New South Wales stood practically alone in the inaugural Parliament when he described claims that Australia was "endangered by the incursion of these hordes of Asiatics" as a "fable" and a "fairy story."[71] On the contrary most understood that danger to be the greatest hazard facing white Australians. When it came to deploring the threat of Asian migration, they vied to surpass one another's alacrity in defense of exclusion. Supporters of the literacy test nevertheless recognized that Australians could not blithely dismiss the British government's concerns, nor could they disregard the Japanese government's inevitable sense of outrage. In many cases opponents of Watson's impolitic amendment simply inverted their colleagues' arguments in defense of the Natal formula: Australians' proximity to millions of potentially dangerous Asian migrants demanded subtlety and restraint, not callousness and bellicosity; yes, providence had bestowed a unique endowment upon white Australians, but Parliament would have to exercise a measure of self-control if they were to fulfill that promise; if the threat from Asian migration was so urgent and compelling, then why risk delay by passing a bill that everybody knew the imperial government in London would reject; and finally, emerging Japanese power in the Pacific certainly posed a threat to white rule on the Australian continent, but that menace warranted tact and sensitivity, not contempt for and indifference to British policies that were designed to reduce tensions and foster peace in East Asia.

Attorney General Deakin delivered one of the most eloquent speeches in support of the government's legislation and against the Watson amendment. He expertly blended an exceptionalist conception of the White Australia

Policy with a realistic appraisal of Australians' international and imperial obligations. Parliament was engaged in establishing a policy of global and historical significance, Deakin claimed, and he expressed confidence that "at the very first instant of our national career we are as one for a white Australia." That policy was to be "the Monroe Doctrine of the Commonwealth of Australia." President James Monroe's declaration warned Europe's imperial powers to respect the independence of the western hemisphere. In contrast Australians were now claiming racial suzerainty over an entire continent. International observers had derided the former policy upon its promulgation in 1823, Deakin reminded his colleagues, yet eighty years later it was diplomatic orthodoxy. Australians' equally pretentious claims would meet with international ridicule, Deakin conceded. European observers would likely watch with "amazement when they regard what appears to be the arrogance of a handful of white men, most of them clustered on the eastern littoral of this immense continent, adopted before they have effectively occupied a quarter of the continent, and with the great bulk of its immense extent little more than explored or with a sparse European settlement."[72] Posterity would judge them more shrewdly.

Deakin praised Japan's recent economic, political, and military development and counseled consideration of that people's national pride. He insisted that it was Japanese migrants' capacity for education, industriousness, and thrift that made them undesirable in Australia, since they threatened to displace white workers who demanded higher wages and better conditions. Deakin left no doubt that they ought to be excluded, but he was adamant that their exclusion had to be handled sensitively. "When it becomes necessary for us to exclude people like the Japanese," he warned, "it is reasonable that we should exclude them in the most considerate manner possible, and without conveying any idea that we have confused them with the many uneducated savages who visit our shores." He was well aware that the debate was being scrutinized by Japanese representatives and was therefore keen to appease Japanese pride, recognizing that "to lump all these peoples together as Asiatics and undesirables would naturally be offensive to a high-spirited people like the Japanese."[73] The Natal formula's adoption and the tactless Watson amendment's rejection constituted the only way to avoid injury to Japan and to ensure Australia's future as a white continent.

The stakes were higher than anybody in Parliament realized. Indeed Hughes had anticipated Britain's strategic dilemma, inadvertently predicting one of the early twentieth century's most shocking diplomatic developments. Unbeknownst to Australian legislators, throughout their deliberations

British officials were secretly negotiating an alliance with Japan.[74] That alliance was designed to neutralize Russian expansion in Asia, of which both parties were increasingly suspicious. Informal negotiations between Britain and Japan began in April 1901, and formal negotiations commenced that October.[75] According to Ian Nish, however, "it cannot be said that the Australian immigration crises in 1901 played any great part in modifying or delaying the alliance." The alliance was simply too valuable to the Japanese.[76]

Thankfully for the success of that effort, a slim majority of House members recognized the sober realism of Deakin's assessment. Given the magnitude of the "Yellow Danger," opposition member Knox admitted the absurdity of offending Great Britain and Japan with one single stroke. Discounting Britain's request for moderation would invite tragedy, Knox counseled, assuring the very calamity that Australians most feared. Australians were defenseless against the intrigues of their Asian neighbors without the Royal Navy's protection: "Where, in the name of all that is good and true, should we be in the face of these menaces at our northern shores, if we had not the British Government to fall back on?" James McCay of Victoria's short-lived Corinella division articulated Australians' predicament. It was precisely because of British support that Australia could even contemplate offending Japan, and without that support nobody would dare unnecessarily antagonize the Japanese. With that in mind, he suggested, legislators should be attentive to British objections. After all, "if we wish to enjoy the benefits of the [imperial] connexion we must also share its burdens." Among those burdens was respect for Britain's global relationships. Richmond's Thomas Ewing concurred. His support for the government's position was simple: "I stand by the Empire, because surrounded as Australia is by hundreds of millions of yellow men, she is powerless to play a lone hand. Without the protection of Great Britain she would be absolutely submerged and destroyed."[77] Those flippant advocates of explicit prohibitions needed to accept this stark but pressing reality.

One of the most ardent speeches supporting the government's position came from a future Australian chief justice and governor-general, Isaac Isaacs. Personally Isaacs favored the direct approach of the Watson amendment. His commitment to a white Australia was beyond reproach, and he was eager "to insure that Australia shall be white, and that we shall be free for all time from the contamination and the degrading influence of inferior races." Nature had drawn the color line, and the stakes, he argued, could not be higher. "It is a white man's war that we must face," Isaacs dramatically intoned, "and I would not suffer any black or tinted man to come in and block the path to progress."[78] He nevertheless rejected the Watson amendment on diplomatic grounds.

Instead he favored appending an emergency provision to the government's bill empowering Parliament to act if the literacy test proved inadequate. His amendment failed.

Despite widespread support, the Watson amendment was narrowly defeated by a 36–31 vote. The Barton ministry did concede that any "European" language should be substituted for "English" in the final bill. As many legislators emphasized, too many Japanese and South Asian migrants could read English. At the same time, not only did this requirement needlessly exclude non–English speakers from Wales, Ireland, and Scotland, but it also alienated prospective northern and western Europeans whose apparently unimpeachable whiteness was an asset to Australia. "Desirable" non-English-speaking emigrants from Scandinavia and Germany might therefore disregard Australia as a destination, despite the tacit understanding in the Australian government that only "coloured" applicants would be subject to the literacy test.[79]

The Imperial and International Aftermath

The British government expressed satisfaction following Parliament's successful defense of the Natal formula. It had not been easy, however, and the Colonial Office needed no reminder of how acerbic the debate had been. The Australian governor-general Lord Hopetoun informed the Colonial Office, "The feeling in Australia . . . is so intense that I cannot blame my Government for having introduced a measure of this kind."[80] And yet imperial authorities felt vindicated. Evidence of Chamberlain's complicity in this masquerade can be found in his response to a petition sent to the Colonial Office on behalf of Victoria's South Asian residents in the autumn of 1901. The petitioners expressed bewilderment at the British government's tacit approval of the immigration restriction bill, then still under debate in the Australian Parliament. "We cannot understand how it is that our own Government now wish to separate us from herself and to put us as strangers along with the outside nations of the world," they wrote, "especially as it is very painful for us to be put along with the Chinese, who are a defeated and dying race." They reminded Chamberlain of India's great sacrifices in the empire's defense. South Asians had demonstrated their willingness "to give their blood wherever the British Government has asked for water." Their petition provides a rare glimpse into the effect of this debate on Australia's small South Asian community. "We are therefore greatly pained that there is so much talk about a white Australia. Is it our fault that the almighty God made us of dark-coloured skin, and are we (who are part of the Empire) to be cast off and put along with the Chinese and Japanese, whilst there is no mention made of the Germans, Russians, French, Italians, or members of other outside nations? Have the outside nations given and done more for the British people than we have given and done? Do the members of Parliament consider the justice of this side of the question?"[81]

Chamberlain offered a disingenuous response that was wholly in line with the deception at the core of the Natal formula. He instructed the Australian governor-general to convey his appreciation of the petitioners' concerns. At the same time, however, he stated the British government's opinion that the immigration restriction bill "does not appear to cast any reflection upon any class of His Majesty's subjects."[82] Australia's desultory acquiescence in the Natal formula had successfully limited British liability. The Australian government was equally dishonest in its response to the petitioners. In their view a careful reading of the bill's provisions would demonstrate that "it contains nothing which couples the Indian with the Chinese races, and that consequently there is no reason for pain on that score."[83] A cursory reading of the parliamentary debates reveals otherwise.

The Japanese government proved more difficult to mollify. Meiji representatives had not hesitated to present their case against the proposed immigration restriction bill, even before the legislative debates began. The Japanese consul in Sydney, H. Eitaki, was a constant antagonist of the Barton ministry on immigration matters and an astute observer of parliamentary proceedings. Eitaki raised the issue with Barton in May 1901, stating the Japanese case against the anticipated legislation. He immediately challenged Australian racial assumptions with some of his own. "The Japanese belong to an Empire whose standard of civilization is so much higher than that of Kanakas, Negroes, Pacific Islanders, Indians, or other Eastern peoples," Eitaki insisted. Conflating the Japanese with these inferior peoples represented an unwarranted insult. He further dismissed the widely held Australian conviction that Japan sought an outlet for its surplus population. Eitaki hoped that Barton would therefore exempt Japanese immigrants from the proposed bill. In June 1901 Eitaki received the support of the Japanese minister in London, who lobbied the British Foreign Office to "advise the Federal Government either to give up the presentation of such a bill or to eliminate therefrom the provisions unfair to Japanese subjects."[84]

Once the debate got under way in Melbourne, the Japanese consul and the Japanese minister in London continued their exertions against discrimination. Predictably Eitaki remained especially concerned by the Watson amendment, but the proposed language change also troubled him. "The

English test," he reminded Barton, "was regarded as courteous to Japan, inasmuch as it placed her on an equal footing with other nations." The proposed change to "any European language" was not, since it constituted an implicit but obvious slur on Japanese speakers.[85]

Unable to elicit a satisfactory response from Barton, Eitaki turned to the governor-general. The substitution of "European" for "English" was "racial, pure and simple," he protested.[86] The Japanese minister in London made similar representations to the British Foreign Office.[87] Eitaki kept his Foreign Ministry apprised of parliamentary debates, and the Japanese Minister in Great Britain, Hayashi Tadasu, was equally distressed by the tenor of the proceedings. He complained to the British Foreign Office that Australian legislators "explain that the measure imposes an educational qualification without distinction of race or colour," yet at the same time "they couple it with such monstrous declarations."[88] Nevertheless in correspondence with the Foreign Office Chamberlain once again expressed his view that the European language stipulation wholly comported with the Natal formula. As such, he could not interfere with Australia's legislation.[89] As Chamberlain speciously told the Foreign Office, "[Hayashi] must take account of the words of the Bill itself, not of words uttered during debate which have no binding force whatsoever."[90] In particular Chamberlain was reportedly concerned that if Britain disallowed the bill, "the only result would be the passage of an even more drastic measure, framed with less consideration for the feelings of Japan, and possibly containing a direct prohibition of the entry of Japanese into Australia."[91] It was left to the British foreign secretary, the Marquess of Lansdowne, to inform Hayashi that his government could not intercede with Australia on Japan's behalf. Based on an earlier argument articulated by Chamberlain, Lansdowne notified the Japanese minister that the Immigration Restriction Act "contains no sign of any discrimination."[92] This did not placate the Japanese Foreign Ministry, which now recognized that "the educational test was likely to be used in such a manner as to discriminate against Japanese immigrants"; they would continue their protests in the following decades.[93]

The Immigration Restriction Act may have provided "a stone wall against the danger of race pollution," as the *Sydney Morning Herald* hoped it would in September 1901, but it had not ameliorated the imperial and diplomatic tensions that afflicted it from the outset.[94] Australian acceptance of the Natal formula—and British acquiescence to the Immigration Restriction Act—in December 1901 did not therefore resolve the issue of racially motivated immigration restriction in Australia. Rather it heralded a new phase in a prolonged imperial and international dispute concerning the rights of Asian migrants to access the British colonies of settlement. Australia, after all, was not alone in legislating against Asian immigration. New Zealand's Parliament finally passed its own Immigration Restriction Act in 1899 after six years of parliamentary and imperial wrangling. That revised legislation sullenly incorporated the Natal formula, thus satisfying the imperial government and joining Australians in restraining Asian mobility by literacy test.[95]

CHAPTER TWO

Mobility and Indenture in Southern Africa

Even as white Australasians initiated measures to stanch the real and imagined networks of Asian labor migration in the South Pacific, a fierce contest erupted over the deliberate introduction of Chinese workers into Britain's newly acquired Transvaal Colony in 1903. Over 60,000 Chinese laborers were indentured to the Witwatersrand (Rand) gold mines between 1904 and 1907, following intense debates that reverberated throughout southern Africa and the broader empire.[1] The colony's Chamber of Mines implemented this system in order to resuscitate the flagging mines of the gold-rich Rand. They did so in collusion with the British high commissioner in South Africa, Lord Alfred Milner, the Transvaal's appointed Legislative Council, mine operators, and the Conservative government in London.[2] Milner in particular came to view Chinese indenture as an essential component of racial, economic, and political reconstruction in southern Africa. The character and causes of the ensuing dispute were markedly different from those prevailing in Australasia and North America, but the consequences were the same: intra-imperial tensions over the soundness of Milner's gambit resounded from the plateaus of the Rand Highveld to the capitals of the empire's white dominions.

The politics of Asian mobility in the Transvaal were contentious, convoluted, and idiosyncratic following the South African War. That conflict had significantly compromised the colonial economy: it dispersed existing workforces, damaged essential infrastructure, and disrupted investment and production throughout the colony's industrial and agricultural sectors. The British military's intentional devastation of the countryside during the war exacerbated these problems.[3] The new colonial leadership therefore prioritized the restoration of lucrative gold mining operations in the Witwatersrand in order to reconstitute the economy. But that effort was beleaguered by serious labor shortages. In the apparent absence of cooperative African laborers—and convinced that whites neither would nor should work alongside blacks—Transvaal and imperial authorities concluded that strictly regulated, indentured Chinese labor represented the only solution to the Rand's labor deficits. Milner especially embraced the idea that Chinese importation would intensify productivity in the Transvaal gold mines, which would in turn entice British immigrants to the colony, thereby ensuring white—and specifically British—dominance in the region.[4]

This case again illuminates the contingencies of Asian restriction politics in the British Empire. Recent scholarship has tended to stress the intra-imperial and transnational resonances of the Chinese importation debate.[5] Instead I argue that specific local, regional, imperial, and international conditions inflected the particular tone and circumstances of the Transvaal campaign against Asian mobility, just as they did in Australasia and North America. The South African experience was therefore atypical, despite similarities in the rhetoric deployed by white activists across continents and despite the inherent transnationalism of both indentured and free Asian migration. The racial and demographic anxieties that predominated throughout colonial southern Africa exerted an especially determinative influence upon the nature of the Transvaal importation debate. The racial politics of the colony fluctuated between raw and inflamed even before the introduction of Chinese indentured labor, thanks to the complex interplay of British colonists, defeated Afrikaners, and diverse African ethnic groups. The introduction of Chinese immigrants provoked a predictably incendiary response, despite Milner's assurances that they would be both legally and physically contained. Fears that Chinese workers would eventually escape the boundaries of their indenture and establish permanent settlements were compounded by the presence of current and former South Asian indentured laborers in neighboring Natal, who now ominously outnumbered whites in that colony.[6]

Perspicacious white South Africans, whether British or Dutch in origin, were cognizant of their tenuous control over African spaces. They feared that a wave of blackness would subsume the continent's whites without the vigilant policing of black bodies and mobility—a system that reached its apogee in the apartheid era.[7] This was the white South African variant of the "yellow peril" that disconcerted so many in Europe, Asia, and the Americas. The former Transvaal state attorney and erstwhile Boer commander Jan Christiaan Smuts often articulated this existential dread in his speeches; he had advocated British and Boer "fusion" on that basis before the calamity of the South African War. He declared during a speech in 1895, "At the southern corner of a vast continent, peopled by over 100,000,000 barbarians, about half a million whites have taken up a position, with a view not only to working out their own destiny, but also of using that position as a basis for lifting up and opening up that vast deadweight of immemorial barbarism and animal savagery to the light and blessing of ordered civilization. Unless the white race closes its ranks in this country, its position will soon become untenable in the face of that overwhelming majority of prolific barbarism."[8] The British-born prime minister of the Cape Colony, Sir Gordon Sprigg, conveyed the same sentiments during the 1897 Colonial Conference in London. Sprigg concluded that white supremacy in southern Africa was already besieged by color and could not sustain a further infusion of nonwhite immigrants. Speaking in support of direct Asian immigration restriction, Sprigg explained to Chamberlain, "With such an overwhelming coloured population as we have in South Africa at the present time we want, if possible, to exclude any addition to that element."[9] Australasian anti-Asian agitators were preoccupied with preserving the already preponderant whiteness of their colonies, while campaigners in the North American West strove to maintain narrower but no less decisive white majorities. Moreover many white Australasians expressed a visceral sense of exposure in the South Pacific, just as some British Columbians and Californians felt vulnerable at the western fringes of North America, but their anxieties were largely hypothetical compared to the lived experience of white South Africans, however distorted those fears might have been in reality.

Besides these crucial demographic and geographic dissimilarities, a cluster of distinct circumstances informed the Transvaal importation debate, further distinguishing it from parallel outbreaks of anti-Asian hostility in the Anglophone Pacific. First, the Transvaal controversy was different simply because it involved the migration of Chinese laborers. Having effectively repressed Chinese immigration in the 1880s, activists in Australasia and North America had since focused their attention mostly on Japanese and South Asian mobility. This made Milner's decision seem especially retrograde because it represented not only the regeneration of an increasingly anachronistic labor system but also the resurgence of a recently dormant source of Asian migration in the British colonies of settlement.[10] Furthermore the decision to import a significant number of Chinese laborers was made intentionally, albeit by an unelected local oligarchy and a distant imperial government. This contrasted with populist outbursts against often conjectural Asian influxes that characterized restriction politics in Canada and Australasia. Active British involvement also differentiated the situation in the Transvaal, with Milner receiving support from his allies in the Colonial Office and from the Conservative-led Balfour ministry in Parliament. The imperial government's complicity astonished the leaders of the Australasian colonies in particular, who remained resolutely opposed to Asian labor mobility throughout the empire. Of course the newly established Transvaal Colony was no organic extension of Greater Britain, as Australians, New Zealanders, and Canadians imagined their communities to be; it was a defeated foreign country with vast gold deposits and without representative self-government. That postwar context of occupation and reconstruction further singularized the Transvaal importation debate.

Finally, the Chinese indenture dispute capsized the typical politics of Asian restriction in the British Empire because Milner and his supporters counterintuitively expected to mobilize flows of gold, capital, and, most important, white migrants by immobilizing imported Chinese workers. They believed that bonded Chinese labor—effectively confined by carefully crafted indenture contracts—would stimulate Rand gold production. This in turn would catalyze networks of colonial, imperial, and international capital, providing much needed investment in railroads, manufacturing, and agriculture. White British migrants would then flock to the Transvaal, enticed by a flourishing economy, abundant land, and employment in supervisory roles with authority over black and Chinese workers. All of this was designed to underwrite Milner's vision for British domination in South Africa and to ensure the political and economic subordination of indigenous Africans and dispossessed Boers. In fact Chinese indentured labor had a quite different effect. It galvanized Boer opposition to Milner's rule and engendered social, economic, and political cleavages among white commercial interests, laborers, and political and economic elites.

As these schisms suggest, a common thread once again at least partially aligned this episode with concurrent Australasian and North American restriction campaigns: the Transvaal importation debate stimulated tension and division across the settler empire, further complicating the already fractious racial politics of British imperialism. Milner's decision provoked outrage among many of the empire's white subjects, from Johannesburg to Cape Town in southern Africa, and from Wellington to Melbourne in Australasia. In southern Africa vigorous protests were lodged by British immigrants on the Rand, by prominent Afrikaners, and by the Cape Colony's government. Australia and New Zealand also joined the fray, bearing witness to the enervating social, political, and economic influence of Chinese immigrants on "white men's countries." According to Seddon and Deakin, the contributions of Australasian colonists to the British war effort in South Africa entitled them to articulate their concerns. Intense debates also raged in Britain, as the measure's Liberal Party opponents and Conservative Party supporters squabbled over the character and intent of Chinese labor importation. So while the causes and substance of the debate were endemic to the Transvaal and the imperatives of British rule in the region, the divisive consequences resonated far beyond the new British colony.

I begin by unraveling the contorted rationale behind Chinese importation in the months following British annexation of the Transvaal. As the deliberations surrounding this decision reveal, Milner predicated the initiative on enlivening local and imperial conduits of white migration, raw materials, finance, and black labor. The revived mobility of these resources depended upon the temporary controlled importation and strict containment of Chinese labor; at least this was the fable that inspired Milner's vision for a British South Africa. Then I examine the counterclaims offered by Afrikaner and British opponents in the Transvaal and the Cape Colony. Three central arguments informed their appraisals of the importation scheme. First, rather than encourage the immigration of desirable white settlers, Chinese importation would inhibit respectable whites from making their homes in the Transvaal. After all, critics contended, what decent white man would wittingly bring his family to a colony perverted by cheap, squalid, and immoral Chinese laborers? Second, antagonists of indenture complained that Chinese miners, no matter how well regulated, would eventually find their way into the Transvaal's wider society and economy—just as Natal's South Asian coolies had supposedly done—thereby further adulterating the racial composition of South African society. Third, they also believed that Chinese labor importation defamed the legacy of those who had given their lives in defense of British rule in southern Africa.

This line of reasoning in particular implicated the Australasian colonies in the Transvaal debate, as the final part of this chapter illustrates. Richard Seddon—still prime minister of New Zealand and still indomitably hostile to Asian mobility in or around the British Empire—became a dedicated spokesman for white resentment toward Chinese labor importation, even as British politicians debated the relevance and justice of the Australasian point of view. While his exertions against Chinese importation briefly rallied supporters from across the empire, imperial authorities ultimately rejected his interference, thus illustrating the limits to such intercolonial networks and interventions as well as the tensions they provoked. The politics of Asian labor mobility in southern Africa were unusual, but their consequences were conventionally far-reaching and disruptive.

Immobilized Chinese Labor and White Supremacy in Southern Africa

Great Britain finally achieved a difficult victory over the Boer republics in 1902, with the assistance of indigenous allies and contingents from Australia,

New Zealand, and Canada. At tremendous cost much of southern Africa now fell under British suzerainty.[11] Following the May 1902 Treaty of Vereeniging, Transvaal and the Orange Free State (now the Orange River Colony) were annexed to the British Empire, administered as Crown colonies, and therefore denied representative self-government. Milner resigned his position as governor of the Cape Colony but retained the post of high commissioner, directly overseeing the two former Boer republics until 1905. His remit included the pacification of hostile populations and the imposition of British cultural and political authority. From his perspective the success of this task hinged upon the immigration of British settlers, which in turn demanded economic reconstruction, which itself depended upon the resumption of profitable gold mining operations in the Transvaal. With the raw materials finally under British rule, Milner hoped to harness the latent prosperity of the Rand to secure British domination of a new united South Africa.[12]

Milner's vision of a white South Africa entwined race, migration, labor, and empire. British supremacy in the region required the suppression of Boer racial identity and nationalism. It also had to contend with the overwhelming preponderance of indigenous Africans vis-à-vis white settlers. Large-scale British immigration ameliorated both of those problems, in Milner's view. Energetic British settlers would inundate Boer influence throughout Transvaal society, while also furnishing manpower for the administration, training, and supervision of black workers. White management of a flexible native labor force would facilitate the resumption of productive mining operations, attracting yet more British settlers. This virtuous cycle of labor and migration would eventually bind the Transvaal—and southern Africa more broadly—to the British Empire.[13] But employers and colonial administrators could neither compel nor encourage blacks to work, Milner and others believed; for example, a September 1902 editorial in the London *Times* alleged that the African native contentedly "luxuriates in his hereditary sloth," lacking any long-term incentive to work.[14] By early 1903 Milner had therefore turned to the short-term importation of indentured Chinese labor to accelerate mine production and boost colonial reconstruction efforts.[15]

The British high commissioner elucidated the assumptions that animated his thinking during a June 1903 meeting with the recently organized White League, which vehemently opposed the indenture proposal. On one hand Milner fully endorsed the League's white supremacist aspirations. He had no desire to see the colony overwhelmed by free Asian immigrants, nor did he countenance granting full and equal rights to Asian residents. He agreed that South African whites faced a stark racial reality considering the demographic predominance of indigenous Africans, and he assured the deputation of his devotion to white civilization in Africa. At the same time, however, Milner criticized the racial obsessions of the colony's anti-Asian politics and counseled restraint among opponents of Chinese importation. Like Chamberlain six years earlier, Milner tried to simply efface the bigotry that characterized colonial hostility toward Asian immigration. His primary motivation for moderating the White League's antagonism, however, was economic. While he adamantly opposed free and permanent Asian immigration, he nonetheless insisted that indentured Chinese were temporarily required to perform cheap unskilled labor in the mines.[16]

Milner then carefully unfurled the convolution upon which he based his entire scheme for white supremacy in southern Africa. The only viable alternative to indentured Chinese labor was a "white proletariat," but this was anathema to the broader racial and economic project unfolding on the continent. A large unskilled white labor force would not only be prohibitively expensive, but it would also imply equality between black and white. The mere suggestion of parity would undermine whites' social, political, and economic hegemony. Yet the Transvaal required an increased amount of "rough labour" upon which to build the colony's future, and temporarily indentured Chinese coolies represented the most prudent and efficient way to fill that void. Firmly controlled Chinese labor would reinforce the white man's elevated place in society by ensuring that whites would not have to toil alongside blacks. The scheme would also create skilled supervisory and management positions that would establish a solid economic base upon which to attract suitable white immigration.[17] The White League's apprehensions were thereby rebuffed by an ironic twist: according to Milner, Anglo mobility, prosperity, and supremacy in southern Africa depended upon the deliberate importation, immobilization, and subsequent repatriation of Asian labor.

Milner accumulated allies for his scheme as the Rand labor situation continued to stagnate. Wartime idleness had already cost the Randlords (as mine owners and financiers were often derisively known) some £30 million in overall losses, and labor shortages, coupled with the declining value of gold, severely inhibited postwar production and profitability. Rising wage levels, exacerbated by the widespread competition for labor, further crippled the Rand mines.[18] Facing these challenges, mine owners, colonial officials, and imperial administrators joined Milner in contemplating alternative sources of labor. By 1903 the concept of employing immobilized Chinese labor to ensure the efficient movement of people (both black and white), money, goods, and resources dominated deliberations over the future of the Transvaal and its place in the empire.

In March 1903, for example, Milner convened leaders of the four South African colonies, along with representatives of Rhodesia and Portuguese East Africa, in the Orange River Colony capital of Bloemfontein for the South African Customs Union Conference, intended to facilitate intercolonial and imperial trade. The delegates in fact spent much of the conference considering interrelated questions of labor and immigration policy. After considering ways to encourage native labor mobility—and after determining that adequate numbers of native workers could not be coaxed into either mines or industry—the representatives contemplated alternative sources of non-white labor. They finally resolved that the temporary importation of strictly regulated Chinese labor might be necessary if the situation did not improve, although "permanent settlement in South Africa of Asiatic races would be injurious and should not be permitted."[19] Like Milner, the delegates concluded that mine operators could mitigate the otherwise deleterious social and economic influence of Asian immigrants by inhibiting their movements and enforcing their removal from the colony upon completion of their contracts.

At the same time, a committee of consulting engineers concluded in a report to the Chamber of Mines that the Rand's prosperity depended upon "an abundant supply of cheap labour drawn from the coloured races." They echoed South African industrial and racial orthodoxy, insisting that whites could not work alongside blacks. Even implicit equality in the workplace threatened the fabric of South African society. It would create a class of degraded white laborers, thereby undermining the white man's claim to racial, economic, and political supremacy.[20] In lieu of white labor the committee offered two possibilities to resume productive operations on the Rand. They suggested the Chamber devote its energies to increasing the African labor force, either through coercion ("legal and moral pressure") or inducements such as increased comforts and higher wages. If these measures failed to compel significant numbers of Africans to take employment on the Rand, then once again the last resort was rigorously regulated Asian labor.[21]

As this critical mass of support gathered among the Transvaal's political and economic elites, the Chamber of Mines dispatched H. Ross Skinner, chairman of the Witwatersrand Native Labour Association, on a fact-finding mission to Asia and the Americas in February 1903. The Chamber tasked Skinner with resolving a long-standing dilemma: How could white settler societies exploit Asian labor without tolerating permanent immigrant communities and the networks of mobility and chain migration that sustained them? For the next eight months he circulated throughout the webs of imperial labor and commerce that braided the Pacific. Skinner knew that colonial and American activists were trying to dismantle the very networks he now explored, and he took for granted the hostility they felt toward Asian migrants. Traveling through California, British Columbia, Japan, Hong Kong, the Malay Peninsula, and China, Skinner nevertheless sought to profit from the mistakes of those who now rued their earlier permissiveness toward Asian labor. He ruminated extensively upon the case against Chinese labor in the United States and Canada, concluding that North Americans' distressing experience was "entirely due to the absence of restrictive legislation at the commencement." Skinner felt confident that the Transvaal could learn from the lessons of California and British Columbia by strictly regulating and controlling Chinese labor in southern Africa at the outset. Echoing the now prevailing orthodoxy among the Randlords, Skinner maintained, "The [Transvaal] Legislature, by their enactments, should make it absolutely certain that the immigrant is securely indentured and his repatriation rendered compulsory on the termination of such indenture."[22]

The urgent impetus to maximize gold production finally seduced the Chamber of Mines into accepting imported Chinese labor as a temporary solution to the colony's labor shortages. One of the measure's most vocal supporters was Sir George Farrar, a prominent Uitlander and chairman of the East Rand Proprietary Mines company. Recently elected president of the Chamber of Mines, Farrar campaigned among his fellow members and the broader white public in support of Chinese importation. In a speech before the East Rand's white miners and residents on March 31, 1903, he outlined the debilitating consequences of continued labor shortages and encouraged the adoption of indentured Chinese as a temporary expedient. "You use to-day coloured labour," Farrar observed, "and what are your special objections to bringing in unskilled Asiatic labour to make up the deficiency?" He assured his listeners that Chinese coolies would not become economic competitors on the Rand upon completion of their indenture; they would be immediately repatriated once their task was finished, "not letting a single man remain behind." Farrar would not support Chinese importation without first securing white laborers, merchants, and tradesmen "perfect immunity from competition, and absolute freedom from the danger that these labourers would settle in this country afterwards."[23] Though he was yet to convince all of the Rand's British and Afrikaner residents, by July 1903 Farrar led a firm majority inside the Chamber.[24]

Milner was also now fully convinced that Chinese importation represented the only way to rejuvenate the Rand. He told Dr. J. E. Moffat in April 1903 that the permanent solution to the Transvaal's labor problems necessitated an "increase of the white population, and in getting rid of the idea . . . that the white man cannot, or ought not to, work with his hands in this country." As unsavory as it might be, therefore, Milner felt it was necessary to "call in the aid of the Asiatics." This was a vital but temporary measure pending the mass immigration of suitable white labor.[25] He remained "dead against the Asiatic settler and trader," he told E. H. Walton: "But without the impetus he would give, I do not see how we are to have that great influx of British population . . . which is the ultimate salvation."[26] As Farrar, Skinner, and others were arguing, Milner envisaged that strict regulation and repatriation was the only way to prevent "the danger of the Asiatic spreading all over the country, settling here permanently, and adding to our already numerous racial difficulties."[27]

The colonial secretary in London was circumspect. Chamberlain wanted to ensure that any attempt to introduce Chinese laborers represented the will of the colony's people, or at least its white people. He acknowledged the widespread opposition during a visit to Johannesburg in January 1903, and he understood the local, national, and imperial difficulties that attended the introduction of Chinese labor on the Rand. Whatever the outcome, Chamberlain demanded a solution to the labor problem, and he felt that it was unlikely to be found among the continent's African population, who in his view were innately allergic to work. During his speech in Johannesburg, Chamberlain opined, "The African alone amongst the great races of the world has been taught by centuries of baneful experience that the only honourable employment for a man is fighting . . . and that labour is the work of slaves."[28] He nevertheless resigned his position in the midst of the debate in order to devote himself to tariff reform, and he was replaced by Milner's close ally, Alfred Lyttelton, in September 1903.[29] With a supporter in the Colonial Office, Milner was able to frame the debate more positively in favor of importation.

Mine owners also leveraged their control over white labor to build support for organizations favoring Chinese labor. As early as August 1903 the Witwatersrand Trades and Labour Council claimed that mine owners were forcing employees to sign petitions in favor of Chinese importation.[30] The Labour Importation Association was among the most effective of these sham advocacy groups.[31] Their manifesto echoed the dogma of the Milner administration: African labor shortages posed a threat to South African development, and Chinese labor was the only solution to the present crisis.

Like Milner they rejected the idea that white supremacy could be maintained on the backs of unskilled white labor. "Remembering what is really meant by a 'White Man's Country,'" the Association declared, "unskilled labour must be left to those alone who are best fitted by race and the conditions of life to undertake it." The Association organized meetings across the Rand and garnered support for numerous pro-importation resolutions throughout 1903 and 1904.[32]

Notwithstanding this growing support the final decision to import Chinese labor ostensibly depended upon the report of a specially convened Transvaal Labour Commission. Commissioned by Milner in July 1903, it was designed to assess the colony's industrial and agricultural needs and to ascertain possible labor sources throughout southern and central Africa. The Commission's majority report concluded that African labor was predominantly characterized by "primitive pastoral or agricultural communities, who possess exceptional facilities for the regular and full supply of their animal wants, and whose standards of economic needs is [*sic*] extremely low." The "only pressing needs of a savage are food and sex," the Commission deduced, therefore blacks lacked any incentive to enter the industrial labor market. The Commission heard a plethora of evidence from white employers across the colony, many of whom proposed antidotes for this imagined native indolence. Recommended solutions included "minor remedies" such as improvements in working conditions to more substantive remedies that amounted to "modifying or destroying" entire indigenous social systems. The Commission concluded that neither approach would render the necessary changes in time to prevent a full-blown industrial crisis on the Rand.[33] It did not explicitly endorse Chinese importation, but it revealed an immediate labor shortfall of 129,000, which "was taken as a thinly veiled vote in favor of the Chinese."[34]

The publication of the Labour Commission's report in November 1903 assured Chinese importation. The findings, coupled with Skinner's report and the support of Milner and Lyttelton, finally pushed the Chamber of Mines into requesting the Legislative Council to act, and a draft importation ordinance was passed before the end of the year.[35] In order to assuage the many concerns of white workers, the Labour Importation Ordinance and the Anglo-Chinese Labour Convention, both of which governed Chinese importation, provided for three-year terms of indenture and bound Chinese laborers to purpose-built compounds, which they could not leave without written permission and only for a limited time. They were required to return to China upon fulfillment of their contract.[36]

Critics of Chinese Importation in the Transvaal

Supporters of the indenture plan claimed that Chinese laborers could be successfully imported, immobilized, contained, expended, and then expatriated. Critics from the Transvaal, Cape Colony, London, and Australasia repudiated each facet of this argument, deriding the racial and economic rationalizations offered by Milner and the Chamber of Mines. Detractors of the proposal broadly condemned Chinese indenture as racial and economic suicide. They claimed that white supremacy in southern African was fragile enough; Chinese importation would further undermine white domination, adulterate the colony's already delicate race relations, and degrade both blacks and whites. The context and substance of their arguments were rooted in the peculiar racial, economic, and political circumstances of postwar southern Africa, but the resultant conflict spread across the Indian and Atlantic oceans.

Opponents of Chinese indenture in the Transvaal specifically contested two essential principles of Milner's argument. First they ridiculed the notion that large-scale white immigration to the Transvaal depended upon Chinese importation. They retorted that the simple presence of Chinese in the colony would discourage self-respecting white immigrants, limit white economic opportunity, destabilize the colony's delicate racial and economic hierarchy, and consign the Transvaal to a future of racial turmoil, miscegenation, and indolence. Second, they scoffed at the Chamber's assurance that the movements of Chinese laborers could be effectively constrained, whether at their workplace or throughout the colony more widely. Either greedy mine owners would negotiate an end to repatriation in order to retain their workforce, or Chinese laborers would simply abscond. Once permanent Chinese settlements became established in the Transvaal, they would inevitably expand at the expense of white and black workers, traders, and retailers as their South Asian predecessors had purportedly done in Natal. In addition to dismissing Milner's claims about white mobility and Chinese immobility, critics offered a claim of their own: Chinese importation dishonored the memory of those soldiers from Britain, southern Africa, and the settler colonies who had given their lives to secure a white South Africa.

On April 1, 1903, White League representative E. O. Hutchinson expounded upon these arguments before some five thousand white laborers at Johannesburg's Wanderers Club, stating that the League was established "to fight all forms of colour and to win the Transvaal for the white man and the white man alone."[37] Its membership derived primarily from poor white traders who felt threatened by Asian competition, and its successful organizing efforts soon attracted trade union support.[38] Hutchinson offered a typically inconsistent case against the Chinese themselves. He decried that "centuries of recession had debased them, had made them servile and cruel." Overpopulation had bred a callously competitive race that ruthlessly contended for advantage, to the enduring detriment of Chinese civilization. At the same time, however, Hutchinson articulated a common and paradoxical corollary that characterized anti-Asian discourse throughout the English-speaking world. While denouncing Chinese laborers' brutal efficiency, he was also forced to admit their industriousness and thrift. He even obliquely conceded that opposition to Chinese immigration was counterintuitive. After all, these supposedly inherent traits were invaluable to a struggling new colony determined to exploit its considerable mineral resources. Hutchinson nevertheless concluded that Chinese indenture's cost was simply too high: whites would be forced to abrogate a millennium of racial, economic, and social development in order to effectively compete with Chinese coolies. That proposition was inconceivable if not impossible.[39]

Hutchinson then mounted a multifaceted case that controverted the high commissioner's assumptions about the reciprocal relationship between Chinese importation and South African renewal. He rejected Milner's claim that immobilized Chinese laborers would mobilize coveted British migrants. On the contrary, large numbers of Asian immigrants would render the Transvaal repellent to prospective white migrants. Desirable white settlers from North America and Australasia had already witnessed the degenerative influence of Chinese immigration firsthand and would never deign to live in a community sullied by Asian immigrants. This augured disaster for the colony. At best the Transvaal's inability to entice white migrants would condemn it to a future of racial integration; at worst the colony would be submerged under an inexorable tide of color.[40]

Hutchinson rebuked the notion that limited numbers of imported Chinese laborers could be corralled in mining compounds across the Rand pending the completion of their contracts. He invoked San Francisco's Chinatown as a example of what happened when white men allowed Asian populations— "so debased, so lawless, so horrid"—to flourish in their midst. He also distrusted the Chamber's promise that only small consignments of Chinese would securely rotate through the colony, repeatedly replenishing the labor force without constituting their own communities. That idea was "ridiculous, impracticable, and absurd," he declared. Before long, he anticipated, ever larger contingents of indentured Chinese would traverse the Indian Ocean, so that eventually the enterprise "would require a larger fleet of steamers than was employed in bringing out the British Army to South Africa." Hutchinson insisted that Chinese importation would demean the sacrifices made by the empire's white soldiers. Britons, Canadians, Australians, and New Zealanders had participated in the South African War to guarantee a white Transvaal. Milner's reckless Chinese importation policy threatened to invalidate their collective sacrifices by throwing the colony open to Asian colonization: "Was it for this that Great Britain gave of her bravest and had accumulated a debt greater than all the debts of all the wars of last century? Was it for this that the Colonies of Australia and Canada had also sent the flower of their manhood to help us?" It was therefore every white South African's duty—British and Afrikaner—to resist this "Chinese curse" in honor of the empire's war dead.[41]

Other Rand organizations also strenuously opposed the Chamber of Mines, and in each case these groups deconstructed the elaborate framework that Milner used to validate Chinese importation. The African Labour League represented commercial interests on the Rand, although it eventually expanded to include trade unionists and even a small number of professionals.[42] Like the White League, its members harbored class resentments toward the Chamber and its cadre of industrialists who would sacrifice white supremacy in the Transvaal for their own economic aggrandizement. According to the League's manifesto, they believed that South Africa was "eminently fitted to become the home of a great white nation." To this end they encouraged the racial synthesis of Britons, Boers, and other white races. They also argued that southern Africa represented a key strategic outpost for the British Empire, and as such "its future must never depend upon a race of helots." They therefore opposed the introduction of Asian labor and instead advocated the intensification of white immigration, combined with a concerted campaign to compel African labor into the mines.[43] They condemned the Chamber of Mines' overweening political and economic influence in a letter to Chamberlain in July 1903, vigorously protesting the Randlords' threatened "deplorable Chinese invasion." Chinese labor might temporarily induce prosperity, but in the long run it would repel white immigrants and inhibit enduring development in the Transvaal.[44] The Pretoria Trades' and Labour Council submitted their own resolution against Asian labor. Claiming to represent 2,000 skilled white laborers, the Council complained that Chinese laborers would defile Transvaal society at every level. Like many other opponents, the Council insisted that a decision of this magnitude should be put before the Transvaal's people, not foisted upon them by Milner, the Randlords, and the imperial government.[45]

Two prominent Afrikaner leaders emerged as ardent critics of Chinese importation on the Rand: Louis Botha, the Transvaal's one-time commanding general, and his compatriot Jan Smuts. These two men represented the interests of the Transvaal's defeated Afrikaners throughout this crisis, and indeed throughout Milner's high commissionership. In July 1903 Botha and Smuts orchestrated a mass meeting against Chinese importation in the former Boer capital of Heidelberg. The meeting resolved against Chinese labor and demanded the colonial administration's commitment to developing South Africa as "a white man's country." Their concerns were by now familiar: they lamented that whites remained a numerical minority and rejected Chinese importation on the grounds that it would "materially strengthen the coloured population of South Africa and will largely contribute to the closing of the Transvaal to white immigration."[46]

Unable to persuade Milner through mass meetings, Botha and Smuts appealed directly to the Labour Commission. Like Milner's other antagonists, the two Afrikaner leaders denied any positive relationship between Chinese importation and British immigration. In an impassioned memorandum sent under Botha's signature in September 1903, they acknowledged the Transvaal's pressing labor needs but insisted that the shortfall was temporary. They implored the commissioners to consider the consequences of mortgaging the colony's racial future on Chinese importation. That policy would "call into life a permanent evil which will weigh as a heavy incubus on the future industrial and social development of this land." Natal's "desperate and ruinous example" provided a case in point. South Asian importation in that colony had been a terrible mistake that discouraged white immigration and suppressed black industrial participation. Botha and Smuts also pointed to the potential imperial and international complications of Chinese importation. Having recently concluded an alliance with Japan, Great Britain might also pursue an alliance with China. The Qing government might then demand the removal of "degrading restrictions" against indentured Chinese, leading to full political and economic rights.[47] Simply put, Chinese importation portended nothing but racial, economic, and political calamity.

Botha and Smuts offered two alternatives. Milner's administration should persuade blacks to work. This would both alleviate the colony's labor shortage and instill the affirming value of work in the indigenous population. Otherwise they would squander labor's civilizing benefits and "simply continue their old life of lazy barbarism." The better solution, however, was an effort to secure "white labour from Ireland, Italy or any other white community in the world." It was striking that Botha and Smuts, having so recently fought in defense of Afrikaner nationalism, now prioritized the indiscriminate encouragement of white mobility to defend white supremacy in the Transvaal. Whichever alternative the Transvaal pursued, it was clear to Botha and Smuts that "the worst day's work that could be done for South Africa will be to add to its black population with its insoluble problems a yellow population with still more insoluble problems." Nothing less than South Africa's future as the "home of a white race" was at stake.[48]

They convinced neither Milner nor the Labour Commission. Smuts grew increasingly despondent when Chinese importation became a reality. In December 1903 he predicted that the impending arrival of the Chinese would "be the beginning of a fresh chapter of disasters for this benighted country."[49] Even his fellow Boers failed to recognize Milner's folly, Smuts complained to his friend the British humanitarian Emily Hobhouse in early 1904. He attributed their apathy to hopelessness but remained convinced that "there burns in the Boer mind a fierce indignation against this sacrilege of Chinese importation—this spoliation of the heritage for which the generations of the people have sacrificed their all." With characteristic melodrama he predicted a new race struggle in southern Africa, one that threatened to eradicate Afrikaner influence and erode British control of the continent. "I see the day coming when 'British' South Africa will appeal to the 'Dutch' to save them from the consequences of their insane policy of today," Smuts counseled, "and I fear—I sometimes fear, with an agony bitterer than death—that the 'Dutch' will no more be there to save them or South Africa."[50] From Smuts's perspective, Milner's Chinese importation policy confounded hopes for white racial reconciliation in postwar southern Africa and condemned both white races to decline.

As Smuts consoled himself, Milner sensed victory. Despite hearing continued grumblings, the high commissioner was confident that significant opposition to Chinese importation had dissipated in the Transvaal by early 1904. He informed Lyttelton that January, "While no one likes the prospect of Asiatic labour, a great majority of the people are disposed to accept it as a proved necessity." The labor crisis had not abated, and he was now convinced that white labor's naïve racial fantasies had finally yielded to economic pragmatism.[51] At the end of January 1904 Milner declared that local resistance had practically ceased. He believed that even Boer opinion was now tacitly in favor of Chinese labor. From the Afrikaner perspective, Milner observed, any negative consequences would invariably redound upon the Transvaal's British authorities if the Chinese experiment failed; if it succeeded, then Afrikaners would reap the benefits.[52] Such cynicism might even have invigorated the despairing Smuts, who bemoaned to Hobhouse in March 1904, "We are so miserably weak, so utterly helpless. We could not even derail the first train coming here with a batch of celestials."[53]

Opposition in the Cape Colony

As the tussle intensified in the Transvaal, the Cape Colony's leaders also expressed disquiet at the proposed Asian influx into a nearby colony. Following the Bloemfontein Conference's tacit acceptance of Chinese importation in March 1903, the Cape Colony's House of Assembly adopted a resolution recording the Cape's "strong opposition to any such importation as prejudicial to the interests of all classes of the people of South Africa." The Cape government's concerns echoed those voiced by anti-Chinese forces in the Transvaal: Asian labor threatened white supremacy not only in the Transvaal but across all southern Africa. The preponderance of blacks already posed grave challenges to white political and economic predominance; Chinese immigrants would further compound that disconcerting dynamic. Moreover Cape opponents feared that Chinese laborers indentured to the Transvaal would inevitably escape their bonds and infiltrate the Cape. Once established, they would slowly supplant white commercial activity across the colony as South Asian indentured laborers had supposedly done in Natal.[54]

The Cape government outlined its concerns to the imperial government in August 1903. Deliberately importing "another coloured race" into southern Africa was simply suicidal. This was especially troubling when Milner's administration was striving to increase white immigration in order to consolidate the European presence on the continent. They warned that Chinese importation would also undermine the Cape's efforts to educate and advance the colony's existing nonwhite populations. The Cape government insisted that it was diligently persuading its black population to meet South Africa's labor needs. "If Asiatics be introduced," they cautioned, "that means of civilization will be checked, and the natives will remain in the state of barbarism from which they are slowly but surely emerging." Finally, and perhaps most ominously, they shrewdly cautioned that Chinese importation threatened to disrupt the movement toward South African federation. The profound divisiveness of Chinese immigration might derail the ultimate goal of British policy in southern Africa, "as it will introduce a highly discordant element between the European communities." This policy might ultimately impede eventual political and racial union of Britain's South African colonies.[55]

John Xavier Merriman emerged as one of the Cape's most ardent critics of Chinese importation. Born in England, he had spent much of his life in Cape and national politics.[56] Merriman identified Chinese importation as a fundamental threat to South Africa's future. Speaking in Paarl on the western Cape in December 1903, he encouraged "all races and colours [to] stand as one man" in opposition. Advocates of Chinese labor were irresponsibly gambling with South Africa's future. The Chinese were inassimilable, he maintained, and their presence would vitiate every soul in the South African colonies. He characterized the proposal as a vast capitalist conspiracy designed to limit the political and economic power of white labor vis-à-vis the Randlords. The stakes were clear: "Are we to be a free South Africa or are we to be a vast slave State, with a few enormously wealthy men at the top, a few mean whites next, and at the bottom a native population left to swelter in its barbarism?" Drawing on his knowledge of anti-Asian campaigns in Australasia and North America, Merriman predicted that Chinese importation would lead to catastrophe.[57] His objections were applauded in Paarl but dismissed by the Transvaal's political and economic leadership.

Unable to prevail upon Milner and the Colonial Office, Cape leaders appealed directly to the Crown. They submitted a petition against Chinese labor to King Edward VII in December 1903 with 3,735 signatures.[58] According to the petitioners, Chinese importation "would bring a new element into a population already weighted with a heavy responsibility arising out of a mixture of races, and would assuredly tend to frustrate the efforts that are being made, not without success, to civilise and elevate the aboriginal natives by means of honest industry." Chinese immigration would also hamper the immigration of desirable whites, turn the Transvaal into a virtual "slave state," and eventually render South Africa "an Asiatic dependency." Ultimately, they warned, "the introduction into this country of persons with alien morals, creeds, and habits of life would operate as a fatal bar to the civilisation and settlement of this portion of your Majesty's dominions."[59] In their analysis the fate of both white and black South Africa was irrevocably entwined in the campaign to thwart Milner's importation scheme.

Their efforts failed. The Cape Colony's British governor, Sir Walter Francis Hely-Hutchinson, dismissed his colony's agitation as politically motivated. From his perspective, the Cape's resistance was orchestrated by the anti-British political party, the Afrikaner Bond, which he believed wanted to unite the colony's black, Afrikaner, and coloured residents against British rule during the upcoming Cape elections. The Bond also wished to undermine British supremacy in the Transvaal, he argued, by impeding that colony's economic recovery.[60] Milner too subscribed to this interpretation. "The natives of the Cape Colony are admittedly hostile to the idea of Asiatic immigration," he told Lyttelton in February 1904, and the Bond wished to capitalize on this sentiment. Milner felt that the Cape's African residents had been "frightened, beyond reason, by the absurdly exaggerated colours in which the numbers and character of the immigrants are depicted to them." He also concurred with Hely-Hutchinson's assessment of the Bond's motives regarding the Transvaal. If South Africa's recalcitrant Boers succeeded in preventing the Rand's regeneration, they could achieve through peaceful means what they had failed to achieve on the battlefield: an end to British supremacy in southern Africa.[61]

The Colonial Office in London also dismissed the Cape's concerns. Lyttelton insisted that the imperial government could not intervene given the urgency of the Transvaal's labor needs.[62] Milner's former Transvaal colonial secretary, Sir George Fiddes, was less tactful and, not surprisingly, echoed Milner's stance. Writing from his new position in the Colonial Office, Fiddes categorically rejected one colony's right to interfere with another's internal affairs; on that basis alone the Cape's apprehensions were irrelevant. More important, he derided the Cape government's efforts to derail Chinese importation as nothing more than a thinly disguised attempt by Bond-affiliated agitators to undermine British power in South Africa. Fiddes declared that there was no viable economic alternative to Chinese labor. The dearth of African labor, coupled with the white man's understandable refusal to toil alongside blacks, meant that "the situation resolves itself into a race between Asiatics and bankruptcy." Indeed the extensive employment of " 'white Kaffirs' would be far worse for South Africa than the worst possible evils of Asiatic immigration," Fiddes contended. He saw the insidious influence of irreconcilable Boers in the Cape's actions. Ultimately, he argued, hostile Afrikaner opinion had no place in this debate. "It would be regarded as an act of unexampled weakness," he warned, "to submit to the decision of those whom we have only just succeeded in conquering the question whether British interests and the British race should continue to be supported in the country which they have just lost."[63]

Richard Seddon and the Imperial Backlash

The debate over Chinese importation could not be confined to southern Africa. The British Empire's annexation of Transvaal—and the participation of Australasian troops in that endeavor—ensured that the dispute became entangled in broader struggles over Asian labor mobility in the empire. Richard Seddon of New Zealand, abetted by his Australian counterpart, Alfred Deakin, launched the most robust intercolonial campaign against Chinese importation and in support of white supremacy in southern Africa. From Seddon's perspective, Milner and his collaborators were threatening the future of a white South Africa, insulting the empire's veterans and war dead, and establishing a dangerous example that could undermine hard-won colonial safeguards against Asian migration and mobility. Such perfidy could not go unchallenged.

The New Zealand premier's intervention was unsuccessful, but his exertions illustrate the ongoing imperial antagonisms engendered by Asian mobility and the process by which those tensions disseminated through the empire. Seddon was the pivot around which much of the intercolonial opposition to Chinese importation revolved, but that also made him a conduit for counterarguments in support of Chinese indenture. His campaign therefore also demonstrates the limits of intercolonial solidarities and activism. While he received support from the Commonwealth prime minister and Australian labor organizations, he also received admonishments from the Colonial Office, the British Parliament, and private individuals with experience in southern Africa. The imperial government had indulged New Zealanders and Australians in their recent convulsions against Asian migration; as self-governing white communities they were entitled to exercise a limited degree of sovereignty over their borders. Imperial authorities were less inclined to cosset Australasian interference in the affairs of other colonies, especially one deemed vital to the exercise of British power in southern Africa.

Seddon rose to defend white supremacy in southern Africa as the debate over Chinese importation intensified. He called Milner's scheme "reprehensible to an extreme degree" and felt compelled to intervene given his colony's own experience with Asian migration. He insisted that New Zealanders and Australians had proven that gold mines could and should be worked exclusively by white men.[64] Moreover he felt obliged to intercede having committed several thousand New Zealand troops to the British war effort in southern Africa. For Seddon the British Empire was a white man's endeavor. During his own colony's restriction debate in 1899, for example, he questioned the prudence of incessant imperial expansion in nonwhite territories: "If we bring these inferior and coloured races under the British flag, it does not follow that we are to admit them into our families. If that is what the extension of the British Empire means to the Britisher, then the less territory we get, and the less coloured races are brought under our flag, the better it will be for the good of the Empire."[65] This was an indictment of capacious imperial citizenship rights and the freedom of movement those rights implied for Asians and Africans under British dominion.

As Chinese importation gained traction among the Transvaal's political and economic elites in late 1903, Seddon joined Deakin to present a united Australasian front against the proposal.[66] In January 1904 the two men sent identical telegrams to Pretoria, outlining their opposition to Chinese labor. The Australasian premiers encouraged Milner's administration to impose outright prohibitions against Chinese immigration; otherwise this racial contaminant promised to pollute not only southern Africa but also the entire empire. "[The] Government of New Zealand foresees grave perils, racial, social, political and sanitary inevitabl[ly] induced by [this] alien influx," Seddon warned. It set a dangerous precedent, one that the white settler colonies had struggled against since the mid-nineteenth-century gold rushes. If the imperial government could force indentured Chinese labor upon the Transvaal, they could do the same to Australia and New Zealand. The Australasian premiers argued that any financial gain would come at the expense of white racial, social, and political integrity. Whether assimilated into white society or excluded from it, the Chinese immigrant constituted a lethal cancer.[67] Seddon and Deakin also expressed their concerns directly to the Colonial Office in London, and the Australian Parliament passed a near-unanimous resolution recording its "grave objection" to Chinese importation, at least until the Transvaal's white population could democratically express its collective preference.[68]

Seddon's efforts received support from white colonists across New Zealand, Australia, and southern Africa. White trade and labor associations from New Zealand applauded his campaign.[69] The Australasian Federated Seamen's Industrial Association's Dunedin section captured the antipathy many white Australasians felt toward Chinese importation in southern Africa. At its 1904 annual meeting the Association endorsed Seddon's protest and condemned Chinese importation as superfluous and detrimental to white labor throughout the empire. They further resolved, "The assistance rendered in men and money during the Boer war by New Zealand and Australia to ostensibly maintain the status of the Anglo-Saxon race entitles these colonies to vigorously oppose [Chinese importation], which is obviously intended to benefit only the mine proprietors and capitalists of South Africa, in whose interests it is becoming alarmingly evident that the recent war was waged."[70] Australian labor associations also registered their support for Seddon. On January 22, 1903, the Carlton Trades Hall Council in Melbourne approved his campaign and resolved that Chinese labor importation disgraced the flag and everything it represented. They inverted Milner's arguments in favor of Chinese indenture, concluding that the introduction of Chinese in South Africa would "be provocative of industrial strife, promote racial animosities, retard the expansion of the country, and prevent the influx of the white races, who alone have the right to be considered." Seddon received similar resolutions from the Brisbane Trades and Labour Council and the Masterton Liberal and Labour Federation in Queensland.[71] The mayor of Sydney reported on a public meeting supporting Seddon's "disinterested and patriotic efforts to maintain the stability of the British Empire by promoting and preserving the racial, industrial, and social integrity of the Anglo-Saxon and Celtic races of the Empire."[72]

Support for Seddon's resistance was not unanimous, however; the premier also received letters encouraging him to moderate his opposition. One New Zealander feared that Seddon's rhetoric might hinder the colony's Christian missionaries working in Asia.[73] An Australian expatriate living in South Africa, F. R. McDonald, asked Seddon to change his position. Labor shortages were devastating the Transvaal's economy, McDonald maintained, and Chinese labor represented the only solution to the crisis. Echoing Milner's unceasing refrain, he insisted that white labor was a chimera in Africa because it meant either "an elevation of the kaffir to the level of the European or the degradation of the unskilled white to the level of the Natives." The social and economic consequences of either alternative were simply "deplorable." Native labor was no more realistic: the African population was too lazy. The only solution was Chinese labor. "You know that my Australian up-bringing has familiarized me with the short-comings of the Mongolian races and I readily admit that the dangers stated exist," McDonald acknowledged. He nevertheless encouraged Seddon to support the well-regulated and strictly controlled importation ordinance then under consideration in Pretoria and London.[74]

In his reply to McDonald, Seddon extolled the redemptive properties of white immigration. Imperial authorities should seize this opportunity to flood the Transvaal with British immigrants since white labor was the only reliable antidote to South Africa's seemingly inveterate racial and economic strife. British immigrants would reproduce, prosper, and finally bring racial, political, and economic stability to South Africa. In this respect Seddon had much in common with Milner. The New Zealander did not, however, share the high commissioner's conviction in the utility of Chinese labor in that equation. British migrants would come only in the absence of Chinese. Otherwise, he lamented to McDonald, "the population of your country will be composed largely of Boers, largely of Chinese, together with a number of Rand mine owners who are not of British origin." Such an outcome would disgrace the sacrifices of the late war and assure enduring British inferiority in South Africa.[75] Seddon expanded his arguments in a letter to W. Hutchinson, a British colonist in South Africa. He was committed to preventing the "yellow agony from spreading in South Africa." The results of Chinese importation were certain: "a debasement of labour and a desecration of the graves of the sons of New Zealand who fought so nobly for freedom, justice, and the flag of our country." The proposed "horde of Asiatics" demeaned the white man's sacrifice in South Africa and would mean "the implantment [*sic*] of the Chinese Dragon on the Union Jack to its disfigurement and dishonour."[76]

Members of the British Parliament considered Seddon's protestations during their own deliberations in early 1904. Prime Minister Arthur Balfour's Conservative government largely supported Milner's scheme, but they faced a serious challenge from parliamentary Liberals, still reeling from their wartime schisms. Liberals portrayed the Conservative-supported importation policy as Chinese slavery, designed in collusion with the Randlords to undermine unionization and reduce white wages in South Africa. For many Liberal MPs the debate over Chinese importation was an opportunity to renew their wartime attacks on Conservative policy in South Africa.[77] On February 16, 1904, Cleveland's Liberal MP, Herbert Samuel, introduced an amendment opposing Chinese importation. The motion sought the Crown's intervention pending a referendum of white South Africans. Samuel derided the proposed indenture ordinance, comparing it to the antebellum American South's slave statutes. Milner and the Randlords "wished the Transvaal and South Africa to remain permanently a country in which an aristocracy of whites was supported by . . . the labour of a servile class of coloured men." There would be no place for the white working man in South Africa under this scheme, Samuel claimed. The fundamental question before the House, he suggested, was "whether the waste-places of the earth under its control should be peopled by Mongolians or should be the home of the white peoples."[78]

Samuel's Liberal colleagues often drew upon Seddon's remonstrations— and the experiences of white settler societies more widely—to bolster their case against Balfour, Milner, and the Chamber of Mines. Concurring that Chinese immigrants diminished the vitality of white men's countries and condemned white labor to destitution, exponents of the New Zealand prime minister's position highlighted the antipathy that white settlers in New Zealand and elsewhere felt toward Asian migrants and mocked Milner's conflation of Chinese importation and British migration. For example, Major John Seely—himself a veteran of the South African War and a future cabinet member—found it inconceivable that Conservatives would endorse the introduction of Chinese labor in South Africa given the recent experiences of Australians, New Zealanders, and Canadians. "So great was the repugnance of all Anglo-Saxon peoples to the admixture of Chinese in the population," he claimed, "that in no single case had Chinese been imported into any country without great efforts being subsequently made to get rid of the influx of Chinese." It was ludicrous to suggest that South Africa should be subjected to "the very thing that every Anglo-Saxon community was doing its utmost to eject and exclude." If British policy was predicated upon creating a "white South Africa," then Chinese immigration would forever preclude that already improbable fantasy.[79]

When Conservative members questioned Seddon's right to interfere in the affairs of another colony, Liberals replied that Australasian colonists' direct experience and selfless support during the late war amply justified their intervention. William McArthur had lived in Australia and he lauded Australasians' contributions to the British war effort, encouraging his colleagues to learn from their experience with Asian immigration: "If we were to estimate the value of . . . the sacrifices made by our colonies in the recent war, surely no opinion had a better claim to be tried than the unanimous opinion of Australia and New Zealand in this matter." Moreover their direct experience of large-scale Chinese immigration entitled them to express their opinions on the issue.[80] Herbert Asquith, the future Liberal prime minister, agreed. Australia and New Zealand had "spilled their best blood on the soil of South Africa in the name of freedom," and that sacrifice alone gave them "a title to speak." More important, Britain's Pacific colonies "have had experience, a close and direct experience, which happily we have been spared, of the contact of yellow immigrant Chinese labour with the daily life of a white community."[81]

Conversely Milner's Conservative Party allies dismissed the notion that the Transvaal could ever really be a conventional "white man's country," thus negating the very premise of Seddon's vexations. Henry Cust outlined the crux of the Conservative case for Chinese labor. He proffered that "the situation in South Africa was a totally new one in the history of modern civilisation." Ostensibly South Africa was a "white man's country," blessed with a suitably temperate climate that was conducive to white settlement. Nevertheless, though it was undoubtedly a place "where white men could live and breed," it also contained "an enormous and overwhelming preponderance of free black men who would not work." This made southern Africa unique, fundamentally different from other "white men's countries." During antebellum America's formative industrial and agricultural development, for example, "the black population were wholly bond and slave," Cust claimed, and in Australia and the western United States "the coloured races of both continents were practically non-existent." This meant that "both were white men's countries, and in both white worked by the side of white in the highest and the lowest labour." In South Africa, however, "a white man would never work at the same task as the black man." Cust was equally dismissive of Seddon's opposition to Chinese importation. "We value our colonies," he affirmed, "but it was somewhat absurd that New Zealand, with a population about equal to that of a provincial town in England, should dictate the policy of the Empire in this matter."[82]

Ian Malcolm, the Conservative member for Stowmarket, expanded on these issues in his speech before the Commons. Malcolm felt that Seddon's and Deakin's grievances were "strangely out of place in the mouths of men who themselves would most violently resent outside interference in the affairs of their own colonies." Australasians had vigorously defended their right to prohibit Asian immigration despite protests from the imperial government. Somewhat disingenuously Malcolm suggested that Transvaal now deserved the same consideration from Seddon and Deakin. Keir Hardie, a founding member of the Labour Party, continued his estrangement from the Liberals by supporting the Conservative position on Chinese importation. From his perspective the argument was ultimately moot. South Africa "was not a white man's country in the same sense that the United States or our own Colonies of Canada, Australia, and New Zealand were white men's countries." The arrival of Chinese labor would therefore not materially affect the white man's position in South Africa. Whites there were already outnumbered by an indigenous majority; this made South Africa distinct from "the United States, where the red man was now practically extinct, from Australia where the Aborigines were practically extinct, and from New Zealand where the Maori were fast going."[83]

Balfour shared Hardie's assessment of South Africa's unique racial composition. Defending his government's support of Chinese importation, Balfour gently dismissed Seddon's and Deakin's concerns: "Australia and New Zealand are colonies of white men which can be permanently made and retained as colonies of white men." Australia's "black races have died away in front of the white race," he noted without regret. Black South Africans, however, "have a resisting power which neither the Red Indian in North America nor the Aboriginal in Australia has been able to show." Ultimately the abiding problem of South African development was "the problem of a great white population living there, having families there, becoming permanent residents, and yet with an incomparably larger number of a wholly different race, who of necessity, from the very nature of things, will have to do the coarse and rough labour of the community." The extensive employment of white labor in South Africa was a dangerous fantasy, Balfour insisted, one that would permanently subvert white supremacy and forever debase the colony's white settlers. "Do not let us aim at an impossible ideal," he concluded, "and do not let us suppose that any conceivable scheme of immigration of white labour is to turn South Africa into a place where the rough work of industrial organisation is to be done by the white instead of the black."[84] In the meantime, if adequate black labor was unavailable, Chinese labor would temporarily suffice.

The imperial government disregarded Seddon's concerns as it had those of similarly disillusioned white South Africans. As the Transvaal's colonial secretary explained to Seddon and Deakin, unskilled South African labor had always been performed by "Native races"; Chinese coolies therefore did not threaten South Africa's extant industrial and racial hierarchy. Moreover South Africa's racial and economic composition was vastly different from Australia's and New Zealand's; Australasian conditions could not simply be superimposed onto the South African industrial landscape.[85] Lyttelton was equally indifferent. Every British colony had the right to determine its internal affairs without interference, and he subtly reminded Seddon, "It is this conviction which has guided His Majesty's Government in its action in regard to the question of alien races in New Zealand and Australia."[86] The implication was clear: New Zealand and Australia should mind their own business.

Lyttelton elaborated this position in the House of Commons. Seddon and Deakin were simply deluded about South African racial and economic realities. "Australia and New Zealand are white communities, and I have a good deal of sympathy with the desire to keep them pure white men's countries," Lyttelton avowed, but the South African case was different. The reality, he affirmed, was that whites would simply not work with blacks, and this would invariably remain the basis of South African industrial and race relations without an overwhelming (and unlikely) increase in white immigration.[87] Hely-Hutchinson reiterated this theme in the Cape Colony. Seddon and Deakin could not understand that "it is the presence and the continued increase of the native races in South Africa which has prevented, prevents, and will always prevent, the establishment of a white labouring class in South Africa." Ultimately "South Africa can never become a white man's country, in the sense that Australia is a white man's country."[88]

Balfour, Milner, and the Chamber of Mines ultimately prevailed. The governments of Great Britain and China concluded the Anglo-Chinese Labour Convention in May 1904, which facilitated the importation of approximately 63,000 Chinese coolies between 1904 and 1907.[89] The vast majority of Chinese recruits came from the northern provinces, especially Chihli (Hebei), Shantung (Shandong), and Honan (Henan).[90] After their arrival in Durban, shipments of Chinese were processed and then herded into strictly regulated compounds in the Transvaal, where they would largely remain for the next three years when not deep underground, which most of them were, for ten hours a day, six days a week. Passive and active resistance to the myriad verbal, physical, and economic indignities inflicted upon them was common among the laborers, and a number of significant riots broke out across the Rand throughout the first years of Chinese importation. Violent abuses and the liberal application of corporal punishment helped to oust Milner from his position in 1905, and he was almost subject to direct parliamentary censure in March 1906 during the ensuing scandal. "Chinese slavery" remained a divisive issue and helped the Liberal Party achieve a sweeping electoral victory in January 1906 following Balfour's resignation the previous month. Sir Henry Campbell-Bannerman's new government began to slowly encourage Chinese repatriation. They were aided by the institution of self-government in the Transvaal in February 1907, when Botha and Smuts's newly formed Het Volk Party constituted a majority government in Pretoria.[91] The system limped on for three more years, until the last Chinese laborers left the Rand in 1910.

CHAPTER THREE

The Politics of Asian Labor Mobility in North America

The debate over Chinese importation in the Transvaal temporarily displaced the focal point of white hostility toward Asian labor mobility from Australasia to southern Africa, from the specter of large-scale South Asian and Japanese immigration to the reality of Chinese importation. The relative calm in the Pacific nevertheless proved illusory, and the fight in the North American West intensified as the struggle in southern Africa subsided. American and Canadian legislators had significantly curtailed Chinese immigration during the 1880s in response to the demands of white gold miners, railroad workers, and local governments. These measures temporarily diminished the energy of anti-Asian politics in North America. Latent racial, economic, and strategic concerns resurfaced in British Columbia and the western United States in the early 1900s, however, rejuvenating long-standing apprehensions toward Asian migrants. In both cases white laborers, newspaper editors, and legislators panicked at the prospect of extensive Japanese—and, later, South Asian—migration, driven in part by their imagination and in part by the Japanese challenge to the status quo in East Asia. And once more the Japanese Foreign Ministry, American diplomats, and British imperial authorities bristled at the persistent humiliations propagated by white racial and economic militants, this time in the North American West.

Recent scholarship has emphasized the transnational networks and relationships that affiliated anti-Asian politics in North America and elsewhere, but this chapter once more underscores the critical and often determinative differences.[1] North American activists certainly used similar language to their counterparts in the South Pacific and the Indian Ocean in describing the distress they experienced when confronted by Asian mobility, and they nourished their attitudes from a similar stock of antipathies. Although redolent of their Australasian and South African analogues, Canadian and American protests were conditioned by a different constellation of local, regional, international, and imperial circumstances, yielding distinct politics, strategies, and consequences. And although their objections to Asian mobility stemmed from the same sources, the Canadian and American campaigns of the early 1900s also unfolded independently of one another. While Canadian and

American activists sometimes collaborated, they too were beholden to different political concerns that more often disconnected them from one another. In this case as in others, then, the most enduring common thread was international and imperial friction. As the *Saturday Review* noted after the 1907 riots, "The relations of British Columbia to the Canadian Government may present analogies to those between Washington and California, but we stand alone in our connexion by treaty with one of the aggrieved parties, and in some cases the victims of racial hatred are our own subjects."[2]

Before examining those differences, however, it is important to acknowledge that an array of commonalities marked the Canadian and American struggles against Asian migration, differentiating them from those ongoing in Australasia and South Africa. Proximity to the Pacific Ocean meant that anti-Asian activism remained primarily, although not entirely, a feature of politics on the West Coast of both Canada and the United States. Western activists often surmised that not enough Asian migrants had ventured beyond the Rockies to stimulate easterners into concerted transcontinental action.[3] As a result campaigners on both sides of the border regularly complained that their eastern compatriots failed to appreciate the threat posed by transpacific Asian mobility. The apparent detachment of easterners in places like New York, Washington, D.C., Toronto, and Ottawa aggravated the isolation and resentment felt by agitators in San Francisco, Seattle, Vancouver, and Victoria. The *San Francisco Chronicle* editorialists complained in late 1906, "However vigorously we here may protest and resolve, we cannot exclude Asiatic coolies until we convince the people of the East that it is desirable to do so."[4] Making matters worse, intensifying aversions toward the scale and character of European immigration in the United States occupied many of those disposed toward restriction in eastern and midwestern cities.[5] Such regional differences were much less pronounced in Australia and New Zealand, where the politics of Asian restriction resonated from coast to coast, thanks to a common sense of exposure and contiguity to the sources of Asian migration. The same was true in southern Africa, where white labor throughout the British colonies balked at Asian immigration, regardless of the origin.

Federalism exacerbated the asymmetry of westerners' anti-Asian fixations in the American and Canadian cases and complicated the implementation of nationwide legislative restrictions. The cynicism of western activists toward perceived eastern indifference therefore also manifested in friction between federal governments in the East and provincial and state governments in the West. British Columbians and Californians in particular campaigned ceaselessly for federal legislation in the early twentieth century, repeatedly instituting local restrictions that were designed to encourage action in Ottawa and Washington, respectively. Federal authorities struggled to balance the demands of western constituents with their diplomatic and imperial obligations. Constitutional disputes over the locus of authority vis-à-vis immigration control compounded these difficulties. Under the terms of the British North America Act, federal authority superseded provincial law in the event of a conflict over immigration. Similarly the U.S. Supreme Court asserted congressional primacy over immigration policy in its 1889 *Chae Chan Ping* decision.[6] Such regional and federal-state tensions were largely absent in Australia and New Zealand. In a unitary state with no formal constitution, New Zealanders determined immigration policy through parliamentary means, while Australians had federated partly in order to institute a unified system of national immigration control across the six constituent states.

The situation in western North America also differed from that in Australasia and southern Africa because relatively large numbers of Japanese and South Asian migrants actually traveled to and through California and British Columbia after the Japanese government's relaxation of emigration restrictions in 1885. Approximately 80,000 Japanese entered the United States between 1900 and 1906, despite a 1900 agreement between the Japanese and American governments that limited Japanese labor emigration.[7] Migrants circumvented that agreement by entering the United States via Hawaii or Mexico, while many others posed as businessmen or merchants to avoid the ban on laborers.[8] British Columbia also served as a gateway for Japanese migration to the United States and increasingly was a destination in itself. For example, around 15,000 Japanese migrants passed through Canada from 1897 to 1901. According to official figures only 4,738 actually remained by 1901, the majority in British Columbia; most were passing through on their way to the United States.[9] This compared to New Zealand, which was home to a mere fifteen documented Japanese immigrants in 1896, and Australia, where some 3,554 Japanese residents lived according to the 1901 census.[10] So as Australasians sought to preemptively close their borders against the possible influx of Asian migrants and as South Africans vented against controlled importations of Chinese, Americans and Canadians worked to seal existing flows of Japanese and South Asians that seemingly threatened to hemorrhage during the first decade of the twentieth century.

As these figures suggest, the Californian and British Columbian campaigns were also linked by geography, a common border, and the mobility of Asian migrants across that border—again distinguishing Pacific Northwest anti-Asian politics from outbreaks in Australia, New Zealand, and southern Africa. This reflected the fact that residents of western North America were enmeshed in and often dependent upon the circuits of Asian mobility that interwove the Pacific during this period. The networks of commerce and shipping that sustained both rural and urban communities in the North American West also conveyed Asian migrants from China, South Asia, and Japan who furnished essential labor and trade for Canadian and American canneries, farms, market gardens, railroads, and fisheries. Hawaii played an especially instrumental role in the movement of people, goods, and culture between Asia and North America.[11] As a hub for Japanese migrants, the islands functioned as a quintessential node of Asian transshipment and mobility in the Pacific. For example, Eiichiro Azuma estimates that 38,000 Japanese migrants entered the United States from Hawaii between 1902 and 1907.[12] White Australasians—and especially Queenslanders—participated in similar networks of Pacific trade and labor, but the White Australia Policy emphatically reversed earlier attempts to exploit Asian workers in the region. For their part, New Zealanders remained largely insulated from actual Japanese and South Asian migration during this period and strove to maintain that isolation.

The strategies used to suppress Asian labor mobility in the Pacific Northwest also differed markedly from those deployed in Australasia and southern Africa. Faced with significant numbers of Asian residents but denied the legal means to expel them, North American agitators instead relied on inventive and sometimes extralegal measures to express their antipathy toward Asian migrants and their frustration toward federal authorities. Lawmakers in Victoria tried to stifle Asian participation in the provincial economy, while Californians attempted to segregate Asian schoolchildren. Exasperated by the repeated failure of legal strategies, some agitators in British Columbia and Washington State turned to violence, instigating race riots in Vancouver and Bellingham in September 1907. These tactics were designed partly to choke Asian social and economic mobility and partly to encourage federal action against further immigration. When the American and Canadian governments finally reacted in 1907 and 1908, they both negotiated restrictions on Japanese labor migrants' transpacific mobility, thus inhibiting migration at the source. This too differed from the strategies used by Australasians, who reluctantly enacted the British government's favored language test to repel Asian migrants at their borders rather than remotely preempting their emigration in the first place.

At the same time, however, there were important differences in the context, tactics, and consequences of American and Canadian approaches to inhibiting Asian labor mobility. Those differences were at once engendered by and constitutive of specific combinations of domestic, imperial, and international politics. For example, British Columbians exercised their legislative prerogatives against two sometimes dissonant sources of sovereignty—Canadian and British—while states pursuing anti-Asian agendas in the American West faced only one: the federal government in Washington. British Columbians therefore grappled with a formidable extra layer of competing authority. Furthermore the British Empire's alliance with Japan required constant and careful mediations by the British and Canadian governments, but it could also help muffle the worst effects of British Columbian insults. On the other hand, Japanese-American relations were far more contentious during this period, which intensified the politics of Japanese restriction in the American West. The expansion of American naval and economic power in the Pacific—exemplified by the annexation of Hawaii and the colonization of the Philippines at the turn of the century—grated against the extension of Japanese imperial power in Korea, Formosa, and China.[13] The Roosevelt administration's sometimes antagonistic relationship with the Meiji Empire therefore exacerbated the consequences of Californians' actions. The Roosevelt administration also had to consider British sensibilities when responding to the mistreatment of South Asian migrants who crossed the U.S.-Canadian border with increasing frequency in the first decade of the twentieth century in places like Bellingham and Seattle. After all, British Columbia was a conduit for Japanese migration to the United States, but it was also an entrepôt for South Asian migrants to the United States.

These domestic, imperial, and diplomatic challenges are the focus of my analysis of anti-Asian politics in British Columbia, California, Washington State, and Oregon. Indeed the actions of Canadian and American activists were a source of tension across the North American continent and across the Pacific and Atlantic oceans. Next to the actual or abstract mobility of Asian migrants themselves, this friction constituted the most durable feature connecting—and often disconnecting—restriction campaigns in the United States, Canada, Australia, New Zealand, and southern Africa. The politics of Asian labor mobility tormented Japanese-American relations at a time when both countries enthusiastically projected their growing military and economic power in East and Southeast Asia. The abuse of South Asian migrants by American laborers in Washington and Oregon stressed Anglo-American relations, even as British officials warily eyed American slights against their Japanese allies. British and Canadian authorities also worked to restrain alienated colonists in British Columbia whose vilifications of Asian migrants irked the Japanese government and encouraged collaborative overtures from American activists.

In the first two parts of this chapter I assess the different strategies adopted by American and Canadian restriction activists in the early twentieth century, though both used segregation to contain the social and economic lives of Asian immigrants. I begin by examining the British Columbian legislature's efforts to curtail Asian economic access at the turn of the century and the complex international repercussions produced by that struggle. Thousands of Japanese migrants entered the region's labor markets during those years. Some intended to settle, but most were transiting the province on their way to the United States. Either way, provincial lawmakers incessantly legislated against their participation in both public and private economic activity in an effort to coerce a federal prohibition on Japanese immigration, prompting domestic, imperial, and international resistance. The second section applies the same multidimensional analysis to the 1906 San Francisco school crisis. The proposed segregation of Asian schoolchildren sparked a serious diplomatic and constitutional crisis, forcing an intervention by the Roosevelt administration, which contrived to unravel the complex domestic and international legalities of the school board's actions. This crisis produced a novel settlement that temporarily pacified both western antagonism and Japanese honor. The so-called gentleman's agreement diverged from the British Empire's usual unilateral strategy of literacy testing for Asian migrants at colonial borders. Instead this arrangement represented a bilaterally negotiated, remote constraint on the mobility of Japanese laborers. The third section addresses another distinctive tactic used by North American restriction advocates against Asian labor migrants: violence and eviction. The fall of 1907 saw the extralegal expulsion of South Asian workers in Washington and Oregon and riots against Japanese, Chinese, and South Asians in Vancouver. These violent disturbances created the urgent context for a separate Japanese-Canadian gentleman's agreement and new constraints on South Asian migration by the Indian, British, and Canadian governments.

Suppressing Asian Mobility in the Canadian West, 1897–1902

White British Columbians had been embroiled in networks of Pacific exploration and commerce for decades before the formal accession of their province to the Canadian Confederation in 1871. Spanish and British expeditions connected the region to the centers of European and North American imperial power in the late 1700s, and the Hudson Bay Company accessed Asian markets via intermediaries in Hawaii by the 1840s. Fur, lumber, and produce from the western reaches of British North America supplied Pacific whaling fleets, Cantonese merchant houses, and European settlers and sailors in Oahu. Returning vessels carried goods and resources from China, India, and elsewhere back to British settlements on the Columbia and Fraser rivers. These connections continued to grow as the region's economy and society matured throughout the mid-1800s.[14] By the time British Columbia became a formal British colony in 1858 following the discovery of gold in the Fraser River Canyon, the area was becoming embedded in what Kornel Chang calls "an imperial circuitry of trade, migration, and communication"; it was a system abetted as much by Asian merchants and brokers as by Europeans and Americans.[15]

Gold and the insatiable labor demands of colonial economic growth encouraged the migration of Chinese laborers in the coming decades, intensifying the entanglements of British Columbia—and North America more broadly—with Asia in the second half of the nineteenth century. By 1860 some 4,000 Chinese had arrived on British North America's Pacific coast in search of gold. As prospectors exhausted the region's deposits, Chinese miners diversified into the colony's canneries, mined coal, participated in land-clearing gangs, operated laundries, constructed roads and ditches, and provided domestic service to affluent whites. Anti-Chinese sentiment intensified when almost 16,000 indentured Chinese workers arrived in British Columbia to help build the Canadian Pacific Railway extension between 1881 and 1884.[16] This surge in Chinese immigration galvanized nationwide support for restriction, especially after the U.S. Congress enacted its own Chinese Exclusion Act in 1882. British Columbians feared the controlled importation of Chinese labor, barred from entering California, would become an uncontrollable flood. Under pressure from the West, the Canadian Parliament finally passed the Chinese Immigration Act in 1885. Echoing comparable Australasian statutes, this legislation imposed a $50 head tax on Chinese entry into the entire dominion and placed a limit of one per fifty tons on the number of Chinese per vessel entering Canadian ports.[17] These measures were designed to incapacitate Chinese migrants by punishing their mobility, penalizing both the individual migrants and those who conveyed them.

The federal government's action heralded a brief lull in anti-Asian activity in British Columbia. That respite was short-lived, however, as increasing numbers of Japanese began arriving in British Columbia during the late 1890s. A combination of factors incited this swell. Disabling Chinese mobility had not disconnected British Columbian industries from the profitable transpacific and imperial commercial networks that enriched the colonial economy. Divested of cheap and supposedly pliant Chinese labor, many colonial producers turned to Japanese laborers to operate their fisheries and lumberyards. Relatively high wages and the purported abundance of employment opportunities attracted the many thousands who made the crossing. Agents, brokers, hoteliers, steamship companies, and successful migrants on both sides of the Pacific facilitated their mobility, providing information, connections, and financial assistance.[18]

British Columbia was also a critical juncture in the networks of commerce and migration that connected Tokyo, Yokohama, Honolulu, Vancouver, Seattle, and San Francisco.[19] The Canadian province was an aperture on the North American continent that channeled Japanese migrants into the United States, where larger Issei communities and more established and diverse economies afforded greater opportunities for new immigrants. A coalition of discontented white British Columbians therefore resolved to excise their province from that network. This proved exceptionally difficult, however, since British Columbians were also ensnared in a web of relationships that precluded a unilateral declaration of Japanese exclusion. British Columbian legislators were constitutionally prohibited from summarily dictating Japanese restriction, and they were obliged to respect Canadian and British relations with Japan.

Determined to suffocate the movement of Japanese migrants through and within the province—but powerless to unilaterally exclude them—provincial representatives endeavored to make life as difficult as possible for them. Their first method—suppressing Japanese economic activity—distinguished British Columbian restriction from its parallels elsewhere. Local legislators hoped that stifling Asian participation in the provincial economy would subdue the flow of Japanese migrants and impress the depth of their commitment to Asian restriction upon Canadian, Japanese, and British authorities. British Columbian lawmakers therefore embarked upon a sustained campaign of petulance in 1897, passing a number of statutes designed to limit Japanese migrants' economic activity. For example, the 1897 Alien Labour Act levied substantial fines on companies that hired Asian laborers on certain public works and utilities projects. Under the terms of this law, penalties accrued daily for each illegally employed Asian laborer, and the provincial government could seize and sell assets, and even imprison employers that proved incapable or unwilling to pay.[20] A succession of similar laws followed. If provincial lawmakers could not thwart Asian mobility at the border, they would deprive migrants of the ability to subsist while living in or traveling through British Columbia.

The broader reaction to these measures clarifies how British Columbian restriction policies determined and were determined by a distinct blend of domestic, international, and imperial politics. Japanese, Canadian, and British representatives across three continents intervened in the ensuing disputes, and each refracted the legislature's actions through the lens of his own local, regional, and global interests.[21] Japanese officials at home, in North America, and in Great Britain protested British Columbians' disdain toward the racial and cultural honor of the Japanese people and the advances of the Meiji Restoration. They reminded Canadian and British officials of Japan's growing economic strength and reiterated the formal and informal commitments that associated Japan with British interests in East Asia and the Pacific. British imperial authorities needed no reminder, especially following recent events in Australasia and southern Africa. Officials from the Foreign Office and the Colonial Office joined with the governor-general in Ottawa to try to ameliorate British Columbian anxieties while finessing relations with Japan. And throughout this crisis Canadian representatives tried to reconcile these irreconcilable interests while protecting their dominion's long-term economic and strategic concerns. Cognizant of British Columbian apprehensions, the Canadian government abstained from the 1894 Anglo-Japanese Treaty of Commerce and Navigation, despite Japan's willingness to forgo the treaty's right of domicile provisions. But federal authorities would not jeopardize Canada's potentially valuable commercial relations with Japan to placate anti-Asian sentiment in the West, nor would they carelessly irritate British relations with the East Asian power.

This unique confluence of politics differentiated British Columbia's relationship with Asian migration from its correlates in Australasia, southern Africa, and the United States. The furor that followed the Alien Labour Act exposes the jumble of domestic, imperial, and diplomatic threads that ensnarled the politics of Asian labor restriction in British Columbia. The Japanese consul general at Vancouver, Nosse Tatsugoro, immediately complained to the British governor-general, the Earl of Aberdeen, that British Columbians' actions constituted "the most unjust and unfriendly measure ever taken by any civilized government against a friendly nation of Great Britain and her dependencies." He also resented that "Japanese subjects are to be discriminated alike the Chinese."[22] This comparison constantly rankled Japanese officials, who believed that their countrymen had proven themselves capable of instituting Western-style social, political, economic, and military reforms; it was insulting to compare this aspiring and modernizing Pacific power to the uncivilized and unsophisticated races of Asia.[23] Canadian officials admitted the validity of the Japanese consul's arguments. The minister of justice, Sir Oliver Mowat, recognized that British Columbians' efforts "might seriously interfere with international relations and federal interests." In addition to undermining Britain's diplomatic relations with Japan, the British Columbian legislature had effectively usurped the federal government's authority over immigration policy. Inaction was the justice minister's solution to the federal, imperial, and international dilemmas provoked by this bill. Mowat recommended to the governor-general that simply reserving his assent rendered the measure inoperative until it could be officially disallowed.[24] By constraining Japanese immigrants' access to the local labor market, then, provincial officials had instigated a transcontinental, transpacific, transatlantic, and transimperial controversy.

Mowat's strategy of inertia failed to curb British Columbians' commitment to Asian restriction, and provincial legislators intensified their program of increasingly brash limitations on Japanese participation in the provincial economy as federal and imperial authorities prevaricated.[25] For the rest of the month Nosse's replacement in Vancouver, Seizaboro Shimizu, doggedly petitioned the Earl of Aberdeen to disallow the province's expanding restrictions on Japanese laborers.[26] After nineteen more acts directed against Japanese economic pursuits, it became clear that Japanese, Canadian, and British officials inside Canada could no longer manage the situation locally, and the governor-general finally appealed to Chamberlain and the Colonial Office for guidance. Chamberlain was of course already sensitive to the politics of colonial Asian immigration restriction, and he urged Aberdeen, "Impress upon your Ministers that restrictive legislation of [this type] is extremely repugnant to the sentiments of the people and Government of Japan." The colonial secretary predictably argued for a federal act based on the Natal formula.[27] This would both assuage Japan's concerns and accomplish British Columbians' objectives. In the meantime, as London, Victoria, and Ottawa tussled over where responsibility lay, the governor-general refrained from vetoing the offending acts in part because Prime Minister Laurier did not wish to antagonize British Columbians by openly advocating disallowance.[28]

Disappointed by the tardy British and Canadian response, the Japanese minister in London finally interceded in August 1898, just as he had two years before in the midst of Australasian campaigns against Japanese migrants. Katō reiterated Shimizu's earlier protests and expressed hope that "such unfriendly and discriminating legislation" would not receive the governor-general's assent. The Japanese minister evidently believed that subtle economic intimidation would prevail where appeals to common sense and international amity had failed. It would be a shame if such an act should "injuriously affect the cordial and commercial relations which now happily exist between Japan and the Dominion of Canada."[29] Katō's threat laid bare the possible consequences of provincial anti-Asian politics. British Columbians could not simply extricate themselves from the conduits of Asian migration without also potentially relinquishing the beneficial trade that flowed through those same channels. This could damage not only the provincial economy but also the Canadian and British economies. But Katō's antagonists in Victoria refused to be intimidated. Encouraged by local labor organizations, in February 1899 the British Columbia legislature expanded existing prohibitions against Chinese coal miners to include Japanese.[30] The legislature once again intensified its anti-Japanese agenda before this latest insult could be satisfactorily resolved, imposing restrictions on Japanese immigrants' right to hold liquor licenses. Previous bills had been directed toward prohibiting Japanese engagement in provincially funded public works programs; the latest act was designed to limit their private commercial activities.[31]

British Columbia's minister of finance and agriculture, Francis Carter-Cotton, defended his province against these intrusions from Tokyo, London, and Ottawa. He maintained that British Columbians had not attempted to restrict Japanese entry; they had merely sought to limit their access to government-sponsored infrastructure projects. Provincial white laborers were enduring a ruinous "influx of Japanese," and while Carter-Cotton regretted that the legislature's actions had embarrassed the imperial government, he nevertheless insisted that British Columbians were actually acting in defense of the empire. It was, after all, "unquestionably in the interests of the Empire that the Pacific Province of the Dominion should be occupied by a large and thoroughly British population." In other words, the restriction of Asian labor mobility was good not only for the province but also for the dominion of Canada and the British Empire.[32] Chamberlain's response reiterated his rejoinder to Carter-Cotton's Australasian counterparts two years earlier. He recognized British Columbians' desire to prevent extensive Asian labor migration, and he agreed that the province must remain British. But he objected to their methods. He once again explained that "it is not the practical exclusion of Japanese to which the Government of the Mikado objects, but their exclusion *nominatim*, which specifically stamps the whole nation as undesirable persons." If British Columbians refused to cooperate, however, the imperial government would force Ottawa to annul the province's legislation under the terms of the British North America Act.[33] Finally, on June 5, 1899, The Canadian governor-general, the Earl of Minto, did just that, officially disallowing the previous summer's objectionable acts, and the Japanese government expressed its satisfaction.[34] Minto disallowed the remaining acts the following year.

The fall and winter of 1899–1900 nevertheless saw a dramatic rise in the number of Japanese arriving in British Columbia: over 7,000 in three months.[35] This increase was partly the result of Hawaii-bound contract laborers being diverted to British Columbian ports by a plague outbreak on the islands. Looming provincial elections further complicated matters, and the situation grew tenser with each arriving vessel.[36] For provincial activists this episode substantiated their determination to disengage British Columbia from the traffic in transpacific labor that connected Japan, Hawaii, Canada, and the United States. It was an abrupt reminder that routes established to convey Japanese elsewhere could easily redirect thousands of undesirable migrants onto Canadian shores, especially as Americans began closing their ports to workers from Japan. The situation took even the Japanese consul general by surprise, as thousands of Japanese arrived in the first three weeks of April alone. In May 1900 Shimizu encouraged his Foreign Ministry to limit the emigration of Japanese laborers to ten per month from each prefecture.[37] At the end of July Japan indefinitely suspended all emigration to Canada and the United States. This policy remained in force for the next four years. According to the British chargé d'affaires in Tokyo, Foreign Minister Viscount Aoki Shūzō was well aware of British Columbian sentiment and made this decision "in order to avoid disagreeable incidents."[38]

Remarkably Japan's unilateral suspension of labor emigration did not placate the British Columbia legislature, which resumed its offensive in late 1900. Having spent the previous three years limiting Japanese migrants' ability to work, legislators now resolved to test the boundaries of federal and imperial power by enacting explicit provincial immigration restrictions. They knew that their efforts were destined to fail, but they hoped to force the federal government into action. Legislators passed two new provincial restriction measures based on a novel reading of the Natal formula. The Act to Regulate Immigration into British Columbia instituted a European language test designed to exclude Japanese laborers on arrival, while the 1900 Labor Regulation Act prohibited any individual or corporation that received "property, rights, or privileges" from the provincial government from employing anybody "who could not read the act itself in a European language."[39] That fall the legislature also reintroduced previously disallowed restrictions on Japanese employment, commercial activity, and political rights.

The remorselessness of the British Columbian legislature initiated urgent responses from every juncture of Anglo-Japanese-Canadian diplomacy. Not surprisingly the audacity of the legislature astonished Shimizu. The Japanese government had only weeks before forbade Japanese labor emigration. In this context, Shimizu wrote, the acts "cannot but be considered as an unfriendly action," and he urged Minto to exercise his powers of disallowance once again.[40] Neither the Crown's representative nor the federal government in Ottawa acted in time, however, and the bills became operative on January 1, 1901. Facing increasing pressure from the Japanese minister in London, Chamberlain impatiently pushed the governor-general into action, insisting that the new legislation violated the British North America Act.[41] The colonial secretary was also under pressure in London: the Foreign Office was preparing to embark on a series of secret negotiations with Japan that would culminate in the 1902 Anglo-Japanese Alliance. Relief came in September 1901 when the governor-general finally disallowed the two most offensive acts.

Laurier's Liberal government also finally yielded to this legislative onslaught in September 1900 by instituting a Royal Commission on Chinese and Japanese Immigration. With Laurier facing federal elections, the timing was no accident.[42] The commissioners visited Vancouver and Victoria and sought testimony in local towns and industries believed to be adversely affected by Asian immigrants. They also traveled to the United States, visiting Washington, D.C., Portland, Oregon, and San Francisco in search of evidence, cognizant of British Columbia's position in a broader transpacific system of migration and commerce. They produced two reports, one dealing with Chinese and the other with Japanese immigration. In each case the commissioners sought witnesses from both sides of the debate and circulated a comprehensive list of questions in local newspapers. They pursued information regarding the vocations, social habits, and civic participation of Chinese and Japanese immigrants as well as tangible evidence of their numbers and their negative impact on white labor, from laundries to land clearance. White witnesses came forward to register their grievances against supposed unfair competition, rampant immorality, and unsanitary living conditions. The Commission also interviewed a small number of Asian immigrants, but their views were given only cursory attention in the final report.[43]

In that report the commissioners carefully distinguished between the unquestionably undesirable Chinese and the "less undesirable" Japanese but nevertheless concluded that Japanese immigrants could not "assimilate with white people." They were hard-working, competitive, independent, and therefore "more dangerous in this regard than the Chinese." The Commission nonetheless recommended that no further action on Japanese immigration was necessary; the Japanese government's moratorium on emigration would suffice. If this proved unsatisfactory, however, they recommended the introduction of a federal Natal Act similar to the one then under consideration in Australia.[44]

British Columbians continued to test London and Ottawa over the coming years. As one British Columbian newspaper complained in 1903, "The only defect . . . apparent in the Japanese system of exclusion is that it doesn't exclude." Given the tangled relationship between the province, the Dominion of Canada, the British Empire, and Japan, the only recourse was continued petulance: "We of this province cannot afford to sacrifice the prosperity of our country for the shibboleth of 'Imperial Reasons.' . . . There is only one way the Japanese can be shut out; that is by the provincial government passing most stringent restrictive legislation, and by re-enacting it every time it is disallowed at Ottawa . . . even though it may mean disruption between the province and the Dominion."[45] The legislature passed four more restriction acts between 1902 and 1905, and each one was subsequently disallowed by the governor-general.[46] Continued pressure from federal and imperial authorities, combined with Japan's voluntary restrictions on emigration, had briefly neutralized British Columbians' exclusionary impulses by 1902.[47] The furor of the previous five years was followed by another five years of relative calm. The resurgence came in 1907, when British Columbian activists adopted a new tactic—mob violence—to convey their contempt for Asian migrants, rejuvenating domestic, imperial, and international tensions throughout the North American West and across the Atlantic and Pacific Oceans.

Containing Japanese Mobility in the American West, 1906–1907

A similarly querulous campaign revived long-standing anxieties toward Asian migrants in the western United States in 1906. Much has been written about these events, and those studies often place American convulsions against Asian mobility in a transnational context, linking protests in California, Washington State, British Columbia, and Australasia through the migrants, activists, and governments that both provoked and reacted to them. I focus instead on the distinctive domestic and international politics that contextualized, shaped, and differentiated Asian labor restriction efforts in the western United States. There the sources and discourses of anti-Asian sentiment were certainly reminiscent of those driving parallel agitations in British Columbia (as well as Australasia and southern Africa). American antipathies demonstrated the same, often contradictory assumptions about innate Asian depravity, asceticism, and inferiority as elsewhere, and they were rooted in similar economic impulses: the rush for gold, infrastructure construction, and the labor-intensive requirements of agriculture, food processing, and resource extraction. Much like British Columbians, activists in the American West felt impeded by their federal government's claims of preeminence regarding immigration policy. But while the causes and ideologies of restriction were similar in the United States and British Columbia, the domestic, imperial, and international contexts differed significantly, which produced distinct and divergent outcomes.

As in British Columbia, earlier anti-Asian movements had focused on Chinese migrants. Following years of escalating protests, petitions, legal constraints, and violence, President Chester A. Arthur signed the Chinese Exclusion Act on May 6, 1882.[48] That statute's ten-year bar on Chinese labor immigration did much to mollify anti-Asian activism in California, but it proved to be only a temporary analgesic for white racial and economic angst. As in British Columbia and Australasia, increasing Japanese emigration—coupled with the East Asian nation's growing military and economic power—revitalized dormant apprehensions. And as elsewhere, this purported new influx derived in large part from the exigencies of colonial, imperial, and global capital. Deprived of Chinese laborers, labor-hungry industries turned to Japanese contract workers.[49] Like Chinese immigrants before them, Japanese immigrants found work in agriculture, domestic service, and railroad construction. They also appeared equally debilitating to the white working man's wage and equally challenging to his dominance in the West.[50]

Hostility intensified in early 1905, as Japanese troops advanced against the retreating Russians in Manchuria. That February, the *San Francisco Chronicle* inaugurated an uncompromising crusade against Asian labor. That newspaper's unceasing invectives fanned racial animosity in the city, and on March 1 the California legislature once again unanimously called upon Congress to enact restrictive immigration laws against Japanese immigrants. The legislature raised the chimera of a clandestine Japanese army posing as legitimate immigrants, claiming that the conclusion of the Russo-Japanese

War would "bring to our shores hordes, to be counted only in thousands, of the discharged soldiers of the Japanese army."[51] In the midst of this growing agitation, on May 6 the San Francisco Board of Education passed a resolution mandating school segregation in the city. The resolution was designed not only to alleviate overcrowding in San Francisco's schools "but also for the higher end that our children should not be placed in any position where their youthful impressions may be affected by association with pupils of the Mongolian race."[52] For the time being, however, the board did nothing to enact this policy. Nevertheless the next day militants in San Francisco established the Japanese-Korean Exclusion League, which spent the following years promoting the outright prohibition of Asian immigration throughout the western United States.[53] These local animosities prompted a national and international crisis the following year.

The San Francisco Board of Education finally instituted school segregation on October 11, 1906. They ostensibly did so to assuage overcrowding in the city's beleaguered schools, following the chaos wrought by that April's devastating earthquake. Japanese and Korean children were thereafter ordered to attend the city's Chinese school, which became the Oriental Public School.[54] The segregation edict was in fact designed to force the federal government to take San Franciscans' anti-Japanese animus seriously. By instigating a diplomatic confrontation with Japan and a constitutional crisis with Washington, San Franciscan activists expected either to compel the Roosevelt administration to negotiate a cessation of Japanese immigration or to induce Congress to pass a federal bar on Japanese immigration analogous to the Chinese Exclusion Act.[55]

This strategy paralleled that of British Columbian agitators, and it was similarly dictated by the strictures of federalism, regionalism, and constitutionalism. At the same time, however, Roosevelt administration officials were compelled to mediate a complex and distinct cluster of competing interests, claims, and responsibilities. These factors distinguished the politics of Asian mobility in the United States from those unfolding in Australasia, but also from those straining Anglo-Canadian-Japanese relations to the north. The school board's actions immediately aggravated the burgeoning transpacific imperial rivalry between the two emergent Pacific powers. Japan invoked its treaty rights under the 1894 Treaty of Commerce and Navigation, providing an urgent international context to the school crisis. That diplomatic fact intersected every other legal, political, social, and economic claim asserted in connection with this dispute, although American representatives at every level and on both sides of the argument denied or downplayed it.[56] Questions regarding the relationship between states' rights, the constitutional treaty-making authority of the federal government, and the rights of alien citizens coalesced in the chaotic, postearthquake remains of San Francisco.

The school board's decision prompted immediate outrage in Japan. Indeed news reached East Asia before it reached Washington, and the American ambassador in Tokyo, Luke E. Wright, quickly alerted his government to the international repercussions of San Francisco's local decree. Japanese public opinion was distressed by newspaper reports relating details of the growing crisis in California. According to the ambassador, moderate Japanese newspapers counseled restraint and exhibited sensitivity toward local racial contingencies in the United States, but less responsible newspapers published inflammatory denunciations of the San Francisco school board's decision and demanded retaliation.[57] In addition the Japanese government expressed concern that immigrant restaurant owners in San Francisco were being subjected to violence, intimidation, and boycotts in the aftermath of the earthquake. The Japanese consul in the city reported seventeen separate assaults on Japanese residents in August alone, and local authorities seemed either unwilling or unable to stem the violence.[58]

Despite these reports, Secretary of State Elihu Root initially failed to grasp the diplomatic significance of the San Francisco school board's actions. Root told his ambassador in Tokyo that the issue was "so entirely local and confined to San Francisco that this Government was not aware of their existence until the publication in our newspapers of what had happened in Japan." He assured Wright that Japanese treaty rights were being respected and that the entire question was a wholly parochial dispute, albeit one exacerbated by the recent earthquake.[59] Nevertheless Wright continued to monitor ominous developments in Japanese popular and official sentiment. Alluding to Japan's recent victory over Russia, he informed Root, "The Japanese are an emotional, proud people, who just at this time have a very considerable opinion of themselves, and who are neither as phlegmatic nor as long-suffering as the Chinese."[60] The Japanese people, press, and government were especially alive to racial insults, and the racially motivated segregation of Japanese schoolchildren was particularly offensive, Wright observed. He wrote on October 31, "The suggestion of the drawing of a color-line in America has created the deepest chagrin."[61]

The Japanese government captured Root's attention by insisting upon redress under article I of the 1894 Treaty of Commerce and Navigation. This treaty guaranteed Japanese citizens "full liberty to enter, travel, or reside" in the United States without "higher imposts or charges in these respects than natural citizens or subjects of the most favored nation."[62] According to the Japanese complaint, the segregated school's quality was immaterial: "The fact that Japanese children, because of their nationality, are segregated in special schools and not permitted to attend ordinary public schools, constitutes an act of discrimination carrying with it a stigma and odium which it is impossible to overlook." The Japanese government maintained this legal position throughout the crisis.[63] The Japanese Embassy also complained that the new "Oriental Public School" was located in a fire-ravaged area of the city far away from Japanese residences. The embassy feared that Japanese children traveling to the school would be subject to harassment and treacherous conditions across the devastated city.[64]

As indifference gave way to focus, Root recognized the interconnected domestic, imperial, and international implications of San Francisco's ostensibly local segregation policies. He articulated his concerns in an unusually blunt memorandum to the secretary of commerce and labor, Victor Metcalf. It was not in America's interest to provoke a war with the Japanese, which he feared would result in "the loss of the Philippines, Hawaii, and probably the Pacific Coast." Roosevelt's successful efforts to conclude the Russo-Japanese War the previous year had already incensed the Japanese public, which Root believed had been intent upon pressing their advantage against Russia. Japanese dominion over Manchuria now represented an unassailable military advantage. Moreover Root privately surmised that the United States had no legal justification in this case "because the things that have been done in San Francisco . . . constitute a clear violation of our treaty with Japan." He concluded, "The Government of the United States can not and will not submit to being forced into an unjust quarrel and subjected to national humiliation and disaster by the action of a few ignorant, narrowminded, and prejudiced men who wish to monopolize for themselves the labor market of San Francisco."[65]

It was also clear that aside from the diplomatic dispute between Japan and the United States the school board had instigated a dispute between California and the federal government. In light of this the Roosevelt administration had to resolve the constitutional conflict between the federal government's treaty-making powers and the state's right to regulate its schools. The board claimed legal justification in California state law. In 1902 the state legislature enacted a statute permitting local school boards to exclude children "of filthy or vicious habits" or children suffering from contagious diseases. The legislature further provided for the establishment of segregated schools for "children of Mongolian or Chinese descent." In the event that segregated schools were established, it was forbidden to allow "Chinese or Mongolian" students to attend any other school.[66]

The State Department solicitor, James B. Scott, addressed this question directly in November 1906. The key issue for the department was Japan's right to challenge San Francisco's restrictions on the basis of the Treaty of Commerce and Navigation's most favored nation clause. Technically, Scott averred, neither the U.S. government nor the Japanese government had any legal justification to oppose San Francisco's segregation edict. However unjust or diplomatically offensive, the law was clear. The Japanese government simply could not "claim a right for its subjects or citizens . . . greater than that accorded to native born citizens of the United States," Scott reasonably deduced. The legal segregation of African Americans in the southern United States—and more specifically the segregation of African American schoolchildren—meant that "a member of an alien race, ordinarily coupled with the Negro in statutes, can claim no greater right than accorded to his fellow sufferer."[67] This was not what Roosevelt and Root wanted to hear.

Roosevelt dispatched Secretary Metcalf (himself a Californian) to San Francisco to assess these problems at their source. Metcalf immediately experienced the confusion wrought by the earthquake and by the city's challenge to both domestic and international law. His first order of business was to meet with the state's supreme court justices, who were unanimous that the school board's actions violated American treaty obligations. They informed Metcalf that if the matter was brought before them they would immediately render a decision to this effect. The court's stance was predicated upon the Treaty of Commerce and Navigation's conferment of most favored nation status on Japan, however, and since the supreme court library had been destroyed in the recent earthquake neither Metcalf nor the justices had access to the actual treaty text. To further complicate matters, the U.S. district attorney in San Francisco, Robert T. Devlin, was not convinced that the treaty had actually extended most favored nation privileges to Japan, at least not beyond the narrow confines of residency rights.[68] From Devlin's perspective, the right to reside in the United States did not necessarily confer the right to education in the same schools as American or European children.[69]

As Metcalf struggled to untangle this constitutional morass in San Francisco, Ambassador Aoki pressed his government's diplomatic case in Washington. The Japanese ambassador complained to the State Department that school segregation represented "a retrograde step in the intercourse of two nations." The San Francisco school board's action was evocative of the despised unequal treaties imposed on Japan by Commodore Perry in 1854 and 1858, he informed Root. Moreover Aoki resented the school board's sweeping racial categorizations: "Japanese racial pride is hurt when they are classed with Mongolians. . . . [The] Japanese are a composite race in which the Mongolian element is no doubt present, but that fact does not justify their classification as Mongolian any more than Englishmen can be regarded as pure Germans."[70] Whatever Metcalf's findings in San Francisco, the Japanese government believed that the 1894 treaty entitled its subjects to equal treatment in the United States—and racial superiority entitled them to better treatment than the Chinese.

Notwithstanding these conflicting legal opinions, Root was now convinced that Aoki's argument was morally and legally compelling. He told the attorney general in November 1906, "The whole purpose and end of the treaty of 1894 was to do away with and prevent just such exclusions as are now provided by the San Francisco School Board." He rejected the argument that separate but equal facilities satisfied America's treaty obligations. Japanese segregation in San Francisco patently constituted discrimination, and it clearly singled out the Japanese for unfair treatment. He was persuaded that San Francisco's actions were "completely subversive of the purpose and spirit of the treaty." More important, Root argued, "it is a discrimination which no proud and sensitive people of a high degree of refinement and civilization can possibly submit to without resentment."[71] Apparently black citizens of the United States had no such rights in the South. Metcalf's final report concurred. Submitted to the Senate in December 1906, the report concluded that if local authorities were unwilling to protect the livelihood or physical safety of Japanese citizens in San Francisco, "it is clearly the duty of the Federal Government to afford such protection." It was incumbent upon the nation to provide "the fullest protection and the highest consideration for the subjects of Japan." But Metcalf's report offered no concrete solution to the crisis and succeeded only in enraging Californians.[72] Defenders of white supremacy in California were already incensed. Three days earlier, in his annual message to Congress, Roosevelt had lauded Japan's recent achievements and denigrated the "wicked absurdity" of San Francisco's segregation order. He now urged all Americans to moderate any "unworthy feeling" toward Japanese immigrants and to afford them equal treatment with European immigrants.[73]

This left the administration still seeking a resolution that would placate both Japan and anti-Asian sentiment in San Francisco (and the western United States more broadly). The gentleman's agreement was born of this diplomatic and constitutional quagmire, although it would take almost two years of negotiations before the agreement reached its final form. Earlier in the crisis Third Assistant Secretary of State Huntington Wilson had suggested the Japanese government might be willing to unilaterally restrict emigration to the United States rather than risk further embarrassment at the hands of Californian labor agitators and school boards. After all, the situation would invariably escalate to the detriment of both the Japanese government and the Roosevelt administration if the U.S. government was forced by public sentiment to impose explicit legislative restrictions on Japanese immigration. Roosevelt and Root now reached the same conclusion.[74] Indeed just four days before Roosevelt's annual message to Congress, California's Everis Anson Hayes had proposed legislation in the U.S. House of Representatives that was designed to expand the Chinese Exclusion Act to include "Japanese, Koreans, Tartars, Malays, Afghans, East Indians, Lascars, Hindoos, and other persons of the Mongolian or Asiatic race."[75]

On November 19, 1906, Root asked Wright to determine if the Japanese government would be willing to deny passports to Japanese laborers bound for Hawaii.[76] On December 28, 1907, Root personally raised the issue with Aoki in Washington.[77] The Japanese government was initially reluctant to unilaterally limit its emigrants, but Root pressed his case, writing, "Without some arrangement, we can see no escape from increased excitement and conditions growing worse rather than better . . . making [the] position of all Japanese on Pacific Coast quite intolerable in ways no government can control directly." In the absence of Japanese cooperation, Root feared that Congress would be compelled to explicitly ban Japanese immigration, much as it had Chinese immigrants.[78] In early 1907 the Japanese signaled their willingness to voluntarily prohibit the emigration of laborers to the West Coast, providing that any diplomatic agreement to this effect was "of a nature such as to prevent the *amour propre* of the Japanese people being wounded."[79]

Amid these exchanges Congress passed a new immigration regulation act on February 20, 1907, imposing a $4 head tax on all immigrants and instituting broad new exclusions on the admission of those considered by immigration officials to be mentally or physically deficient, criminally inclined, or otherwise morally suspect. The act also authorized the president to refuse admission to foreign nationals attempting to enter the continental United States from America's insular possessions or any foreign country if their entrance was "to the detriment of labor conditions."[80] Since the majority of Japanese immigrants traveled to the United States either directly from Japan or via Hawaii, the act's intent was clear. According to Roger Daniels, Roosevelt drafted this particular clause himself.[81] "Under this authority," Root told

Wright that evening, "the President will enforce limitations on passports issued by [the] Japanese Government." The San Francisco School Board agreed to rescind its segregation order on March 13, 1907.[82]

The basic principles of the gentleman's agreement were now in place. The president was entitled to limit Japanese immigration from Hawaii, and Foreign Minister Hayashi Tadasu indicated his willingness to withhold passports from all Japanese laborers intending to travel to the continental United States.[83] On March 17 Roosevelt enacted an Executive Order officially prohibiting the immigration of Japanese immigrants whose passports entitled them to travel only as far as Hawaii, Mexico, or Canada.[84] From the Japanese foreign minister's perspective, his country would obtain more favorable terms if negotiations on a formal treaty resumed during a quieter period.[85] Negotiations continued for another year, culminating in a Japanese pledge to prohibit labor emigration to Hawaii.[86]

Anti-Asian Violence in the Pacific Northwest, Fall 1907

The gentleman's agreement was an extraordinary international solution to the transnational problem of Japanese migration, a diplomatic settlement that administratively terminated the transpacific labor circuit connecting Hawaii and the United States. It therefore represented a departure from the undiplomatic prohibitions preferred by white activists and the tactful but dishonest literacy test favored by the British government. It successfully ameliorated U.S.-Japanese tensions for over a decade, until Japanese diplomats challenged the prejudicial status quo at the Paris Peace Conference in 1919 and American lawmakers summarily canceled the agreement five years later. From the perspective of American and Canadian activists in the borderlands of the Pacific Northwest, however, the gentleman's agreement did not resolve two urgent problems that continued to plague the region: Japanese and Chinese immigrants had already settled among them, and a new network of South Asian migration purportedly threatened the livelihoods of white laborers in Washington and Oregon. Eager to redress these breaches, anti-Asian campaigners throughout the Pacific Northwest turned to violence in 1907. British authorities floundered in response, unsure of the legal status of South Asian migrants in the United States and embarrassed by parallel outbursts in British Columbia. The Japanese government, on the other hand, proved characteristically emphatic in defense of its subjects abroad.

Small numbers of South Asians began to arrive in the United States in the late nineteenth century, mostly from British Columbia. Some sought political refuge from the repressions of British India, while others pursued economic opportunity in the extractive economies of the U.S.-Canadian border region. In the absence of explicit restrictions those deemed physically healthy found it relatively easy to immigrate to the United States, and almost 1,000 entered between 1903 and 1906, 600 in the latter year.[87] This growing trickle soon compelled the American consul in Vancouver to warn his superiors of a potential deluge. In November 1906 L. Edwin Dudley encouraged the State Department to consider "that there are at least three hundred and fifty millions of these people, laboring for very small wages, who can easily be induced to cross the Pacific." He warned Washington, "There is every indication that there will be an enormous influx of these people upon the Pacific Coast within a very short time, unless it is checked, either by the Canadian or American governments."[88] As in Australasia and British Columbia, a small cluster of Asian migrants apparently represented the vanguard of a teeming horde.

Many of these migrants—predominantly Sikhs from the province of Punjab—were drawn to the lumber mills of Bellingham, Washington. Declaring themselves incensed by local mill owners' apparent preference for "Hindoo" laborers over whites, in August 1907 the city's white workers declared that continued employment of South Asians would not be tolerated after the upcoming Labor Day. In celebration of this holiday, a thousand of Bellingham's white workers demonstrated their intent by parading through the town. Isolated assaults on South Asian workers followed, and several boardinghouses were attacked.[89] Two days later, on September 4, Bellingham's South Asian residents were subjected to five hours of violence and intimidation at the hands of some 500 whites, intent on "[escorting] them to the city limits with orders to keep going."[90] That evening the mob swept through Bellingham's boardinghouses and mills, forcibly marching clusters of terrified South Asians to the city's jail, where 202 huddled for the night under the mayor's protection.[91] The following morning the majority of Bellingham's Sikh residents chose to leave their homes and workplaces despite assurances of safety from the mayor. Some struck for the relative safety of Seattle, carrying all the belongings they could handle. Many more headed toward British Columbia, which at least offered the ostensible security of the British Crown. One group apparently set off on foot, following the railroad tracks toward British Columbia. According to the *Bellingham Herald*, the "bitter mob of turbaned Asiatics" that elected to wait for the afternoon train to Vancouver was dispatched to the sound of "jeering and the cries of 'good' and 'don't come back.'"[92] The city's few remaining South Asian residents followed over the coming days, either heading north to Canada or south to Seattle and California.[93]

White laborers in Bellingham had corralled and then expelled South Asian immigrants in a visceral protest against their mobility, their access to the local economy, and their settlement in white communities. Sixty miles to the south, Sikh residents in Everett feared similar treatment. Upon hearing of the violence in Bellingham they petitioned the British vice consul in Seattle for protection.[94] James Laidlaw, the British consul in Portland, informed his ambassador in Washington, James Bryce, that he feared a duplication of the Bellingham violence in other parts of the state. Concerned that local authorities could not adequately protect the city's South Asian residents, Laidlaw proposed asking the federal government to bolster state and municipal authorities.[95] Indeed sporadic violence had already broken out in Seattle. Thirty-three Sikhs trying to escape the violence in Bellingham were reportedly prevented from boarding a steamer bound for Alaska, while one hundred more apparently engaged in a melee with "20 Scandinavians," resulting in five arrests.[96] Over the coming weeks Laidlaw reported isolated incidents of intimidation against South Asians in the state capital, Olympia, and in Danville near the Canadian border, but nothing that approached the ferocity of the Bellingham riot. However, he observed an abiding hostility toward South Asians in state newspapers and in his informal interviews with municipal officials.[97] The mayor of Everett, for example, rebuffed the fears of his town's South Asian residents, while at the same time urging Laidlaw to "discourage any further immigration at the present time under present conditions."[98]

Within weeks serious violence broke out again in Washington and Oregon. In scenes that recalled the Bellingham disturbances (and despite the mayor's assurances) over forty of Everett's Sikh residents were placed under protection in the city jail on the night of November 2, following warnings of impending violence. The hundreds of white laborers who assembled that evening attacked South Asian boardinghouses since they were denied the opportunity to commit violence against their inhabitants.[99] The *Everett Daily Herald* was unequivocal regarding the causes and solution to the state's ongoing anti–South Asian violence: "The truth of the matter is that the whole story is told when it is said that this 'is a white man's country.' We feel that we can't assimilate the Hindus, and we don't wish to try. . . . Race prejudice is as old as the world, and were there no economic considerations, it would be a most potent argument against the coming of the Hindu; the two together make a strong case. Everett does not wish the Hindus, but it wants no violence in getting rid of them."[100] As in Bellingham most of Everett's South Asian residents chose to leave the town rather than face further harassment and violence.

Ambassador Bryce was reluctant to lodge a formal protest with the State Department for a number of reasons that reveal the overlapping layers complicating the international politics of Asian restriction in the Pacific Northwest. First, as Bryce and the Foreign Office understood it, the 1815 "Anglo-American Convention to Regulate the Commerce" applied only to subjects from Britain's European territories, and this treaty still enumerated the rights of British citizens in the United States in 1907. Britain's South Asian subjects therefore were exempt from the treaty's diplomatic protections. This was compounded, Bryce noted, by U.S. legal rulings that denied citizenship to nonwhites (with the exception of "aliens of African nativity" and "persons of African descent"). Though Bryce did not take the logical next step, it is clear that Britain's South Asian subjects became effectively stateless upon entering the United States. Second, even if Britain's colonial subjects were entitled to diplomatic protection in the United States, Bryce doubted that the Foreign Office could penetrate the gauze of federalism that governed state and federal relations. Given the numerous, competing sources of authority in the region, the British ambassador felt it was "likely to prove impossible to secure the immunity of these British Subjects from interference in their employment or even from violence." Third, British authorities in Washington, London, and India were increasingly concerned about South Asian sedition in the United States. A number of South Asian individuals and organizations had been under surveillance in Boston and New York since 1905, and there was growing evidence of collusion between Irish and South Asian nationalists.[101] The situation worsened over the coming years, but the inchoate stirrings of rebellion did not escape the British government's attention. Fourth, as the *New York Times* trenchantly observed on September 7, if the British government registered a formal grievance with the American government, it was "likely to find itself embarrassed . . . because of the ever-present danger of similar attacks upon East Indians, who are numerous in British Columbia." It would set an uncomfortable precedent "if they in turn are called upon to pay damages for injuries to persons and property sustained by the Hindus . . . at the hands of British colonists."[102]

Bryce knew the issue would continue to fester: "The continuance of [South Asian] immigration into the Pacific Coast states cannot but be a cause of grave anxiety to this Embassy . . . and it would appear that their immigration to British Columbia is equally open to objection."[103] As a result of anti-Asian agitation in the western United States, the India Office offered to promulgate a public announcement in India euphemistically stating, "Industrial conditions in the United States are unfavourable to British Indian immigrants." The Foreign Office concurred, hinting that it might be advisable to simply stop issuing passports for South Asians to travel to the United States.[104] There appeared to be at least some truth in the India Office's statement. In addition to those South Asians subject to direct harassment over the previous months, Bryce was reporting a growing number of unemployed and destitute Sikhs seeking repatriation in California and Oregon.[105]

Events in Vancouver soon proved the striking prescience of the *New York Times*' analysis. The Japanese government's temporary suspension of labor emigration ended following the conclusion of the Russo-Japanese War in 1905, and by the end of 1906 over 2,000 new Japanese immigrants arrived in British Columbia. By then the position of the province's exclusionists was complicated by two recent developments. Concluded during the Japanese government's emigration pause, the Anglo-Japanese Alliance severely circumscribed British Columbia's legislative options. Moreover Laurier's government had finally signed the Anglo-Japanese Treaty of Commerce and Navigation in 1906, which technically entitled Japanese subjects to domicile and work privileges throughout Canada. The promise of increased commercial benefits placated many British Columbians, but others interpreted the federal government's actions as tantamount to prostrating the province before a flood of Japanese immigration.[106] Increasing numbers of South Asian immigrants also irritated white sentiment in British Columbia. Late 1906 witnessed intensifying demonstrations in Vancouver as vessels arrived carrying South Asian laborers. Complaints to Ottawa yielded nothing, and another attempt to institute a provincial literacy test floundered before federal and imperial opposition while the clamor against South Asian and Japanese immigration continued to grow.[107]

In the face of this ostensibly mounting threat, over 700 white Vancouverites assembled to protest Asian immigration on the evening of September 7, 1907. The demonstration had been conceived in August and designed to coincide with the proposed visit to Seattle of Ishii Kikujirō, director of the Japanese Foreign Ministry's Bureau of Commerce. He abruptly changed his plans upon hearing of Vancouver's proposed protest. The movement was nevertheless given extra momentum in September by the rumored approach of 700 Sikh exiles from the United States, displaced by the violence in Washington and Oregon. The protest gained extra potency from rumors describing approaching vessels filled with Japanese, South Asian, and Chinese immigrants.[108]

As the crowd marched toward city hall, the number of protestors swelled to some 8,000, motivated by their opposition to nonwhite immigration and determined to "stand for a White Canada." As the evening progressed, the protestors thronged around City Hall, where an international panel of speakers railed against the evils of Asian immigration, including local agitators from across the political spectrum, such as C. M. Woodworth of the Vancouver Conservative Association, Harry Cowan of the Vancouver Trades and Labour Council, Asiatic Exclusion League members, and local clergymen. The American anti-Asian movement's leading members were also present, including A. E. Fowler, secretary of Seattle's Asiatic Exclusion League, and the American Federation of Labor's W. A. Young. One particularly well-received speaker, J. E. Wilson, had recently arrived in British Columbia from New Zealand. He regaled the crowd with tales of Australasia's unwavering commitment to anti-Asian immigration policies.[109] There followed a night of violence during which Japanese and Chinese homes and businesses were attacked by mobs inflamed by the evening's meeting. The situation intensified when the *Monteagle* arrived four days later, carrying over 900 South Asian passengers along with 114 Japanese and 149 Chinese. The Japanese passengers disembarked at Victoria when Vancouver authorities were unable to guarantee their safety. As British subjects, however, the 914 South Asians were eventually allowed to land.[110]

If the British response to American assaults on South Asians was tepid, the Japanese reaction to new attacks on their subjects in British Columbia was strident and swift. Consul General Nosse immediately registered his government's disappointment. He blamed the violence on persistently "inflammatory remarks" in the British Columbian legislature and the Canadian press in general. In particular he expressed regret that "while things are getting tranquil down at San Francisco . . . the 'epidemic' has taken possession of British Columbia, and that epidemic is freely taken up for the political purpose without thinking how dangerous it would be . . . from the international point of view." He demanded Ottawa's immediate intervention and requested prompt action to protect Japanese lives and property. The Chinese chargé d'affaires in London lodged a similar complaint at the Foreign Office.[111]

In response Laurier conveyed the Canadian government's regret to the Japanese emperor. In his accompanying telegram to the British ambassador, however, Laurier stressed, "It must not be forgotten that amongst the people on [the] Pacific Coast there are strong racial prejudices which though greatly to be regretted . . . have to be taken into consideration by all those who desire to cultivate best relations between Canada and [the] Orient." His admission of the underlying racial motivations for these attacks stood in stark contrast to the American government's insistence that analogous sentiment in that country was primarily economic in origin.[112]

The many petitions Laurier received before and after the riot from British Columbian citizens left him in no doubt as to the prevailing feeling in the province. The Rossland Miners Union, for example, insisted, "Asiatic immigration is an unmixed evil, detrimental alike to the country and the people, as it would in time reduce the bulk of the white population to the low plane of Asiatics." It was preferable "to have a portion of our great natural resources lie fallow, a heritage for the Caucasians of the future, than to have them developed by Asiatic labor and a plague spot planted in our midst."[113] Ten days after the riot the Trades and Labour Congress of Canada petitioned Laurier to abrogate Canada's adherence to the Anglo-Japanese Treaty of Commerce and Navigation. It was responsible for the recent influx of Japanese immigrants, the Congress complained, and would inevitably lead to the "utter loss and ruin not only of British Columbia, but all Canada."[114] Laurier needed no reminder of the issue's sensitivity. In a letter to Francis J. Deane of the *Daily News* the prime minister lamented British Columbians' contradictory desire to retain lucrative trade links with Japan while vilifying and humiliating their subjects in Canada: "[The Japanese] will not be treated with contempt; they want to be treated as a civilized nation and if we will not treat them in that way, they will simply resent our action and shut off communication with us."[115]

In response to the Vancouver disturbance, on Laurier's recommendation the Canadian Privy Council dispatched the minister of labor (and postmaster general) to Japan. Rodolphe Lemieux arrived in Tokyo on November 15, 1907. His goal was to secure Canada's own gentleman's agreement with Japan. During his meetings at the Japanese Foreign Office, Lemieux was accompanied by Claude MacDonald (the British ambassador in Japan) and Joseph Pope, Canada's undersecretary of state for external affairs. Hayashi and Baron Chinda, his vice minister, represented Japan along with Ishii. The British government was content to allow the Canadian representatives a relatively free hand in their discussions with the Japanese government. Representing the Foreign Office, MacDonald was instructed to support the Canadian proposals, which he felt were appropriate and likely to receive Japan's acceptance.[116]

Lemieux argued that Japan was partly to blame for British Columbian attitudes. Since 1902 the Japanese consul general in Vancouver had repeatedly assured the Canadian government that, as in the American case, the Japanese government was limiting the issuance of passports to Canada. Only returning legal residents and their families, students, merchants, and tourists were entitled to enter Canada under Japan's euphemistically titled Emigrant Protection Law. Moreover since Canada had joined the Anglo-Japanese Treaty of Commerce and Navigation in 1906 the Japanese government had done little to inhibit emigration despite its tacit acceptance of limits. Japanese laborers also circumvented existing restrictions by immigrating to Canada from Hawaii. But like his prime minister, Lemieux did not deny that racial prejudice inspired anti-Asian immigration sentiment in Canada. Speaking of Asian immigrants, he asserted, "As in every Anglo-Saxon community, there exists a deep-seated popular determination to exclude from the sparsely-settled territories, the concentrated masses of the Orient." Economic concerns were not incidental, but racial antagonism played a prominent role, Lemieux admitted.[117] He also suggested that British Columbia's geographic isolation from the rest of Canada (and its proximity to the western United States) exacerbated these anxieties. He informed Hayashi in a separate memorandum, "In a community where one man in four is of a foreign race, and where the disparity is rapidly growing less, there is some ground for the uneasiness of the people of British Columbia."[118] Lemieux requested that Japan vigorously enforce its extant Emigrant Protection Law and limit the emigration of laborers and artisans to 300 per year.[119]

Negotiations continued for over a month; finally, on December 23, the Japanese government offered to voluntarily restrict emigration to Canada. Hayashi was unwilling to officially relinquish the rights of Japanese immigrants to reside and work in Canada, rights that were guaranteed by Canada's accession to the Anglo-Japanese Treaty of Commerce and Navigation. Nevertheless the foreign minister proclaimed that "it is not the intention of the Imperial Government to insist upon the complete enjoyment" of those rights, especially when "that would involve disregard of special conditions which may prevail in Canada from time to time." "Acting in this spirit," Hayashi announced, "and having particular regard to circumstances of recent occurrences in British Columbia, the Imperial Government have decided to take efficient means to restrict emigration to Canada."[120] Under the terms of the Japanese proposal, previously domiciled Japanese immigrants would be allowed free entry into Canada, along with their wives and children. Domestic servants and farm laborers possessing contracts to other Japanese would also be allowed to enter the dominion. Laborers possessing other types of legitimate employment contracts approved by the Canadian government were similarly free to immigrate. Hayashi intimated that their numbers would not exceed 400 per year. Finally, merchants, tourists, and students would be exempt from the agreement's restrictions.[121]

Lemieux faced misgivings from his government once he returned to Ottawa, and Laurier insisted upon a public statement from Japan prohibiting all contract laborers.[122] Lemieux, however, was resolute. The only realistic alternative to Hayashi's proposal was Canadian abrogation of the Anglo-Japanese Treaty of Commerce and Navigation, which would then allow Ottawa to impose federal restrictions. But such measures, Lemieux warned, "would mean a very serious breach in the treaty of alliance between the Mother Country and Japan." Canada would also have to sacrifice its new and potentially lucrative commercial relationship with Japan. Hayashi's proposal therefore represented the best alternative, Lemieux insisted. He observed, "Can we consistently ask the allies and friends of Great Britain to brand themselves before the whole world as an inferior race?"[123] Having considered Lemieux's report in its entirety and content that Japan was publicly committed to voluntary restrictions, Laurier and his ministers acceded to the gentleman's agreement on January 14, 1908.[124] Diplomatic notes confirming the arrangement were exchanged six days later.

At the same time, Laurier sought to inhibit the continued immigration of South Asians into Canada. On November 11 Governor-General Earl Grey informed the secretary of state for the colonies, the Earl of Elgin, that Laurier was considering imposing restrictions on South Asian immigrants. Under Laurier's terms no South Asian immigrant would be allowed to enter Canada without £200 in their possession. The prime minister understood that this measure singled out British subjects for exceptional treatment, and it was therefore likely to be disallowed by the imperial government. Nevertheless he cleverly forced the British government's hand by suggesting that any disorder "against the Hindus would extend to the Japanese who would defend themselves . . . [and] much bloodshed might ensue." If the British government wished to avoid this measure, Grey suggested, Laurier was willing to accept a declaration from British authorities in Asia that no South Asian emigrant would be allowed to leave imperial ports without a passport designating Canada as the destination. In addition, Grey suggested, the Canadian, British, and Indian governments should set strict limits on the number of passports issued to South Asian emigrants.[125]

As the Indian government considered Laurier's cleverly disguised ultimatum, the Canadian government concocted another ingenious—and thoroughly disingenuous—alternative that promised to block South Asian migration to Canada. On January 8, 1908, Ottawa announced that all prospective immigrants must travel to Canada by continuous journey from their place of birth or citizenship. In addition all immigrants were required to purchase direct tickets at their point of origin. In the absence of direct steamship passage from India to Canada, the order in council represented a de facto ban on South Asian immigration and further bolstered the newly imposed restrictions against Japanese laborers, who might circumvent the gentleman's agreement by way of Hawaii. The Indian viceroy, the Earl of Minto, tacitly accepted the Canadian ruse on January 25. Laurier's government had cleverly avoided enacting explicit restrictions against Britain's South Asian subjects, thus satisfying the British and Indian governments.[126] This order in council was eventually enshrined in new immigration legislation in 1910.[127]

In order to avoid any misunderstanding, however, the Canadian government sent Deputy Minister of Labour William Lyon Mackenzie King to London in early March 1908. The previous year King had chaired two royal commissions, one charged with assessing damages incurred by Chinese and Japanese immigrants during the Vancouver riots and another with conducting a wide-ranging inquiry into the causes of Asian immigration into Canada.[128] Now King was tasked with securing British support for Canada's new restrictions. Based upon his interviews with imperial officials and members of Parliament, he concluded that Canada's "desire to restrict immigration from the Orient is regarded as natural." Moreover "that Canada should remain a white man's country is believed to be not only desirable for economic and social reasons, but highly necessary on political and national grounds." With regard to South Asian immigration, King concluded, "The native of India is not a person suited to this country." The climate, South Asian immigrants' inability to assimilate into Canada's predominantly European population, and labor competition rendered them unsuitable immigrants. It was therefore in these South Asians' best interests that they be discouraged and ultimately prevented from making the journey to Canada. King concluded that this was a humanitarian policy entirely in accord with Great Britain's stewardship of the Indian subcontinent and its subjects.[129]

Whether veiled by gentleman's agreements or disguised by ingenious travel requirements, duplicitousness had once again succeeded in suppressing the international and imperial friction engendered by white activists' disdain for Asian migrants. By 1908 restrictions on Asian labor mobility interlaced the major white settler communities of Australasia, North America, and southern Africa. White activists throughout these communities certainly shared similar conceptions of the dangers and inadequacies inherent to Asian immigrants, but in each case a specific constellation of political, economic, geographic, and diplomatic considerations had shaped and conditioned the contours of distinctive restriction regimes. These separate exclusion campaigns were nevertheless united by the deleterious imperial and international consequences they fostered, and those repercussions continued to escalate in the coming years, as the rest of this book demonstrates.

CHAPTER FOUR

The Limits of Anglo-American
Solidarity and Collaboration

A flurry of accusations caromed across the transatlantic news wires in the aftermath of the Bellingham and Vancouver riots. Some in the British press speculated on the involvement of American activists in Vancouver and mused that white labor in British Columbia must have succumbed to a California strain of the anti-Asian contagion. One London *Times* correspondent concluded, "The whole affair bears the hall-mark of Yankee-doodleism." Not surprisingly the *New York Times* rejected claims of American responsibility for the Vancouver disturbances, sardonically recommending that British leaders get their own house in order before casting aspersions on American labor. To that newspaper's editorialists British suspicion of American malfeasance revealed a deeper betrayal. The riots had demonstrated that "British sentiment allies it more nearly with Anglo-Saxons and whites everywhere than with the ally bound to it by a paper bargain." British Columbian workers had taken a noble stand for white solidarity against Asian encroachment, and yet Great Britain continued to privilege its alliance with Japan over the natural racial affinities that bound the white diaspora globally. While the *New York Times* advocated transnational racial solidarity, the London *Times* counseled respect for international and imperial interests, editorializing that wherever responsibility lay, the Vancouver riots were by no means symptomatic of a singularly American disease; the racial and economic anxieties that engendered such violence suffused colonial sentiment far beyond British North America. While remaining convinced of American complicity, the English newspaper's editorialists nevertheless castigated those British colonists who had exploited racial resentments without regard "for the embarrassments and the dangers which they prepare for the Empire at large."[1]

In this chapter I shift my analysis away from the distinctiveness of regional restrictions on Asian mobility and adopt a larger frame, one that encompasses white anti-Asian activism on both sides of the Pacific. I examine unsuccessful efforts to cultivate both transnational and international cooperation among Americans, British colonists, and the British government in the wake of the Bellingham and Vancouver disturbances. As the divergent newspaper responses suggest, for some contemporary observers and present-day scholars alike the turbulence in Washington and British Columbia represented a connected—and possibly even coordinated—outburst of transnational white solidarity against Asian labor migration.[2] The spatial and temporal proximity of the riots and the presence of some prominent American restrictionists in Vancouver implied a cross-border conspiracy between American and Canadian militants that threatened to resonate beyond the anti-Asian spasms plaguing North America that September. Yet this proved to be only a transitory moment of collusion. In fact it was difficult for activists on either side of the border—or on either side of the Pacific—to capitalize on the shared animosities that energized their common resistance to Asian migration.

To be sure, some individuals continued to promote Anglo-American partnership against the threat of Asian labor mobility, despite the substantial political and diplomatic obstacles. Most notably Theodore Roosevelt proposed collaboration during negotiations over the American and Canadian gentleman's agreements with Japan. He hoped to leverage Britain's alliance with the East Asian power in order to pressure the Japanese into unilaterally enacting prohibitions on their labor emigrants. More dramatically the president further probed British and Canadian interest in pursuing a coalition against transpacific Asian migration in early 1908 during a series of meetings with the Canadian deputy labor minister William Lyon Mackenzie King.[3] While British and Canadian officials balked at these suggestions, some in Australasia saw opportunity in the projection of American naval power across the Pacific later that year. In the minds of Australasia's most ardent exclusionists, the visit of Roosevelt's "Great White Fleet" to Auckland, Sydney, and Melbourne in August and September 1908 augured a forceful rejection of Asian—and especially Japanese—labor mobility in the Pacific.

But these undertakings remained largely aspirational. A blend of domestic, imperial, and international political considerations ultimately precluded meaningful cooperation at any level in the wake of the 1907 riots, and pretensions of transnational white solidarity disintegrated when confronted with the imperatives of diplomacy and empire. Instead of galvanizing American and British Columbian agitators in fellowship against Asian migrant mobility, therefore, the Bellingham and Vancouver riots had the opposite effect. The revulsion expressed by British and Canadian authorities toward the use of violence against Japanese allies and South Asian subjects in British colonial spaces chilled whatever warmth might have existed between American restriction organizations and the Vancouver Exclusion League, thwarting future transborder agitations in the Pacific Northwest. Fear of being labeled disloyal to the empire convinced members of the Vancouver League to repudiate their largely prospective institutional links with their American counterparts. At the international level British and Canadian authorities abstained from cooperating with the Roosevelt administration in deference to the Anglo-Japanese alliance and in suspicion of American motives regarding that oft-maligned pact. Australasian expectations of American intervention in the Pacific also atrophied as the Great White Fleet steamed away for Manila and Yokohama, and any interest Roosevelt may have entertained in nurturing U.S.-Australasian solidarity against Asian migration dissipated with the end of his presidency.

Whatever possibilities for future transnational or diplomatic alliances might have existed amid the Bellingham and Vancouver protests therefore wilted before the exigencies of diplomacy and empire. British imperial authorities could not countenance the appearance of Anglo-American collusion if they wished to preserve their strategically important alliance with Japan. Collaboration between the United States and the colonies of settlement also made British officials uneasy. In this regard international and imperial friction once again constituted the most robust, enduring, and unwelcome thread linking the Australian, New Zealand, South African, Canadian, and American campaigns against Asian labor mobility. Those tensions soured the transnational solidarities professed by white activists across the British Empire and on both sides of the 49th parallel and precluded intergovernmental compacts against Asian migration; they irritated Anglo-American relations and briefly conjured images of secession and disintegration beyond the Rockies; and they inflamed already overwrought interimperial rivalries in the Pacific and East Asia, further straining Japanese-American and Anglo-Japanese relations in the process.

I begin by exploring British and Canadian efforts to expose the role played by American agitators in the Vancouver riot and demonstrate that the prospects of consolidating a transnational white labor alliance against Asian mobility waned in the aftermath of the 1907 riots. The British ambassador in Washington, James Bryce, and the Canadian prime minister in Ottawa, Wilfrid Laurier, both suspected American involvement in the ranks of the British Columbian anti-Asian movement, although their investigations never conclusively revealed how determinative that influence might have been in directing the violence in Vancouver. While Bryce sifted through reports from the Pacific Northwest, Laurier engaged the enthusiastic services of a willing infiltrator, Thomas Robert Edward McInnes, who worked to uncover American malfeasance and British Columbian treachery. Concerned by the implication of sedition, the leaders of the Vancouver Exclusion League denied any ties to their American counterparts and declared fidelity to the Canadian Constitution and the British Crown.

As the possibilities for cross-border collusion withered in the North American West, American officials in Washington sought collaboration with British and Canadian authorities against Japanese migration in particular. Roosevelt proved especially eager to cultivate Anglo-American cooperation. But despite his repeated efforts to nurture mutual Canadian-American hostility toward Asian labor mobility, Roosevelt's clandestine appeals proved futile. British and Canadian officials would not risk alienating their Japanese ally by openly aligning with the United States, especially as Japanese-American and Japanese-Canadian negotiations continued in Tokyo. Despite these disappointments, some Australians and New Zealanders sought succor in the increased Pacific naval presence of the United States in late 1908. However, not everybody felt comfortable lauding a putative transpacific racial alliance that both excluded Great Britain and isolated the Japanese. Ultimately neither transnational nor international coalitions against Japanese labor mobility gained traction, even as the struggle against Asian migration crested in the Pacific.

The Vancouver Riots and the Limits of Transnational Solidarity

In the weeks and months following the Bellingham and Vancouver riots, British and Canadian authorities struggled to unravel the multifaceted politics that underpinned the turmoil. They were especially determined to ascertain the extent of American involvement in British Columbian restriction politics. But American orchestration proved difficult to substantiate since much of the evidence derived from rumor, innuendo, and anecdote. In the midst of the chaos in Vancouver, for example, British, Canadian, and American correspondents filed conflicting reports on the exact source of the trouble. Honest British and Canadian observers admitted that large numbers of British Columbians harbored their own racial and economic animosities toward Asian immigrants. Yet they imagined those antagonisms could never have manifested so violently without goading from outside the province. The *Spectator* articulated this theory, insisting that American labor leaders had traveled directly from Bellingham to incite their brethren in British Columbia.[4] The *Victoria Daily Colonist* also blamed Seattle's A. E. Fowler for inciting British Columbians to vent their resentments against Asian-owned businesses and properties. This "alien agitator" had crossed the border solely to propagate enmity between the British and Japanese governments.[5] Former prime minister Sir Charles Tupper was the most candid in his assertion of American responsibility, declaring, "These rascals, I have no hesitation in saying, do not belong to British Columbia, but are foreigners from the United States."[6] On the other hand, American reporters stoutly denied that their compatriots were responsible for the violence, "except in the sense that example is more effective than precept." British Columbian activists needed no encouragement to exercise their deeply entrenched antipathies toward Asian immigrants, the *New York Times* reflected, and no Americans were arrested in commission of violence during or after the riots.[7]

The British ambassador to the United States contemplated these issues as the rancor on the streets began to subside. Relaying details of the disturbances to London, Bryce suspected American responsibility for the disorder in Vancouver, but he could not prove it. "It would be incautious at present, and it would probably prove incorrect," he told his foreign minister, "to infer any deliberate policy on the part of any American in authority to embarrass the relations between Great Britain and Japan." He did sense an undercurrent of American resentment while digesting the stream of consular and newspaper commentary that flowed from the Pacific Northwest. Bryce deduced that the American press at the very least relished "the coincidence of the attacks on Orientals under British protection in Washington State with those on Oriental allies of Great Britain in Vancouver," and he concluded, "It would not be too much to say that there has evidently been no feeling of regret that the anti-Oriental agitation in British Columbia, with its expected effects on Anglo-Japanese relations, has been greatly aggravated by American agency." As he mulled the possibility of American complicity in the Vancouver disturbances, Bryce was therefore convinced that at least some Americans now savored the prospect of obliging Great Britain to choose between its strategic alliance with Japan and its racial alliance with white colonists. He claimed that Americans had long begrudged Britain's alliance with Japan since it ostensibly provided a shield for Japanese commercial and strategic predominance in the Pacific. He also assumed that this spiteful attitude derived from lingering bitterness over the previous year's crisis in San Francisco. During that dispute the British press had expressed incredulity toward the apparent impotence of the federal government in the face of state and municipal mistreatment of Japanese immigrants. "It is therefore natural," Bryce admitted, "that the [American] press should now endeavour to show that the Dominion Government is in a similar dilemma with regard to the action of the populace of British Columbia."[8]

Bryce was not alone in speculating about the "extent to which the anti-oriental agitation on the Pacific Coast from California to British Columbia is coordinated and controlled."[9] Prime Minister Laurier also expressed concern regarding possible links between American and British Columbian activists. Four days after the Vancouver riot Laurier received a letter from Thomas Robert Edward McInnes, a British Columbian barrister (and poet) whose brother was a leader of the Vancouver League. He offered to provide Laurier with secret intelligence concerning the League's activities and transnational connections.[10] He most portentously claimed in a letter to the prime minister in November 1907, "There is an American element at work in Vancouver whose movements should be carefully watched and *anticipated* by some person or persons qualified to do so."[11] McInnes, of course, was just the person to undertake that task.

McInnes conducted his investigation with Laurier's consent, and it culminated in a largely circumstantial case against the ongoing influence of American militants in the British Columbian restriction movement. Despite his earlier suspicions, McInnes determined that Vancouver's Exclusion League was "not now in any way under American control or direction." He nevertheless concluded that Fowler and a small group of associates from Seattle had helped incite the riot in Vancouver, and he ventured that Americans might try to further inflame existing British Columbian hostilities toward the Japanese "until that feeling reach[es] a stage where the British Columbians forget they are British and look upon their interests as identical with those of California, Oregon, and Washington." In addition to potentially losing the allegiance of white British Columbians, McInnes warned, Great Britain might also lose its alliance with Japan. Despite his conviction that militant American and Canadian protesters were guilty of fostering transnational, imperial, and international animosities, he called upon the Japanese to ease the tension.[12]

Whatever the veracity of Bryce's suspicions and the value of McInnes's surveillance, the leadership of Vancouver's Asiatic Exclusion League was eager to erase any suggestion of American influence over their organization. Confronted by the intimation of disloyalty to Canada and Great Britain, the most vigorous force for Asian restriction in British Columbia quickly and clearly abandoned its transnational pretensions—but not its ultimate goal of Asian exclusion from the Canadian West. On February 7, 1908, McInnes reported on the recently held Conference of Asiatic Exclusion Leagues of America in Seattle. The American representatives reportedly desired an international executive, designed to influence Mexican, American, and Canadian immigration policies. McInnes related that only one Canadian representative actually attended the meeting, and he grandiosely professed to having "thwarted their plans completely as regards Canada."[13] A few weeks later, following Lemieux's mission to Japan, the Vancouver League's secretary, Gordon M. Grant, introduced a resolution repudiating the organization's previously stated aspiration to forge institutional links with their American counterparts. The resolution further recommended that the League "make no alliance with any other than an exclusively British organization" and declare its "loyalty to the British Empire, and its faith in the British Constitution as an efficient instrument for securing full protection against the evils confronting the citizens of British Columbia from the coolie labor of Asia."[14] Grant later told Laurier, "The American element is working energetically among the rank and file of the League," and he promised to disband the organization and purge its pro-American faction if the resolution failed. The resolution passed.[15]

Although some American agitators continued to envision a broader transnational movement that spanned the North American West, British Columbian militants recognized that cooperation with Americans threatened the entire exclusionary enterprise in Canada. The secret to the Vancouver League's success ironically impeded its ability to forge ties with its American counterpart. The League had recruited its leadership from Vancouver's professional classes in an effort to lend credibility to the organization in the eyes of British Columbian and Canadian elites. Those same individuals quickly recoiled when the association's alleged ties to Americans brought their allegiance to the dominion and to the British Empire into question. One British Columbian periodical noted in January 1908, "Such men . . . cannot afford to be associated with alien agitators and professional demagogues."[16] Chastened by the wanton violence of the September 1907 riots—and embarrassed by the intimation of disloyalty—Grant promised Laurier "defeat of the American plan to control the Vancouver League . . . and a lifting of the methods of the League to a higher plane of constitutional agitation."[17] The Vancouver and Bellingham disturbances therefore represented the zenith of cross-border activism in the Pacific Northwest, and that activism collapsed as quickly as it peaked.

The Limits of Anglo-American Diplomatic Cooperation

Attempts to foster international arrangements between the British and American governments continued, even as transnational solidarities between

American and Canadian laborers and activists diminished. The impetus came exclusively from American officials, who tried to take advantage of Britain's ongoing diplomatic tribulations with Asian migration on numerous occasions during those tumultuous months. In early October 1907 Third Assistant Secretary of State Francis Mairs Huntington-Wilson was among the first to advocate Anglo-American intergovernmental cooperation. Just weeks after the Vancouver riots Huntington Wilson encouraged Root to broach the possibility of forming a united front against Japanese immigration with Bryce, "lest we should miss profiting by the present very delicate position in which Canada has placed the British Government."[18] A month later, in the midst of American negotiations with Japan, Roosevelt suggested that the State Department remind their East Asian interlocutors "that their staunchest ally, England, is in precisely the same position; that her colonies British Columbia, New Zealand, and the Australian Commonwealth take precisely the same position as our Pacific Coast States take; that it is an economic question."[19] Roosevelt minimized white racism, but his intent was clear: to exploit Britain's relationship with Japan—and its colonies' anti-Asian impulses—to mitigate American activists' injurious influence on Japanese-American relations. The following month, during Lemieux's negotiations with the Japanese Foreign Ministry in December, the American ambassador in Tokyo approached his British counterpart "with a view to make a common case . . . stating that he was well aware that the United States could not get better terms than Canada, in view of the alliance existing between Great Britain and Japan." The British government declined this American appeal to unite in support of exclusion.[20] The British ambassador in Japan believed "it would have had the worst effect with the Japanese if anything like joint action had been taken by England, Canada, and America."[21]

Roosevelt would not easily abandon attempts to foster Anglo-American cooperation, however, and his most audacious proposal came in January 1908. That month he invited Canadian deputy labour minister Mackenzie King to visit him at the White House. Roosevelt was keen to discuss the issue of Asian immigration with Mackenzie King, having learned about his recent reports on the subject from a mutual American acquaintance. With Laurier's permission, Mackenzie King traveled to Washington with the understanding that his interview with Roosevelt was "purely a personal and unofficial one." He dined with the president on the afternoon of January 25 and recorded his version of events the following day. During their meeting the president conveyed his concern that anti-Asian agitation in the North American West might ultimately result in the Pacific states' secession. "This may seem like a strong statement," Roosevelt reportedly told Mackenzie King, "but I believe that if the people east of the Rocky Mountains in the United States were indifferent to the situation, and the British were indifferent to the feelings of the people of British Columbia, there would be a new republic between the mountains and the Pacific."[22]

Aware that Mackenzie King would soon travel to England, Roosevelt once again hoped the British government would relay to the Japanese the American president's support for exclusion. "The Japanese must learn that they will have to keep their people in their own country," Roosevelt told the Canadian. "England's interests and ours are one in this matter." Roosevelt made it clear that his recent decision to dispatch the American battle fleet around the world was partly designed to demonstrate his resolve against Japanese immigration. He also lamented Lemieux's decision to decline the American ambassador's request for cooperation in Tokyo, since Roosevelt apparently believed that this allowed Japan to "play off England against the United States, and the United States against England in this matter." Since both parties received generous terms from the Japanese, Roosevelt's apprehensions were misplaced, but his persistence reflects his view that Britain's alliance with Japan might yet benefit the United States. The president then invited his secretary of state to question the Canadian minister. Root echoed Roosevelt's sentiments, although Mackenzie King remembered that the secretary "was less direct than Roosevelt in his plea for British assistance." "What at once surprised and impressed me," Mackenzie King recalled, "was the emphatic manner in which the President indicated that there was a possibility of serious trouble with Japan" and that British intervention might help avert conflict. The president invited his guest to attend the annual Gridiron Club dinner in Washington before returning to Canada. If Roosevelt's earlier request for British help had surprised the Canadian minister, the president's speech that evening "startled" him. Roosevelt chided the press for their irresponsibility toward the sentiments of "foreign powers," but he also warned that once the United States had exhausted polite diplomacy, it would be time to "send the fleet into the Pacific."[23] Mackenzie King then returned to Ottawa and relayed the substance of his extraordinary interview to Laurier.

Roosevelt's unorthodox diplomacy astounded Laurier and his deputy minister. The latter later told the British foreign secretary, "The discussion with the President was due entirely to the President's initiative, which had been so pressing as to be a little embarrassing."[24] In order to further probe Roosevelt's intentions, Laurier sent Mackenzie King back to Washington, conveying his belief that Canada's recently concluded arrangement with

Japan to voluntarily restrict the immigration of Japanese laborers had practically settled the question from the Canadian point of view. He nevertheless recognized that Canadian and American interests converged on the issue and expressed his desire to assist the American government. Laurier stressed, however, that this could be done only after consultation with the imperial government in London.[25]

Mackenzie King arrived back in Washington on January 31, whereupon this remarkable episode in Anglo-American-Canadian diplomacy resumed. He discovered that since his last visit the American government had largely secured its own gentleman's agreement with Japan. He once again met privately with the president, who reiterated his appeal for British cooperation on the question of Japan, and he repeated his preference for a peaceful resolution while still insisting that the U.S. Fleet's voyage around the world was designed to impress the Japanese. Roosevelt also revealed his awareness of the question's broader global implications, expounding upon the situation in Australia. Speaking like a true devotee of the White Australian ideal, the president voiced concern over the declining white birth rate in that Pacific colony: "If the population of the country is not increasing and strengthening, how can it defend itself against the blackbird and or the yellow-skin?" The following day Roosevelt invited Mackenzie King and Bryce to a White House lunch, where he once again affirmed his commitment to the resolution of the Asian mobility problem. He impressed upon his guests the potential for cooperation should Japan renege on its recently concluded agreements with Canada and the United States. Roosevelt ruminated upon the possible consequences of war between the United States and Japan and suggested that British Columbia would almost certainly demand British support against Japan.[26] According to Bryce, Roosevelt continually "emphasized the identity of feeling and of interests (real or supposed) between the Canadian inhabitants of the Pacific Coast and their neighbours in the Pacific States of California, Oregon, Washington, and Nevada." While he expected Japan to honor its commitments, Roosevelt insisted that "hostility towards Oriental labourers . . . was too strong to be resisted either by Canada or the United States' Government." If Japan broke its word, "it might therefore be a good thing if His Majesty's Government, as an ally of Japan, were to convey to that country their knowledge of the serious view which the United States' Government took of the position." Bryce assured the president that his government was attuned to the significance of the issue, especially given Britain's experiences with Canadian, Australasian, and South African laws and demonstrations.[27] Roosevelt further reminded Bryce that the British ambassador's own writings had been devoted to fostering common interests among the English-speaking peoples. Roosevelt evidently believed that the Japanese immigration question provided an opportunity to act on Bryce's suggestion.[28]

Bryce communicated the details of this meeting to his superiors in London and found the British foreign minister once again reluctant to intervene. Grey surmised that Japanese-American negotiations had reached a successful conclusion, and he suggested that if the British government intervened at this stage it might appear to imply "a doubt whether Japan would keep her assurances to Canada as well as to the Government of the United States." Concerned that Japanese leaders would recoil at American, British, and Canadian collusion, Grey did not wish to unnecessarily provoke or alarm the Meiji government.[29] Bryce accepted his foreign secretary's decision but was struck by Roosevelt's and Root's vehemence. He warned Grey that the Roosevelt administration, "if it should think it is being trifled with," might provoke a showdown with Japan. If the situation deteriorated to that point, Bryce pessimistically recommended that the Foreign Office should reconsider its position.[30]

When Mackenzie King met with the president again on February 24, Roosevelt had not relented in his desire to secure British support. The president said that the Australian prime minister, Alfred Deakin, had invited the U.S. Fleet to visit. Roosevelt correctly interpreted this as directly related to Australia's own apprehension toward Japanese immigration. The president then offered to send the fleet to Victoria and Vancouver, an offer that Mackenzie King professed he could not accept without consulting his government. The following day Mackenzie King met with Roosevelt for the last time. The president once more pressed for cooperation: "What I would like to accomplish is not merely an understanding for today, but some kind of convention between the English-speaking peoples, whereby, in regard to this [immigration] question, it would be understood on all sides that the Asiatic peoples were not to come to the English-speaking countries to settle, and that our peoples were not to go to theirs." Ultimately, Roosevelt concluded, "if Japan understands that in this question the English-speaking powers, Great Britain and the United States, have a common interest, there will be peace." Despite Britain's reluctance to intervene, Roosevelt felt it was essential that Mackenzie King impress upon the Foreign Office the question's importance. Despite Grey's confidence, Roosevelt insisted that the recently concluded gentleman's agreement had not settled the question, and it was incumbent upon Britain and the United States to remain vigilant and united in opposition to Japanese immigration.[31] However, Roosevelt's earnest calls for cooperation went unanswered. From Great Britain's perspective, foreign policy considerations precluded overt participation in an anti-Japanese alliance with the United States; Laurier well understood that sensitivity and deferred to the imperial government.

Two Colonial Office memoranda from this period encapsulate the complexity of the Asian immigration issue from Great Britain's perspective and further elucidate the imperial government's reluctance to embrace Roosevelt's proposal. The previous year's riots had alarmed the British government, which tasked Sir Charles Prestwood Lucas to undertake a systematic appraisal of the "coloured immigration" problem as head of the Colonial Office's Dominions Department. After surveying the historical development of anti-Asian legislation in the British dominions, he concluded that while the imperial government had empathized with colonial attempts "to keep the self-governing Colonies for the white race," they had nonetheless tried to ameliorate the colonies' worst excesses on behalf of the empire's nonwhite subjects and allies. Nevertheless the self-governing colonies remained committed to Asian exclusion without regard to nationality and continually demonstrated "no great regard for the feelings and susceptibilities of the coloured races as regards methods of exclusion." The situation promised nothing but internecine imperial and diplomatic friction. First, South Asians' resentment of their treatment at the hands of fellow imperial subjects might provoke a reckoning in which Britain would be forced to choose between the Raj and its white empire. Second, the British alliance with Japan might be compromised. Japan's emergence as a first-rate power in particular had "given the Eastern races a new status which has been won by force and not conceded as a matter of grace," and the Japanese would not suffer inferior treatment indefinitely. Third, as had become clear the previous year, the issue was likely to cause friction between the United States and Great Britain, either in the form of American complaints regarding South Asian immigration (or Britain's alliance with Japan) or British complaints regarding "interference on the part of the United States in our relations with the Dominions."[32]

Acknowledging the problem's enduring significance and complexity, Prestwood Lucas turned his attention to possible resolutions. "It is a question which is perpetually looking acute," he worried; "it is a question second to none in difficulty and importance." In this complicated global context, Britain's options were limited and the temptation to do nothing was appealing. The dangers of doing nothing, however, were too serious to ignore. Potential American involvement was of special concern. Prestwood Lucas feared

Britain's marginalization by direct American involvement with the colonies: "If we do not take the initiative, the United States may stand out on and through this question as the leaders of the English-speaking peoples in the Pacific as against the coloured races." During the already arduous history of this vital question, Prestwood Lucas identified only one initiative that proposed to address Asian immigration's imperial dimension. This involved setting aside a specific portion of territory somewhere in the empire "for coloured immigration and colonization as a set off against their exclusion from the self-governing dominions." This solution would provide a suitable outlet for South Asians and other nonwhite migrants while segregating them from the white colonies. Prestwood Lucas rejected this proposal, however, as economically impractical and unlikely to meet the white dominions' approval, whom he suspected would seek favorable economic concessions in these Asian reservations. Instead he proposed encouraging colonial participation in treaty negotiations designed to prohibit undesirable immigration. In addition he recommended that India and the self-governing colonies should reciprocally negotiate treaties of exclusion. It would be another ten years before the British Empire adopted the latter suggestion.[33]

The U.S. Fleet in New Zealand and the Limits of Transpacific Collaboration

Prestwood Lucas's vexations regarding possible American usurpation of British influence in the white dominions were also inspired by the voyage of the American battle fleet. He wrote as that flotilla steamed west across the Pacific toward Australasia, where it was scheduled to spend six weeks during its year-long circumnavigation of the globe. Just as Prestwood Lucas worried, the Great White Fleet's visit to Australia and New Zealand expanded the scope of potential collaboration against Asian mobility and immigration beyond North America. Many Australians and New Zealanders interpreted the fleet's visit as a gesture of transpacific white racial solidarity against Japanese power in the region, a tangible filament connecting American and Australasian anti-Asian sentiment and activism. Others saw the vessels' arrival as a wedge that threatened to needlessly provoke Japanese anger, which would force a rupture between Britain and its Australasian colonies.

The fleet's reception in New Zealand is particularly instructive. Some in that British colony's parliament and press energetically acclaimed Roosevelt's display of naval might, eagerly anticipating American support for New Zealand's anti-Asian exclusion efforts. The enthusiastic and explicitly racial welcome in that colony was tempered, however, by those who remained confident in the Royal Navy's protection and respectful toward the imperial government's alliance with Japan. Moreover some within New Zealand's indigenous Maori community expressed reservations about American racial attitudes and wondered aloud whether that country's color line was too sharply drawn. As the fleet left New Zealand's shores, those who looked forward to closer cooperation with the Americans against Asian mobility in the transpacific were disappointed. As the excitement of the visit subsided, so too did hopes of Australasian-American collaboration against Japanese labor mobility.

British authorities expressed uncertainty and suspicion about Roosevelt's motives even as the fleet prepared for its departure in Virginia. When Bryce first heard reports of the voyage he suspected that Roosevelt was acting to "impress" the Japanese government with a show of American naval strength. The risk, Bryce warned the British foreign secretary, derived from "the danger of exciting an irresponsible press and public opinion," which in his view was "always sensitive and often impetuous."[34] Bryce later speculated that Roosevelt was acting to bolster the electoral prospects of his party's presumed nominee, William H. Taft, in the western United States. More fantastically the British consul-general in New York reported rumors that Roosevelt himself sought a second elected term in office and was willing to provoke war with Japan by demanding the total exclusion of Japanese immigrants at the barrel of the fleet's guns in order to satisfy his western critics.[35]

The fleet departed Hampton Roads, Virginia, on December 16, 1907, bound for San Francisco via Trinidad, Brazil, Chile, Peru, and Mexico. Almost six months later, on May 6, 1908, the vessels arrived in San Francisco. During this time British representatives in the United States continually speculated about Roosevelt's motives and closely monitored American press attitudes. By January 1908, as the fleet steamed from Rio de Janeiro to Punta Arenas in Chile, Bryce was finally convinced that war between Japan and the United States was merely a fiction of the American and European press. Such chauvinistic speculation represented nothing more than a "morbid passion for 'news' and the total loss of sane judgment which that passion induces."[36] While the British military attaché in Washington, Lieutenant Colonel B. R. James, interpreted the fleet's transfer as calculated to bolster America's position in ongoing negotiations with Japan over the gentleman's agreement, he also concluded, "This in no way implies a probability of war."[37]

Roosevelt himself was notoriously vague regarding his motivations for the fleet's voyage. He almost certainly hoped to inspire domestic support for naval development while providing an opportunity to test the tactical and strategic capabilities of the U.S. Navy.[38] This was especially important while the Panama Canal remained under construction. Until the completion of that waterway, American naval vessels were still forced to circumnavigate South America through the Strait of Magellan in order to defend the Pacific and Atlantic oceans, a long and potentially treacherous journey. Yet Roosevelt did not hesitate to stress the voyage's diplomatic purpose, as his meetings with Bryce and Mackenzie King demonstrated. He reiterated this theme during a meeting with British Columbian legislators in February 1908, when he reportedly told the visiting members of Parliament during a discussion of Japanese immigration, "We have got to build up our western country with our white civilization, and (very vehemently) we must retain the power to say who shall or shall not come into our country." In the meantime, Roosevelt declared, "I thought it wise to send that fleet around to the Pacific to be ready to maintain our rights." "That fleet is there in the interests of the whole Pacific Coast," he insisted, and it was intended to protect "the interests of British Columbia as well as those of California. . . . It is in the interests of Australia as well." When asked if the Monroe Doctrine applied to the Pacific coast of North America, Roosevelt affirmed that it did, and reportedly intimated that it would apply to Australia as well if necessary.[39]

Whatever Roosevelt's evolving intentions, many white Australasians interpreted the voyage of the U.S. Fleet as an expression of transpacific racial solidarity against Asian, and especially Japanese, immigration. On January 24, 1908, Deakin contacted the American ambassador in London, Whitelaw Reid. He stated his desire to welcome the fleet to Australia since the voyage was "an event in the history not only of the United States, but of [the Pacific] Ocean." A month later Deakin finally submitted a formal invitation through the Australian governor-general. A visit by the Americans, he remained convinced, "would be a further token of the close alliance of interests and sympathies which already exists between the two countries and might in some degree operate to make it more complete." The American government accepted Deakin's invitation on March 22.[40] Root suggested to Roosevelt why diverting the fleet to Australia was "good business": "The time will surely come, although probably after our day, when it will be important for the United States to have all ports friendly and all causes of sympathy alive in the Pacific."[41]

New Zealand's government presented its own invitation through the British Embassy in Washington in March 1908, and the Roosevelt administration quickly accepted.[42] Members of New Zealand's Parliament debated the meaning and significance of the American fleet's visit in the months before its arrival. Their often contentious deliberations reveal the possibilities, but also the limits, of an imagined Anglo-American racial alliance in the Pacific. Members of the majority Liberal Party followed the striking example of their long-serving and recently deceased former prime minister, Richard Seddon: they resoundingly espoused the dangers of Asian labor mobility and celebrated the symbolism of American naval power. Sir William J. Steward captured the essence of white New Zealanders' anxiety and their anticipation of American assertiveness in the South Pacific. Like many of his colleagues, Steward believed that "the brown and yellow races will challenge the white race for the possession and occupancy of large areas of the earth which are not at present fully populated." He echoed a widely held apprehension that neither New Zealanders nor Australians could withstand a concerted wave of Asian immigration. It was clear to Steward and many of his contemporaries that both "White New Zealand" and "White Australia" would therefore exist only as figments of the imagination unless Australasians augmented their defenses.[43] The visit of the U.S. fleet, then, provided a timely opportunity to strengthen the white man's hold on the South Pacific.

Steward's Liberal colleagues were equally vehement on this point. John Hornsby was unusually blunt, announcing his gratitude "that Uncle Sam has come into the Pacific to keep the yellow and brown men busy if there is to be any trouble." "I would rather live in the most abject manner under Uncle Sam's flag," he proclaimed, "than I would tolerate the monkey-brand any time." Moreover, he argued, Great Britain's alliance with Japan effectively meant New Zealanders had "been handed over to the Japs" and faced "Armageddon" without protection from the Americans. Despite the Anglo-Japanese Alliance and British imperial interests, Hornsby saw the visit as an opportunity for New Zealand to finally and explicitly restrict Asian immigration over British resistance. In less apocalyptic terms Andrew Rutherford echoed Hornsby's interpretation of the fleet's cruise. The Americans were "not coming here on a business visit": "They are coming here to help the European races to show the coloured races of the East that they are not to have it all their own way in the Pacific." Rutherford thought this message would be reinforced if other white powers emulated the Americans' tour of the Pacific. Auckland's Thomas Thompson also looked forward to the American visit on racial and strategic grounds. From a racial point of view, New Zealanders and Americans "spring from the same stock," he argued. Strategically Thompson embraced the Americans' foray into the Pacific "because it lessens our danger of Asiatic aggression and tends to strengthen the grounds of our national existence." Ultimately, he declared, America must be "regarded as a British Power, and is united with our Empire by ties of commercial, racial, and sentimental interests."[44]

The independent member from Dunedin North, George Thomson, also celebrated the prospect of New Zealand–American cooperation against Asian encroachment. "We never know what the brown and yellow races together may do," Thomson warned, and therefore New Zealanders must do their part to "draw together the two great branches of the English-speaking people." New Zealand's one million whites were defenseless against 700 million Asians, and the dominion's future depended upon the "solidarity of the white race." Josiah Hanan agreed. Hanan was an Invercargill native, and his South Island constituents, like those in Dunedin, had long imagined themselves victims of a Chinese invasion. A forceful American naval presence in the Pacific unquestionably helped New Zealand, he argued: "It lessens our danger of Asiatic aggression and tends to strengthen the grounds of our national existence."[45]

Others in the New Zealand Parliament, especially among the Conservative opposition, felt that the U.S. fleet's impending arrival had caused some New Zealanders to disregard the broader imperial perspective. The most outspoken of these was Thomas M. Wilford, who strenuously objected to spending public finances on entertaining the Americans.[46] The United States had done "absolutely nothing for our benefit," Wilford maintained. The only thing that Americans recognized was "the almighty dollar," and it was nonsense to suggest that racial brotherhood animated New Zealand–American relations. In fact, Wilford proclaimed, prohibitive American tariffs and arbitrary immigration laws worked to the detriment of New Zealanders. Yet even while he derided the U.S. fleet and the nation it represented, Wilford remained dedicated to a vision of white cooperation against the imagined Asian horde. "The only time there will be any real friendship between Britain and America," he declared, "will be when China and Japan join forces and the rest of the world combines against a common foe."[47]

Wilford was not alone. William Fraser also felt embarrassed by his colleagues' rhetorical embrace of the United States. He was motivated primarily by his commitment to the empire, which he believed offered New Zealanders the most reliable protection. Fraser acknowledged that legitimate feelings of racial amity animated much of the enthusiasm, but he cautioned that exponents of racial brotherhood were overzealous: "We are not going to Auckland to welcome the American fleet as the future saviours of this Dominion from the yellow fiend." To that end some parliamentarians would gladly supplicate the approaching Americans at the expense of New Zealand's traditional guardian, Great Britain, Fraser chided, as if "John Bull is too old and feeble now to protect us; we come to you, Uncle Sam, to save us from the Chinese and the Japanese." Such sycophancy was not only unseemly and unnecessary; it was also detrimental to New Zealand's relationship with Britain. If his colleagues feared an impending race war, they ought to recognize that all white powers, not just Americans, would have a vested interest in its satisfactory conclusion. Fraser speculated, "If the time does come when the white race has to fight the yellow one . . . the white races will have joined together, and it will not be only the Stars and Stripes that will float in the Pacific Ocean—the Union Jack will be there also to the front as usual."[48] Alfred Barclay echoed this sentiment: "I am unable to understand quite why we should prostrate ourselves in adulation . . . before the visiting navy. I am unable to understand why the whole country should be turned upside down about this matter." Americans served their own interests and no other's, Barclay insisted, and it was absurd to suggest that New Zealanders could expect unflinching American support in the event of a Pacific crisis.[49]

New Zealand's press was equally concerned with the racial implications of the American visit, and none was more vocal than the *New Zealand Herald*. Its August 8, 1908, editorial encapsulated the racial anxieties and possible diplomatic implications of the fleet's tour. The *Herald* applauded the "universal emotion of jubilation and goodwill" that accompanied the fleet's arrival in the colony and reiterated the widely held sentiment that "the Americans are not and cannot be 'foreigner' to the British peoples." In this new atmosphere of international Anglo-Saxon brotherhood, the *Herald* downplayed earlier stereotypes of Americans as the product of a "mongrelized" race and was willing to marginalize French Canadians and the South African Boers in their rush to bind the United States into this fantasy of racial unity. "In spite of certain ethnological modifications made in the national composition of the American people by the recent immigration of other than North European peoples," the *Herald* equivocated, "they are still much more closely akin to our stock than are certain sections of the self-governing dominions of the Empire." The *Herald's* embrace of "Brother Jonathan" indicated the extent to which the Japanese in particular and Asians in general were seen as a very real threat to white supremacy in New Zealand. Shared language, customs, laws, and religion were enough to unite the Pacific's English-speaking peoples, but under the present circumstances "our welcome is more than friendly." In the *Herald's* estimation, "Upon this we are not divided by political lines, nor divorced by revolutions. We welcome the American fleet with more than warmth, because we all realise that the English-speaking peoples of the Pacific are moving simultaneously and spontaneously in a tacit understanding which Governments cannot but acknowledge and recognise; and that to-day the American fleet, not less than the British Navy, stands for the racial integrity of every English-speaking State in the Pacific."[50]

The *Auckland Star* was similarly infatuated by the American visit's implications. The preparations under way in Auckland were animated by a profound sense of racial kinship, "a spontaneous warmth of feeling, and that sense of fraternal kindliness and confidence which . . . we reserve for brothers in blood and brothers in arms alone." The *Star* disregarded any lingering political animosities between Britons and Americans because "when all is said and done, there is no tie so permanent, no feature of national character so ineffaceable, as that which springs from community of racial origin." The *Star* hoped the visit would "inaugurate a closer union in feeling and purpose between the two great branches of the Anglo-Saxon race."[51] The *New Zealand Times* concurred: "Above and beyond all else, the visitors will be honoured because their presence in our waters is a bold, emphatic assertion of the dominance of the White Race."[52] Ultimately America and "Greater Britain" shared a "strong, binding, and abiding community of interest" based on "the command of the Pacific by the white race," and there was no "better herald of the white reign" than the American fleet's visit to Auckland. The Yellow Peril was real, close, and unpredictable, the *Times* warned, and the Anglo-Japanese Alliance was insufficient protection against the tide of Asian immigration.[53] As the paper suggested, after the fleet left for Australia Britain's alliance with Japan would not endure forever, and Britain would be forced to "play different cards" in the Pacific once that treaty was allowed to lapse. "One of those cards has just been played by the Dominion of New Zealand," the *Times* proudly boasted. Their invitation to the Americans represented "the first move on the white side in the game of 'White and Yellow.' "[54]

As in Parliament, however, there was dissent in the press. The conservative *Dominion* was especially circumspect and disdainful of any suggestion that the visit promised American complicity in Australasians' racial fantasies. The notion that "America will assist Australasia in carrying out its policy of excluding Asiatic immigration and protect it in the event of Asiatic invasion" was nothing more than "mischievous nonsense." Such rhetoric only undermined New Zealand's relations with Great Britain.[55] The *Dominion* continued its campaign against this anti-Japanese, pro-American rhetoric throughout the fleet's stay in New Zealand. While the fleet's presence in Australasia would undoubtedly "restore the mental balance of the people who are haunted by bad dreams of an Asiatic invasion," the *Dominion* observed on August 14, it was unlikely that Americans intended to "fold a great white arm round the timorous people who seem lately to have forgotten that there is such a thing as a British Navy, with British honour behind it."[56] Talk of racial alliance with the United States was offensive, counterproductive, and dishonorable. The *Dominion* took particular solace in a warning issued by Britain's *Spectator* magazine, which cautioned that "mischief-makers" should not be allowed to "represent the [American] navy as a weapon to be used in [a] race-feud between English-speaking peoples and Asiatics."[57]

The response of New Zealand's Maori community was equally conflicted and offers yet another corrective to the enthusiasm exhibited by many white New Zealanders. As the *New Zealand Herald* pointed out, the fleet's visit engendered debate concerning Maori participation "on account of the rigid drawing of the 'colour line' in the United States."[58] One of the most vocal critics of American racism and its implications for Maori involvement in the festivities was Apirana Ngata, member of Parliament for the Eastern Maori District. In his capacity as a New Zealander and MP, Ngata supported the government's invitation. As a Maori, however, he opposed what he saw as the exploitation of Maori culture for the proposed celebrations. His objections were twofold. He resented American racial attitudes: "We cannot close our eyes to the fact that in America the treatment of the coloured races has not been such as has been the treatment of the Maoris by the British race in New Zealand. . . . We cannot as a people be expected to spontaneously extend a great welcome as from the Maoris of New Zealand to the American fleet." According to Ngata, for example, Rotorua's Arawa people unanimously refused to take part in the official ceremonies once they were told of Americans' mistreatment of their own indigenous and African population. Ngata also expressed frustration at the government's tendency to "trot out our Maoris to be exhibited for the entertainment of tourists, and we want to put a stop to that."[59] Ngata believed the exploitation of Maori traditions for the amusement of visiting dignitaries enfeebled Maori culture.

Continuing his crusade for "calm and cool reason" toward the fleet's visit, Wilford also derided American racial attitudes on behalf of New Zealand's Maori population: "But need I dwell upon the feelings of the Americans towards the black or the coloured races? Need I refer to the attitude of the American Press or to the attitude of American politicians in regard to the President of the United States inviting Mr. Booker Washington to dinner with him? Knowing the feeling of the American people towards coloured races, I . . . ask the Government to prevent any exhibitions by the Maori people for the delectation of these American visitors."[60] One concerned New Zealander also expressed apprehension about the impending arrival of so many American sailors, "as they come from a country where dark blood is looked down upon." The only way to prevent these "low whites" from exploiting native goodwill, he argued, was to place Maori settlements under government supervision until the visitors' departure.[61]

Ngata's and Wilford's concerns prompted some of their colleagues to defend American race relations. Charles Major disputed Ngata's understanding of American history. Unlike Europeans in New Zealand, European settlers in North America "were dealing with quite a different race." American mistreatment of Native Americans was entirely justified, Major claimed, because "it was a question of reprisals against one of the most cruel and ruthless races of people in the world." New Zealand's prime minister, Sir Joseph Ward, also rejected Ngata's assessment of American attitudes. "The racial difference between the whites and negroes is entirely different from ours," Ward observed, and it was incongruous to compare Pakeha (European)–Maori race relations with those prevailing in the United States. George Laurenson too challenged Ngata's and Wilford's claims. The fleet represented "a visit from the greatest branch of the English-speaking family to the Pacific," and that in itself was worthy of celebration. More important, however, the cruise was "a demonstration that, whoever dominates the Pacific, the white races are to dominate it," and this was especially important as Japan and China strengthened themselves. Laurenson was equally offended by Wilford's claims of American racism. Antipathy toward blacks was one thing, but he insisted that "the American race has as much respect and love for the Red Indian as we have for the Maori." Laurenson was astonished that Wilford could not appreciate "what this demonstration by the American fleet really means to every white man and woman who lives on the borders of the Pacific Ocean."[62]

Not all Maori representatives were as unenthusiastic about the fleet's arrival as Ngata. Another Maori leader, Te Rangi Hiroa (Dr. Peter Buck), rejected Ngata's pessimism. A prominent Maori physician, Buck was the son of an Anglo-Irish immigrant father and a Maori mother and maintained close links to both his Pakeha and Maori ancestry. Maori exclusion from the festivities, he argued, "would not be representative of the desirable unity of the two races." In fact it "would be a direct insult to the Maoris, and belittling them as an, apparently, unimportant factor." Buck recognized that "the Americans are prejudiced against coloured people, but that is in America, where they are of negroids, descended from generations of slaves." Instead "the Maori people are of Caucasian descent, and should not be identified with the objects of the American's aversion."[63] King Mahuta Tawhiao Potatau

Te Wherowhero was also enthusiastic about the prospect of his people's involvement in the fleet's welcome. Mahuta envisaged an unprecedented gathering of Maori tribes from across New Zealand to meet the Americans as "the original owners of the soil."[64]

Despite these reservations the official banquet honoring Admiral Charles S. Sperry and his officers espoused the theme of Anglo-Saxon amity. Indeed testaments to the "special pride in our old Anglo-Saxon race" suffused the celebrations and found echoes in almost every official and unofficial pronouncement that week. In finally welcoming the fleet to New Zealand, Prime Minister Ward set the tone. He celebrated the fleet's arrival as testament to Anglo-Saxon racial brotherhood. The ships assembled in Auckland's harbor were a tribute to the vigor of "a people we delight to think sprang from our own old Anglo-Saxon blood, from a people speaking our language, and sharing our own traditions, institutions, and national aims," and Sperry would emulate these sentiments whenever he was called upon to speak in New Zealand or Australia.[65] Although he publicly raised a glass to racial solidarity, Sperry privately confided to his wife that his New Zealand hosts "have a big 'Yellow Peril' scare, and are eagerly speculating as to whether we will make common cause with them." While he was willing to embrace a transpacific "*community* of *commercial* interests" with New Zealand, he was "careful not to go farther than that."[66] Undoubtedly the words of his commander in chief, Theodore Roosevelt, resonated with him in the South Pacific. "I need not tell you that you should exercise the most careful watch at all times both before and after you leave the Orient," the president had warned Sperry in March 1908.[67] For all his public and private admonitions against the dangers of unhampered Asian migration, Roosevelt was keen to avoid unnecessarily antagonizing the Japanese as American battleships cruised toward Japanese waters.

Ultimately New Zealanders and Australians would be disappointed. The fleet's visit did nothing to foster closer Anglo-American-dominion cooperation vis-à-vis Japan, and the Anglo-Japanese Alliance remained Britain's primary strategic and diplomatic crutch in the Pacific. Nonetheless the prospects of increased American involvement in Pacific affairs briefly stimulated anticipation of American support for Australia's claims to white supremacy. Keen to capitalize on the success of the fleet's visit, Deakin's government acted quickly to cement relations with their "British kindred" across the Pacific. In a letter to Roosevelt, which was to be conveyed by the British government to the ambassador in Washington in accordance with imperial protocol, the Australian government lauded the U.S. Fleet's "power and efficiency" and invited Roosevelt to visit Australia during his proposed postpresidency world tour. The Foreign Office was unsure of how to deal with this request. Prestwood Lucas objected to the "grovelling tone" of Australia's message, and others found it "wanting in dignity." They could not, however, conceive how to avoid sending it.[68] Thankfully, from the British point of view, Roosevelt declined the invitation.[69]

Undeterred, Deakin's successor, Andrew Fisher, captured the lingering atmosphere of optimism and anticipation, even while contemplating the worst. If Australia was threatened by "a European or Asiatic power," he observed, there was no guarantee that Great Britain would be able to defend her vulnerable southern dominion, especially if Britain's own security was imperiled. Australians therefore required additional support, preferably from a powerful nation attuned to their particular circumstances and anxieties. "In this connection," Fisher suggested, "thoughts naturally turn to the people speaking our own language already deeply interested in resisting foreign aggression in the Pacific—the people of the United States of America." To this end Fisher proposed a seven-point agenda designed to cultivate American support. In addition to encouraging American trade and investment, Australians ought to promote American immigration "of the right sort" and foster closer ties through visits of American dignitaries. It would also be essential "to join with them as far as we may in keeping the Pacific for the Anglo-Saxons" and to "take every opportunity to make them consider themselves our own kinsfolk."[70] The threat to Australia's survival would recede, he expected, in the relative safety of this sympathetic transpacific embrace.

Despite Fisher's optimism, the previous two years' events did not bode well for increased cooperation among the Pacific's "white men's countries." Rather than bind them together in a racial community of interest, the tumultuous period between 1906 and 1908 had vividly demonstrated the domestic, imperial, and international tensions and divisions wrought by immigration exclusion. The American and Canadian gentleman's agreements with Japan had temporarily mollified the issue's force and salience in the North American West. It would be another six years before the issue of Asian immigration forcefully reasserted itself on the world stage. The folly of restrictive colonial immigration policies was once again brought into sharp relief as World War I raged throughout Europe, Africa, and Asia from 1914 to 1918. And once again Britain and its white dominions experienced the enormous challenges engendered by colonial activism against Asian labor mobility in the Pacific.

CHAPTER FIVE

The Politics of Asian Restriction in a World at War

The years immediately following the Bellingham and Vancouver riots were relatively calm in the imperial and diplomatic struggle over transpacific Asian labor mobility, at least compared to the seemingly incessant turbulence of the previous decade. The barriers erected by white activists over the preceding twelve years had temporarily quelled the most offensive extravagances of colonial and American anti-Asian politics. American and Canadian agreements with the Meiji government suppressed Japanese labor emigration, which in turn anaesthetized the hostility toward Japanese migrants that had recently gripped the North American West. White British Columbian anxiety toward South Asian migrants similarly receded after the Vancouver riot, thanks to the success of Canada's continuous journey regulation. At the same time, Australasian literacy controls had effectively subdued regional Asian labor networks, thereby muting the clamor for direct enumerated prohibitions in Australia and New Zealand. The context and strategies of these restriction campaigns were distinct, but they all shared one thing in common: British, Japanese, American, and Canadian officials had contested the most egregious of these initiatives in order to ameliorate imperial and international tensions, and the absence of racially explicit immigration controls in all of these cases owed much to those interventions.

Nevertheless this opposition obscured rather than erased the ongoing toxicity of white colonial and American prejudice, and in this chapter I explore the resurgence of imperial and diplomatic tensions immediately before and during the First World War. In two important episodes discord over existing anti-Asian restrictions exasperated British imperial and foreign relations: the 1914 *Komagata Maru* crisis in British Columbia and the wartime deterioration of Japanese-Australian relations. The arrival of the *Komagata Maru* and its 376 passengers off the coast of Vancouver in May 1914 represented a direct challenge to Canadian prohibitions on transpacific South Asian mobility. Indeed it constituted a literal (if failed) attempt to create a new circuit of South Asian migration between the Indian subcontinent and the North American West. If that ill-fated expedition illustrates the friction that hampered imperial politics during this period, the degeneration of Japanese-Australian relations exemplifies the adverse diplomatic and international implications of dominion restriction following the outbreak of war in August 1914. Escalating antagonism between Britain's antipodean colony and its key Asian ally in the Pacific set the stage for open hostility between Australian and Japanese representatives at the postwar peace conference in Paris. As these examples illustrate, racial and economic antipathies continued to churn throughout the self-professed white enclaves of the Pacific Rim, and Asian migrants continued to challenge the onerous restrictions imposed upon them by white colonial governments.

The *New Statesman* encapsulated the imperial burden of colonial racism just before war broke out, declaring in June 1914, "The Indian immigrant has ceased to be a local difficulty; he has become an imperial portent." South Asian manpower was vital to imperial defense, and the embarrassment of exclusion threatened to undermine Indian allegiance to the armed forces of the empire. Moreover restive South Asian nationalists bristled at discriminatory treatment toward their compatriots in the white dominions.[1] Yet the stakes were no less momentous from the dominions' point of view. The Canadian interior minister, Frank Oliver, remarked during a federal parliamentary debate in March 1914, "If we introduce into Canada a larger number of people having an Asiatic civilization than we have . . . people of European civilization, then Asiatic civilization becomes dominant at the expense of European civilization."[2] This was the great imperial riddle: How could the British government harmonize colonial racial and economic anxiety with the imperatives of imperial rule over nonwhite subjects in Africa and Asia? That abiding enigma continued to bedevil the empire as the war raged.

Similar tensions simmered in the diplomatic sphere in the weeks before the outbreak of war. In May 1914 the British inspector general of overseas forces, Sir Ian Hamilton, inadvertently highlighted the ongoing sensitivity of racial discrimination in Anglo-Japanese relations. Speaking before an audience in Wellington, Hamilton injudiciously described the Pacific as the fulcrum in a struggle between Asians and Europeans for world supremacy. He compounded his indiscretion by announcing that "British countries were being invaded by foreigners who lived on rice."[3] His imprudent remarks riled the British and Japanese governments. One British official wryly observed, "The speech was not tactful considering that we have a rice-eating Asiatic for an ally."[4] Japan's prime minister Count Ōkuma Shigenobu and foreign minister Baron Katō Takaaki commented on Hamilton's transgression in the following days, as did the Japanese press. Tokyo's *Nichinichi Shimbun* pronounced that many in Great Britain and its white dominions "believe in the irreconcilableness of the white and yellow races" and warned ominously, "Should the white races continue to uphold their racial prejudice, the challenge must be accepted."[5] The British ambassador in Tokyo, Sir Conyngham Greene, considerably understated Japanese antipathy when he observed, "There is a little feeling of pique observable here in connection with the sore subject of racial prejudice," and the British foreign secretary, Sir Edward Grey, complained to Prime Minister Asquith, "It is becoming a serious matter that [Hamilton's] loose tongue and pen should affect our relations with Japan."[6]

Existing studies of the international disputes surrounding Asian migration tend to gloss over the war, skipping instead to the fractious debates of the Paris Peace Conference.[7] Yet the First World War only intensified the politics of Asian restriction, especially for the British Empire, and that conflict represents a major turning point in the imperial and diplomatic history of Asian labor restriction. The war capsized prevailing assumptions about white supremacy, entitlement, and infallibility and energized new and existing currents of anticolonialism throughout Asia and Africa.[8] The vital contributions of South Asian, Japanese, and Chinese laborers, sailors, and soldiers raised the expectations of British allies and subjects alike.[9] Victory in the struggle against Germany earned tangible rewards for the Japanese, including control of former German colonies in China and Micronesia and influence in the reconstruction of postwar international order. These developments in turn aggravated the apprehensions of white colonial agitators, who feared a devastating backlash after years of anti-Asian chauvinism and discrimination. Rather than tempering their provocative restriction regimes in response to increasing Japanese and South Asian assertiveness, however, white activists instead redoubled their commitment to Asian exclusion.

I begin by exploring the local and imperial consequences of the *Komagata Maru*'s tempestuous confinement off the Vancouver coast in the summer of 1914. According to its architect, the vessel's voyage signified the inauguration of a new conduit of South Asian migration across the Pacific that would challenge the legality of Canada's 1908 continuous journey order. This nascent migrant network was conceived not by the labor demands of imperial or global capital, as previous networks were, but by Baba Gurdit Singh, a South Asian expatriate and activist from Hong Kong. While Singh failed to achieve his objective, he did instigate a serious imperial crisis that unsettled the empire on the eve of hostilities in Europe. This episode therefore provides a striking example of the negative repercussions stimulated by years of formal and informal efforts to immobilize South Asian migrants in the British colonies of settlement.

I then chronicle the gradual decay of Japanese-Australian relations over the course of the First World War and highlight the diplomatic connotations of Asian restriction in the British Empire as seen through the prism of this relationship. Upon the declaration of war in August 1914, Japanese observers optimistically expected that their participation would finally engender international equality and respect for the Japanese people. That optimism was short-lived. Propelled into an uncomfortable alliance with their erstwhile antagonists, many Australians feared the Japanese would exploit this awkward partnership and press for concessions against the White Australia Policy. Japanese territorial gains in the Pacific and the Australian acquisition of New Guinea brought Japanese military forces closer to Australia, which inflamed existing anxieties regarding the Commonwealth's proximity to East Asia and its relative isolation from Europe and the Royal Navy. As the conflict wore on, increasingly resentful Japanese commentators criticized Australians' refusal to moderate their discriminatory immigration policies, leading them to question the value and sincerity of the Anglo-Japanese Alliance. The Australian government lent further credence to these critiques when it extended the purview of the White Australia Policy to encompass its new South Pacific dependency in New Guinea and rejected Japanese requests for moderation.

Challenging South Asian Immobility in North America: The *Komagata Maru*

Canada's continuous journey regulation had successfully inhibited South Asian labor immigration since 1908, and it remained an effective prohibition as long as direct, uninterrupted travel between India and Canada was impossible.[10] That provision faced multiple challenges in the months before the First World War, however, the most potent of which came from South Asian immigrants and migrants themselves. In the year before war broke out in Europe, small groups of South Asian activists from across the British Empire tried to reconstitute the migration networks that had been abolished by the 1908 order. These efforts culminated most emphatically in Gurdit Singh's audacious voyage aboard the *Komagata Maru* and yet another British Columbian campaign to fortify provincial and federal borders in the summer of 1914. While the forces of restriction once again prevailed, these protests against South Asian immobility embarrassed the Canadian and British governments, illustrated the continued salience of British Columbian antipathy toward Asian migrants, and inspired already aggravated Indian nationalists in North America and beyond.[11]

Incremental attempts to erode the continuous journey provision and re-suscitate some measure of transpacific South Asian mobility gained traction in May 1913. That month representatives of Canada's small South Asian community lobbied the Colonial Office in conjunction with their compatriots in London for repeal of the provision. They framed their argument in moral and imperial terms. The Canadian mandate prevented legally domiciled South Asians from reuniting with their families, the petitioners argued, which imposed an unfair hardship on British subjects in both India and Canada. The Canadian government rebuffed these claims. The Privy Council assured the imperial government that the regulation did not inflict an invidious burden upon South Asians because it applied to prospective immigrants of every nationality, regardless of race. They of course neglected to acknowledge that continuous passage was impossible for South Asians, but not for Europeans, and this ruse fooled nobody. The India Office registered its dissatisfaction and warned that Canadian intransigence threatened to "exacerbate Indian popular feeling," which was already inflamed by South Africa's recent refusal to grant full rights to its South Asian immigrants.[12]

Unsubstantiated rumors of a planned direct steamship service between Calcutta and Vancouver further alarmed white activists and Canadian authorities in the midst of this exchange. Such a service would invalidate the continuous journey provision and revitalize the imperial and domestic embarrassment of South Asian restriction. Incensed white British Columbians immediately seized upon the reports and sprang into action. Vancouver's Grandview Ratepayers Association, for example, directly petitioned the Canadian prime minister, complaining that the provision's abnegation would facilitate a renewal of South Asian immigration that would eviscerate the social, economic, and moral character of British Columbia and prove "destructive to all forms of higher civilisation."[13] Stimulated by white anxiety—and with no evidence as to the rumor's origin or veracity—the Privy Council swiftly appealed to both the imperial and the Indian government. Without intervention from London, Canada would be forced to unilaterally "prevent any considerable immigration into this Dominion of a race, unfitted alike by their constitution, temperament and habits, for permanent residence in this country."[14] This entreaty contained a tacit threat: if the imperial government did not quietly block the alleged route, white dissidence would erupt once again in the Canadian West. The rumored steamship line never materialized, but in November 1913 a far more startling challenge emerged when the British Columbian Supreme Court declared the "continuous journey" regulation unconstitutional on a legal technicality. Parliament quickly rewrote the provision to the court's satisfaction, but in the meantime over sixty South Asian detainees awaiting deportation were released.[15]

Faced with these mounting challenges, the federal government confronted a familiar conundrum: proponents of exclusion in British Columbia stridently demanded South Asian migrants' absolute exclusion and threatened to act independently if Ottawa failed to preserve the continuous journey regulation, but the British government remained steadfast against explicit racial prohibitions of Asian migrants, especially those bestowed with imperial citizenship. Sensing a potentially lethal challenge to its South Asian restriction regime, the Canadian government sought yet another ostensibly objective administrative device to reinforce the apparently faltering continuous journey provision.

For five years the Canadian government had shrewdly exploited seemingly objective realities of geography and transportation to blockade the circuits of South Asian migration to North America, and Canadian authorities once again resorted to subterfuge. In December 1913 the government promulgated a temporary prohibition on the immigration of all laborers into British Columbia, citing labor market contractions in the province.[16] While in principle the order applied to Europeans and Americans as well as Asians, it had no practical effect on the former as they rarely arrived in Canada via British Columbian ports. It was another ingenious and seemingly impartial manipulation of transportation, circumstance, and space. The Privy Council's sleight of hand did not deceive the Hindustani Association of Vancouver Island, however, which complained to the India Office that "economic expediency in lieu of fundamental justice and fair play to Hindustani subjects of His Majesty . . . will not tend to cement India more closely to the Empire." "Our status is ignored," they lamented, "and [the] racial colour bar [is] imposed against us." The Colonial Office nevertheless colluded with the Canadian government, insisting that the order was not racially motivated since it applied to all laborers, regardless of race and nationality.[17] As usual, the imperial government was content to acquiesce in its dominion's deception, providing the illusion of imperial justice and equality remained intact.

Singh decided to test Canada's de facto preclusion of his South Asian compatriots' mobility against this already volatile backdrop. In the summer of 1914 he personally chartered a Japanese steamer named the *Komagata Maru*. He originally intended to board migrants in Calcutta and make directly for Vancouver, thereby actually satisfying the requirements of the continuous journey provision. Hong Kong, however, was home to a large number of South Asian expatriates, and it was there that Singh formulated and advertised his scheme. Not surprisingly his potential passengers were either un-willing or unable to travel to Calcutta to begin their journey to Canada. Forced to amend his plan, Singh resolved to sail directly from Hong Kong in con-travention of Canadian immigration regulations. The *Komagata Maru* de-parted on April 6, 1914, with 165 passengers. In a testament to the global reach of South Asian migrants, the vessel picked up more passengers in Shanghai, Moji, and Yokohama. By the time the *Komagata Maru* began its Pacific cross-ing, bound for Vancouver, there were 376 predominantly Sikh migrants on board. Having initially intended to test Canadian authorities by satisfying the conditions of the continuous journey decree, Singh now determined to flout the regulation and challenge its validity in the Canadian Supreme Court.[18]

The Canadian government first heard of Singh's intentions on March 30 in a telegram from the governor of Hong Kong. The government belatedly re-plied a week later that the ship's passengers would not be allowed to land. By then the *Komagata Maru* had already left Hong Kong en route for British Co-lumbia. When it arrived in Vancouver harbor on May 23, waiting immigra-tion officials denied its passengers permission to land. Reluctant to grant Singh his grandstand case against the continuous journey regulation, British Columbian officials cited the Privy Council's temporary ban on im-migration. All but twenty-two of the 376 passengers were detained on board pending deportation proceedings, the small group being legally domiciled returning immigrants. The standoff began when Singh, in conjunction with representatives of Vancouver's increasingly agitated South Asian community, challenged the deportation orders in court.[19] Conditions on the vessel wors-ened over the coming weeks as food, water, and basic supplies ran low. Un-able to disembark, those 165 passengers who boarded in Hong Kong had now been at sea for over two months. In response to inquiries from the king—with whom Singh communicated via the Canadian governor-general—Canadian authorities insisted that racial enmity had no bearing on the passengers' de-tainment. In fact the Privy Council's labor exclusion order, the undersecre-tary of state for external affairs fraudulently maintained, "applies not only to Hindus, but to all others as well, including English-speaking peoples in the United States."[20]

White activists in British Columbia immediately moved to seal this pos-sible fracture in their border, and their reaction guaranteed that Singh's in-trigue would produce an imperial crisis. Vancouver's federal representative in Parliament, Henry Herbert Stevens, articulated the sentiments of his fel-low westerners. He was an outspoken critic of Asian immigration and a vigorous proponent of a "white Canada," but he also clearly understood the imperial and international sensitivities engendered by colonial hostility toward Asian immigration. Canada was forced "to choose between two evils," he acknowledged, as the *Komagata Maru*'s passengers languished in Vancouver Harbor. On one hand the dominion faced "the possibility of causing some slight offence to these people from across the seas." He recognized that India, Japan, and China resented exclusion, and he admitted that Canadians could not easily disregard their indignation; as a British dominion, Canada was obliged to respect Britain's imperial and international interests. On the other hand, however, Stevens refused to countenance unrestricted Asian immigration, even at the risk of offending the British government.[21]

Vancouver had once again become the site of strident anti-Asian agitation. On the evening of June 23 protestors staged a public meeting against Asian immigration at the city's Dominion Hall. White Vancouverites registered their opposition to the landing of the *Komagata Maru*'s passengers, who had now suffered in the harbor for a month. Vancouver's mayor, Truman Smith Baxter, insisted that local opposition to South Asian immigration was in no way racially motivated; it was simply a reflection of widespread unemployment in the city. Moreover, he protested, the province's ordinance against immigration made no specific mention of any nationality; therefore it could not be construed as discriminatory. Like Baxter, almost every speaker tried to efface the racial undertones of their opposition to Asian immigration, tacitly acknowledging the imperial and diplomatic implications of the standoff.[22]

Stevens was the evening's real draw. He did not disappoint the crowd, nor did he disguise his bigotry. In a way his Australasian contemporaries would have recognized, he underscored the dangers inherent in the province's proximity to "800 millions of Asiatics," contending, "The very least tremor from that source would unquestionably swamp us by weight of numbers." The 354 Indians now trapped aboard the *Komagata Maru* represented the vanguard of an inexorable flood that threatened to overwhelm not just British Columbia but the rest of Canada as well. Without white British Columbians' continued vigilance "Canada today would have been swamped with Orientals and there would be left today practically not a vestige of the civilization of which we are so proud." To great applause he insisted that Asian migrants were socially, culturally, economically, and racially inassimilable: "And I hold that in every one of these phases it would be detrimental to the civilization we hold so dear to allow any large influx of Orientals into this country." Resurrecting earlier frustrations, Stevens chided that authorities in Ottawa and the eastern provinces were slow to recognize these facts of geography and demography, while the imperial government sought merely to avoid conflict with Japan, China, and India. Nevertheless it was imperative that the white men of the West remain resolute, regardless of the imperial and international consequences. To the crowd's delight, Stevens adamantly declared, "I intend to stand absolutely on all occasions on this one great principle of a white country and a white British Columbia."[23]

As these remonstrations highlighted, even the most vociferous opponents of Asian immigration understood the intricate balance of imperial and national interest that federal authorities had to navigate. They also demonstrated, however, that Asian restriction was deemed too vital an issue to sacrifice before Britain's imperial and diplomatic interests. Following this rambunctious meeting, the crowd carried a resolution condemning Asian immigration as "detrimental and hurtful to the best interests of the Dominion from the standpoint of citizenship, labor and moral conditions." From their perspective, the *Komagata Maru*'s passengers symbolized a breach in the dike of Canadian white supremacy, and their admission would signal the dissolution of Canadian racial, social, and economic order. The crowd therefore demanded the passengers' immediate deportation and the enactment of a stringent, explicit, and unassailable restriction regime.[24]

Compelled by the previous evening's events, the following day British Columbia's Conservative premier, Richard McBride, outlined his own opposition to landing the passengers before the federal prime minister in Ottawa, Robert Borden. Notwithstanding the tremendous local aversion to Asian immigration, McBride told Borden, there was already widespread unemployment among Vancouver's current residents and little prospect of improvement. In order to avert future crises, McBride believed, Canadian authorities must assert their right to control immigration at both the provincial and the federal level. He understood this had to be done with sensitivity toward British, Japanese, South Asian, and Chinese views, so he suggested precisely the measure Stevens had outlined the night before: reciprocal exclusion. "In this way," he insisted, "no offence can be charged against national dignity."[25] McBride's telegram was only the beginning, for Stevens's call to educate federal authorities in the East fell upon fertile ground. In the coming days Borden received a number of resolutions, petitions, and telegrams, lauding Stevens's position as the will of Vancouver's white residents. From the board of directors of the Vancouver General Hospital to the Vancouver County Loyal Orange Lodge, Borden was inundated with letters "seeking the total expulsion of all Oriental immigration into this Dominion."[26]

The Canadian prime minister understood their concerns. During his time in opposition Borden had himself argued that Canada's sheer enormity necessitated the careful selection of appropriate migrants from only "the best emigrating races of the world." Only under these circumstances could the dominion cultivate and preserve a vigorous national character. Fully cognizant of the issue's sensitivity, Borden articulated a careful defense of Asian exclusion in 1908, which highlighted the complex interconnections of race, nationalism, imperial relations, and diplomacy:

> Let us have a due sense of Imperial as well as Canadian interests; let us appreciate the sanctity of treaty rights which must always be observed, and the respect which must be paid to a great nation like Japan, the ally and friend of Great Britain. . . . [But] British Columbia must remain a British and Canadian province, inhabited by men in whose veins runs the blood of those great pioneering races which built up and developed not only Western, but Eastern Canada. And while we recognize our duty to the Great Empire whose flag shall always float above us, we respectfully and loyally maintain that Canada in so vital an essential as this must be accorded a freedom of judgment as perfect and unfettered as that exercised not only by the other great dominions of the Empire, but by Great Britain herself.[27]

As much as he might have once commended his petitioners' conviction, as prime minister Borden was now forced to mediate these seemingly intractable impulses.

Vancouver's South Asian community and white opponents of Asian immigration hardened their positions as the weeks wore on, and the Colonial Office in London feared the consequences for British rule in India as Borden ruminated in Ottawa. The day after Stevens's speech, Secretary of State for the Colonies Lewis V. Harcourt telegraphed the Canadian governor-general, reminding him that as long as the *Komagata Maru* remained in British waters it was "very desirable to avoid use of force which would have extremely bad effect in Punjaub [*sic*]."[28] It was clear that Singh recognized the imperial implications of his vessel's protracted stay in Vancouver Harbor. He wrote to the governor-general on July 8 that the passengers' forcible return to Asia would undoubtedly produce a "bad impression to native armies." "To save India from troubles" Singh urged the governor-general to provide a tract of land for their settlement and cultivation.[29]

On July 10 Sir Charles Hibbert Tupper offered Borden a solution. Tupper was a former member of Parliament and Canadian solicitor general now practicing law in Vancouver. His firm represented the Japanese owners of the *Komagata Maru*, who feared they would face legal liabilities if conditions on board the ship deteriorated any further. Acting on their behalf, Tupper suggested that the federal government assume responsibility for resupplying the ship in preparation for its return to Hong Kong.[30] Though reluctant to provision the vessel, lest this encourage copycat voyages, Borden signaled his willingness to adopt this plan if Tupper guaranteed the immediate departure of the *Komagata Maru* upon resupply.[31] Tupper responded affirmatively and suggested the operation take place outside Canadian waters in order to limit publicity and liability for all concerned, and Borden agreed.[32] With a resolution in place, the Board of Inquiry charged with determining the passengers' fate ruled in favor of the government. On July 17 the prospective immigrants were informed of the decision, and officials ordered the ship's Japanese captain to leave Vancouver Harbor and make for Hong Kong.

With their legal options exhausted and deportation proceedings complete, the passengers' situation grew more desperate. Faced with expatriation, they seized control of the ship. The following day Vancouver's immigration inspector, Malcolm Reid, assembled a force of over 175 armed police and former soldiers. Intent upon forcing the *Komagata Maru* to sea, Reid and his boarding party approached the vessel aboard the tugboat *Sea Lion*. They were met with a hail of debris as they attempted to embark the much larger ship. According to a report by the assistant superintendent of immigration, the passengers injured twenty officers aboard the *Sea Lion* in a "shower of coal, iron bars, clubs and pieces of machinery." Apparently they also fired shots at the officers. No bullets hit their target, and the officers did not return fire, no doubt cognizant of their disadvantageous position some ten feet below the deck.[33] Unable to overwhelm the passengers, the *Sea Lion* finally retreated in defeat. On July 21 an exasperated Borden finally authorized the HMCS *Rainbow* to compel the *Komagata Maru*'s departure. As one of two ships in the Canadian Navy, the *Rainbow* was sorely outdated. Yet it served its purpose. Resupplied by the Canadian government, the *Komagata Maru* finally left Vancouver Harbor on July 23, two months after it arrived.[34]

However, the consequences of the *Komagata Maru*'s incarceration in Vancouver Harbor had just begun. Every British-controlled port in East Asia rejected the vessel, and its passengers were finally forced to disembark in India. In a cruel and ironic inversion of the "continuous journey" provision— and despite the fact that most of the passengers had no home on the subcontinent—British authorities in India decreed that they would be sent to Punjab. There representatives of the Raj would decide upon appropriate punishment. A detachment of police greeted the ship when it finally made landfall at the town of Budge Budge in West Bengal. Their attempted arrest of Singh provoked a riot, resulting in the deaths of twenty-six people, with thirty-five more injured. Though Singh escaped, the deaths provoked anger in Punjab and galvanized regional nationalists.[35]

The episode underscored the stubbornly combustible imperial politics of South Asian restriction and the possible dangers they portended for the integrity of the empire. The impending European conflict only accentuated the vulnerabilities engendered by colonial intolerance. On the same day the *Komagata Maru* limped out of Vancouver Harbor, the German government was encouraging Austria to deliver its fateful ultimatum to Serbia, following Archduke Franz Ferdinand's assassination one month earlier. War broke out just over one week later, as the disconsolate Indian refugees sailed toward uncertainty in Asia. Canadians would soon find themselves defending the empire alongside South Asian troops, men the sentinels of a White Canada would sooner see confined to the Asian subcontinent. Across the Pacific, Australians now found themselves in an equally uncomfortable alliance, setting the scene for an equally debilitating challenge to British diplomacy in East Asia.

Australia's Uneasy Wartime Alliance with Japan: Japanese Optimism, 1914

The rest of this chapter elucidates the increasingly grievous wartime implications of the White Australia Policy and the broader colonial politics of Japanese restriction that it epitomized. Japanese-Australian relations deteriorated over three distinct phases. The war began with a semblance of optimism and enthusiasm, as Japan officially entered the fight against Germany on August 23, 1914. According to Count Ōkuma, his country had entered the war "to show the West what it is slow to believe, that we can work harmoniously with great Occidental powers to support and protect the highest ideals of civilization."[36] In this context both Japanese and British officials anticipated a relaxation of Australian racial attitudes. But that optimism had evaporated by early 1915, only to be replaced by growing animosity. By then the Japanese conquest and occupation of former German colonies in the Pacific had in fact exacerbated Australian trepidations. The Commonwealth government therefore proved unwilling to yield and actually expanded the White Australia Policy into New Guinea. By 1917 Japanese-Australian relations were trending toward disarray. It became clear that Japan—with Britain's blessing—intended to retain custody of their new Pacific possessions, and the cantankerous and indelicate Australian prime minister William Hughes began a campaign against real and perceived Japanese interference in the regulation of Australian borders.

All of that was to come. In the meantime the Japanese government signaled its willingness to defend its ally's interests following Britain's declaration of war on Germany on August 4, 1914.[37] Germany's small Pacific empire fell within months. By the end of October Japan had seized the Caroline, Mariana, and Marshall Island groups to the north of the equator. One month later Japanese troops successfully defeated German forces at Kiaochow, on China's Shandong Peninsula. South of the equator Australian forces seized German New Guinea and the islands of the Bismarck Archipelago.[38] The British colonial secretary, Lewis V. Harcourt, moved swiftly to ensure the smooth transition of these territories from German control and to preclude inadvertent hostilities between Japan and Australia. He instructed the Australian governor-general, Sir Ronald Munro Ferguson, to prevent Australian operations above the equator. Harcourt also encouraged Munro Ferguson to prepare his Australian charges for Japan's postwar retention of their conquests.[39]

These early victories aroused expectations of improved Australian-Japanese relations in the Japanese press. The *Jiji Shimpō*, for example, suggested in a January 1915 editorial that Japan's success would erode Australian racial prejudice. The *Nichi Nichi* concurred and celebrated a new "gospel of the Pacific," in which Japan's "justice and humanity" were now widely recognized on all sides of the ocean. Even Australians, they claimed, acknowledged that Japan was "animated by nobility of principle" and entertained no designs on Australian territory.[40] The following April the *Mainichi Shimbun* even detected "a marked growth of pro-Japanese tendencies" in Australia, reporting, "It is assuredly no slander to say that the world wide anti-Japanese sentiment had its beginnings in Australia; and its disappearance in that country must as a matter of course lead to its disappearance in all other quarters of the globe." The war had irrevocably changed global race relations: "White men are mostly slaves to racial prejudice, and hold that white can only ally with white. But the present war is a war of white versus white, while racially alien Japan has given proof of loyalty to her British ally. White Germany is the foe of white Australia, coloured Japan the friend of white Australia; those of one race are foes, those of alien races friends. Their bond of union is not the colour of the skin but quality of heart."[41] Writing from Tokyo, Ambassador

Greene noted "a general impression that Australian feeling has now undergone a material modification in the direction of a more sympathetic attitude to this country." In his view this softening in attitude derived from Japan's participation in conveying Australian troops to Europe.[42]

The prospects for improved Australian-Japanese relations were such that in January 1915 Foreign Minister Baron Katō Kōmei instructed his ambassador in London to press once more for Australian adherence to the Anglo-Japanese Treaty of Commerce and Navigation. The Treaty had been in place since 1894, but successive Commonwealth governments had rejected invitations to subscribe to its terms, primarily because they feared that accession would abjure their right to restrict Japanese immigration. Canada had finally assented to the Treaty in April 1913, stipulating that its adherence in no way inhibited its right to control immigration. Flush with victory in January, Katō informed Ambassador Inoue Katsunosuke that Japan recognized Australia's reluctance to sign the Treaty because of the immigration issue. Consequently Japan was willing to grant Australia the same terms as Canada.[43] Fearing that even these magnanimous terms might undermine their carefully cultivated restrictions, the Australian government declined the Japanese invitation.[44]

Reporting from Australia, Munro Ferguson felt there was still cause for optimism. In a letter to King George V he observed that while Australians' commitment to a white continent remained robust, he expected that Japan's contributions to the imperial war effort would eventually moderate Australian attitudes.[45] Following the Japanese victories in the Pacific, Munro Ferguson even reported a "profound" shift in Australian attitudes toward their Asian allies. "The immense service rendered to the Empire in general and to Australia in particular by Japan and also by India," he predicted, "will have to be recognised."[46]

Much of this early optimism proved to be wishful thinking. More pessimistic—or perhaps realistic—observers soon recognized that wartime alliance did not guarantee the relaxation of Australians' attitudes toward their East Asian ally. Indeed Japan's initial offer of support initiated a debate among British officials regarding the possible implications of Japanese involvement for Australia. Japan's prestige, the efficacy of its naval power, and the consequences for China were among the most important issues under consideration. Concerns regarding Australian security also featured in the discussion. There were two schools of thought. The British minister to China, Sir John Jordan, wanted to avoid a Japanese declaration of war; he feared that China would lose territory in the event of Japanese participation. In making his case Jordan also warned that Japan would inevitably seize Germany's

Pacific possessions, with potentially negative consequences for Australian security.[47] Conversely, another Foreign Office official speculated that the Japanese would be offended if Great Britain declined their offer of assistance. In response the Japanese might act independently in China, and "by strengthening Japanese interests in the Pacific threaten ours in Australia."[48] Whichever analysis proved correct, both alternatives perceived Australia as the potential target of an opportunistic Japan, which might use the Commonwealth's contemptuous racial attitudes to justify aggression.[49]

Indeed the wartime alliance did nothing to dispel long-standing Australian racial anxieties toward Japan, and Japan's seizure of Germany's Pacific island colonies was bound to engender anxiety and distrust in Australia. According to one Australian senator, whose thinly veiled reference to Britain's ally evaded the censors in October 1914, "If the people of this Commonwealth still maintain their high standard of national aspirations, they will have to be prepared to embrace with both arms a policy which will have for its object the filling up of this continent. . . . While European civilization is exhausting itself, the power of another civilization is becoming greater, and it does not require any large amount of prescience to foresee that there are many grave problems confronting, not only the people of our Empire in general, but the people of this Commonwealth in particular."[50]

Even Munro Ferguson's sanguinity was short-lived; within weeks he detected that Australian public opinion remained "strong" concerning the White Australia Policy due to the sudden proximity of Japanese military forces.[51] As the Crown's representative in Australia, the governor-general was privately disdainful of Australians' white continental fantasy. Although he acknowledged the visceral attraction of racial exclusion to Australians in a March 1915 letter to Secretary Harcourt, Munro Ferguson nevertheless denounced the White Australia Policy as "unsound economically and dangerous to the interests of the Empire."[52] It undermined Australian economic development (especially in the Northern Territory), antagonized Britain's allies and the imperial government, and "together with the discouragement of white immigration . . . it leaves us an empty continent, while it invites occupation by other peoples." He sensed, however, a unique opportunity in the new proximity of the Japanese military, which might finally dispel the policy's hold: "This fool's paradise needs a rude awakening, and if a Japanese naval base near the [equator] should act as a solvent then it would be a blessing in disguise!"[53]

Despite his personal antipathy toward the Commonwealth's racial politics, Munro Ferguson understood that an explicit challenge to the White

Australia Policy would elicit serious opposition. He feared that Japan might press Australia for concessions on the immigration question. "It is hard to say how far the Japanese may put pressure on us during the war . . . for the admission of coloured races to Australia," he mused in a letter to Harcourt's successor, Andrew Bonar Law, in December 1915. "Any relenting in the White Australia Policy would bring any Government here to grief, for to whatever extreme this policy has been pushed, few would acquiesce without a fight in opening up Australia to coloured races." Cognizant of British distaste for Australians' racial fantasies and mindful of the empire's racial diversity, Munro Ferguson also echoed Australians' concerns that they could not rely upon British support in the event of Japanese aggression.[54]

Strains in the Alliance, 1915–1917

Optimism quickly succumbed to anxiety and resentment on both sides. Among Australian leaders the Japanese conquest of former German colonies provoked particular consternation. Munro Ferguson canvassed prominent Australian political figures about their opinion of Japan's new position in the Pacific during the spring of 1915. He identified two fundamental objections. First, many Australians were clearly apprehensive about the prospect of Japanese naval bases in the captured islands; a distance of 1,400 miles from the Caroline Islands to the Australian continent was evidently too close for comfort. Second, he observed uneasiness regarding the possible commercial advantages that Japan might accrue from their new possessions. For his part Munro Ferguson believed that "the best antidote to a return of the Yellow Peril Scare would be the realization of the cost and difficulty of administering the whole Pacific."[55]

Two reports by Australia's Naval Intelligence Department in late 1915 reveal the depth and scope of Australians' concerns. The first identified Japan as the primary threat to Australia in the Pacific. The authors nervously observed the hardening grip of the Japanese on the captured islands. Most important, they feared that the Japanese harbored expansionist designs toward the Australian continent. The authors acknowledged that Australian policies antagonized their Pacific neighbors, and they understood that this friction might eventually compel Japanese aggression. In their view Japan was an overpopulated island nation that lacked sufficient arable land, and its people therefore coveted the Australian mainland: "The existence of a huge half-empty area in the southern temperate zone, almost defenceless except for fleets six weeks away, is a constant temptation to the more excitable among Japanese publicists." The White Australia Policy provided a convenient pretext for aggression since it offended Japanese sensibilities and damaged the nation's prestige. While mature Japanese leaders might accept the dominion government's prerogative to control immigration, many Japanese were aggravated by Australians' association of them with "Chinese and Hindu coolies and with African negros." As if this were not enough to tempt Japanese expansionists, Australia's northern coastline was an excellent base from which to protect the East Asian power's flank. The Naval Intelligence Department therefore expected the Japanese to pressure Australians into ameliorating their Immigration Restriction Act.[56]

These defense planners did not expect British support in the event of a concerted Japanese political (or military) assault on the White Australia Policy. They feared that British public opinion would be at best apathetic toward Australians' plight should Japan "claim as a reward for her services during the war the free admission of her citizens to any part of the Empire." The authors also doubted whether subjects in the wider empire could be persuaded to defend the policy. "If the White Australia policy antagonized Japan alone," they mused, support might be forthcoming. In reality, however, "there are communities within the Empire, which also have taken part whole-heartedly in the war, that believe the Australian policy to be harmful to their interests—and gratitude to Australia would be more than counterbalanced by the combination of gratitude to India and to Japan with the existing London prepossession in favour of modifying the White Australia policy." Consequently Australians had to be in a position to defend themselves after the war.[57]

A second report two months later sounded similar themes. Produced by the Department of the Navy, it reiterated an enduring Australian belief that imperial naval policy should abandon the long-held British conviction that "the seas are one" and instead reflect the particular strategic exigencies of the Pacific Ocean. Japan had emerged as a contender for regional naval supremacy. Although in deference to the wartime alliance they never mentioned Japan by name, the authors obtusely acknowledged Japanese scorn toward the White Australia Policy and expressed their hope that imperial policy would take cognizance of the Pacific dominions' determination to maintain their "racial purity." The British government and press, however, apparently disagreed: "The interest of maintaining in the Pacific a purely British stock, free from the admixture of Asiatic or other races whose ideals and ethical bases are incompatible with British morals, manners and institutions, seems to be regarded by a great many British publicists as hardly an Imperial interest at all."[58] Their solution to this problem was a designated Pacific fleet, based in Australia and therefore sensitive to the Commonwealth's particular racial aspirations and objectives.

The Australian military's fear of a Japanese quid pro quo on immigration proved prescient. In February 1916 the secretary of the Australian Department of External Affairs, Atlee Arthur Hunt, reported an informal conversation with the Japanese vice consul, Eiji Amau. According to Hunt, Amau tried to discern whether Australia's opposition to Japanese immigration had waned. He was particularly eager to achieve a moderation of restrictions on temporary Japanese visitors, such as merchants and tourists. Amau's overture reflected mounting pressure in Japan to weaken Australian immigration laws. One member of the Japanese Diet successfully introduced a resolution pressing his government to eliminate "anti-Japanese action in Australia and the British South Seas and to ensure that Japanese subjects may, subject to no special restrictions, freely proceed thither and engage in enterprize." In particular this legislator bemoaned the "truly outrageous idea" that Japanese were subject to the same treatment as Chinese and South Asians under Australia's 1901 Immigration Restriction Act.[59] Hunt actually believed that it was in Australia's interests to consider this limited accommodation, especially if the Commonwealth could preempt an official request.[60] The Australian government summarily rejected his suggestion. One unnamed respondent (probably Hughes, the new prime minister) declared, "We cannot overlook the fact that the most effective way of peacefully penetrating a country, with a view to its ultimate occupation, is by the immigration of a virile and fighting class."[61] The door therefore remained firmly closed to Japanese immigration despite the pressure of the wartime alliance.

The Japanese press also began to reconsider its earlier optimism. In June 1916 Rentaro Kayahara ("Kwazan") published an article in *Chūōkōron* advocating the abandonment of the Anglo-Japanese Alliance in favor of an alliance with Germany. Japan's central foreign policy problem, Kwazan mused, was overpopulation, and the solution to this crisis was extensive emigration to the Australian continent: "If Japan should make a Japanese Colony of Australia, which is capable of accommodating a population of at least 200 millions, she might transfer thither the whole of her 50 odd millions, and there would still be room to spare. Would not Japan's problem of population and livelihood be naturally solved in the twinkling of any eye?" To this end the Anglo-Japanese Alliance was an impediment to future Japanese development, and cooperation with Germany constituted the only appropriate strategy.[62] In another article published that September in the *Third Empire* newspaper,

Kwazan pressed the Japanese Foreign Office to "compel the Americans and British to admit our people." If the Foreign Office was unwilling to act, the navy was more than up to the task. The Japanese people demanded the right to emigrate, and if that could not be achieved peacefully it must be achieved "by force of the iron hand and mailed fist." The recently conquered German islands were of little value to Japan, Kwazan insisted, and even the American possessions of Hawaii and the Philippines were not worth Japan's attention. Rather "Japan's sphere of extension lies beyond the equator in Australia, New Zealand, and Tasmania. They are sufficient for a new Japanese Empire and offer an easy solution of Japan's over-population and hardship of living."[63]

The Australian director of military intelligence, Edmund Piesse, suspected that the Germans were using Kwazan's writings to foment trouble between Japan and Australia. There is no doubt that German periodicals attempted to exploit Australian racism. The *Korrespondenzblatt*, for example, reported in September 1916, "Australians complain that the barriers against Japanese immigration into 'the White Man's country' will soon have to fall. . . . The Entente has Japan as an ally, but at what a price!" The moderate *Japan Advertiser* recognized that such impolitic rhetoric in the Japanese press might undermine Japan's position. On August 6, 1915, for example, the *Chronicle* opined, "Colonial jaunophobia is sometimes very ridiculous, but some of the Japanese papers, though it offends them, do all they can to warrant it."[64] In order to combat negative articles in the Japanese press, the British government contracted the services of an unnamed British author who was responsible for producing pro-British articles and pamphlets in Japanese newspapers and periodicals. To aid him in his duties, Greene was keen to obtain Australian speeches and newspaper articles that reflected an improvement in Australian-Japanese relations, "if such evidence exists."[65]

Similar rhetoric proliferated elsewhere in the Japanese press. Dr. Tomidzu Hiroto fiercely criticized the Anglo-Japanese Alliance in *Yamato*: "The treatment of the Japanese in Australia is far worse than that of those who are in America. The white people in Australia are treating the Japanese there like beasts." The Japanese people had been forced to submit to these indignities due to the relative weakness of their country, but the war had demonstrated Japan's growing power. Tomidzu cautioned that this continued national and international humiliation would ultimately lead to war with Great Britain and the United States.[66] Even moderate Japanese newspapers demanded accommodation. Tokyo's *Asahi Shimbun* lauded the significance of Japan's contribution to the allied war effort in an August 1916 article. The transportation of Australian and South Asian troops, patrols in the southern Pacific, and operations against Germany's possessions in China and the Pacific all demonstrated Japan's central role in the British campaign. As a result of their contribution "it has become no longer necessary for Japan to acquiesce in disadvantages and inconveniences in her relations with the British Colonies . . . and it would furthermore not be wrong for her to plead the need for the adoption of measures to do away with them."[67]

One of the most withering Japanese critiques of the White Australia Policy appeared in the *Chūōkōron*. According to that publication, "with an area of one-seventeenth of the globe Australia has less than a one three-hundredth part of the world's population, and this disproportion of land to population is a particular cause of uneasiness to white Australians." "The reason," the *Chūōkōron* surmised, "is that the coloured races who are excluded by Australians out of racial prejudice number 800 millions or half the population of the earth, and these 800 millions warningly and enviously encompass maternity-shirking Australia with her small population of 5 millions." This undermined not only international relations but also Australian national development: "Brandishing a kind of preferential right they exclude all races but the white and their superstition of endeavouring to establish a so-called White Australia is in fact the cause of the disease of slackness and stagnation, affecting Australian civilization." It was therefore Japan's duty to impress upon its ally the folly of the White Australia Policy.[68] This was actually no different from what Australians had been saying ever since the inception of the Immigration Restriction Act, but such rhetoric from Japanese sources did nothing to alleviate Australians' apprehensions; rather it confirmed their darkest fears.

In contrast Australian newspapers and politicians were under a system of strict censorship regarding Japan, enacted on April 15, 1916, which forbade them from "publishing any matter likely to cause trouble with the Japanese Government." References to "Asiatic immigration" and "nonwhite labour" received special attention.[69] According to Lieutenant George G. McColl, Australia's deputy chief censor, "Prior to the establishment of the Censorship there were many anti-Japanese articles published and strong measures had to be taken to suppress them."[70] The experience of one House of Representatives member, James H. Catts, illustrates the scope of this censorship, especially against the kind of anti-Japanese rhetoric that was commonplace in the Australian Parliament before the war. One of the worst offenders, Catts was censored seven times for making anti-Japanese statements. He frequently lambasted the government's censorship and saw himself as the prophet of a defining struggle for Australian national survival. In one parliamentary speech (which was subsequently censored from Hansard), Catts stated that Australians should no longer send their soldiers to Europe, "in view of our geographical position, and the growing menace of international friction in this quarter of the globe."[71] His rhetoric was even more vitriolic outside Parliament. During a speech in Armidale, New South Wales, in November 1917 Catts warned of a coming race war with Japan and lamented the white racial suicide taking place on European battlefields.[72]

Catts was not alone. By the end of 1917 the deputy chief censor had recorded twenty-four incidents. Even the new prime minister was subject to censorship. Hughes had of course railed against Asian immigration since the inauguration of the Commonwealth Parliament in 1901, and he remained absolutely committed to the White Australia Policy for the rest of his life. The censor reportedly struck part of an August 1916 pro-conscription speech in which Hughes declared, "We have lifted up on our topmost minaret the badge of a White Australia, but we are as it were a drop in a colored ocean ringed around with a thousand million of the colored races. How are we to be saved? What arrogance and what futility it would be to emblazon White Australia on our banners if we are not prepared to fight for it."[73]

The debate over conscription in Australia was often marked by racial overtones and concern for the integrity of the White Australia Policy, as Hughes's speech suggests. The bogey of Japanese invasion was employed by both sides of the debate.[74] After the rejection of conscription by referendum in October 1916, for example, one irate member of Parliament echoed the prime minister's censored remarks two months before:

> By our action in turning down conscription we have neutralized for ourselves the benefit of our association with the Empire. We have written our death warrant as a free white community. . . . Remember for a minute the position of Australia. Here is a country occupied by a handful of white people, who are intruders upon an area which, geographically, belongs naturally to the yellow and black races. There are around our northern shores countless millions of those races who regard with ill-concealed hatred the attitude we have taken up towards them. It is an arrogant attitude, as they regard it and naturally so, to exclude them from a part of the world belonging by right to those races, and not to us.

In refusing to institute conscription, Australians had foresworn the "moral support and sympathy of the white races of the rest of the world," upon whose protection and forbearance the White Australia Policy ultimately rested. Unless conscription was initiated, he concluded, "we shall go down dishonoured and disgraced beneath the yellow race, more virile than we."[75] Privately Munro Ferguson concurred with this assessment. Australians would need support if they wanted to maintain their claim to white supremacy, and "not one of those sections of the community who are fighting the Government have any conception of the danger incurred in endeavouring to hold Australia with 5,000,000 of people or of the madness of so doing without the concurrence of the rest of the Empire and the protection of the British Fleet."[76]

Critics of conscription also used the threat to white supremacy in their campaigns. The Australian Labour Party's platform for 1918 (which itself was subject to censorship) decried "the serious depletion of Australia's most virile manhood through her share in the war." Their rationale was defensive, and they used precisely the same argument as was put forward two years before in favor of conscription: "As the one outpost of white civilization whose nearest neighbors in enormous numbers are anxious to find more elbow room, we are in grave danger of being swamped out of existence by the mere weight of their numbers, should we allow them free ingress. . . . To restrict the influx of these races is vital to Australia's existence as a free community. To maintain those restrictions we must be able to defend ourselves against the aggression of those whose interests are opposed to that policy. . . . The only reliable defence of Australia must be a local defence."[77] This was a long-standing dilemma in Australian political and military discussions, and the war had only exacerbated the predicament.

By the end of 1916 even Munro Ferguson perceived that Japan was emboldened by its role in the war. He warned Bonar Law of "a peaceful penetration by Japan which may at any time develop some aggressive form." The Japanese vice consul in Sydney had even intimated to him that Japan's commitment to the alliance might wane unless Australians exhibited some willingness to reconsider their restrictions on Japanese immigration.[78] Munro Ferguson remained ambivalent, however, about the implications of Japanese aggression. As he told the king, this might provide an opportunity to teach Australians a lesson for their intolerant and counterproductive immigration policies: "This should give food for reflection to a Community which can put five Divisions in the Field when its existence is at stake and cannot, even for these, find adequate reinforcements."[79]

Mounting Japanese-Australian Antagonism, 1917–1918

Australian-Japanese relations approached their nadir in 1917. The Australian government's determination to project Asian restriction into New Guinea and the Japanese government's insistence upon commercial openness in the Pacific once more brought the two into conflict. Japanese frustrations intensified in proportion to Australian obduracy over these issues, and the Japanese military's advanced deployment in the Micronesian islands further roused Australian angst toward its nominal ally. The Australian prime minister only heightened the tensions by reaching out to the Americans, whose own relationship with the Japanese deteriorated following Japanese wartime expansionism in China. It is not surprising, then, that the dispute over racial equality and the rights of Japanese migrants would come to dominate Japanese and Australian participation in the postwar negotiations.

The end of 1916 brought political changes in both Japan and Great Britain. Ōkuma submitted his resignation as Japanese prime minister in October, and David Lloyd George replaced Asquith in Great Britain the following December. Shortly after, in February 1917, Britain and Japan concluded a secret agreement in support of each other's claims to Germany's former Pacific colonies.[80] During these negotiations the British government urged Australians to refrain from injurious statements regarding Japanese retention of its captured German colonies. In response the Australian government agreed to "carefully abstain from doing or saying anything likely to strain or make difficult the relations between His Majesty's Government and Japan." They also reiterated Hughes's pledge that Australians would not oppose the postwar occupation of captured German islands by the Japanese.[81]

This settlement precluded an embarrassing public protest from Australia and bolstered Commonwealth claims to New Guinea. Hughes and his government viewed their own spoil of war as a potential lookout station and military base to warn of impending (Japanese) attack. The capture of New Guinea and the surrounding islands, however, provoked new tensions in the Australian-Japanese relationship. One of the most serious questions pertained to the extension of the White Australia Policy into New Guinea. Japanese immigration had been permitted under German rule. By 1917, under the pretense of wartime conditions, the Australian government tried to close the islands to the Japanese, with the exception of "female relatives" of Japanese laborers already on the island.[82] After protests from the Japanese government, Australia agreed to allow Japanese laborers who wished to leave New Guinea and return at a later date to do so. Those who chose to leave permanently could be replaced on a one-for-one basis.[83] Nevertheless the Japanese government continued to press for concessions, arguing that British traders were allowed access to islands under Japanese occupation, a claim contested by the Australians.[84]

Munro Ferguson also turned his attention to the captured islands. His primary concern during this period was consolidating Britain's South Pacific possessions, and he tirelessly campaigned to vest administration of the empire's Pacific islands under the Australian governor-generalship. To this end he proposed the creation of a high commissioner of the Pacific. In order to convince the British government of his proposal's efficacy, he invoked the threat of Japanese expansion, with all the flair and indignation of his Australian charges. Unless administration of the Pacific possessions was consolidated, Munro Ferguson warned the king, they could not be "defended in face of the urgent necessity of adequately meeting Japanese trade aggressions."[85] He expanded on this theme in a letter to the new secretary of state for the colonies, Walter Hume Long, in October 1917:

> The more one comes into contact with the Japanese the more one recognises their efficiency and the helplessness of Australia if left alone with them in the Pacific—a helplessness by no means understood by the Australians themselves—who one fears might blunder into a quarrel with Japan, more especially should the Federal Government be put in charge of British dependencies in the Pacific. Steps should undoubtedly be taken promptly to unify British administration in such Pacific Dependencies as we have or may have. . . . A first class Pacific power watches every move of the game in commercial and territorial expansion and is ready to pounce down upon a quarrelsome neighbour, a helpless prey and an empty continent.[86]

Some Japanese expansionists sensed just such an opportunity. Writing in *Shin Nippon*, Shimatani Ryosuke observed, "The fact that Indians, Chinese and Japanese are meeting with similar treatment at the hands of the Anglo-Saxon people is gradually awakening in the minds of these eastern peoples a dim vision of an East for Eastern peoples." This emerging pan-Asiatic rhetoric was nourished by the British dominions' racist immigration policies, Shimatani argued, and it provided Japanese exponents of empire with a powerful propaganda weapon.[87]

The Japanese press and diplomatic corps, however, was largely concerned with American opposition to their East Asian policy during 1917. This opposition was exemplified by the U.S. response to Japan's "twenty-one demands," presented to the Chinese government in January 1915. This opportunistic attempt by Japan to politically, economically, culturally, and strategically dominate China was met with consternation by the Wilson administration. Resolution finally came on November 2, 1917, when Secretary of State Robert Lansing and Ambassador Ishii Kikujirō agreed to respect Chinese territorial integrity and maintain the "open door," while at the same time recognizing Japan's "special interests" in China.[88]

This settlement was met with uncertainty in Australia. On one hand, the American challenge to Japanese hegemony in mainland Asia was a further source of anxiety for the Australian government during the war. For Edmund Piesse, the Lansing-Ishii accords implied that Japan—confounded by American intransigence on the Asian mainland—might turn its attention elsewhere. As long as Japan looked to China as an outlet for its surplus population, the sanctity of the White Australia Policy was assured: "Expand somewhere, Japan must—unless fortunately her population should cease to increase. Clearly it is to Australia's interest that Japan should expand on the continent of Asia, rather than to the South." If this outlet was closed, however, Piesse feared that advocates of southern expansion in Japan would seize the initiative: "And if they do, is it not certain that the relations of Australia and Japan will come into question—to the extent at all events of the restrictions of the White Australia policy and of further opportunities for Japanese trade?"[89] Southern expansion, Piesse assured his superiors, would mean an increasingly determined Japanese challenge to Australian immigration policies. On the other hand, if Japan was successful in dominating China, with its resources and manpower, "she will certainly be the dominant Power in the Pacific." Southern expansion might still prove unnecessary, but Australia must nevertheless prepare to face a strengthened and aggrieved postwar adversary.[90]

But Hughes saw an opportunity in America's vocal opposition to Japanese expansion. The Australian premier brought his concerns regarding Japan's enhanced strategic position to the United States while en route to Great Britain for a meeting of the Imperial War Cabinet in August 1918. Hughes wanted Wilson's support for Australia's territorial claims in New Guinea, and he no doubt expected a sympathetic hearing for his warnings regarding Japan. In a speech before the Pilgrims Society in New York on August 31, Hughes outlined his justification for what became his "Australian Monroe Doctrine." Ostensibly directed toward German recovery of its Pacific colonies, Hughes announced, "Hands off the Australian Pacific is the doctrine to which by inexorable circumstances we are committed. And against all predatory nations we shall strive to give this doctrine effect to the last ounce of effort at our disposal." He sought American backing for this policy against "any pred-atory power," and if the islands were not to be in Australian hands, they "should be in the hands of friendly and civilized nations."[91] Hughes did not directly impugn Japan, but the implications of his speech were obvious to the Japanese. In response to his call for an Australian Monroe Doctrine, the *Asahi Shimbun* reported, "Whatever the views of Australians may be with regard to the Pacific, to exclude Japan who is at present entrusted with its safeguard-ing is a palpable impossibility." The war, in the editorialist's opinion, had fundamentally changed the strategic balance in the Pacific, and Japan was now a pivotal power in the region. Hughes's remarks, the *Asahi* suggested, only provided Germany with a desperate propaganda tool in trying to drive a wedge between Great Britain and its ally.[92]

An editorial in the *Osaka Asahi* went further, castigating Hughes for his speech, which the newspaper interpreted as "a sure manifestation of the an-tipathy of the Australians towards the Japanese." The speech also provided an opportunity to chastise Australians for their exclusionary immigration policy, which the *Asahi* editorialist contested was "inimical to the material interests of the Japanese" and "highly objectionable to the Japanese as a ci-vilised nation." It was clear at this point that when a peace conference was finally called, Japan would protest these intolerable conditions: "Japan has a legitimate right to protest strongly against such discrimination, both from the viewpoint of international etiquette and international justice."[93] Nor was the *Japan Chronicle* fooled by Hughes's oblique references. "There is good reason to believe that Mr. Hughes' scheme plans to exclude another Power from the South Pacific in addition to Germany," the newspaper's editorialist contended, and he meant to obtain American support if possible. It was clear that Hughes feared Japanese invasion and that "only by keeping the South Pacific as 'white' as Australia itself" could his exclusion plan be achieved.[94]

Munro Ferguson was more concerned that Hughes's pandering to the United States might eventually impel Australia out of Britain's orbit. "I can almost foresee the day," he told Long in June 1918, "when there will be a Party in Australia who will advocate a 'White' Pacific guarded by two great Repub-lics on either side acting in close alliance."[95] At the same time, however, he encouraged Long to get tougher with Hughes, observing, "It is doubtful whether [the] U.S. will want to protect Australia from Japan. Moreover, when Australia is brought to face facts she is more likely to prove herself a chip off the old block than she has done under spoon feeding."[96] He was right on both counts. Sir John Latham, head of the Australian Naval Intelligence Service, was already reflecting on the problems that British foreign policy would face in the Pacific once the war was finally won. Among the most pressing issues, of course, was Australia's relationship with Japan. It was not simply an Australian problem but one that concerned a community of interest across the white fringes of the Pacific. "The policy of White Australia and the determination of Australasia to keep the yellow races at a distance must receive support from Canada and the United States," Latham asserted, "and despite the present treaty between Great Britain and Japan (though it can hardly be renewed in the future) the British Empire must be very much influenced by the Dominions Overseas."[97]

The period 1914–18 demonstrated that some Australians would sacrifice imperial unity and Britain's alliance with Japan—even in the context of the most destructive war in history—in order to preserve their racial fantasies. The White Australia Policy remained paramount, even when it threatened to alienate a key wartime ally and partner. At the same time, the Australian premier's intransigence and lack of regard for British imperial and international interests exasperated Munro Ferguson. He complained to Long in April 1918 that Hughes was not even willing to entertain a gentleman's agreement with Japan, as Canada and the United States had done a decade earlier. Hughes, the governor-general grumbled, wanted it both ways. He seemed content to rely on Great Britain to negotiate on Australia's behalf and expected "that the whole force of the Empire is to be employed in keeping an empty Australia white." "This does no doubt represent faithfully the Australian view," Munro Ferguson told Long, "which is that 5 millions of people should be allowed to pursue an exclusive policy within this Continent and over all adjacent area of the Pacific they covet, without interference from the rest of the Empire and with immunity from Foreign interference secured by the British Fleet."[98] At the same time, however, he understood that the White Australia Policy would be maintained and defended at all costs after the war: "Coloured immigration is at once highly controversial and impracticable. Australia would fight against 'colour' with greater spirit than against Germany."[99] From the governor-general's point of view, the Australian position was increasingly untenable.

With peace finally in sight, Japanese writers also began to address the problem of racial prejudice in the British dominions and the United States. Greene summarized a representative article from the *Kokumin Shimbun*: "For Japan the most important question in connection with President Wilson's League of Nations is the mode of dealing with the racial discrimination idea. The object of the League's formation will not be fully realised it would seem, so long as Japan and other coloured races are differentially treated in white communities."[100] The Japanese delegation to the Peace Conference would endeavor to rectify these racial insults with the insertion of the "racial equality amendment" into the League of Nations Covenant. Despite Munro Ferguson's complaints, however, Hughes would be true to his word. Indeed throughout World War I Australians had maintained that without constant vigilance they would face a rapacious and debilitating onslaught of Asian immigrants, and Australia's commitment to white supremacy continued to elicit tension with Japan and Great Britain as the drama shifted to the halls of Versailles.

CHAPTER SIX

Making Peace with Asian Immobility

London, Paris, and Washington

The end of the First World War raised expectations of social, economic, and political change across the globe. The weakening—and in some cases the outright collapse—of the world's most powerful empires implied the realization of long-denied national ambitions for colonized communities throughout Europe, Asia, Africa, and the Middle East. The American president's rhetoric lent possibility to those hopes. His oratory offered relief from the carnage of the previous four years, and for a brief period his ideals seemed to presage the reform of an antiquated imperial order and the liberation of millions. Indeed Wilson's principles of diplomatic and economic openness articulated what many throughout those regions had already concluded.[1] Japanese and South Asian contributions to the allied war effort, for example, heightened opposition to the Eurocentrism of contemporary international relations and intensified Asian resentments against the discriminatory impulses of supposed white allies. This sense of anticipation nevertheless conceded to disappointment, especially for those who expected the removal of constraints on Asian labor migration. Four empires disintegrated in the wake of allied victory, but the exclusionary aspirations of many white Americans, Australians, Canadians, New Zealanders, and South Africans remained stubbornly intact.

In this chapter I elucidate how the fractious politics of Asian labor immobility ruptured the pretense of peace, reconstruction, and reform after the First World War. I specifically examine the ongoing salience of Asian immigration restrictions during three major wartime and postwar conferences, all of which played a determinative role in redefining the character and meaning of imperialism and diplomacy after the war: the 1917 and 1918 Imperial War Conferences in London, the 1919 Peace Conference in Paris, and the 1921 Naval Conference in Washington. Usually studied in isolation, taken together these meetings illustrate that South Asian, Japanese, and Chinese participation in the war did not temper colonial and American anxiety toward Asian migrants, nor did it diminish the indignation felt by Asian subjects and diplomats when confronted by white prejudice. On the contrary the imperial and international politics of Asian migration intensified in the aftermath of the Great War, compelled by the inflexibility of white economic jealousy and racism and by the increasingly confident resistance of Asian migrants and envoys. In the end, while these conferences provided an international platform for colonial and American arguments against Asian mobility—and for Asian grievances against restriction—they did not reduce the tensions engendered by those contradictory claims. Instead postwar peacemaking legitimated colonial chauvinism, disillusioned Asian hopes for reform, and inscribed discrimination, injustice, and animosity onto the mechanisms of postwar international and imperial governance.

In the war and the peacemaking that followed, then, white activists' commitment to Asian immobility continued to beleaguer imperial and international diplomacy, and the global discord provoked by white racial and economic angst continued to fester after the armistice. The lingering acrimony of the *Komagata Maru*'s ill-fated challenge to Canadian restriction laws reminded British and Indian officials that colonial enthusiasm for South Asian exclusion still vexed intra-imperial relations, despite attempts over the previous two decades to subdue and conceal those tensions. Australians' deteriorating relationship with the Japanese—and their unyielding dedication to exclusion—set the stage for a dramatic showdown between erstwhile allies at the postwar peace proceedings. Beyond the British Empire, the Wilson administration's wartime resistance to Japanese expansion in China, coupled with the ongoing convulsions of white activism in the American West, soured Japanese-American relations on the eve of the Paris Peace Conference.

Those charged with reconstructing the postwar international order struggled to find a solution to these tenacious problems, as had their predecessors. David Lloyd George assembled an Imperial War Cabinet in 1917, summoning the colonial premiers to London in the waning years of the war. The British prime minister also convoked two Imperial War Conferences, in 1917 and 1918. These innovations facilitated deeper dominion involvement in wartime strategy and imperial governance.[2] They also provided a forum in which imperial authorities could finally confront—or, more accurately, camouflage—colonial antipathy toward South Asian migrants. As British leaders endeavored to mitigate the effects of colonial racism in London, delegates from around the world convened in Paris. The future of Germany and the establishment of the League of Nations dominated the proceedings, but the Japanese appeal for racial equality placed Asian mobility rights at the center of postwar discussions. The Australian prime minister's unrepentant crusade against the Japanese delegation's relatively modest request—and his promotion of the White Australia Policy's extension into Germany's former South Pacific colonies—strained his Commonwealth's already difficult relations with Japan and forced the British government to tacitly support racial discrimination, not only throughout its empire but also throughout the world. In the wake of these impassioned disagreements, British, Australian, and American officials planned for a renewed Japanese challenge to their restrictive immigration regimes after the United States proposed an international conference to discuss the future of the Pacific in 1921.

During the 1917 and 1918 Imperial War Conferences British imperial authorities once again tried to mask the intercolonial antagonisms engendered by Australasian, Canadian, and South African prohibitions on South Asian labor mobility. Like his father before him, the secretary of state for India, Austen Chamberlain, sought a remedy that would both countenance colonial impropriety and mask the insolences inflicted upon South Asian subjects. Unlike his father, he struck upon a device that dominion representatives would willingly adopt: reciprocal, economically motivated exclusion rights for both white colonial governments and the government of India. As fraught as these debates were, imperial and colonial representatives could at least confront the question of South Asian mobility internally and discreetly. Events at the Paris Peace Conference, on the other hand, publicly revealed existing animosities, disclosing the diametrical assumptions about race and restriction that plagued the peacemaking process. The Japanese delegation arrived in Paris determined to challenge constraints on the movement of Japanese migrants. The deputation's proposed racial equality clause represented a seemingly innocuous strategy by which they could pierce that shroud of colonial and American immobility. The Australian prime minister opposed the Japanese challenge and worked tirelessly—and successfully—to thwart adoption of the racial equality amendment.

Even as he campaigned against the Japanese equality clause, the Australian leader also attempted to expand the reach of the White Australia Policy in the South Pacific. Hughes proclaimed that the former German colonies of New Guinea, the Bismarck Archipelago, and Bougainville in the Solomon Islands represented natural dependencies of the Australian Commonwealth. They provided an additional layer of security against potential threats from the north and lucrative commercial opportunities for the British and Australian people. Hughes also argued that existing circuits of Asian labor migration in those former German possessions, especially in and around New Guinea, would terminate under Australian suzerainty. His proposed extension of the White Australia Policy to these territories further irritated the Japanese peace delegation, press, and government. Hughes's repeated public affronts to Japanese prestige and ambition—coupled with the Japanese military's new strategic position in Micronesia—served only to inflame Australian anxieties about Japanese intentions in the immediate postwar period. These apprehensions manifested in the imperial debate over continuation of the Anglo-Japanese Alliance and in concerns that the Japanese would resuscitate their frustrated racial equality claim at the Washington Naval Conference in late 1921. British, Australian, and American diplomats were relieved when the Japanese did not broach the subject, but tensions and anxieties lingered in the aftermath of these international conferences.

The Imperial War Conferences and South Asian Immobility, 1917–1918

Over one million South Asians participated in the British war effort from 1914 to 1918, serving in almost every theater from France to German East Africa. In addition to manpower, the empire's South Asian subjects contributed millions of pounds to Britain's dwindling wartime treasury. To nationalists like Mohandas Gandhi, his compatriots had amply demonstrated their loyalty and earned equal status with white colonists. Gandhi understood the invidiousness of colonial bigotry better than most, having devoted his prewar legal career to expanding the rights of South Asian immigrants in Natal. Lloyd George also recognized that India's contributions had fundamentally transformed the dynamics of empire, observing after the war, "Fighting alongside white soldiers and against white enemies . . . had created a new self-consciousness among Indians that showed itself in a demand for greater recognition."[3] In this context of Indian national consciousness, the imperial government understood that the vexatious question of intra-imperial mobility rights would invariably reemerge as thoughts turned to peace.

These sentiments nevertheless clashed with a renewed sense of nationalism in the self-governing dominions, the leaders of which sought to maintain white privilege while protecting and enlarging their legislative autonomy as they gathered in London in 1917. They therefore persisted in their commitment to the impermeability of colonial borders. The sanctity of the White Australia Policy remained paramount for Prime Minister Hughes. He had the robust support of New Zealand's premier William Ferguson Massey and Canada's prime minister Sir Robert Laird Borden, both of whom asserted the right of their respective dominions to maintain discriminating—and discriminatory—immigration policies. Still fiercely devoted to white supremacy in South Africa, Jan Smuts not surprisingly concurred with his colleagues, rejecting any challenge to his recently unified dominion's fragile racial power structure.

Faced with this colonial intransigence, Chamberlain deployed a strategy similar to that employed by his father twenty years earlier. He knew he could not convince the self-governing colonies to abandon their restrictions. He also understood that he could not impose South Asian mobility by bureaucratic fiat. Chamberlain therefore proposed the adoption of an ostensibly neutral and reciprocal policy that immobilized both white and South Asian migration between the colonies of settlement and India. To this end the secretary submitted a resolution at the first Imperial War Conference in April 1917, simply stating that the assembled representatives "[accept] the principle of reciprocity of treatment between India and the Dominions." He stipulated that neither the imperial nor the Indian government sought to force unrestricted South Asian immigration upon the white dominions, and he acknowledged the desire of colonial leaders to "preserve the homogenous nature of their population and the special civilisation which they have striven to cultivate."[4]

Chamberlain asked the colonial premiers for only three concessions, none of which he believed would jeopardize their restrictions. First and foremost, he wanted assurances that British subjects of Asian descent would "not be less favourably treated than other Asiatics." Second, he sought a guarantee that educated South Asians would be entitled to temporarily travel and study in the dominions. Third, he requested that South Asians already legally resident in the dominions be treated with respect and consideration as British subjects.[5] According to the India Office, South Asians wished only to exercise the privileges of imperial citizenship and "do not understand why, on the ground of race, they are excluded from large tracts of the Empire, and worse treated in some matters than Asiatics who do not belong to the Empire." Canada's continuous journey regulation had effectively prohibited South Asian immigration to Canada since its promulgation in 1908, for example, and yet the dominion's gentleman's agreement with Japan entitled some four hundred Japanese laborers to enter each year. This was manifestly unfair, especially given the wartime contributions of the empire's South Asian subjects.[6]

This strategy of mutual immobility allowed the Indian government to reciprocally exclude white colonial labor migrants, expressly stating, "It would be clearly recognized that the exclusion in either case was not motivated by race, but was in fact the outcome of different economic conditions."[7] The dominion premiers unanimously accepted this motion (in the notable absence of their Australian colleague) but seized the opportunity to reiterate their perpetually obstinate positions. Borden was quick to note Chamberlain's recognition of the "ideal and the aspiration of the self-governing Dominions with regard to their present social order and the type of civilization which they are desirous of building up." Smuts used the occasion to assert his abiding stance on South African race relations. "We are a white minority on a black continent," he somberly reminded his colleagues, "and the settlers in South Africa have for many years been actuated by the fear that to open the door too widely to another nonwhite race would make the position of the few whites in South Africa very dangerous indeed."[8] Despite their grumblings, however, Borden, Massey, and Smuts each acceded to the reciprocity principle and committed themselves to its implementation at an unspecified future date.

Of course reciprocity was nothing more than a shrewd sleight of hand rooted in two decades of deceit. Few white Australians, New Zealanders, Canadians, and South Africans sought to make their home in India, but the illusion of reciprocity promised to resolve the issue without further injury to the dignity of South Asian subjects. Chamberlain was willing to accept this fiction, in part because colonial antipathy toward South Asian immigration had thus far proven impervious to resolution, and in part because the India Office was at that time considering an implausible but nonetheless attractive scheme to divert future South Asian migrant flows to the recently seized colony of German East Africa. Once it became clear that Britain would claim suzerainty over Germany's former African possessions, Chamberlain had urged London to allow "free and unimpeded" South Asian migration there. A successful community already existed in the colony, and thousands of South Asian soldiers had participated in the conquest of the possession. Just as important, the dominions' commitment to exclusion "makes it the more necessary to find some other field of expansion to which Indians may freely go for trade or settlement."[9] As the India Office observed in its supporting memorandum, the redirection of intra-imperial South Asian migrant flows to East Africa would "remove some of the bitterness which [colonial exclusion] has engendered in the minds of Indian publicists and politicians."[10] The Committee of Imperial Defence agreed: dominion racism posed a threat to the integrity of the empire, and "there can be no doubt that the situation would be greatly relieved if an outlet for Indian emigration could be found in a country which, as in the case of German East Africa, is of large extent, is thinly populated, and is apparently suitable for Indian settlement."[11]

The potential palliative of South Asian colonization in East Africa would nevertheless have to await the end of the war. In the meantime the India Office submitted a revised resolution during the second Imperial War Conference, held in London in July 1918. The amended proposal further elucidated the central deception of the reciprocity formula, declaring, "It is an inherent function of the Governments of the several communities of the British Commonwealth, including India, that each should enjoy complete control of the composition of its own population by means of restriction on immigration from any of the other communities." This clarification removed any ambiguity concerning the Indian government's right to reciprocally restrict white immigrants. In addition the new resolution stated that the families of lawful South Asian residents in the dominions would be allowed to reunite and that students, tourists, and commercial representatives would also enjoy entry privileges.[12] The Indian representative at the Imperial War Conference, Sir Satyendra Prasanno Sinha, made the case for these expanded rights after introducing the new resolution. All the Indian government desired, Sinha assured his colleagues, was recognition that Britain's South Asian subjects "should not receive a less favourable treatment than other Asiatic people who are not subjects of the British Empire."[13] Ultimately, Sinha concluded, the reciprocity formula "will help us to allay the agitation which, particularly at a time like this, is a source of grave embarrassment."[14] Dominion premiers unanimously passed this new resolution.

The reciprocity provision constituted the core of a new modus vivendi among the imperial government, the Raj, and the dominions, although they delayed its enactment pending the conclusion of the war. On one hand, it validated white colonial discrimination, even as it conjured the illusion of reciprocity. On the other hand, the imperial and Indian governments hoped this deception would finally eliminate the stigma of South Asian exclusion and at least nominally elevate the status of Indian subjects. The India Office nevertheless continued to press for an East African sphere of colonization. Among its desiderata at the Paris Peace Conference was its intention to secure German East Africa as a means to reward those who had rallied to the colors. Based on decades of experience they understood that while reciprocity purported to ameliorate the sting of dominion restriction, "the fact remains, and every Indian knows it, that His Majesty's Indian subjects are not welcomed, and indeed barely tolerated, in many of the countries flying the British flag."[15] Although this imagined Indian colony never materialized, the perseverance of its advocates illustrated their suspicion that colonial restrictions on South Asian migrants would continue to foster intra-imperial acrimony.

Japan, Australia, and the Racial Equality Amendment, 1919

The Paris Peace Conference officially convened on January 18, designed to both terminate the war and eliminate the sources of international conflict. But the British and American delegations also implicitly engraved race, discrimination, and immobility into the reconstructed—and supposedly reformed—postwar international order. They did so by rejecting a Japanese amendment to the League Covenant, which called for the recognition of national and racial equality. The Australian prime minister in particular contended that this clause portended the free movement of nonwhite migrants, and he maintained this conviction throughout the conference. Following Hughes's lead, the *Melbourne Herald*'s Versailles correspondent, Keith Murdoch, misrepresented the tone of the Japanese proposal, claiming that the Japanese insisted "that all countries in the world must permit free ingress to all peoples."[16] In reality the proposition made no direct reference to migration. Japanese officials in fact indicated that immigration policy was a purely domestic prerogative, and therefore beyond the purview of the proposed amendment. Nevertheless the Japanese call for global racial equality portended disastrous implications for an international community still anchored upon imperialism, discrimination, and inequality.

Historians have offered a number of reasons to explain why Japan presented its racial equality claim in Paris. The long-standing quarrel over colonial restriction is widely cited as the most important precipitating factor. This is not surprising, given the primacy of the issue in Anglo-Japanese and Japanese-American diplomacy during the previous two decades. A second explanation interprets the proposal as a genuine attempt to enshrine a capacious principle of racial equality in the new League of Nations Covenant. However, this interpretation ignores twenty years of Japanese diplomacy on immigration exclusion, during which Japan had consistently resented its association with other, "less civilized," nonwhite races. A third account perceives the racial equality amendment as a function of Japanese domestic politics. In this view the proposal represented a necessary salve to anti-League sentiment in Japan. The proposal was alternatively interpreted as a cynical bargaining chip, introduced by the Japanese delegation to barter for Shantung and the former German Pacific colonies. This was a view held by some among the European and American delegations.[17]

The Japanese government's submission of its racial equality proposal likely constituted a blend of these various motives, but a final and more likely interpretation construes the proposal as being motivated by the Japanese desire to achieve recognition as a thoroughly civilized great power, equal to their European and American counterparts. Ever since their victory over Russia in 1905, the Japanese people had struggled to obtain international recognition, and this was consistently reflected in the travails of its emigrants abroad. Immigration rights were therefore an important marker of Japanese advancement and acceptance in an international community still dominated by white, Western empires. This was the argument presented by the Japanese ambassador to the United States, Viscount Ishii Kikujirō, during a speech in New York. Racial equality posed no threat to existing arrangements and simply represented an issue of "legitimate pride and self-respect." His countrymen were committed to "straightening out the existing injustice of racial discrimination," the ambassador assured his American listeners, but were willing to do so "independently of the question of labor or immigration."[18]

Even before the delegates officially convened in Paris, the British ambassador in Tokyo perceived an impending Japanese challenge to colonial and American restriction. Sir Conyngham Greene alerted the British foreign secretary to a troubling emergent consensus on the Japanese government's proposed peace terms the day after the armistice. Based on his examination of local press commentary, Greene concluded that the Japanese, emboldened by Wilson's rhetoric, intended to confront the discrimination that underpinned colonial and American immigration laws. The *Kokumin* newspaper editorialized on November 3, 1918, "The object of the League's formation will not be fully realized, it would seem, so long as Japanese and other coloured races are differentially treated in white communities." Americans and Australians would be compelled to modify their unfavorable policies toward Asian migrants if President Wilson's recent pronouncements were reliable.[19] That same newspaper reported on November 30, "A justice and humanity which fails to solve the racial question is a spurious justice and humanity. A world league of peace built upon a spurious justice and humanity is a house built on the sand."[20]

Greene sent further warnings to the dominion and imperial governments just days before the Paris Peace Conference began. The Japanese press was adamant that any prospective League of Nations be founded upon the principle of racial equality. In support of this contention, Greene forwarded a leading article from the *Asahi Shimbun* by Shigetaka Shiga, a prominent Japanese intellectual. Shigetaka surmised that his nation's wartime contributions had eroded anti-Japanese sentiment in Australia and New Zealand, and he hoped that this would provide an opportunity to eliminate the "numerous evils which arise out of the immigration question and which are the cause of so many international enmities."[21] Greene continued to forward disquieting reports once the conference began. On January 10, 1919, the ambassador conveyed an article by Dr. Toda Kaiichi of Kyoto Imperial University, who chided Canadians, Americans, and Australians for greedily hoarding vast expanses of undeveloped territory while nations like Japan and China struggled with surging population growth and insufficient arable land. Notwithstanding the starkness of white territorial and commercial gluttony, Toda maintained that it was Japan's responsibility to advocate racial equality during the peace conference as the "only international force among the colored nations." More important, the future success and integrity of the League necessitated the elimination of racial discrimination. Otherwise, Toda assured his readers, it would "simply degenerate into a means of oppression of the coloured races by the white."[22] The following month Greene reported that approximately 500 people from across the Japanese political spectrum had gathered in Tokyo to demand the abolition of racial discrimination.[23] Momentum was building toward a reckoning in Paris.

Imperial authorities scrambled to contrive a preemptive response that would satisfy both the Japanese and white militants in the colonies. Greene personally felt that the racial equality question was "perhaps the most difficult and delicate that can be imagined for physical, ethical, and sentimental reasons," and he was unsure whether the conference or even a future League of Nations could adequately address the full scope of the question.[24] Lionel Curtis, an acolyte of the secretary of state for the colonies, Alfred Milner, and advocate of imperial federation, presented a possible solution in December 1918. The British Empire had already concocted a palatable remedy for South Asian exclusion in the dominions, and that reciprocity formula offered an expedient proposal with which Britain could counter any Japanese complaint. In this way, Curtis suggested, Japan "can be offered the same terms as those which India and the Dominions have made with each other; but she cannot be offered better terms." The India Office reiterated this suggestion the following month on its own initiative.[25]

Both the Foreign Office and the Colonial Office rejected this recommendation as premature and imprudent. Writing from the former, Max Muller recommended that the imperial government simply avoid discussing the issue with Japan, since India and the dominions had not yet finalized arrangements governing intra-imperial migration. Moreover Muller had it on good authority from the former British naval attaché in Tokyo that the Japanese delegation would not even raise the issue in Paris; it was merely a fiction of Japan's opposition press.[26] Secretary Milner was similarly disinclined to broach the reciprocity proposal with Japan, trenchantly observing, "It is not necessarily a good answer to claims of foreign governments that certain classes of British subjects are subject to special restrictions as to right of entry."[27]

Despite Muller's skepticism, on February 13 the Japanese delegation submitted their anticipated proposal to the League of Nations Commission as an amendment to article 21 (on religious equality) of the League Covenant: "The equality of nations being a basic principle of the League of Nations, the High Contracting Parties agree to accord, as soon as possible, to all alien nationals of States members of the League, equal and just treatment in every respect, making no distinction, either in law or in fact, on account of their race or nationality."[28]

Baron Makino Nobuaki gave a poignant and measured speech in support of his delegation's amendment. His statement embodied the spirit of a new diplomatic era, inspired by the American president's salubrious vision of a postwar order characterized by open diplomacy, self-determination, and international comity. The respected Japanese diplomat warned his fellow conferees that racial discrimination threatened to undermine the very peace they had convened to restore. He conceded the sensitivity of the problem and insisted that his delegation neither demanded nor expected immediate redress. Rather his nation's proposal should "be regarded as an invitation to the governments and peoples concerned, to examine more closely and seriously, and to devise some acceptable means to meet a deadlock which at present confronts different peoples." The war had stirred global aspirations that world leaders could not ignore, and Makino reminded the commissioners that they were designing a system of collective security in which the defense of one nation's people might demand the supreme sacrifice of another's. It was therefore only just that every citizen and subject "should be placed on an equal footing with people he undertakes to defend even with his life." Indeed throughout the recent war, men of all races had fought together for the same cause, "irrespective of racial differences." After such a transformative experience, "the principle at least of equality among men should be admitted and be made the basis of the future intercourse."[29] Rather than admit that basic principle, the commission removed article 21 from the League Covenant entirely.[30]

The League Commission's procedural maneuver only temporarily impeded the Japanese delegation's proposal, and the deputation remained committed to the adoption of their amendment. Following that first setback, a Japanese Foreign Office spokesman proclaimed his government's belief that "in the future among the civilized nations, at least, racial discrimination is to be abolished."[31] The Japanese government even considered removing its own restrictions on Chinese labor and foreign landownership in preparation for a renewed assault on racial discrimination in Paris.[32] A report in the *Asahi* outlined the stakes: "Of 1,500,000,000 population of the world, the white races are only 600,000,000, the rest of the 900,000,000 being yellow, dark, and red races." As the only "coloured" power among the big five at Versailles, it was "up to Japan to stand resolutely, even sacrificing her interests, to see that the present unfair condition be removed." The Japanese Diet's Executive Committee for the Abolition of Racial Discriminations held an impassioned meeting in Tokyo, unanimously resolving that Japan should refrain from joining the League in the amendment's absence. The *Hochi Shimbun* refused to accept defeat and encouraged Japan's delegates to overcome the opposition, warning its representatives that "if they fail in this task, the Japanese people will not welcome them home."[33]

Japanese disappointment deepened when the Commission presented its League Covenant proposal to the final drafting committee on March 26, absent the racial equality amendment. Melancholy and contempt characterized the response to this second major rebuff. Though critical of their delegation, many Japanese blamed Australian and American intransigence for the amendment's defeat. According to the *Hochi* newspaper's editorialists, William Hughes and Australian "selfishness" constituted the real barrier to discrimination's abolition, and they were largely correct.[34] Hughes stood resolutely opposed to racial equality and had signaled his hostility before even arriving in Paris, telling Acting Prime Minister William Alexander Watt just days before the armistice, "I want an absolutely free hand to hold up our end for our Pacific policy and White Australia policy."[35] On February 2 Hughes reiterated his opposition in a memorandum to Britain's chief League Commission delegate, Lord Robert Cecil. Australia would "absolutely decline to accept" any mechanism that included compulsory arbitration on the White Australia Policy, Hughes stated, and throughout the conference he remained vigilant against any Japanese attempt to revive the issue.[36]

The Japanese delegates knew that their success or failure depended upon persuading the Australian prime minister to temper his uncompromising devotion to white supremacy. Baron Makino and Viscount Chinda Sutemi met with Hughes in early April, seeking his support for yet another revised proposal. This new amendment conveyed a simple endorsement of national equality and mentioned neither racial equality nor discrimination, modestly stating, "The equality of nations being a basic principle of the League of Nations, the High Contracting Parties agree to endorse the principle of equal and just treatment to be accorded to all alien nationals of states members of the League." In an effort to impress the depth of Japanese public opinion upon Hughes, Makino and Chinda shared a telegram relaying the declared intent of the Executive Committee for the Abolition of Racial Discrimination to overthrow the Japanese government and effect Japan's immediate withdrawal from the League of Nations if the Japanese delegation failed to secure the amendment's inclusion in the Covenant. Unmoved, Hughes flatly rejected the entreaty.[37] Regardless of Japanese assurances, he saw nothing more than a surreptitious stunt designed to facilitate the resumption of Japanese labor migration and the eventual colonization of vulnerable white communities around the Pacific.

Other British Empire delegation members, though opposed to Asian immigration, attempted to broker a compromise. Smuts suggested the call for "equal and just treatment" for all "alien nationals" be changed to "equitable treatment of all nationals," while Cecil preferred to find "some words expertly limited to discrimination between nationals of foreign states *actually resident in the state*."[38] On April 11 Makino met once again with Hughes, Smuts, and Louis Botha, and once again Hughes refused to concede. The Japanese representatives made it clear that their room for compromise was also limited. Although they had stated that they did not wish to deny any member state's right to regulate immigration, they refused to accept a British suggestion including this proviso in the League Covenant.[39]

Unable to overcome Hughes's tenacious opposition, the Japanese delegation once more diluted its proposal following a feisty debate.[40] What began as an explicit statement of racial equality was now reduced to an "endorsement of the principle of the equality of nations and the just treatment of their nationals."[41] Makino introduced this exhaustively revised and thoroughly insipid amendment at a League Commission meeting on April 11. Tacitly recognizing American and British dominion aversion to any perceived interference in their immigration laws, the Japanese delegate stated that his government had no desire to "encroach on the internal affairs of any nation." The revised clause was merely intended to establish "an aim in the future international intercourse."[42] Speaking on the British delegation's behalf, Cecil sheepishly announced that he was unable to vote for the Japanese proposal on the spurious grounds that it represented a potential intrusion into the domestic affairs of member states.

The American president's statement on the Japanese proposal was a master class in prevarication and equivocation. According to Wilson, it was preferable to simply ignore the racial equality issue for the time being, lest the delegates find themselves engaged in a bitter dispute, and for that reason he refused to vote in favor of the amendment. Eleven members of the Commission ultimately affirmed their support for the Japanese proposal, leaving the United States and the British Empire among six that did not.[43] As chairman of the League Commission, Wilson announced defeat of the measure, unilaterally declaring that a vote of this nature required unanimous consent. This enabled him to defeat the proposal without having to explicitly vote against it.[44] The Japanese delegation again faced bitter disappointment, despite having comprehensively attenuated their original amendment. Following its final failure, Makino reluctantly announced that Japan would no longer press the proposal's adoption. He proclaimed, "The Japanese government and people feel poignant regret at the failure of the Commission to approve of their just demand for laying down a principle aiming at the adjustment of this long standing grievance." Racial equality was a "deep-rooted national conviction" for Japan, Makino insisted, and his country reserved the right to reintroduce the amendment at future League meetings.[45]

Japan, Australia, and the Pacific Mandates

Safeguarding the White Australia Policy domestically was not enough for Hughes; he also demanded the retrenchment of Asian mobility rights in Germany's former South Pacific colonies then under Australian control. From his perspective, and from the perspective of Australian military planners, New Guinea, the Bismarck Archipelago, and the German Solomon Islands were new outposts of Australian racial, economic, and strategic suzerainty.[46] As such, Hughes and others demanded the immediate disengagement of these islands from the circuits of South Pacific labor and commerce and their transformation into Australian-sponsored nodes of Asian immobility. These demands compounded the indignities perpetrated by the Commonwealth's opposition to the racial equality clause and further injured the already strained relationship between the Australian and Japanese governments.

Hughes vigorously defended his Commonwealth's claims to these islands in an address before the House of Lords' Empire Parliamentary Association during his extended wartime stay in London. No discussion of Australian social, political, and economic development could ignore the Commonwealth's precarious geopolitical position in the South Pacific, he began.

Encouraging the assembled peers to invert the spatial and racial geography of their empire, Hughes submitted that Australia was not a remote and isolated antipodal outpost but "in the very middle, or at the very gates of, that part of the world in which the greater part of its population live." With this in mind, he encouraged his listeners to recognize the bleak truth that animated his and others' devotion to the White Australia Policy: Australia was "a white spot in a coloured ocean." This fact had conditioned Australia's development from the outset, forcing its leadership to "adopt a policy of protection of the white people settled in Australia against this tremendous ocean of mankind which is settled roundabout." Australians frequently disagreed on a range of issues, he admitted, but they rarely diverged on "the question of the retention of Australia for the white race." In Hughes's mind, then, Germany's former colonies were essential to the defense, economic security, and continued whiteness of the Australian continent. Unless the Commonwealth obtained permanent dominion over these islands, he cautioned, a hostile power could strangle Australian trade or "swoop upon Australia herself." While he failed to identify from where this putative threat might descend, he left little doubt that Japan—then occupying the Marshall, Caroline, and Marianas Islands to the north—posed the biggest threat to Australians' safety.[47]

Hughes's peace claims centered on obtaining outright control of Germany's former Pacific colonies that had been under Australian occupation since the outbreak of the war. He made his case to the British Empire delegation on February 6, 1919, outlining the strategic, racial, and economic importance of those possessions to the Australian people. Reiterating the themes of his Lords speech, Hughes urged his fellow delegates to recognize that Australia was an island continent of five million whites, remote from Europe but alarmingly close to the "teeming millions of Asia." In light of these conditions Australians had necessarily adopted restrictive immigration policies designed to exclude "large populations of widely different race, type, and habits of life—a population which cannot, without the most disastrous social and racial consequences, either be absorbed or remain unabsorbed." Surrounded and perpetually vulnerable, the Commonwealth's leaders were adamant that "at any cost and at any sacrifice, Australia shall be kept free from these evils." To protect the racial integrity and security of their Commonwealth, Australians were determined to claim sovereignty over the Pacific islands that encircled them. "In particular," Hughes demanded, "she must have full power to control immigration into these territories," as well as full jurisdiction over the islands' trade.[48] For Hughes and his government, direct annexation and implementation of the White Australia Policy was the only acceptable solution to Australia's persistent strategic and racial anxieties. Hughes expected opposition from Wilson but remained confident that he could persuade the American president to relent. Wilson "is a man firm on nothing that really matters," Hughes told Munro Ferguson as the Peace Conference got under way in Paris. "Give him a League of Nations and he will give us the rest."[49]

Wilson proved more determined than Hughes expected. Keen to avoid the odor of territorial aggrandizement or blatant imperialism, the conference adopted a mandatory system in January 1919. Under this arrangement—devised by Smuts and Wilson—the former German colonies would be administered by individual states on behalf of the League, although Germany's Pacific islands were eventually rated "C-level mandates," meaning they could be administered by the mandatory power practically as colonies.[50] Publicly Hughes expressed disappointment. The proposed mandatory system did not provide sufficient guarantees for the Commonwealth's security, he grumbled, nor did it assure the well-being of the native populations. The territories were simply too scattered and the League of Nations' power too immature to ensure the efficacy of the mandates. If the conference insisted on instituting this folly, however, he would begrudgingly accept, providing his dominion secured mandatory powers for all the islands in question.[51]

Privately Hughes had actually reconciled himself to the mandatory principle. As he admitted to Watt in a cable on January 31, at least this prevented Japan from fortifying its own former German colonies to the north. Even as he fought vigorously in public for direct annexation, Hughes quietly urged his colleagues in Melbourne to accept the mandate system. Still he advised Watt not to publicly indicate Australia's satisfaction.[52] Watt and his colleagues expressed "bitter disappointment" with the decision and urged Hughes to continue fighting for complete control. If he could not convince the conference, the cabinet exhorted Hughes to ensure that the proposed mandates' terms empowered Australia with complete control over immigration. "If this is not specified," Watt worried, "Australia's racial policy will be challenged and injured, if not destroyed." It would also engender widespread miscegenation in the Pacific islands, to the detriment of both the native peoples and their white administrators. The acting prime minister advised Hughes to exploit American racial fears on this question. "Surely America must sympathise with a people isolated and adjacent to unnumbered colored millions, but resolutely facing its duty to keep this fertile continent and its intimately associated islands for the selected white races."[53]

In fact the Japanese delegation had inadvertently aided Hughes in his campaign to secure the new Australian mandates against Asian intrusion.

Makino had insisted upon the right of mandatory powers to govern their new charges under domestic law during the initial negotiations over Class C mandates. This allowed him to overcome opposition from within his own government and to reassure his superiors that "the mandate system in essence will be no different from annexation." This ruse ultimately backfired on the Japanese diplomat, however, since it also allowed Australia and New Zealand to strictly enforce domestic legislation in their mandates south of the equator, which included their restrictive immigration laws.[54] Australia and New Zealand worked diligently thereafter to abjure Japanese labor and commercial interests in their new mandates. Japan had failed to secure the racial equality amendment; now they failed to prevent Australasians from extending racial inequality to their new mandates.[55]

Munro Ferguson raised a number of concerns regarding Australia's new mandates. He informed Milner in February 1919 that Asian restriction remained a powerful force in Australian politics and, "though not so outspoken as Mr. Hughes, most politicians are anxious that the Southward expansion of the Japanese should be combated." He correctly assumed that, given the opportunity, Australia would formally extend the White Australia Policy to the islands.[56] This would invariably complicate Anglo-Japanese relations. He told Milner in May, "The antagonistic attitude of Australia to Japan is a further complication which will greatly extend the risk of misunderstanding unless guarded against by the Imperial Government."[57] In an attempt to prevent these potential diplomatic difficulties, Munro Ferguson continued his wartime campaign to establish a high commissioner for Great Britain's Pacific possessions, which would include the recently established Australian and New Zealand mandates. From his perspective this was especially important in the wake of Hughes's impolitic treatment of Japan at the Paris Peace Conference. Now serving as undersecretary for the colonies, Leopold Amery was coming to a similar conclusion in London. Australian and New Zealand racial attitudes were simply too abrasive to entrust them with the islands. He told Milner, "There is much to be said for putting all the islands under a joint Imperial Australian and New Zealand Council sufficiently detached from local Australian and New Zealand politics to be able to carry on a rational policy of development."[58]

Munro Ferguson was convinced that Australians were unable to grasp the potential dangers engendered by their exclusionary immigration policy. He told Milner in March, "My experience of Australia leads me to believe that the general public remain unperturbed by the dangers to which the country is exposed by reason of the smallness of her population, the vastness of her uninhabited areas and the proximity of hundreds of millions of coloured peoples anxious to exchange their own over-crowded demesnes for the fertile and extensive lands from which they are excluded more by the Immigration Restriction Act of the Commonwealth than by force of arms."[59] Australians were entering a volatile and dangerous phase in their relations with the Japanese, and Munro Ferguson recognized the grim implications this augured for British foreign policy. "Risk of friction with Japan is serious," he warned King George V, especially since "Australian external policy is apt to be ill-considered and aggressive." The governor-general also fretted that Australian racial attitudes rendered it an unsuitable mandatory power. The dominion's intense color consciousness, he felt, would necessarily hamper effective administration in the newly acquired islands. He told the king, "The 'white Australia' methods of Government are not suited to the [circumstances] of a subject population."[60] This was a potentially toxic brew when combined with Hughes's exploits in Paris, the extension of Japanese exclusion to the islands, and Australia's already tenuous strategic position in the Pacific.

Other perspicacious Australians doubted the sagacity of the Commonwealth's new mandatory power. Rupert W. Hornabrook, a prominent anesthesiologist with experience in South Africa and Great Britain, was concerned that Australia was shouldering a responsibility for which it was neither prepared nor particularly well-suited. For one thing, the islands' administration was likely to cost too much. For another, Australians were simply "too impulsive" to handle this new responsibility. One need only recall Hughes's performance in Paris, Hornabrook counseled, to realize "how very unsuited we really are to deal with delicate international questions on our own." A third and related concern was that Australia's presence in the islands would bring it even closer to Japan, which now controlled the former German islands north of the equator. The Commonwealth government should turn Australia's responsibility over to imperial authorities, he suggested, which were immeasurably more qualified to administer the islands.[61] Hornabrook kept up a steady stream of opposition in the Adelaide *Mail* throughout the summer of 1919, albeit to no avail.

As Munro Ferguson and Hornabrook predicted, the Australian government did extend the White Australia Policy to its mandates, much to the chagrin of Japanese officials, who frequently raised objections to this policy in the immediate aftermath of the Peace Conference, especially in New Guinea, where Japanese commercial interests had previously thrived under German rule.[62] By August 1920, however, the Japanese had relented to the Australian government's demands, seeking instead a bilateral arrangement, similar to the gentleman's agreements then governing Japanese migration to Canada and the United States. Nevertheless Japan remained resolute that its subjects residing in New Guinea should enjoy the same privileges they had enjoyed under German dominion. The Japanese government also sought the relaxation of wartime restrictions that prevented their subjects from owning and operating copra plantations in the mandate and from having equal access to port facilities at Rabaul. If Japanese residents were subjected to inferior treatment under Australian authorities, Viscount Uchida Kosai, minister of foreign affairs, informed his ambassador in London, "there is no doubt that public opinion in Japan would become highly agitated and the government would be confronted with a very delicate situation."[63]

Hughes once again rejected Japan's proposal, believing the Japanese were attempting to "introduce [the] thin end of [the] wedge of racial equality." "We are starting with [a] clean slate," the Hughes government declared, adamant that it would govern as it pleased.[64] With regard to its mandate in German Samoa, the New Zealand government cabled its "complete agreement" with the Australian position to the British government shortly after.[65] When the new League agreed upon final terms for the C mandates in December 1920, Japan announced that it would not protest the absence of a clause facilitating equal opportunity for all member states in each League mandate. Nevertheless the Japanese government insisted that their decision "should not be considered as an acquiescence on the part of His Imperial Japanese Majesty's Government in the submission of Japanese subjects to a discriminatory and disadvantageous treatment in the Mandated territories."[66] In reality it was exactly that.

Reaping the Whirlwind: The Aftermath

Hughes returned to Melbourne in August 1919 and triumphantly proclaimed before Parliament, "White Australia is yours. You may do with it what you please."[67] His tenacious defense of Australians' racial, economic, and strategic prerogatives in Paris had seemingly preserved one of the most treasured founding principles of the Commonwealth. Yet his confident declaration belied the continued tensions engendered by Australians' commitment to a white continent. His exertions had thwarted what he perceived to be the Japanese delegation's surreptitious attempt to undermine the White Australia Policy, but his victory was pyrrhic. Hughes had made himself solely responsible for standing against racial equality and, more ominously, Japan's aspirations for the postwar international order. The rush of victory soon gave way to fear and anxiety. Hughes's tactless opposition to Japan's proposed amendment aggravated tensions between Australia and Japan, while his successful claims on the former German colony of New Guinea—and the extension of Japanese power into the Marshall, Caroline, and Marianas islands—increased Australian concerns of Japanese expansion by bringing the two antagonists into closer proximity.

The ordinarily chauvinistic Sydney *Bulletin* captured the essential dilemma of Hughes's Parisian diplomacy in an unusually shrewd editorial published not long after the prime minister's return to Australia. Hughes had vocalized the Australian people's cruder nationalist and racial impulses during his time in Paris. Those impulses were indisputably authentic, but Australians needed more astute leadership if the dominion was to "hold her own against the alien forces surrounding her." "No intelligent Australian believes that Australia's safety will be secured merely by shouting at Japan across the ocean," the *Bulletin* editorialist observed with uncharacteristic sagacity. The editorialist admitted that Hughes had performed a "brilliant stunt" by orchestrating the defeat of the racial equality amendment and securing at least some of Germany's former Pacific colonies for Australia, but it represented clumsy and potentially dangerous diplomacy to unnecessarily incur Japanese resentment. Hughes's "inability to mobilise the nations interested in the policy of racial exclusion" constituted his most egregious diplomatic blunder. Instead of quietly cultivating American, Canadian, South African, and New Zealand support for Australia's position vis-à-vis Japan, Hughes had recklessly and rambunctiously rushed headlong into the fray, alienating Japan, Great Britain, and the United States in the process. Australia was now needlessly "exposed and isolated" in the Pacific, the *Bulletin* feared, and a tantalizing target for Japanese expansion.[68]

Hughes also came to realize that his open hostility toward the racial equality amendment had shielded Massey, Borden, Smuts, and especially Wilson from criticism. The American president's attempt to evade culpability especially incensed the Australian premier, and Hughes believed that Wilson had privately blamed him for the equality amendment's defeat in front of the Japanese delegation, even claiming that he personally favored adoption of the proposal. "He is Mr. Facing-both-ways," Hughes complained to Watt two days after the Commission's final vote.[69] His suspicions were well-founded. Wilson's confidante Colonel Edward House had earlier confided to his diary, "It has taken considerable finesse to lift the load from our shoulders and place it upon the British, but happily, it has been done."[70] Wilson's doctor, Cary

Grayson, recorded a similar sentiment in his diary on March 22. "It was not necessary for the United States to take a stand in this connection," he wrote of the racial equality amendment, "because the British government, backing the opposition of Australia and New Zealand, declared they could not accept any such plan."[71]

Hughes had received ample warning of his diplomacy's potential shortcomings. In January 1919 Tokyo's *Nichi Nichi* newspaper published a forceful denunciation of Australia's postarmistice attitude. Australians had resumed their hostile prewar posture by excluding Japanese immigrants and commercial interests from New Guinea, the *Nichi Nichi* complained. Such ingratitude was difficult to fathom, since without Japanese help German warships would have decimated Australian troopships, crippled Australian trade, and plundered the continent's exposed coastal cities with impunity. Australian disrespect toward its erstwhile ally "should not be lightly regarded."[72] The *Nichi Nichi* denounced Hughes's uncompromising and unfriendly approach in another editorial, published on January 27, 1919, in which the writers accused Hughes of personally obstructing Japanese war aims and impeding the cause of peace. The Australian premier "persists in his anti-Japanese attitude, clings to his principles of racial prejudice, and much to our surprise is entirely devoid of the characteristic magnanimity of a great Empire," the editorialists protested. If Hughes continued to frustrate the Japanese delegation's endeavors in Paris, they warned, "the root of future calamity will not have been eradicated and Mr. Hughes will not achieve his purpose however violent his agitation may be."[73] Japanese observers understood what Hughes was slow to recognize: rather than ameliorate Australians' security concerns, his obstinacy had actually exacerbated them.

The Japanese delegation imparted a similar warning on April 7, 1919, just as Hughes's remonstrations against the Japanese amendment reached a crescendo. Following an interview with Makino, the reporter Keith Murdoch wrote of being "strongly impressed by [Makino's] grave warning that public opinion in Japan will hold Australia accountable" for the failure of the equality amendment. Makino insinuated that Japanese-Australian relations would be "seriously compromised by the Australian government's attitude." Japan's proposal, the delegate assured Murdoch, posed no threat to the White Australia Policy and merely represented an "assertion of man's equality." Murdoch tried to convince Makino that Australia was being "used to pull the chestnuts out of the fire for the greater Powers, which equally dislike the amendment," but Makino remained convinced that Australian intransigence represented the real obstacle to racial equality.[74]

Murdoch's published report shocked the Australian government in Melbourne. Watt quickly cabled Hughes to express his cabinet's concern that Australians were being held responsible for the defeat of the Japanese proposal. Indeed Japanese press reports suggested "growing irritation in Japan against Australia's reaffirmation of its principles." Watt also received a stream of intelligence from the British Embassy in Tokyo, indicating resentment of Hughes's stalwart resistance to racial equality. The British Minister Plenipotentiary in Tokyo, Sir Beilby Alston, reported from Japan that the subject was "practically the one topic of discussion."[75] Watt subtly admonished his prime minister that "public activities or utterances calculated to inflame Japanese feeling against Australia ought to be moderated or eliminated" since relations between Japan and Australia seemed to be developing "new and dangerous features."[76] Hughes predicted that he could deflect these criticisms. It was nothing less than "a contemptible lie" propagated by the Americans, he insisted, to suggest that Australian opposition alone had doomed the racial equality amendment. Wilson had taken the unprecedented step of requiring a unanimous vote on the issue, which in Hughes's mind proved the American president's complicity. He assured his colleagues that he had fully apprised the Japanese press of Wilson's duplicity and that Makino was now aware that their amendment would have succeeded if Wilson had not changed the rules. "Do not worry," Hughes cheerfully reassured Watt.[77] Hughes had indeed taken the unusual step of typing a statement for submission to the *Tokyo Asahi*, outlining Australia's position on Japanese immigration on solely economic terms and fiercely denying that he alone had defeated the amendment.[78]

Hughes's optimism did not allay everybody's concerns. Edmund Leolin Piesse, director of the recently established Pacific Branch of the Prime Minister's Department, also doubted whether Hughes had served Australians' best interests in Paris. He privately told the Royal Navy's Commander Bertram Home Ramsay in June 1919 that Hughes and the Australian delegation had been "unwise" to so vehemently and brazenly resist Japan's call for racial equality: "There is of course no question of abandoning the essentials of White Australia—on that we will fight, whether we are ready or not, but it would have been quite safe, in my opinion, to have accepted one of the innocuous forms in which they put it forward." Hughes had unnecessarily inflamed Japanese public opinion and "may have rendered her ready to pick a quarrel with us," he feared.[79]

Many British officials expressed similar views. In response to Makino's speech one Foreign Office official noted, "I am afraid we have made trouble for the future by rejecting the very innocuous amendment [Japan] last proposed in the Commission." As Makino implied, Japan could insist on much stronger language in the future. The Foreign Office's Ronald Macleay concurred; after all, if the amendment had been accepted, it was unlikely that Japan would ever have "dared to accuse" any other country of violating it, "as they are well aware that they live themselves in a glass house and that as long as they discriminate against Chinese labour and against foreigners generally in the matter of land tenure they cannot afford to throw stones."[80]

The Australian governor-general also sensed a growing uneasiness in Melbourne following Hughes's successful Parisian campaign. In a letter to the king's private secretary, Baron Stamfordham, Munro Ferguson admitted that Hughes's stance was popular with the "man in the street," especially since ordinary Australians assumed the Royal Navy would protect them against Japanese ire, "and therefore rather rejoices to see 'the little brown men of Japan' being put in their proper place by [their] valiant P.M." But Australian ministers evinced discomfort as they contemplated the consequences of alienating their increasingly powerful neighbor.[81] Nothing positive would come from estranging Japan. The governor-general playfully cautioned Hughes on April 29, "The Rising Sun is I fear a more formidable luminary than the Spangled Stars—therefore I trust a form of words may be found to soothe wounded feelings, while in no way endangering the whiteness of Australia." More seriously, he chided, "It is very desirable that Australia should not be inscribed permanently—as a result of the Peace Conference—in the Black Books of 'the little brown men of Japan.'"[82]

Hughes's performance in Paris had clearly intensified Australians' fear of Japanese intentions, and cynicism, anxiety, and peevishness characterized the Commonwealth government's postwar relations with Japan. In the months following the Peace Conference Australian officials viewed Japanese motives with suspicion and apprehension occasionally bordering on paranoia. In October 1919 Hughes urgently telegraphed the first lord of the Admiralty in London, Sir Walter Long, to request that Britain immediately dispatch a Royal Navy battle group to Australia. The small Australian fleet was practically inactive due to coal, oil, and ammunition shortages, and Hughes expressed alarm that it was unable "to undertake any effective action in the Pacific for the present if an emergency rose." Reports suggesting that the Japanese fleet was unusually active in its home waters stoked his fears. Long curtly dismissed the Australian premier's request. Dissatisfied, Hughes reiterated that British support was urgently required. "It is a long way from Tokio to Whitehall," he reminded Long, "but we are within a stone-throw."

Australia was in no position to defend itself against a Japanese attack, Hughes warned, and the situation was becoming acute. "We profoundly distrust Japan," he fretted. Hughes also reminded Long that Japan's "strong animosity has been roused by our opposition to her desire for an equal treatment of her [immigrants] and their entry into Australia." Despite Hughes's vociferous entreaties, however, the British government declined his request yet again.[83]

Others Australians also sensed Japanese treachery around every corner. In December 1919, for example, Victoria's premier reported the Japanese consul's request for a panoramic photograph of Melbourne, intended for publication in a Japanese geography textbook. The Department of Defence granted this request with the proviso that "some excuse should be invented for withholding views of the Port."[84] Similarly, in January 1920, the Japanese Ministry of War dispatched two army officers to Australia and New Zealand "to help consolidate friendship with Japan." The Australian government complained to Lord Milner, expressing surprise that "military officers should be entrusted with [a] mission to consolidate friendship with Australia," and declared itself "very much embarrassed by the proposed visit."[85] In response Milner insisted that it would do more harm to prevent the officers' visit and suggested that they be accompanied by an Australian officer on their tour.[86] The Japanese government ultimately canceled the visit. According to the Japanese consul in Sydney, hostile Australian public opinion toward Japan had rendered the visit futile.[87]

Australian intelligence officials expressed concern that Japanese steamers loading coal in Newcastle, New South Wales, were engaged in espionage. One intelligence official reported in August 1920 that Japanese crews sightseeing in the region around Newcastle appeared "rather too businesslike and frequent." They frequently rented motor cars and took extensive trips around the Hunter River Valley, brandishing cameras wherever they went, which, according to Captain Longfield Lloyd, "indicates either a most remarkable liking for photography on the part of the Japanese, or a careful and consistent encouragement in the use of the camera by their Government." It was also clear to Lloyd that the fertile Hunter River Valley, with its easy access to the coast and coal mines of New South Wales, would be a tempting target, "especially for a race of grain eaters."[88]

Even estimations of Japan's wartime contributions became cause for concern. In November 1920, for example, Piesse informed Hughes that British and Japanese authorities were overstating Japan's contributions to Australian defense during the late war. Piesse was particularly offended by the postwar claim of the British ambassador in Tokyo that the Anglo-Japanese Alliance had "assured the safety of Australia, New Zealand, and the Pacific coast of Canada" throughout the hostilities. More important, references in the Japanese press continually suggested that Japan's wartime naval support was a singular reason why Australia must moderate its attitude toward its Pacific ally.[89] Officials in the Australian Navy Department were equally resentful of British and Japanese claims that Japan had provided heroic and indispensable protection to Australia's troopships and commercial vessels and even continental defense during the Great War. Japan's contributions were woefully meager and greatly overstated, the Department insisted.[90] Such episodes highlighted the unintended consequences of the Australian prime minister's Parisian diplomacy. Hughes's reckless disdain for Japanese racial sensitivities had actually aggravated rather than assuaged Australians' apprehensions of Japan's postwar aims.

The 1921 Imperial Conference, the Anglo-Japanese Alliance, and the Washington Naval Conference

As Australians agonized over countless imagined perfidies, the British government prepared to host dominion leaders at the 1921 Imperial Conference in London to determine the future of the Anglo-Japanese Alliance. This extraordinary pact had irritated colonial leaders since its ratification in 1902, and for almost two decades it had impeded their attempts to explicitly and entirely exclude Japanese immigrants.[91] They were not alone. Many Americans shared their exasperation, suspecting the alliance of emboldening Japanese expansionism in East Asia and inhibiting American commercial and financial interests in China. Chauvinistic American editorialists also griped that Great Britain would be forced to intercede on its ally's behalf if war broke out between the Japanese and Americans. Even some Japanese had begun to express bitterness toward the alliance, cognizant of the glaring absurdity of their association with an empire whose colonists stridently discriminated against Japanese subjects. One Japanese observer noted in 1915, "The antagonism of the colonies to Japanese laborers, on the one hand, and the resentment felt by the Japanese people for the humiliation of their compatriots on the other, might place the British Government in an extremely awkward position if the Japanese Alliance is continued."[92] And yet the alliance had persevered for twenty years.

The latest iteration of the treaty was due to expire on July 13, 1921, however, and by 1920 the pact had largely outlived its usefulness. The German and Russian threats animating the alliance had evaporated in defeat and revolution, while American unease intensified toward this increasingly dissonant artifact of the prewar international order. Aware of his southern neighbors' aversion to the alliance, Canada's new Conservative and Unionist prime minister, Arthur Meighen, forcefully advocated for abrogation.[93] Both British and Japanese officials also recognized that their alliance jarred with the League of Nations' new spirit of collective security, something they acknowledged in a joint communiqué to that body in July 1920.[94]

The British government's strategic calculus in the Pacific had also changed. Plans were under way to construct a new naval base in Singapore, both to defend that strategic outpost (possibly from Japan, whose aggressive wartime diplomacy toward China had distressed British officials) and to offer better protection to Australia, New Zealand, and Britain's Asian colonies. Finally the British Foreign Office understood that the "colour bar—racial equality claim—baffles agreement between Japan and the Dominions, and meets with implacable opposition in Australia, New Zealand, South Africa, and Canada." It was clear by 1920 that the British government faced a difficult decision between alliance with Japan and friendship with the United States. Ultimately, the Foreign Office recognized, "our future course lies between our ally with whom our interests conflict, and our friend who is united to us by race, tradition, community of interests and ideals."[95]

Britain alone would not determine the alliance's future, however, and Australians in particular demanded a say in its repeal or renewal. Watt made the case for consultation during a May 1920 visit to London. Brandishing a familiar and versatile Australasian trope, the Australian treasurer avowed that "Australia was in the neighborhood of 800,000,000 Asiatics, and must be placed in a position to make her opinion known before any further Anglo-Japanese arrangements were made."[96] It may have seemed counterintuitive that Australasians would demand anything other than abrogation given their continued antagonism toward Asian immigration and their long-standing distaste for the alliance, but discerning observers knew that the situation was far more complex. After all, for over two decades Australasians had audaciously and relentlessly demeaned the people and government of Japan, and some now realized that a despondent ally was preferable to a disgruntled, indignant, and revisionist adversary. A June 1920 *Argus* editorial captured the ambivalence with which perspicacious Australians viewed the agreement. On one hand, Australia had "a large body of people who regard Japan with apprehension, fearing her imperialistic aims and the possibility of her penetrating into the Commonwealth." On the other hand, the alliance had unquestionably benefited the Commonwealth over the years, and in its absence Japan might seek unfriendly allies to protect its interests in the Pacific.[97]

And yet if the alliance was to continue, many within the Australian press clamored for bold revisions that would countenance the Commonwealth's devotion to racially delimited borders, Asian restriction, and white supremacy on the continent. As the *Sydney Morning Herald* reported in June 1920, Australian interests required that "no treaty between Japan and Britain shall contain in it anything inimical to the policy of a White Australia." Whatever form the final treaty revisions took, the *Herald* argued, "it should frankly face the racial security of Australia, and should be conditioned by the great ideal of Anglo-American friendship."[98] The *Melbourne Herald* was even more forthright. That newspaper's editorialist thundered in March 1920 that any revision of the Anglo-Japanese Alliance required dominion approval and an unequivocal endorsement of the White Australia Policy by both Britain and Japan. Moreover Japan must abandon the folly of racial equality and withdraw its claims to commercial and immigration rights in Australia's South Pacific mandates. After all, "these claims are an invasion of Australia's sovereignty, and their persistence is a menace to racial and economic independence." Unless Britain and Japan revised the alliance with reference to dominion—and American—concerns, the alliance would persistently beleaguer efforts to avert war in the Pacific. East and West might be driven toward conflict by "cosmic and racial processes whose operations are hidden from the puny intelligence of mankind," but Britain and Japan had an opportunity to forestall that seemingly inevitable race war if they tackled the admittedly difficult issues that plagued the Pacific.[99] The *Sydney Telegraph* was more diplomatic but nevertheless reiterated calls for Australian involvement in the revision process. Japan must understand that "racial exclusion does not imply any sense of inferiority"; the White Australia Policy was merely an acknowledgment of the dominion's preference for European civilization. Furthermore preemptive Japanese exclusion was preferable to the alternative, which was racial discrimination toward Japanese residents living in Australia.[100]

Australian officials also inclined toward retaining the alliance. Piesse prepared a memorandum in May 1920 at the British foreign secretary's request, outlining the advantages and disadvantages of renewal from the Australian perspective. He prefaced his response by listing the ways Japan had proven itself to be "an unworthy ally." Most egregiously Japan had imposed the disgraceful twenty-one demands upon China without reference to Great Britain and in the midst of war, and Japan's "self-regarding and perfunctory" participation in the war effort exacerbated their dishonor. The Japanese were clearly intent upon expansion in Asia and beyond, Piesse claimed, and their policies were largely directed by an undemocratic military and bureaucratic oligarchy. Despite this litany of treacheries, Piesse recognized that the alliance served a useful purpose from Australians' standpoint. Cancelation of the treaty might placate China and the United States, but it would stimulate bitterness in Japan, and possibly endanger Britain's Far East possessions. Renewal might allow Britain to moderate Japanese policies and permit Australians to extract concessions from its unpredictable ally. Piesse recognized that the White Australia Policy had long encumbered Anglo-Australian-Japanese relations, but he now saw an opportunity to assuage those tensions. Through renegotiation of the treaty, Britain could finally secure Japanese recognition of Australian immigration policies. In addition Piesse suggested that Britain might obtain a Japanese guarantee that they would not raise the "racial equality amendment" again, at least not "in a form objectionable to Australia." Finally, Australia wanted Japan to refrain from encouraging financial and commercial investments south of the equator. This would be "an important step towards the Monroe Doctrine for the South Pacific." Piesse understood that the last two requests were unlikely to receive a hearing, but they were central to Australia's Pacific policy.[101]

The British ambassador to Japan expressed similar sentiments. Charles Eliot strongly urged the British government to renew the Anglo-Japanese Alliance. His reading of Japanese public and official opinion suggested the alliance was widely supported in Japan, and good relations with the Japanese were essential to Britain's continuing strategic, commercial, and imperial interests in the Far East. Eliot believed the Japanese would not introduce their enmity toward the dominion's exclusionary immigration policies into the treaty discussions and seemed content "to accept that legislation in silence." Ultimately, he concluded, the alliance's renewal "cannot but be beneficial to our Dominions, for at least it must tend to moderate any ambitions of the Japanese in the Pacific, which would obviously be detrimental or disagreeable to their Allies."[102]

Some Japanese observers interpreted the alliance in the same way. Writing in the Japanese periodical *Diplomatic Review*, Count Soyeshima Michimasa challenged Australian suspicions of Japanese motives: "The British colonies are apt to regard Japan as a predatory Power, and Australia, more particularly, is seized with intense Japanophobia. But if Japan really entertained designs upon the British colonies, she would have seized the great opportunity offered by the Great War." From Soyeshima's point of view, the alliance exerted a restraining influence upon proponents of Japanese expansion, and in this respect "the British Colonies are the great beneficiaries under the Anglo-Japanese Treaty of Alliance."[103] The *Osaka Mainichi* similarly hoped the alliance's renewal could provide an "antidote for the Japanophobia of the Australians": "Since they are subject to this disease even while the Alliance is in existence, it can easily be imagined how violent their fits will be when the pact has come to grief."[104]

As he prepared to leave once more for London, Hughes outlined his Commonwealth's position on the Anglo-Japanese Alliance in a speech before the Australian Parliament on April 7, 1921. It was a remarkable speech that demonstrated a newfound perspicacity on Australian-Japanese relations, perhaps enlivened by the previous two years' anxiety. He told his colleagues that the Anglo-Japanese Alliance had become an essential component of the Commonwealth's defense policy. Australians had "boldly announced that we intend to retain this continent for ourselves, and we have set up the banner of a White Australia." This was a fundamental principle of Australian national life that could never be compromised. Nevertheless he finally recognized that "it can hardly be expected that the overcrowded countries of the East can see the matter from our point of view." Without British protection, therefore, White Australia would be nothing more than a figment of the imagination. Since Great Britain could not afford to extend its naval protection around the entire empire, it was imperative to remain on reasonable terms with Japan. "No man can deny," he told his colleagues, although he had vigorously denied it in the past, "that it is a thing more precious than rubies that we should have an alliance with the greatest Power in the East." Hughes intoned with characteristic melodrama, "We must steer our barque between Scylla and Charybdis."[105]

Piesse reported that Hughes's statement was favorably received in Japan.[106] The *Osaka Asahi* even accepted the Australasian premiers' proposal that renewal should codify Japan's acceptance of the White Australia Policy and the White New Zealand Policy. The Japanese newspaper disregarded the earlier racial equality amendment as "idealism": "Japanese statesmen know full well that from the standpoint of real politics, not only is the race equality proposal impossible of realisation but may even produce much evil." With this chimera dispelled, "there can ... be no reason why the British Dominions in the Pacific should feel any menace from Japan."[107]

Prime Minister Lloyd George opened the Imperial Conference in this unpredictable context on June 20, 1921. He signaled the importance of continued good relations with Japan in his opening speech. The Pacific was destined to become the center of postwar great power relations, he predicted, and it was in the interests of every nation to avoid a costly and destructive arms race in the region. Given the significance of the Pacific, Lloyd George stressed the importance of attenuating racial antagonism: "No greater calamity could overtake the world than any further accentuation of the world's divisions upon the lines of race." Such schisms were also potentially lethal to the British Empire itself: "Our foreign policy can never range itself in any sense upon the differences of race and civilization between East and West. It would be fatal to the Empire."[108] Lloyd George clearly directed his remarks to the dominion premiers and their often reckless public statements regarding Asian immigration.

After decades of Australasian complaints, it may have shocked some observers to hear Hughes and Massey defend the once-despised treaty, and yet that is precisely what they did in London. Hughes was uncommonly conciliatory toward Japan, a nation he had recklessly castigated just two years before. In his opening speech before the Imperial Conference, he admitted that Australians did not have "a clean slate" as far as the Anglo-Japanese Alliance was concerned, but in his view "the case for renewal is very strong, if not indeed overwhelming." He remained committed to appeasing the Americans and counseled that any Anglo-Japanese treaty must be revised to assuage American concerns. But he was also strongly committed to extending the alliance. He advised his fellow premiers, "Should we not be in a better position to exercise greater influence over the Eastern policy as an Ally of that great Eastern Power, than as her potential enemy?" Hughes then imparted sage advice he himself should have heeded two years earlier in Paris: "Now, if Japan is excluded from the family of great Western nations—and, mark, to turn our backs on the Treaty is certainly to exclude Japan—she will be isolated, her high national pride wounded in its most tender spot. To renew this Treaty is to impose on her some of those restraints inseparable from Treaties with other civilized nations like ourselves. We will do well for the world's peace—we will do well for China—we will do well for the Commonwealth of British nations to renew this Treaty. We want peace."[109] New Zealand's William Massey also expressed his commitment to the alliance, although he made it clear that his support for the treaty "does not in the very slightest affect the fact that in New Zealand we stand by our right to choose our future fellow-citizens."[110]

Despite the Australasian premiers' support, the British and Japanese governments ultimately allowed the alliance to lapse. Both understood that unless Americans could reconcile themselves to its continuance, the alliance would remain a barrier to improved Anglo-American and Japanese-American relations.[111] The Four-Power Treaty, which was concluded at the Washington Conference the following year, effectively supplanted Britain and Japan's twenty-year alliance and assuaged colonial concerns. The new treaty promised to restrain Japan while drawing the United States into closer cooperation with Britain and the British dominions in the Pacific.[112]

From November 1921 to February 1922 delegates from the United States, the British Empire, Japan, France, Italy, China, Belgium, Portugal, and the Netherlands convened in Washington at President Warren G. Harding's invitation to discuss the problems afflicting their respective interests in the Pacific, ranging from commercial access in China to naval disarmament.[113] British and American diplomats conspired to ensure that Asian immigration restriction remained off the agenda, despite its enduring centrality to Pacific politics. To this end in July 1921 Secretary of State Charles Evans Hughes made a "discreet inquiry" regarding the British government's objectives. Hughes envisaged a capacious conference program encompassing "all such Pacific and Far Eastern problems as are of international concern," but he explicitly stipulated that Washington would not provide a forum for the discussion of "purely domestic matters such as immigration, a point which must be frankly stated if necessary." Not surprisingly the British foreign secretary, Lord Curzon, concurred.[114]

The Japanese government's intentions remained obscure. In response to Harding's invitation, the Japanese Foreign Ministry recommended that "problems such as are of sole concern to certain particular powers or such matters that may be regarded as accomplished facts should be scrupulously avoided."[115] It was unclear from this ambiguous reply whether immigration and racial equality constituted accomplished facts from the Japanese perspective. While the Foreign Ministry dissembled, the Japanese press urged their government to mount a direct challenge to anti-Japanese restrictions, and Japan's wartime prime minister, Ōkuma Shigenobu, spoke for many when he denounced the "racial prejudice which is latent in the breast of the white race" and their "yellow peril agitations."[116] Cognizant of these visceral public sentiments, Ambassador Eliot speculated that Japan might seek redress in Washington, although he predicted that they would reserve their ire for American restrictions since, in his view, the Japanese "specially object to certain American laws which implied that Japanese are of a lower status than white races."[117]

Concerned that the Japanese might revive their campaign for racial equality, the British foreign secretary ordered a comprehensive review of Asian immigration restrictions across the British Empire and the world in preparation for the Washington conference.[118] Requests for information were sent to British officials in Africa, Asia, North America, Latin America, and Australasia in preparation for potential Japanese or Chinese complaints.[119] Frank Ashton-Gwatkin of the Foreign Ministry's Far Eastern Department assembled the resulting memorandum. He had earlier identified Asian immigration restriction as "the most difficult question" facing the British Empire in the Pacific, and his latest investigation corroborated that assessment.[120] He assiduously surveyed the extraordinary surfeit of restrictions in the British Empire, the United States, Latin America, and the French and Dutch empires, as well as restrictions imposed upon foreigners in China and Japan. After chronicling the historical trajectory and contemporary manifestations of "racial discrimination and immigration" across the world, Ashton-Gwatkin concluded that the issue's most invidious complications affected relations between the United States and the British dominions, on one hand, and Japan, China, and British India, on the other. While he recognized the question's economic and political aspects, he ultimately admitted that Asian restriction was essentially a racial question: "The white and the coloured races cannot and will not amalgamate, and countries where the white population is in power have determined from a sure instinct for self-preservation that they will never open their doors to the influx of a coloured race, which might eventually become dominant."[121]

Ashton-Gwatkin concluded that while China and India lacked the diplomatic influence to redress the opprobrium directed toward their emigrants, Japan's emergence as the "only nonwhite first-class Power" ensured its continued resistance to colonial and American racism. And yet Japan's growing strength could never elide racial discrimination's devastating and inexorable logic, since "however powerful Japan may eventually become, the white races will never be able to admit her equality." The Japanese were permanently and irredeemably "colored," and no measure of military and economic power could negate that fact. That essential inequality was destined to continually plague the white powers' relations with Japan, Ashton-Gwatkin pronounced. He predicted that the Japanese would exploit white racism if necessary; they could not erase white prejudice, but they could "ultilise it as a stalking-horse to obtain other ends." The Japanese could be expected to invoke their opposition to racial discrimination if the Western powers imposed excessive disarmament demands or sought robust economic concessions in China at Japan's expense. If Japan did raise the issue, for either diplomatic or domestic gain, it would be hard to ignore. After all, the conference was designed to address the "Pacific question," and there was simply "no subject more fundamental in the ultimate settlement of that problem." Ashton-Gwatkin concluded, "It therefore remains in Japan's power at any time to foil the Conference by this means. Whether she will use the weapon or not depends upon whether the Conference is bringing her loss or gain. Should she decide to renounce the Conference and all its works she could probably find no better rallying cry for public opinion at home, and no better propaganda for the purity of her motives abroad, than an appeal for 'racial equality.'"[122] Despite the British and American delegations' trepidation, Japan chose not to revive the thwarted racial equality proposal, nor did it challenge dominion and American restrictions upon Japanese migrants.

The politics of Asian immigration restriction in the years following the Great War pulsed with angst and resentment. The imperial and international conferences of the period had failed to make peace with Asian mobility and immobility, with the notable exception of the devious imperial reciprocity formula. Hughes's unceasing belligerence at the Paris Peace Conference had transformed the festering sore of racial inequality into an open wound, and only Japanese reticence had prevented the issue from undermining the Washington Naval Conference three years later. In the meantime the dominion governments were quietly reinforcing their restrictive immigration regimes. More ominously, an even greater challenge to Japanese racial sensitivity was emerging in the United States. That country's legislature would soon deal a crushing blow to Japanese dignity, souring Japanese-American relations for the next two decades.

CHAPTER SEVEN

Reinforcing Asian Immobility
on the Pacific Rim

Shortly after the First World War the American eugenicist Lothrop Stoddard published a lurid racial jeremiad entitled *The Rising Tide of Color against White World-Supremacy*. According to him, four years of "White Civil War" had weakened the world's imperial powers, but they now faced an even greater challenge in the wake of that tragedy. The threat came neither from hunger nor radicalism but from an impending wave of Asian migration that promised to oust whites from their position of global domination and privilege. The temporary frailty of white civilization had emboldened the world's "brown and yellow peoples," who prepared to assail the British and American empires in search of wealth and land. In Stoddard's estimation, the menace of renewed Asian mobility portended a global race struggle that would recast the international balance of power and consign white civilization to degeneration and ruin. Stoddard was nevertheless confident that this threatened torrent of Asian migration would ultimately crash upon levees of white settlement in the North American West, Australasia, and southern Africa. Those communities constituted "race frontiers" that stood between white racial purity and annihilation, as long as their vigilant inhabitants braced the fragile racial barriers that separated Asia's hordes and the certain inundation that threatened the white races globally. "Nothing is more striking," Stoddard enthused, "than the instinctive and instantaneous solidarity which binds together Australians and Afrikanders, Californians and Canadians, into a 'sacred union' at the mere whisper of Asiatic immigration."[1]

As Stoddard's invective suggests, Asian exclusion campaigns reached their apogee along the white fringes of the Pacific during the first half of the 1920s. The vicissitudes of both war and peace had intensified colonial and American resistance to Asian mobility, propelling the issue back into the center of domestic, imperial, and international politics. Domestically continued racial angst, economic dislocation, and the prospect of renewed global migration instigated a roiling surge of postwar nativism that climaxed in revived demands for Asian exclusion in New Zealand, Canada, and the United States. Internationally Japan's growing power and assertiveness rekindled the suspicions of white racial militants throughout the Pacific who dreaded the possibility of an emboldened, aggrieved, and expansive Asian adversary enforcing the free movement of its migrants. Similar concerns animated fears of South Asian migration within the British Empire's white settler colonies, despite broad agreement over the reciprocity formula concocted by imperial authorities at the end of the war. Concerned legislators therefore renovated their existing restrictions in response to this pervasive sense of alarm and in spite of the potentially damaging consequences. Once again white agitators' commitment to their racial and economic supremacy bedeviled good sense and reason, deepening the domestic, imperial, and international tensions that had accompanied their efforts since the late nineteenth century.

In this chapter I analyze this final significant outbreak of white activism against Japanese, South Asian, and Chinese mobility from 1920 to 1924, which culminated in effective Asian exclusion throughout the white communities of the Pacific. In doing so I draw the main arguments of this book back together. On one hand, Stoddard's "sacred union" remained as elusive and illusory as ever after the First World War. Despite underlying symmetries in the context and language of their concomitant debates, protestors in New Zealand, Canada, and the United States once again adopted distinct new strategies of restriction, independently from one another and under quite different circumstances. On the other hand, these campaigns illustrated the continued disdain with which white militants in the British and American Pacific regarded Asian migrants, confirming the worst assumptions of Japanese, South Asian, and Chinese observers. In fact the most significant commonality uniting these separate cases was not a sense of transnational white solidarity and cooperation but rather a more conspicuous atmosphere of imperial and international acrimony, resentment, and tension that would linger for decades to come.

The exclusionary spasms of the postwar years therefore demonstrate the distinct strategies embraced by anti-Asian militants across the Pacific and the international friction that those restrictions continued to engender. I begin by examining postwar debates over the adoption of a new system of remote Asian immigration restriction in New Zealand. While the Immigration Restriction Act remained an effective deterrent in Australia, New Zealanders discarded their literacy test in 1920 with scant regard for imperial or international sensitivities. Precipitated by fears of an impending surge of South Asian migration from the British colony of Fiji to the north, this policy promised to stanch the flow of Asian migrants before they ever embarked for Auckland or Wellington. The new bill required non-British immigrants to apply in advance from their country of residence, whereupon the colonial customs minister would determine the applicant's "suitability." A small number of legislators from across the political spectrum objected on imperial and international grounds, but it nevertheless became law in late 1920. This regulation embossed an ostensibly objective and racially neutral veneer over New Zealanders' anti-Asian sentiments until the latter half of the century. The second section of this chapter recalls Srinivasa Sastri's tour of Australasian and Canadian South Asian communities in 1922. The Indian statesman's expedition was dedicated to improving the social, economic, and political conditions of the white dominions' small South Asian diaspora, and it revealed the bitter success of colonial efforts to curtail and contain the mobility of South Asian migrants in the white dominions.

The third part of the chapter illustrates the Canadian government's very different approach toward immobilizing what remained of Asian migrant pathways in British North America in 1923. Despite the continued profligacy of British Columbian rhetoric, Canadian officials maintained their relatively diplomatic approach toward Japanese migrants while further limiting their numbers. Federal authorities bilaterally renegotiated their gentleman's agreement with the Japanese, revising downward the number of Japanese laborers permitted to enter the dominion each year. Chinese migrants received no such consideration; Canadian legislators took advantage of China's continued diplomatic weakness to almost entirely prohibit immigration from that country. Unable to act so robustly toward South Asian migrants, the federal government instead enacted new restrictions on international travel and family reunification, ensuring that Canada's dwindling South Asian diaspora could neither replenish nor sustain itself. The methods may have differed from those adopted by New Zealanders, but the outcome was the same: practical Asian exclusion in Canada by 1923.

Finally and most dramatically Japanese-American relations deteriorated in the wake of the U.S. legislature's decision to unilaterally abandon the 1908 gentleman's agreement with Japan in 1924. Members of Congress imposed an almost total prohibition on Japanese immigration and settlement by denying entry to anybody deemed "ineligible for citizenship." This legal contrivance indirectly but effectively prohibited Japanese immigration to the United States, coming in the wake of Supreme Court decisions that disqualified Asians from the rights and privileges of U.S. citizenship. Protests by the Japanese government and its aggrieved subjects—with support from Secretary of State Charles Evans Hughes—only entrenched congressional resolve, which calcified around conceptions of sovereignty and the absolute right of states to control domestic policy without interference from foreign powers or organizations. This was a dubious construction given the inherent international and transnational nature of immigration, but it succeeded in allaying American liability despite ongoing Japanese exasperation. The edifice of sovereignty would become the centerpiece of future American and colonial defenses of their exclusionary immigration regimes and the key to finally subduing—but certainly not eliminating—international and imperial tensions over Asian mobility restrictions.

Remote Restriction in New Zealand, 1920

In April 1920 New Zealand's *Auckland Star* reported that a deluge of South Asian migrants threatened to inundate the dominion. According to that newspaper's unsubstantiated reporting, some 50,000 South Asian migrants stood poised to descend upon New Zealand from the nearby British colony of Fiji. Thousands of indentured South Asians had labored on the islands' sugar plantations since the 1880s. That system had ended during the First World War, and many discharged laborers now lacked the funds to return to India. Unable to repatriate themselves, these unemployed and unwelcome migrants reportedly contemplated the relatively short journey to New Zealand. According to the *Star*, unidentified third parties were systematically training Fiji's Asian coolies to pass New Zealand's flimsy dictation test, and the dominion faced an overwhelming racial and economic crisis unless the government acted immediately to confront the threatened onslaught. "If this country has made up its mind to remain white, to avoid the terrible evils arising from mixture of races that afflict America and South Africa," the editorialist admonished, "it should take measures accordingly and act boldly."[2] The *Star* joined a chorus of veterans organizations, trade unions, and parliamentarians, all of whom urged Prime Minister William Massey's Reform Party government to tackle this impending scourge.[3]

In response Massey introduced the Immigration Restriction Amendment bill in August 1920. This new legislation abandoned the Natal formula, which had been the central feature of New Zealand's anti-Asian immigration regime since 1899, and instead effectively immobilized unwanted migrants at the source. The bill endowed the minister of customs with the power to remotely regulate Asian migration to New Zealand instead of waiting until migrants arrived at the border. It required all prospective non-British immigrants—in practical terms all nonwhite immigrants—to apply in writing from their country of residence, explaining their qualifications for settlement in New Zealand. The customs minister could summarily reject their application if he deemed the candidate "unsuitable." This ensured that all suspected non-white migrants would be denied entry to New Zealand by ministerial fiat before they even left their home. This innovation was a major departure from the colony's earlier restriction methods and further distinguished New Zealand's border control system from those of its contemporaries across the Tasman Sea and the Pacific Ocean.

The debate over remote restriction in 1920 bore a striking resemblance to the controversy instigated by Richard Seddon in 1896, when the premier had invoked an almost entirely fictional flood of Chinese migrants to justify pre-emptive prohibitions on Asian mobility in and around New Zealand. British and Japanese opposition had impaired Seddon's goal of enumerated Asian exclusion at that time, and he was forced to adopt the Natal formula. Twenty years later Massey announced that 174 South Asian immigrants had entered New Zealand in the past six months, compared to just 193 throughout all of 1919. In keeping with two decades of disingenuousness and hyperbole by his colonial and American counterparts, Massey cited this negligible increase to demonstrate that New Zealand's one million whites faced an imminent and potentially unstoppable torrent of Asian migrants unless Parliament acted quickly and decisively. The new legislation, Massey remarked on September 14, 1920, reflected "a deep-seated sentiment on the part of a huge majority of the people of this country that this Dominion shall be what is often called a 'white' New Zealand." New Zealanders did not wish to cast aspersions upon any race or nationality, the prime minister maintained; they merely sought to ensure that all prospective immigrants "shall be people of whom we shall be able to approve."[4]

Massey and his ministers knew that they risked the imperial government's opposition by discarding the Natal formula. Imperial authorities had cleaved to the literacy test since 1897, seeing in it a way to harmonize imperial and international obligations with white colonial racism and economic protectionism. Moreover the recent war had only heightened the injustice felt by the victims of colonial discrimination. India's substantial assistance to the imperial war effort had strengthened South Asians' claims to imperial citizenship while simultaneously rousing nationalist emotions throughout the Raj and beyond, while the wartime contributions of the Japanese had reinforced their Great Power status and predominance in East Asia. In order to preclude interference from London and as a tacit concession to Japan, the Massey government therefore granted the dominion's governor-general power to exempt entire "nations and races" from the provisions of the act.[5] This ploy permitted New Zealanders to reject individual Japanese immigrants without extending the stigma of explicit national exclusion to all Japanese. Prohibition of South Asian migrants presented another possible impediment to the imperial government's consent, and Massey cited the recently approved reciprocity formula to counter this concern. That resolution, he reasoned, had adorned South Asian exclusion with an imperially sanctioned fig leaf.[6]

Massey's supporters employed familiar arguments in favor of stemming this alleged revitalization of Asian labor mobility in the South Pacific. As during earlier debates, advocacy for more durable immigration controls was born of New Zealanders' proximity to existing imperial circuits of Asian migration—in this case, indentured South Asians in the Fijian plantation economy—coupled with isolation from the centers of white power and population in the northern hemisphere. As usual, proponents argued that even one successful South Asian, Chinese, or Japanese immigrant was too many, that singular presence constituting a bridgehead for the exponential chain migration of family, friends, and neighbors. This was especially dangerous given the large numbers of itinerant South Asians purportedly awaiting an opportunity to leave Fiji. The South Asian presence in that neighboring British colony especially disconcerted Edward Kellett, an independent Labour MP who had seen this menace for himself on a recent visit to the island's plantations. Based on his observations, Kellett mused that New Zealand would become an Indian colony if even modest South Asian transmigration from Fiji gained momentum. According to his wildly erroneous calculations, the progeny of America's first slaves had multiplied so potently that blacks now outnumbered whites in the United States by a ratio of three to one. Notwithstanding his flawed statistics, Kellett's claims bespoke the underlying anxiety engendered by Fiji's recently dispossessed South Asians. Their immigration to New Zealand would invariably escalate to epic proportions unless the dominion firmly closed the door against even the slightest intrusion.[7]

Similarly apocalyptic premonitions, rooted in the same long-held assumptions about New Zealand's geographic location, occupied many of Kellett's colleagues, and their remonstrations cut across party lines. Most dramatically the Liberal Party member from Invercargill, Josiah A. Hanan, foresaw a global racial conflict that would put New Zealand on the front lines of an inevitable civilizational struggle. "I believe . . . that ultimately we will have war between the coloured races and the white race," he cautioned his colleagues; New Zealanders therefore had an obligation to preserve the vitality and dynamism of the white race in preparation for that fight. Anything other than total exclusion invited racial deterioration and a migrant invasion that would render the colony an outpost of Asian colonization without the discharge of a single weapon. Richard McCallum concurred with his Liberal Party colleague's dour assessment. Sparsely populated New Zealand remained irresistibly alluring to Asian immigrants, whom he imagined clamored to escape their congested homelands. "I agree with the policy of Australia," McCallum avowed, "namely, if we can possibly do it we should keep New Zealand 'white.'" Only Asian exclusion, coupled with the promotion of British immigration, could reify that ambition. Even Apirana Ngata, speaking on behalf of the Eastern Maori District, applauded the chamber's support for Asian immigration restriction. "As a representative of the aboriginal race of New Zealand," Ngata affirmed, "I sympathize with the first immigrants to this country—the British—in the attitude they have taken up with regard to the influx of Chinese and other Asiatics." From Ngata's perspective, British civilization was morally superior to all other forms, and it was therefore preferable that British settlers colonize the "waste places of New Zealand and Australia." The British dominions had been far too diplomatic in the past; it was now time to categorically enforce exclusion.[8]

These admonitions did not prevent some representatives from questioning the tact and necessity of the proposed legislation. Their concerns highlight another enduring platitude of Australasian restriction efforts, one that remained as relevant in 1920 as it had been during the restriction campaigns of the previous century. The majority of legislators clearly understood the imperial and international problems engendered by New Zealanders' claims to white racial and economic supremacy, even as they professed their commitment to Asian exclusion. Opponents therefore challenged the government's indiscretion while still bemoaning Asian migrants' deleterious effect on white communities. It was a stubborn contradiction that thrived on the emotional potency of anti-Asian sentiment and a shrewd recognition of New Zealand's particular geographic, political, and strategic circumstances.

Independent Charles Statham could therefore encourage his colleagues to treat the subject of restriction with the "greatest delicacy," even as he lamented Asian immigrants' degrading influence on white social and economic development and advocated the strict segregation of East and West. Like almost every other critic of Massey's proposal, the Reform Party representative Alexander Malcolm remained unambiguously "anxious that we should keep this country white" but promoted a negotiated approach to exclusion. After all, thousands of South Asian troops had fought for the British Empire during the Great War, and it was offensive to disregard their sacrifice while crafting New Zealand's border control policy. George Mitchell of Wellington South likewise saw the supposed recent Asian influx as a "menace to the race," and yet the Massey government's rash and inelegant solution perturbed him as it did others. "In our dealings with other nations I think we should be very careful indeed not to hurt their feelings and sow the seed of future trouble," Mitchell warned. New Zealand was simply too small to continue offending Asia's emerging centers of power, and the dominion had "neither cause nor right to be in any way offensive to the people we are going to exclude."[9]

If these legislators stood up in support of a more diplomatic exclusion regime, a small minority actually challenged the entire artifice of Asian restriction. In the process they contested some of the greatest shibboleths of Australasian restrictionists. Most remarkably the leader of the recently formed Labour Party, Harry Holland, questioned his colleagues' reflexively racialized attitudes toward Asian migrants. In a statement that raised hackles among the White New Zealand Policy's most devoted custodians—and even within his own party—Holland proclaimed, "Biologically speaking, the same red blood of humanity flows in the veins of all of us, no matter what piece of land we happened to be born upon." The Labour leader certainly favored restrictions on the numbers of South Asian and Chinese laborers who entered the dominion, along with strict educational tests upon entrance, but he called upon members of his party to transcend their racial jealousies and forge class alliances with New Zealand's legally settled "coloured workers." If all New Zealand's South Asian laborers were unionized and paid wages equal to whites', Holland argued, they would pose no threat to the colony's living standards and the entire basis of restriction would evaporate.[10] This constituted a relatively bold, coherent, and sensible solution to New Zealand's "race problem," and it was summarily rejected by Parliament.

Holland's Labour colleague from Auckland, Michael J. Savage, challenged another enduring Australasian cliché in support of legislative prudence. New Zealanders were living "practically within a stone's throw of teeming millions," Savage reminded his colleagues, yet both they and their Australian compatriots harbored countless acres of deserted and undeveloped land. For decades this rhetorical device had been used to justify exclusion, lest Asia's multitudes establish a foothold in Australasia's empty spaces. Now Savage was arguing that Great Britain's South Pacific outposts could no longer ignore the potential international implications of their covetousness. It was a dangerous and untenable conceit that was increasingly difficult to sustain, especially in light of the widely held assumption that overcrowding impelled Asian labor migration.[11]

William Downie Stewart of Massey's Reform Party confronted yet another long-standing pillar of the White New Zealand Policy. Since the new
legislation granted the government almost unlimited power to exclude undesirable immigrants, was it then necessary to retain the existing and offensive
poll tax on Chinese immigrants, "an enactment which is regarded as inhu-
man and an insult to a great nation"? As he observed, "China is a country of
four hundred million people on the borders of the Pacific, and one with
which we cannot afford to quarrel needlessly." If the new proposal erected an
unassailable barrier against Chinese immigration, as its proponents claimed,
then perhaps it behooved New Zealanders to eliminate this reprehensible affront. "I am as strongly in favour of a 'white New Zealand' policy as is anybody
in the House," Downie Stewart insisted, "but I want to give effect to it without
needlessly offending the representatives of a great power."[12] His colleagues
disagreed, and the poll tax persevered as an added layer of discrimination
against prospective Chinese immigrants until the Second World War.

Despite these lucid critiques, advocates of stricter controls prevailed. Anti-
Asian sentiment was apparently so strong in the dominion that Governor-
General John Jellicoe did not even consider withholding the act pending the
imperial government's assent. New Zealanders considered the bill to be a vital and urgent measure, he told the secretary of state for the colonies, Lord
Milner, and postponement would merely create a "feeling of soreness" between the dominion and imperial governments. "The [New Zealand] Government has been careful to avoid any distinction between the different
nations or coloured races," Jellicoe assured Milner, so there was no cause for
alarm.[13] British authorities in India were not so easily convinced and expressed
their aversion to the new act in May 1921.[14] New Zealand's attorney general,
Sir Francis Bell, deflected their concerns, asserting, "The Government of
India is not fully cognisant of the anxiety felt by the Commonwealth of Australia and the Dominion of New Zealand at this juncture." The new
legislation was not explicitly directed against South Asians: "It was directed
against the colonization of our territories by persons of Asiatic race of whatever country." The government merely wished to preserve New Zealand for
"men and women of British extraction." The Indian and imperial governments ultimately relented. New Zealand would continue to allow temporary visits by South Asians, and students would be permitted to enter the
dominion for educational purposes, but any further permanent settlement
was forbidden.[15] The rationale of "unsuitability" and the strategy of remote
exclusion remained the foundation of New Zealand's stringent border controls until the 1970s.

V. S. Srinivasa Sastri's British Dominion Tour, 1922

New Zealand's brazen rejoinder to the Indian government confirmed a new reality in British imperial politics: the fiction of reciprocity had replaced the Natal formula as London's preferred answer to racial prejudice against South Asians in the dominions. Having finally acquiesced to South Asian restriction, the Indian and imperial governments now turned their attention to securing equal treatment for those relatively small numbers of South Asian immigrants already legally domiciled in the empire's white dominions, a policy affirmed by colonial representatives (with the exception of South Africa) at the 1921 Imperial Conference in London.[16] To this end, and at the dominion premier's invitation, the respected Indian statesman and educator V. S. Srinivasa Sastri embarked on a tour of Australia, New Zealand, and Canada in the summer of 1922.[17] His task was neither to contest nor to depose restrictions on South Asian migration to those British territories. Instead Sastri's remit authorized him to investigate the political, economic, and social inequities suffered by legitimate South Asian residents. His final report reveals the success of colonial restrictions on South Asian migration and mobility, and illuminates the suffocating effect of those controls on the size, growth, and development of colonial South Asian communities.

Sastri arrived in Australia on June 1, 1922. He quickly discovered that the Commonwealth's small South Asian community—which numbered between 2,000 and 3,000 people—enjoyed limited social and economic rights, but their public lives were deeply circumscribed by widespread political and economic disenfranchisement. Some state governments barred all Asians from owning land reclaimed and irrigated under the state's aegis, while others precluded South Asian employment in specific industries and agricultural pursuits. The Commonwealth government also denied South Asian residents access to federal pensions. Sastri was struck by the sanctity with which an overwhelming number of Australians held the White Australia Policy, and he encountered particular hostility from labor unions and political organizations who were convinced that his visit foreshadowed an effort to force a resumption of South Asian migration. Despite securing no immediate reforms, Sastri did obtain pledges from state and Commonwealth authorities, who promised to reduce the burdens borne by Australia's South Asian residents. He then sailed for New Zealand to investigate conditions facing that dominion's approximately 600 South Asian residents. Unlike their counterparts in Australia, New Zealand's South Asian community enjoyed full suffrage. As in Australia, however, they were disqualified from the dominion's pension system and faced numerous barriers to employment. Despite these institutionalized obstacles, Sastri ascribed widespread South Asian unemployment to their comparatively recent arrival in New Zealand. Since the dominion's South Asian population remained relatively small—and since the recent Immigration Restriction Amendment Act had effectively curtailed future growth—Sastri found little to criticize. After all, he glibly observed, the dominion's rigid new restrictions ensured that New Zealand's South Asian community would naturally dwindle into obscurity in the coming years.[18]

On July 25 Sastri departed for British Columbia, where the vast majority of Canada's South Asian residents lived. He once again found a community in decline, their numbers decreasing precipitously from over 6,000 in 1914 to 1,200 by 1922. Most of the province's South Asian residents had either surreptitiously entered the United States or returned to India after the war. Those who remained, Sastri discovered, worked either in the British Columbian lumber mills or in agriculture. He focused his efforts on securing the franchise for them. While the federal government did not explicitly withhold voting rights on the basis of race, it disallowed those not legally entitled to vote in their province of residence. Since most lived in British Columbia, this provision virtually excluded the entire dominion's South Asian population from the national franchise. Although many provincial governments instituted exemptions for those who had served in the Canadian armed forces during the war, British Columbian legislators made no such concession. Based upon his interviews with provincial and federal officials, Sastri expected they would soon rectify this injustice. The remaining grievances derived from the Canadian government's refusal to admit the children and relatives of current South Asian residents to the dominion.[19]

Sastri concluded that his tour was a success. Although he achieved minimal tangible advances, he believed his visit had edified the white populations of Australia, New Zealand, and Canada. "The average citizen of a Dominion still regards India as a land of mixed poverty and splendor," he observed, "barbaric in outlook and aspiration as well as in magnificence." He hoped that his visit had corrected this flawed perception. In reality he had explored a South Asian diaspora totaling fewer than 4,000 across the three Pacific dominions. Those communities were dwindling due to old age, the trickle of returnees, the small number of female immigrants, and the practical exclusion of future immigration. But he remained sanguine that "personal intercourse" was the "best solvent of prejudice."[20] From the perspective of many white colonists, however, even this small number of South Asian immigrants represented the thin end of a much larger wedge. Faced with what they saw as a potentially immense tide, the dominion leaders continued to believe that exclusion and repatriation was the best solvent for prejudice.

Reinforcing Canadian Restrictions, 1923

Despite Sastri's optimism, the postwar period saw the revival of anti-Asian sentiments in Canada, just as it had in New Zealand. While New Zealanders strove to extinguish potential new circuits of South Asian labor migration in Fiji, Canadians worked to prevent the dominion's existing Asian immigrant communities from propagating new networks of migration. From the perspective of white activists and legislators, requests by resident immigrants for new family reunification provisions, stable residency privileges, and expanded travel rights were a devious attempt to circumvent the dominion's exclusion laws. Canadian legislators also acted to prevent the fraudulent exploitation of existing exemptions for merchants, tourists, and students. Each successful Asian immigrant—legal or otherwise—represented a potential new node of mobility for relatives and friends, and these loopholes only encouraged further deception. Faced with these purported challenges, Canadian authorities tightened their anti-Asian border controls in 1923 and consigned existing Chinese, Japanese, and South Asian communities to retrenchment and isolation.

As usual, British Columbian activists inflamed long-standing racial and economic passions. White workers, retailers, trade unions, veterans organizations, newspapers, and local political leaders continued to bellow—with little justification—that untrammeled Asian mobility, aggressive economic diversification, and fraudulent immigrants threatened the province. They once more pressed their grievances upon federal authorities in Ottawa, demanding immediate action.[21] Since the late nineteenth century British Columbian campaigners had maintained that federal ministers ignored their fulminations because Asian migrants rarely traveled east beyond the Rockies. Simon Fraser Tolmie of Victoria complained during the 1923 debate, "One of our principal troubles in the past has been I think the inability of the people east of the Rocky mountains to grasp the Asiatic situation in its full significance."[22] But anti-Asian anxiety in Canada's central and eastern provinces had swollen with every Chinese and Japanese immigrant that traversed the interior in search of opportunity during the war, and British Columbian entreaties now reached a receptive audience.[23]

On July 1, 1923, the Canadian Parliament passed a new Chinese Immigration Act. The government repealed the despised poll tax but imposed draconian new limitations that made further Chinese immigration practically impossible. Under the new regulations only visiting Chinese diplomats, students, and businessmen with $2,500 in Canadian investments were allowed to enter the dominion. Children born in Canada to one or more Chinese parents were permitted entrance, although no provisions were made for family reunification.[24] Even this meager gesture met resistance. New Brunswick's John B. Baxter opposed allowing children of mixed Chinese and European descent entry into Canada. "Do we want half any more than we want full-bloodied Chinese?" Baxter inquired. "If whites choose to let down the racial standard to that extent, should not they keep their progeny in the East instead of bringing them in here?"[25]

As in New Zealand, nobody doubted the necessity of stronger legislation; debate in the parliamentary committee responsible for crafting these new restrictions instead centered on erecting the most robust barriers against future Chinese immigration while mitigating their harmful effect on Canadian imperial and international relations. The recently elected prime minister, William Lyon Mackenzie King, was well versed in the international complications engendered by the White Canada Policy, having been immersed in the issue since the battles of 1907–8. He firmly opposed further Chinese immigration, but he urged his colleagues to balance their entrenched racial and economic resentments with Canada's broader responsibilities. He warned the committee on April 30, 1923, "If . . . we lose sight of the international aspect and use expressions—either unguardedly or for other reasons—which are certain to be repugnant to peoples of another part of the world, I am afraid that instead of helping to relieve a very serious situation we shall only be creating . . . a situation which will be infinitely worse." King hoped that abrogation of the poll tax, with exceptions for students and merchants, would soothe Chinese resentment, thus allowing Canadians to maintain their lucrative trade links while implementing more effective legislative measures against permanent Chinese immigration.[26]

Despite the prime minister's appeal for restraint, the committee's British Columbian members remained unapologetic in their support for stricter anti-Chinese controls, and in fact urged their extension to all Asian immigrants. Tolmie maintained that his province's representatives were devoted to preserving Canada's international relations, but not "at the expense of giving up our country to the Asiatics." The Chinese were devious and conniving foes and had manipulated every available exception for decades. The time had come for Ottawa to implement complete and utter exclusion. John A. MacKelvie too believed that Parliament should stop all "oriental" immigration, even if Canadian commercial and diplomatic relations with Asia suffered. He questioned the efficacy of exemptions, declaring, "The wily oriental has found some means or subterfuge to circumvent any regulations that may have been imposed upon him." If they allowed even a modest number of Asian immigrants to enter Canada, he sarcastically suggested, then "in a very short time indeed there will be very few white people in British Columbia with whom any oriental can carry on trade." In his view King's preoccupation with the legislation's possible international repercussions was nothing more than a chimera, since every country had an internationally recognized right to control immigration. Caribou's George McBride concurred, declaring that Asian migrants were intent upon colonizing the entire Pacific coast of North America. The whole region would be lost unless the government permanently terminated all Asian immigration. In his estimation all of British Columbia's Chinese, Japanese, and South Asian residents should either be paid to return to Asia or be officially segregated from white society. "If the good Lord had intended orientals and white people to live in the same country," McBride quipped, "he would not have put the Pacific ocean between them."[27]

Only Winnipeg's James Shaver Woodsworth openly opposed the march toward total Asian exclusion. An ordained Methodist minister and prominent social progressive, Woodsworth derided his British Columbian colleagues' animosity toward Asian immigration and encouraged them to temper their prejudices. Invoking Stoddard's recently coined refrain, Woodsworth accepted that Canadians faced "a rising tide of colour," yet he challenged the exclusionary impulse that animated his colleagues' response to that deluge. It was, he argued, "a dangerous proceeding for a comparatively small portion of the human race to attempt by physical force to beat back the great masses of the coloured and darker people of the world."[28] Not surprisingly his fellow members ignored his pleas, and Parliament passed the legislation soon after. According to one estimate, between the statute's enactment on July 1, 1923, and its eventual repeal in 1946, only twenty-five Chinese were actually allowed into Canada. Henceforth July 1 became known as Humiliation Day among Chinese Canadians.[29]

As the committee debated the appropriate scope of Chinese exclusion—and threatened to expand its purview to all prospective Asian immigrants—the Canadian government endeavored to further restrict Japanese immigration by diplomatic means. Since late 1907 the Hayashi-Lemieux Agreement had curtailed Japanese immigration to Canada. This device had operated smoothly since its inception, but popular resentment of even severely limited

Japanese immigration grew, especially in British Columbia. Recent injudicious calls in Parliament for a Japanese Exclusion Act prompted renewed negotiations between Tokyo and Ottawa. Eager to avoid unilateral and explicit prohibitions on Japanese immigrants, the Canadian government sought a downward revision of Japan's annual quota of 400 laborers. Similarly the Japanese government remained committed to precluding overt legislative exclusion in the British dominions. Once again, then, Canada and Japan amicably negotiated the restriction of Japanese immigration.[30] In August 1923 Japan announced its intention to limit emigration to just 150 agricultural laborers and domestic servants per year.[31]

The continuous journey provision remained an effective barrier to large-scale South Asian transpacific migration, but this regulation also made it difficult for legitimate residents to leave and return to Canada. Since 1920 the Canadian government had required all naturalized South Asians to register upon leaving the dominion; those who did not lost their right to domicile and were unable to return. Shipping companies plying the Pacific route between Hong Kong and Vancouver regularly refused to carry South Asian passengers bound for Canada, even if they possessed residency rights. In addition to denying reentry to legal South Asian residents, Canadian regulations made it difficult for wives and children to join their husbands and fathers.[32] To rectify these injustices the Indian and Canadian governments collaborated to create a more effective passport system for naturalized South Asians. The new regulations were supposed to facilitate the reunification of families and ensure that all of Canada's South Asian residents could leave the dominion for extended periods and still retain their residency.[33] In practice, however, Canada's South Asian community remained small (just over 1,000 in 1921), overwhelmingly male (approximately forty female immigrants in 1921), and subject to arbitrary discrimination and prejudice.[34]

Japanese Exclusion in the United States, 1924

The U.S. Congress instituted Japanese exclusion in May 1924, despite the continued efficacy of the 1908 gentleman's agreement and despite objections from Japan. This last major convulsion against Asian mobility was also the most diplomatically disruptive. Characteristic of previous restraints on Japanese migration, American legislators concealed their intent, relying upon the unique judicial innovation of "aliens ineligible for citizenship" in lieu of explicit enumerated exclusion. When faced with remonstrations from both the Japanese legation in Washington and their own State Department, legislators buttressed this inventive legal device with seemingly incontestable appeals to the sovereign right of independent states to determine domestic policy without outside interference. These innovations culminated more than two decades of colonial and American agitation against Asian mobility and triggered a final diplomatic dispute that tainted Japanese-American relations until after the Second World War.

Even as New Zealanders and Canadians imposed new restrictions on Asian mobility, they had nevertheless heeded the Japanese government's resentment toward explicit and unilateral legislative exclusion. Japanese authorities had unfailingly resisted overt restrictions on their migrants ever since the first expressions of antagonism emerged throughout the white periphery of the Pacific in the late nineteenth century. Successive Japanese governments had instead exhorted their colonial and American antagonists to accept bilaterally negotiated restrictions. The gentleman's agreement between Japan and the United States (and its Canadian analogue, the Hayashi-Lemieux Agreement) exemplified this abiding tenet of Japanese diplomacy. For fifteen years this delicate compromise had insulated Japanese-American relations against the defamatory polemics of racial activists in the western United States. This measure never entirely assuaged the embarrassment engendered by white racial attitudes or the Japanese government's determination to contest prejudice against its people, but it veiled the most painful consequences of white discrimination in the American West.

That façade finally collapsed under the weight of American nativism in 1924. The demand for stringent new restrictions sprouted during the war and flourished in a postwar climate of eugenics, economic recession, and antiradicalism. Even Americans' comparatively tolerant attitude toward European immigration wilted under the intensity of fear and antipathy during those challenging years. Restrictions tightened as the war raged in Europe. Congress imposed a literacy test on all potential immigrants in 1917 over President Wilson's veto. Legislators also extended an unprecedented "barred zone" around much of Asia that same year, thus prohibiting all Asian immigration to the United States with the exception of Filipinos and Japanese. The growing U.S. restriction regime distended further in 1921 when Congress enacted the Emergency Quota Act. Since southern and eastern Europeans now appeared to many Americans to be morally, politically, culturally, and even racially suspect material for citizenship, this measure severely limited all European immigration based on quotas derived from the 1910 census.[35] The U.S. Supreme Court further delimited the boundaries of citizenship in 1922, ruling in *Ozawa v. U.S.* that a Japanese immigrant and long-term resident, Takao Ozawa, was ineligible for citizenship under the Naturalization Act of 1906. He was neither white nor of African ancestry; therefore the Court pronounced him disqualified from U.S. citizenship.[36]

Like the British Empire's Natal formula, this concept of "aliens ineligible for citizenship" allowed Congress to obliquely prohibit Japanese immigration while avoiding the diplomatic indiscretion of explicit exclusion. The House Committee on Immigration grasped that opportunity in 1924. Emboldened by the *Ozawa* decision and convinced that the gentleman's agreement was nothing more than an illusion foisted upon the American people by an imperious president with State Department collusion, the committee summarily annulled that sixteen-year-old truce between Japanese prestige and American xenophobia. Representative John C. Box reported to his fellow members, "I doubt whether the Gentlemen's agreement made by President Roosevelt . . . has any force or has ever had any force that America ought to recognize. To say that the President can by some secret understanding hidden in his bosom or by some written memorandum hidden in the archives of the Department of State, never submitted to the Senate, establish a law, a supreme law of the land, binding on the legislatures of States, binding on this body and the whole country, would be most extraordinary."[37]

The committee concluded that the gentleman's agreement had simply failed to exclude Japanese immigrants, which meant that "in certain portions of the Pacific coast the white race confronts the very conditions foreseen by Roosevelt." The committee determined, "It would appear from these facts that the United States has been grossly lax in permitting the increase in her territory of an unassimilable population ineligible for citizenship, and that she has deferred too long the adoption of remedial measures."[38] Awash in testimony that decried Japanese duplicity, economic rapacity, and racial inassimilability, the committee members included the "aliens ineligible for citizenship" clause in their immigration restriction bill, thereby enacting Japanese exclusion by deception. From the perspective of congressional restrictionists, at least, they had not violated the delicate compromise inherent in the mysterious gentleman's agreement since there was no mention of Japan in the final act.

Japanese officials contested this thinly veiled ruse. Though shrouded in legal obfuscation, the new law's intent was obvious, recorded in hours of congressional testimony and reams of press commentary. The Japanese ambassador in Washington, Hanihara Masanao, lodged a formal protest before the committee even published its final report. He complained to Secretary of State Hughes that the impending adoption of the "aliens ineligible for citizenship" clause unilaterally repudiated the gentleman's agreement and contravened the 1911 Japanese-American Commercial Treaty. This constituted "an arbitrary and unjust discrimination reflecting upon the character of the people of a nation, which is entitled to every respect and consideration of the civilized world." His government recognized the right of Congress to regulate immigration, but this domestic entitlement had foreign policy implications. American legislators had raised a fundamental question of global import: "whether Japan as a nation is or is not entitled to the proper respect and consideration of other nations."[39] Once more, as so often in the past, a Japanese ambassador was compelled to justify the quality and character of his people in the national capital of an ostensible friend.

Hughes and the State Department immediately strove to mitigate congressional insensitivity. In a letter to Representative Albert Johnson, Hughes gently chided the committee's disregard for Japanese-American relations and criticized its disregard for the likely reaction in Japan. Despite the committee's assessment, the gentleman's agreement had successfully inhibited Japanese labor mobility to the United States for the past sixteen years. More important, Hughes insisted, it had balanced Japanese dignity against the exclusionary impulses of white agitators. The committee's arbitrary dismissal of that arrangement would undermine decades of diplomacy and violate American treaty obligations. The Japanese government sought no special treatment for their emigrants: Why not simply apportion Japan the same quota as every other nation?[40]

Hughes's reasoned and constructive letter initially promised to restrain this discriminatory approach to Japanese exclusion. The Senate appeared especially amenable to Hughes's testimony, even as House members remained unmoved.[41] The *New York Times* reported positively on the secretary of state's rational retort, calling for a "fair basis for limitation" that would avoid "unnecessary affront to the Japanese."[42] Johnson received letters from the general public applauding Hughes's tact and encouraging the House Committee on Immigration to temper their injudicious approach. "There are fair ways of protecting our interests other than going out of our way to hit the Japanese in the face," wrote one correspondent. David Starr Jordan, the former president of Stanford University, sent Johnson a point-by-point refutation of the case for Japanese exclusion, lamenting the committee's disregard for the issue's foreign policy implications. "The international interests of the United States cannot be safely left at the mercy of [a] haphazard local referendum," he wrote. "One can hardly imagine a more reckless way of dealing with international affairs." Other letter writers were less circumspect. Franklin

Arnold of Hoquiam, Washington, like many others, bemoaned Hughes's opposition to exclusion: "Secretary Hughes has not lived on this coast, therefore his opinion is worthless. He naturally wishes to avoid a conflict with Japan, but ask him whose country this is!"[43]

Hughes and Hanihara then committed an unwitting and ultimately calamitous blunder in their attempt to balance domestic demands for restriction with the foreign relations imperatives of mollifying an increasingly aggrieved and disappointed Japanese government and populace. Things began innocuously enough. Hughes met with the Japanese ambassador in March 1924, shortly after Johnson's committee published its final report. Hanihara remained conciliatory despite the committee's discouraging and disparaging statements, telling Hughes that he would refrain from issuing a formal protest unless the bill actually became law. The secretary of state then suggested that the committee's misunderstanding of the gentleman's agreement was the main impediment to a satisfactory resolution of this emerging rift between their two countries. Partly out of respect for Japan, the agreement had never been published, but the settlement's apparent secrecy had allowed opponents of Japanese immigration to question its efficacy and even its existence.[44] Hughes therefore proposed that if they together publicized and demystified the substance of the agreement, they might succeed in assuaging public and congressional anxiety.[45]

Hanihara agreed, and the following month he composed a thirteen-page letter to Representative Johnson and his Senate counterpart, LeBaron B. Colt, outlining the history and content of the agreement. Hanihara dutifully described its provisions, stressing the Japanese government's faithful commitment to its terms and even suggesting its willingness to revise the arrangement if necessary. The ambassador then reiterated that congressional avoidance of an overt injunction against Japanese immigration did not fool his government. After all, the Japanese remained the only Asians "ineligible for citizenship" who were not already explicitly barred by other legislation. In this context any legislation designed to exclude all Japanese immigrants from the United States outside the bounds of the gentleman's agreement would be "mortifying" to his compatriots.[46]

Notwithstanding the measured tone of Hanihara's communiqué, proponents of Japanese exclusion fixated on the final paragraph of the letter. It was there that Hanihara reflected upon the "grave consequences which the enactment of the measure retaining that particular provision would inevitably bring upon the otherwise happy and mutually advantageous relations between our two countries."[47] Hostile elements in the press and Congress seized upon Hanihara's invocation of "grave consequences." The ensuing out-cry revitalized anti-Asian forces in the House and Senate. In the minds of even some fair-minded observers, Hanihara seemed to have resorted to in-timidation. Hughes saw nothing of the sort. As he told the American ambas-sador in Japan, this was nothing more than an "innocuous expression of regret that would be felt in the event of any impairment of the happy rela-tions between the two countries."[48]

Senate support for the gentleman's agreement suddenly evaporated, espe-cially after Henry Cabot Lodge denounced Hanihara's "veiled threat." Senti-ment quickly veered from diplomatic sensitivity toward Japanese dignity to outrage and indignation. The Senate sponsor of the bill, David Reed, re-marked, "The letter of the Japanese Ambassador puts the unpleasant burden upon us of deciding whether we will permit our legislation to be controlled by apprehensions of 'grave consequences' with other nations if we do not follow a particular line of legislative conduct." This threat to American sovereignty represented an intolerable intrusion into the American legisla-tive process by Japan, something no member of Congress could endure. Despite being the bill's cosponsor and initially supporting Hughes's call for restraint, Reed switched his vote.[49] The Senate Immigration Committee's bill, which provided for the continued operation of the gentleman's agree-ment, was subsequently crushed by a vote of 76–2.

This outcome shocked Hanihara and Hughes. The two men quickly ar-ranged for Hanihara to clarify his comments. Read in context, the ambassa-dor noted, it was difficult to comprehend the Senate's outrage: "I simply tried to emphasize the most unfortunate and deplorable effect upon our traditional friendship which might result from the adoption of a particular clause in the proposed measure."[50] But it was too late to rescue Hughes's compromise in Congress. Thereafter, as Hanihara and Hughes tried to salvage Japanese-American relations, momentum shifted to Johnson's tactless House bill. Sen-ate exclusionists revived an earlier amendment offered by the junior senator from California, Samuel M. Shortridge. The Shortridge amendment incor-porated the House's "ineligible for citizenship" formula into the final Senate immigration bill, which passed the chamber on April 15, 1924.[51]

When news of the Senate's rancorous response to Hanihara's supposed threat reached Tokyo, Minister of Foreign Affairs Matsui Keishirō tried to control the damage, expressing the Japanese government's sincere alarm and regret over the Senate's interpretation of Hanihara's remarks. The recent fu-ror was nothing more than a misunderstanding, Matsui insisted. Hanihara had simply failed to comprehend the possible negative connotations inherent in his allusion to "grave consequences." He assured the American ambassador in Tokyo, Cyrus Woods, that Japan would never presume to interfere in the American legislative process and that his government harbored no retaliatory intentions even if Congress chose to pursue explicit exclusion.[52] Matsui repeated the same sentiments to the British ambassador in Japan, Charles Eliot, who reported that the foreign minister was "grave and despondent" and appeared to have "lost his confidence in the friendship of the United States . . . and did not feel sure that they would respect the dignity of Japan." More ominously, Eliot informed London, the Japanese foreign minister suspected that some senators were willing to sacrifice Japanese-American comity for electoral gain.[53]

Woods reported growing resentment in the Japanese press as this saga unfolded in Washington. One usually moderate Japanese newspaper intoned, "No nation retaining the least trace of its self-respect could tolerate the discrimination aimed at by the Johnson Bill. [It] strikes at the very foundation of American-Japanese friendship." The news from Washington had even temporarily displaced the acrimonious general election then under way in Japan. It was becoming clear, Woods warned Hughes, that "the Japanese have felt the blow to their pride even more keenly than was expected and their sullen resentment will be hard to overcome." One member of the American Embassy staff in Tokyo found a leaflet in his car after visiting the Japanese Foreign Office, purportedly left by the "Japanese Strenuous Efforts Society." The leaflet, entitled "Awake! Japanese Nation!," called for the Japanese people to rise up in opposition to America's "arbitrary" actions and to "punish the hypocritic and cruel America." On April 18 Woods reported an atmosphere approaching "national crisis" in Japan.[54] He feared that the situation would deteriorate if President Coolidge signed the immigration bill into law, especially in the context of Japan's looming general election: "It would be entirely erroneous to assume that Japan is already resigned to the situation or to underestimate the bitterness of the feeling of her resentment."[55] At that very moment, for example, the Nagoya Association for Conducting Agitation for People's Diplomacy against the United States had passed a resolution denouncing America's hypocritical claims to be the bastion of liberty and equality. Americans, the Association asserted, demanded access to Asian markets while denying immigration rights to Asian citizens. While preaching equality, Americans subjected their own black population to "abominable" treatment. It was left to the Japanese people "to dispel the prejudices of the white people and to establish the spirit of true humanity."[56]

The apprehensions engendered by this congressional rebuke were not confined to Japan. The American ambassador to China, Jacob Gould Schurman, also expressed concern. He believed this insult to the Japanese threatened to destabilize the balance of power in East Asia. "The gravest consequences will follow in China and the Orient," Schurman warned, if Japan was left "sullen and resentful" by American actions. Japanese antipathy toward the United States would inevitably threaten the "open door" policy in China, disrupt American trade, and provide sustenance to anti-Western impulses throughout Asia.[57] Chinese newspapers were also expressing hostility toward Americans' anti-Asian attitudes. On April 29, for example, the Harbin *Dawning* observed the "malignity existing between the white and the yellow race." The epicenter of white animosity had now shifted to the United States, the *Dawning* suggested. After the late war's intraracial bloodletting, it was clear that the "strength of the white race remains intact in the American people." In the event of a global race war, "the malignity harbored by the American people toward the yellow race is the more pernicious and far reaching."[58] It was clear to Schurman that American immigration policy had global implications far beyond the West Coast, Washington, D.C., and even Tokyo.

Schurman was correct. The South American press also expressed unease about the U.S. decision to exclude Japanese immigrants. Their fears were not based on the possibility of Japanese-American conflict; rather South American editors expressed concern that their own republics might become an alternative destination for Japanese immigration. Indeed U.S. officials in Peru were reporting a growing campaign in the Brazilian press to force similar measures in that country. According to the Peruvian newspaper *El Tiempo*, the Brazilian press feared that Japanese immigration would be diverted to Latin America now that the United States was closed to them: "Is it convenient for the Latin American nations to count in their midst a large nucleus of Japanese? We do not think so." The U.S. ambassador in Uruguay reported similar sentiments in that country's *El Pais* newspaper.[59] Colombia's *El Nuevo Tiempo* foresaw a potentially analogous situation: "Asiatic immigration is not appropriate from any aspect for the republics of the New World, and it is essential that all of them follow the example of the senators in Washington for this guarding of their ports."[60]

Not surprisingly the British government closely monitored the deteriorating situation between the United States and Japan. Reflecting upon the Senate's inappropriately passionate response to Hanihara's letter, the British ambassador in Washington, Sir Esme Howard, could barely conceal his contempt: "Their indignation knew no bounds, moderation gave way to extreme jingoism, and it was decided that here was a Heaven-sent opportunity to administer a stinging rebuke to a Government which had dared to raise its voice against the possible enactment of a measure under consideration by the elected representatives of the American people." Howard nevertheless expressed amazement that Hughes had not foreseen the Senate's violent reaction to Hanihara's reference to "grave consequences." From the British ambassador's perspective, the entire incident was indicative of the "wholly irresponsible attitude of Congress towards international affairs and their utter contempt for the susceptibilities of other nations." This was a dangerous tendency, Howard observed, especially since 1924 was an election year in the United States. In his estimation, however, it was "merely one of those occasional squalls for which any foreign representative in this country must be prepared."[61]

More ominously the British ambassador in Japan reported a troubling conversation with the Japanese foreign minister on May 16, 1924. Matsui intimated his expectation that the British dominions would not emulate the United States by unilaterally excluding Japanese immigration. He informed Eliot that the Japanese government had never objected to negotiated restrictions on Japanese immigration. Japanese objections derived from the American decision to legislate independently against Japanese immigration. Eliot told his foreign secretary, Ramsay MacDonald, "I am sure that if any British colony acts in the way [Matsui] described as offensive to Japan it will be a severe blow to Anglo-Japanese friendship."[62] Eliot reiterated this concern the following month and predicted that Japan would seek anti-European and anti-American alliances with other Asian states and colonies "if the white races persist in their antipathy to Asiatics." This would be especially likely if Canadians and Australians chose to imitate the Americans.[63] In response to Eliot's repeated entreaties, the imperial government shared this warning with the dominions on June 9, 1924.[64]

As one Foreign Office official observed, Japanese concern regarding the dominions probably derived in part from the former Australian prime minister's recent activities.[65] In February 1924 William Morris Hughes embarked on an American lecture tour. That still vigorous defender of White Australia was therefore preaching his gospel of Asian exclusion throughout the American debates over immigration restriction. As he told one audience, Americans were right to finally and firmly restrict immigration in general and Japanese immigration in particular. Australians had done the same at their Commonwealth's inception because "those whom we exclude cannot merge into the body of Australian society" largely because their "economic, social, racial ideals and standards are entirely different."[66] The United States and Australia therefore shared a common goal. He declared during another American speech, "We feel that in the American people we have friends who understand our aspirations, who out of the fund of their own experience subscribe to them, and will if necessary lend support to them. . . . It is better that the problem of a crowded Japan should remain temporarily unsettled, or find solution in some other way, than we should discard those basic principles of freedom upon which America was founded, and Australia has developed." Hughes remained convinced that Australians faced an incomparable threat from "colored" immigration. After all, he insisted, "Australia is within a few days' sail of over a thousand millions of Asiatics. Total exclusion is the only remedy." Nevertheless, he warned, Americans could not rest on the laurels of the Johnson-Reed Act. The Japanese were already beginning to colonize South America, and Americans needed to act preemptively lest the western hemisphere face an overwhelming influx. Hughes asked his American audience, "To what extent is or can such immigration be compatible with the Monroe doctrine?" In case he had not sufficiently conveyed his point, he concluded, "If Western civilization is a thing as precious as we deem it to be then it is not to the interests of mankind that Australia the farthest outpost of White civilization, [nor] America its chief citadel, should be submerged in a yellow sea."[67] The former premier's speeches were widely reported in the United States, and they were especially favorably received on the West Coast.

As the ramifications of congressional pique reverberated around the world, Charles Evans Hughes made one final attempt to forestall Japanese exclusion, writing directly to President Coolidge on April 25, 1924. Neither Japan nor the State Department wished to interfere with the right of Congress to control immigration, he told the president; in fact both parties accepted the need to limit Japanese settlement. But unilateral legislative exclusion promised only to embitter Japanese-American relations. It would destroy the delicate diplomatic accord engendered by the gentleman's agreement, encourage illegal Japanese immigration, and unnecessarily offend the Japanese people. Congress had apparently ignored the last consideration, approaching the immigration question "as though it were simply a matter of dealing with Orientals." This was a dangerous assumption, Hughes told Coolidge, since Japan had emerged from the Great War as a first-rate power. Indeed the United States had recognized Japan's elevated stature at the recent Washington Naval Conference. Ultimately American strategic, commercial, and diplomatic interests depended upon continued cooperation with Japan. "The danger to our interests in destroying this good will and creating in its place racial resentment of a powerful nation," Hughes insisted, "is obvious."[68]

Despite protests from the State Department and the Japanese government, both houses of Congress passed the Immigration Act on May 15, 1924. As the bill awaited Coolidge's signature, Hughes scrambled to assuage the Japanese government's inevitable exasperation. Summoning Hanihara to the State Department on May 23, Hughes insisted the act derived solely from Congress's conviction that the country's immigration policy must be codified by legislative action, not by international treaties or agreements administered solely and clandestinely by the president. It did not reflect American enmity toward Japan, he assured Hanihara. Even as the secretary strove to soothe Japanese irritation, however, he was forced to inform the ambassador that Coolidge had no choice but to sign the legislation. Congressional sentiment was so strong that members would almost certainly override the president's veto, Hughes explained, which would inevitably trigger an even more hostile debate. Moreover the 1921 Emergency Quota Act was due to expire on June 30. If Coolidge stalled the enactment of new legislation, it would wreak havoc upon the country's immigration system.[69]

According to Hanihara, the Japanese Foreign Ministry would likely understand the president's predicament, but the Japanese people would feel the "keenest disappointment," which he feared might ultimately manifest in violence and disorder.[70] In fact Hanihara was already under pressure from his government in Tokyo. The recent Japanese election, held on May 10, had returned a coalition government for the first time in Japanese history. Hanihara did not expect the present government, led by Count Kiyoura Keigo, to survive. As the ambassador told one State Department official on May 15, Kiyoura's government was itself under increasing pressure to encourage moderation of the American government's stance.[71]

Nevertheless, as expected, Coolidge signed the Johnson-Reed Act on May 26. In his statement Coolidge said he regretted the exclusion provision but stressed Americans' continued "admiration and cordial friendship for the Japanese people." He expressed his preference for the gentleman's agreement, which in his view had proven a more effective and congenial method of controlling Japanese immigration. What Coolidge objected to was the means Congress had chosen to control Japanese immigration. "There is scarcely any ground for disagreement as to the result we want," he acknowledged, "but this method of securing it is unnecessary and deplorable at this time."[72]

Not surprisingly the president's equivocation did little to temper popular feeling in Japan. Writing from Tokyo, Woods (who had recently tendered his resignation, ostensibly due to his mother-in-law's illness but more likely in protest) reported that the legislation's enactment had "aroused the deepest bitterness and resentment here." Early press reports were "caustic," Woods related, since many Japanese had apparently harbored the hope that Coolidge would veto the bill. By June 4, however, Woods discerned a moderation in tone. There was a pervasive sense of futility in the press since it was clear that no amount of remonstrating would reverse the American government's decision. Individual acts of protest mounted, however, and Woods reported two suicides and a growing call for the boycott of American goods. Over 30,000 people apparently demonstrated in solidarity with one man who took his life in protest on the grounds of the former American Embassy, which received troubling information that American missionaries around Tokyo feared for their safety.[73]

In the meantime, on May 31, the Japanese government lodged an official protest with the State Department, declaring that it was obvious the legislation's "ineligible for citizenship" provision was manifestly directed toward Japan and as such constituted an affront to the Japanese people. While Japan resented the economic motivations that animated American legislators' actions, "still more unwelcome are discriminations based on race." The argument articulated by American restrictionists—that Japanese immigrants were inassimilable in the United States—was specious since barely one generation of Japanese immigrants had settled in the country. This space of time was simply "too short to permit any conclusive judgment being passed upon the racial adaptabilities of those immigrants in the matter of assimilation." Moreover assimilation was possible only "in a genial atmosphere of just and equitable treatment." Yet Japanese assimilation in the United States had been continually impeded by "invidious discriminations" in the western United States: "[Thus] it seems hardly fair to complain of the failure of foreign elements to merge in a community, while the community chooses to keep them apart from the rest of its membership." Aside from the act's inherent racial injustice, the United States was also guilty of unilaterally abrogating the 1911 Commercial Treaty's key provisions, not to mention the 1908 gentleman's agreement. With regard to the latter, it seemed that "the patient, loyal, and scrupulous observance by Japan for more than sixteen years, of these self-denying regulations, in the interest of good relations between the two countries, now seems to have been wasted."[74] Apparently the patient and cordial personal diplomacy pursued by Hughes and Hanihara for the previous two months was also wasted. Hanihara resigned his post in protest.

Hughes responded to Japan's official protest on June 16. Faced with the reality of Japanese exclusion, he was now forced to pragmatically deflect Japanese criticism. He ignored the charge of racial discrimination, choosing instead to focus on America's sovereign right to legislate immigration policy. Since Japan had already acknowledged that right in its correspondence with the State Department, Hughes effectively avoided addressing the crucial and most difficult diplomatic issues raised in the Japanese protest.[75] The Japanese press also noted this glaring omission, according to Jefferson Caffery, the interim American chargé d'affaires in Tokyo following Woods's resignation. Hughes's defense of American actions was simply "too legalistic," the Tokyo *Jiji* complained, and ignored the "spirit" of previously successful diplomatic efforts to curb Japanese immigration to the United States.[76]

Sporadic outbreaks of anti-American sentiment continued in the coming days. On July 1, for example—the date the new restrictions took effect—the embassy in Tokyo reported an "anti-America day" celebration attended by over 12,000 people. Protests were lodged at the embassy throughout the day, and Americans were advised to remain in their homes during the evening's mass meeting. The American consul in Nagoya reported that at least one Japanese department store had refused to stock American goods. The general atmosphere of anti-American agitation caused anxiety among the city's Christian missionaries.[77] Caffery dismissed the boycott as the work of domestic producers and local jingoistic organizations who were attempting to exploit the situation to their own benefit.[78] The consul in Nagasaki observed similar demonstrations and protests, including a lantern procession designed to mark the shame of July 1.[79] Periodic and isolated reports continued in the coming weeks and months, although anti-American agitation was largely confined to Japan's cities. Indeed when the new American ambassador to Japan, Edgar Bancroft, assumed his post in November 1924, he noted the immigration issue's continued "live and burning" significance in the Japanese press, even if sadness and disappointment now characterized the Japanese public's attitude.[80]

The passage of the Johnson-Reed Act in May 1924 culminated almost thirty years of white activism against Asian labor mobility in the United States and the British Empire. Cognizant of the deleterious domestic, imperial, and international consequences of Asian restriction, British and American authorities had labored to mitigate their subjects' and citizens' most embarrassing compulsions throughout that period. Denied the opportunity to enact the explicit exclusion laws they craved, colonial, state, and federal legislators instead adopted an array of deceptive regulations designed to conceal the racial, economic, and strategic anxieties that animated popular animosity toward Asian migrants. From literacy tests to reciprocity agreements, duplicity and disguise had characterized these efforts from the outset. In this respect the Johnson-Reed Act's enactment of Japanese exclusion through the "aliens ineligible for citizenship" clause was a fitting end to decades of diplomatic dissemblance and legislative truculence. The contours of white exclusion regimes that would persist for decades to come were now in place. The racial agitators who cried for restriction across the Pacific's white periphery had triumphed over the patient petitions of Japanese diplomats, individual immigrants, and even their own governments. And yet their victory was quintessentially pyrrhic, coming at the expense of international comity, morality, and wisdom.

Conclusion

The Burdens of White Supremacy

Whether intended as solemnity or satire, Rudyard Kipling's 1899 ode to the American colonization of the Philippines ostensibly encapsulated the white races' duty to civilize, educate, and nurture the colonial world's "half-devil and half-child" peoples, and his titular "White Man's Burden" became a shorthand justification for the European and American imperial projects.[1] I argue, however, that the domestic, imperial, and diplomatic tensions engendered by restrictive immigration regimes constituted the real burden of white supremacy. Those involved in British imperial administration clearly understood that fact. Joseph Chamberlain, Alfred Milner, Ronald Munro Ferguson, David Lloyd George, and countless bureaucrats in the Foreign Office and Colonial Office regularly confronted the consequences of dominion racism as they sought to manage both the Anglo-Japanese Alliance and the Indian subcontinent's loyalties. When Lloyd George remarked to dominion premiers during an Imperial War Cabinet meeting in 1918, "The colour question does not disturb us as it disturbs you," he glibly summarized the key divergence between the exigencies of British imperial management and the dominions' tenacious racial and economic anxieties.[2] Of course Lloyd George and his dominion colleagues elided the fact that the "color question" was really a question of white social, economic, and political supremacy.

Those responsible for managing American foreign relations also recognized the dangers inherent in Asian exclusion. Theodore Roosevelt, Elihu Root, Woodrow Wilson, and Charles Evans Hughes often faced the diplomatic and domestic implications of western U.S. racism as they juggled the expansion of American power in the Pacific with the rise of Japanese power in East Asia. As the U.S. Fleet departed Honolulu en route for Auckland in July 1908, President Roosevelt told the naval officers that their country's large immigrant population invariably led to "points of friction between this country and other countries, such as exist in no other nation." This was an unusually candid acknowledgment that immigration policy and American foreign relations were inextricably and often adversely connected.[3] His admission was no less accurate for being so uncommon, as this book has shown.

Despite their obstinate attempts to enforce restriction regardless of the consequences, state and dominion leaders, legislators, and even implacable racial activists also knew that their efforts constantly destabilized imperial and foreign policy. Richard Seddon, Wilfrid Laurier, Jan Smuts, and William Hughes, among many others, clashed with imperial and Japanese authorities over the folly of restriction throughout the early twentieth century. On almost every occasion they acknowledged the implications of their discriminatory impulses before proceeding to outline the racial, economic, and strategic necessity of exclusion. As Australian legislators finalized their Immigration Restriction Act in late 1901, for example, the supportive *Sydney Morning Herald* recognized that "between the Scylla of the Commonwealth's will respecting the guarantee for a 'white Australia' and the Charybdis of Imperial policy some careful steering will be required."[4] More often than not, the role of Odysseus fell to British and American officials, who struggled to navigate the hazardous politics of Asian restriction in conjunction with Japanese diplomats.

And of course the Japanese understood only too well the toxic and injurious nature of anti-Asian immigration politics. As I have demonstrated, the victims of discrimination did not passively tolerate restriction, and the Japanese government made one more attempt to redress dominion and American exclusion in the fall of 1924. Their opportunity came during League of Nations Assembly discussions concerning the Protocol for the Pacific Settlement of International Disputes. This proposal clarified how League members adjudicated disputes among signatory (and nonsignatory) states. The Protocol's supporters hoped it would establish a mechanism for preventing war and thus finally facilitate the elusive goal of disarmament. With this objective in mind, the Protocol recommended two modifications to the existing League Covenant: an "obligatory" arbitration system under the jurisdiction of the League's Permanent Court of International Justice and the application of sanctions against states that refused mediation.[5]

While these proposed changes raised general legal and political concerns among many representatives, a successful amendment secured by the Japanese delegation engendered particular consternation among dominion and American observers. Introduced by Adachi Mineichirō, the Japanese amendment potentially brought previously excepted domestic questions under the League's jurisdiction: "If the question is held by the Court or by the Council to be a matter solely within the domestic jurisdiction of the State, this decision shall not prevent consideration of the situation by the Council or by the Assembly under Article 11 of the Covenant."[6] The right to restrict immigration clearly figured among those previously disqualified domestic questions, although Adachi and his colleagues carefully avoided the subject during the debates.

Critics of the amendment immediately exposed the ruse, complaining that the Japanese delegation intended to collapse the sovereign boundaries that precluded the League's consideration of the immigration question, among others. Australian observers were especially unnerved. The *Sydney Morning Herald*'s normally taciturn editorial writers concluded, "To bring immigration policy within the purview of the League would involve such a grave invasion of domestic sovereignty that it would in all probability lead to the dissolution of the League itself."[7] William Hughes, the former prime minister whose remonstrations had thwarted Japan's earlier attempt to mobilize League support for immigration liberalization, launched a predictably vigorous counterattack in his latest role as Nationalist Party MP for North Sydney. Imagining a possible future ruling by the Court of International Justice, Hughes carped, "If these gentlemen should decide that Australia should open its doors to the East, with its 1,000,000,000 of people, that would be the end of Australia, and the future of the civilized world would be profoundly changed."[8] Whether the Japanese amendment actually rendered such a decision legally possible—and many dispassionate observers doubted that it did—was beside the point. Despite the American government's abstention from the League, Japan's ploy met a similarly skeptical reception in the United States.[9]

League members ultimately failed to ratify the Protocol, but this episode is nevertheless significant because it represents the last serious attempt to negotiate an end to restrictions on Asian labor mobility by white governments. Like their South Asian and Chinese counterparts, Japanese authorities had challenged their antagonists' slurs throughout the incendiary debates of the previous three decades. They had done so initially by diplomatic means, protesting discrimination while negotiating bilateral limitations on Japanese emigration, as evidenced by the 1907–8 gentleman's agreements with Canada and the United States. The Paris Peace Conference occasioned a new tactic, one based upon the assertion of racial and then national equality, but that approach had floundered before both overt and clandestine British and American resistance. The Japanese turned to the newly established League of Nations when traditional diplomatic interventions failed once again during the early 1920s. In doing so they adopted a new strategy of deception, emulating the subterfuge practiced by their colonial and American adversaries during the restriction campaigns of the previous thirty years. This final disappointment meant that negotiation, internationalism, and trickery had all failed to dislodge white antipathy toward Japanese migrants.

Ever since the Meiji Restoration, Japanese leaders had endeavored to secure Western acknowledgment of Japan's status as a "civilized" peer in the international community, but they were constantly rebuffed. The failure of Adachi's final gambit in the League exacerbated the ongoing sting of exclusion, most recently perpetrated by the U.S. Congress. According to Akira Iriye, American exclusion undermined the spirit of cooperation inaugurated by the 1922 Washington Conference, marginalized proponents of American-Japanese comity in both countries, emboldened nationalistic elements in the Japanese military, and revitalized jingoistic political forces that were committed to colonial expansion and martial strength.[10] Restrictions on the mobility of Japanese migrants did not directly cause the imperial and military adventurism that followed, but they undoubtedly contributed to a continuing sense of alienation from the norms and strictures of the international community and generated support for Pan-Asian alternatives among Japanese intellectuals and diplomats.[11]

The Geneva Protocol's failure also illustrated another new reality. For the previous thirty years white agitators in Australia, Canada, New Zealand, South Africa, and the United States had flailed against the largely imaginary threat of prodigious Asian mobility, stubbornly constructing their monochromatic communities regardless of local, imperial, and global opposition. Fueled by their chronic racial and economic anxieties, defiance and deceit had characterized these efforts from the outset. By 1924, however, activists had finally shrouded their restriction efforts in an apparently impervious camouflage: sovereignty. Rooted in centuries of custom and law, sovereignty provided an ostensibly unassailable and dispassionate façade behind which white militants could conceal the unsavory racial and economic realities of restriction.[12]

Since the late nineteenth century American and colonial activists had employed a diverse array of restriction strategies, ranging from the subtlety of administrative literacy tests, bilateral negotiation, and remote application to the bluntness of violence, segregation, and protest. Now they had finally found a reliable and universally applicable alternative. Dominion and American legislators had often invoked their sovereign right to control Asian mobility, but they deepened their reliance on that principle after the First World War. As Mae Ngai has argued, that conflict had "simultaneously destabilized and entrenched nation-state boundaries, ushering in an interstate system based on Westphalian sovereignty, which sanctified the integrity of the territorial nation-state and the principle that no nation can interfere in the affairs of another."[13] The new League of Nations also heightened that sensitivity, as members (and nonmembers) jealously policed their sovereign rights against possible infringements or violations. Enshrined in Article 10 of the League Covenant, "territorial integrity" helped guide peacemakers and nation-builders alike in their efforts to constitute new states, new borders, and new protectorates amid the crumbling wreckage of the German, Austro-Hungarian, Russian, and Ottoman empires.[14] At the same time, it hardened old borders against the apparent dangers of radicalism, poverty, economic disorder, and the prospective resumption of large-scale emigration from the war-ravaged ports of Europe in the immediate postwar years.

Appeals to sovereignty did not quench the combustible politics engendered by enforced Asian labor immobility, of course. Even as overt racism dissipated, Asian immigration restriction remained an enduring feature of political, economic, and cultural life throughout Great Britain's self-governing dominions and the United States well into the second half of the twentieth century. Given this book's rendition of the torrid international politics that accompanied restriction, it is at once surprising and predictable that these discriminatory immigration controls finally yielded, at least in part, to the shifting objectives of international relations in the years following the Second World War.

Americans were the first to begin dismantling their racist immigration architecture. Motivated by the wartime alliance with China, Congress finally repealed the Chinese Exclusion Act in 1943, after six decades of prejudice and discrimination. This was a minor concession since under the new legislation Chinese immigration was still subjected to an infinitesimal quota, totaling only 105 immigrants annually. The Magnuson Act did grant citizenship rights to those Chinese residents who could prove they had entered the country legally, but this was a difficult proposition since legal Chinese immigration had been impossible since 1882. Nevertheless this represented a major departure for U.S. naturalization law.[15] Similar concessions were made to immigrants from the Philippines and India in 1946, with new quotas of 100 per year granted to both nationalities. More important, Filipino and South Asian immigrants were also finally granted the right to become American citizens.[16]

Americans continued to moderate their immigration laws in the postwar years in a process driven largely by cold war imperatives.[17] Faced with increasing criticism from the Eastern Bloc and eager to gain allies among the decolonizing nations of Africa and Asia, successive congresses and presidents were forced to reach beyond the boundaries of exclusion both at home and abroad after the Second World War.[18] In 1952 the Immigration and Naturalization Act (McCarran-Walter Act) eliminated racially motivated prohibitions on Japanese (and Korean) immigration. This legislation, although far from generous, finally removed the stain of exclusion that had burdened U.S.-Japanese relations since the late nineteenth century. Japanese immigrants were subject to the same nominal 100 per year quota as Chinese and South Asian immigrants, but the act also granted naturalization rights to Korean and Japanese immigrants. As other scholars have demonstrated, the McCarran-Walter Act was largely inspired by the new geopolitical realities facing the United States in Asia and was at least partly designed to "cement the loyalties of the 'good Asians' (Republican Chinese, South Korea, and a reconstructed Japan) against the 'bad Asians' (Chinese and other Communists)."[19]

Canadians were next to formally eliminate their racial barriers against Asian immigration and naturalization. Following the Second World War the Canadian government gradually moderated its restrictions on South Asian and Chinese voting rights and naturalization (1947), Japanese voting rights and naturalization (1948), and family reunification (1950).[20] The end of these limitations on Asian participation in Canadian national life effectively terminated the White Canada Policy that British Columbians in particular had so vigorously pursued since the mid-nineteenth-century gold rushes. Canada's Japanese, South Asian, and Chinese residents were now able to live, work, and vote without the ignominy of the myriad legal restrictions that had hitherto circumscribed their lives.

It still remained for the Canadian government to overhaul and modernize its immigration system, which Lester Pearson's Liberal government finally did in 1967. Immigration regulations introduced that year instituted a bold and innovative new arrangement based on a points system rather than racial or national origins. This system was effectively color-blind. Prospective immigrants were (and still are) allocated points based on their education, age, language skills, work experience, and the availability of employment in Canada.[21] Following the new regulations, Canada's immigration policy no longer discriminated against Asian immigration, officially ending the White Canada Policy.

Australians and New Zealanders moved much more slowly toward officially repealing their whites-only immigration policies. Australians remained committed to their White Australia Policy in the wake of the Second World War. As the postwar Labor government's immigration minister, Arthur Calwell, declared, "The flag of White Australia will not be lowered."[22] Unlike in the United States, the burgeoning cold war actually augmented the Commonwealth's traditional geographic and racial anxieties, especially after the Communist victory in China in 1949.[23] The yellow peril was now tinged with red. In 1958, however, Australians abandoned the notorious dictation test that had enclosed the Commonwealth since 1901. At the same time, the government began to relax restrictions on Asian naturalization.[24] In addition to Australia's growing economic and political engagement with Asia in the 1950s, this change was prompted by growing opposition among Australians themselves. The most concerted campaign against the White Australia Policy came from the University of Melbourne's Immigration Reform Group, founded in 1959. This group published a provocative report in 1960 entitled *Immigration: Control or Color Bar*. The authors assailed Australia's racially motivated immigration policy and called for a relaxation of the Commonwealth's restrictions. This was essential, the Group insisted, not only because Australians would benefit from increased interaction with Asian people and cultures but also because the White Australia Policy was an international liability and a nineteenth-century anachronism.[25] The government reduced restrictions on Asian naturalization in 1966 and announced that non-Europeans with necessary education and skills would be encouraged to immigrate.[26] Minor changes followed, most of which remained hidden from the Australian people, but it was clear that Australia's economic future lay in Asia. Faced with this new reality, Gough Whitlam's new Labor government finally announced the termination of the White Australia Policy in 1973.[27]

New Zealanders remained similarly committed to their whites-only immigration policy after the Second World War. A postwar study concluded that New Zealand's immigration policy should retain its preference for white British immigrants. This stood in contrast even to Australia, where limited southern European immigration became acceptable as part of the Commonwealth's postwar "Populate or perish" campaign.[28] Indeed, as James Belich observes, "New Zealand managed to edge out even Australia in the persistence of a racialist immigration policy."[29] The government did grant citizenship rights to New Zealand–born Chinese in 1952, but for the most part New Zealanders preserved the contours of the Massey government's 1920 Immigration Restriction Amendment Act, which allowed the dominion to remotely restrict Asian immigration on the basis of "undesirability" rather than race.[30]

As global attitudes toward race began to shift during the 1950s, however, it became difficult to maintain the fiction of nondiscrimination that had sustained New Zealand's immigration policies since the late nineteenth century. Reverend Dr. Rajah B. Manikan of the International Missionary Council succinctly captured the essence of New Zealand's position when he correctly observed, "New Zealand is slightly shrewder than Australia, and does not use the 'White Australia' expression which infuriates all Asian people. . . . The policies, however, are exactly the same."[31] Since at least 1899 New Zealanders had largely avoided the international opprobrium incurred by Australians thanks to the latter's tactless and strident commitment to their White Australia Policy. As Australians slowly moderated their stance in the 1950s, however, New Zealanders could no longer hide behind the rhetorical and legislative indiscretions emanating from across the Tasman.

Small but increasing numbers of Pacific Islanders pierced the first holes in the White New Zealand Policy in the 1960s. Immigrants from the Cook Islands (a New Zealand protectorate from 1901 to 1965) were New Zealand citizens by virtue of their colonial relationship, and Western Samoa (formerly a League of Nations Mandate that gained independence from New Zealand in 1962) negotiated a quota system following independence. As Belich notes, since immigrants from the Cook Islands and Samoa were considered to be racial relatives of New Zealand's Maori population, their immigration did not necessarily challenge the country's imagined racial balance.[32] Asian immigrants, however, remained beyond the bounds of acceptability until much later. New Zealand made a nominal concession toward racial sensitivity in 1961, when the Immigration Amendment Act required anybody who was not a citizen of New Zealand (including British citizens, but not Australians) to obtain a permit before entering the country. This new law was supposed to highlight the fairness of New Zealand's immigration law, but as Donald Denoon and Philippa Mein-Smith point out, it remained difficult for Asian visitors without existing familial ties to New Zealand citizens to enter the country.[33] Like Australians, however, New Zealanders were forced to reconsider their position following Great Britain's entry into the European Economic Community in 1973. Faced with losing privileged access to its traditional export market, New Zealand turned to Asia, and in 1974 the Kirk government announced that racial considerations would no longer guide the country's immigration policy.[34]

White South Africa embarked upon a very different path. Whereas the postwar international climate slowly fostered changes in the racial policies of the United States and Britain's Pacific dominions, White South Africans intensified their commitment to whiteness by instituting a thoroughgoing system of apartheid following the National Party's electoral victory in 1948.[35] While South Africa's newly constructed segregation regime did not directly affect Asian immigration, which was practically prohibited in any event, apartheid did apply to the country's South Asian population. As one National Party statement announced, "Indians are a foreign and outlandish element which is unassimilable. They can never become part of the country and must therefore be treated as an immigrant community."[36] This sentiment was, in fact, nothing new. South Africa's South Asian population had been subjected to this attitude since the first indentured plantation workers arrived in Natal in 1859. South Asians gained political representation in 1984 within a new tricameral legislature. This concession came as part of P. W. Botha's "Total Strategy," designed to limit the growing power of the African National Congress. South Asian representation under this new—and still racialized—system was limited, however, and blacks remained barred from the franchise.[37] Not until Nelson Mandela's dramatic electoral victory in 1994 did the walls of restriction finally crumble in South Africa. Only then did full social, political, and economic participation become a possibility for millions of black and Asian South Africans.

The final dismantling of anti-Asian restrictions did not eradicate the anxieties inspired by migrant mobility, of course, and vestiges of this early twentieth-century angst retain their salience in the twenty-first century. Immigration control remains a contested, complicated, and vexing question for governments—and migrants—around the world. Sovereignty endures as the constrictive framework within which discussions of immigration reform take place, despite migration's inherently transnational nature. In 2011, for example, the Obama administration turned its attention toward comprehensive immigration reform. The administration's proposal, Building a 21st Century Immigration System, offered a range of bureaucratic, economic, and technical reforms focused on "restoring responsibility and accountability to our immigration system."[38] Yet the proposal—much like the fantastical wall along the U.S.-Mexican boundary proposed by American presidential candidate Donald Trump in 2015—imagined that immigration policy exists in a vacuum, bounded and contained by U.S. borders.[39] As I have demonstrated, that assumption is an unsustainable fiction that ignores the lessons of the late nineteenth- and early twentieth-centuries paroxysms over Asian restriction. International relations, diplomacy, and migration are thoroughly entangled, and any effort to reform the politics of immigration must take cognizance of that fact.

Notes

Abbreviations

AMEL	Leopold Amery Papers, Churchill Archives Center, Churchill College, Cambridge University
ANZ	Archives New Zealand, Wellington
CAB	Cabinet Office Records, National Archives, London
CAC	Churchill Archives Center, Churchill College, Cambridge University
Cd.	British Parliamentary Command Papers
CO	Colonial Office Records, National Archives, London
CP	Records of Commonwealth Persons, National Archives of Australia, Canberra
CPD	Commonwealth of Australia, *Parliamentary Debates*
CUL	Cambridge University Library, Cambridge
DCPD	Dominion of Canada, Parliamentary Debates
FO	Foreign Office, National Archives, London
IT	Island Territories, Archives New Zealand, Wellington
LAC	Library and Archives Canada, Ottawa
LOC	U.S. Library of Congress, Washington, D.C.
NA	U.S. National Archives and Records Administration, College Park, Maryland
NAA	National Archives of Australia, Canberra
NARA	U.S. National Archives and Records Administration, Washington, D.C.
NLA	National Library of Australia, Canberra
NLNZ	National Library of New Zealand, Wellington
NSWPD	New South Wales, Parliamentary Debates
NZPD	New Zealand, Parliamentary Debates

RBP   Robert Borden Papers

RCMFP   Ronald Crawford Munro Ferguson Papers

RG   Record group, U.S. National Archives and Records
           Administration, College Park, Maryland

TNA   The National Archives, London

UKPD   United Kingdom, Parliamentary Debates

VPD   Victoria, Parliamentary Debates

WLP   Wilfrid Laurier Papers

WMHP   William Morris Hughes Papers

Introduction

1. For a recent exposition on the relationship between mobility and empire, see Ballantyne, "Mobility, Empire, Colonisation." For the relationship between imperialism and openness, see Bacevich, *American Empire*.

2. Bender, "Commentary," 610. For an overview of the motives behind this "historiographic revolution," see Iriye, *Global and Transnational History*. For examples in imperial history, see Ballantyne and Burton, *Empires and the Reach of the Global*; Fojas and Guevarra, *Transnational Crossroads*; Magee and Thompson, *Empire and Globalisation*; McCoy and Scarano, *Colonial Crucible*; McGuiness, *Path of Empire*; Kramer, *The Blood of Government*; Ballantyne, *Orientalism and Race*; Kaplan and Pease, *Cultures of United States Imperialism*. For works on migration that illustrate the uses of this transnational frame, see Hoerder, *Migrations and Belongings*; Gabbacia, *Foreign Relations*; Gabbacia and Hoerder, *Connecting Seas and Connected Ocean Rims*; Chang, *Pacific Connections*; Geiger, *Subverting Exclusion*; Fujita-Rony, *American Workers, Colonial Power*; McKeown, *Chinese Migration Networks and Cultural Change*; Hsu, *Dreaming of Gold, Dreaming of Home*. Examples of this approach in international relations history include Manela, *The Wilsonian Moment*. For exemplars in global history scholarship, see Bender, *A Nation among Nations*; Bayly, *The Birth of the Modern World*. For the Pacific as a site of transnational mobility and exchange, see Armitage and Bashford, *Pacific Histories*; Kurashige et al., "Introduction"; Igler, *The Great Ocean*; Matsuda, *Pacific Worlds*; Cumings, *Dominion from Sea to Sea*. Comparable developments have also invigorated almost every geographic subfield. Many recent interventions in British imperial history, for example, are oriented around far-reaching conceptions of the British world, while an expansive "United States in the world" framework now vies with ostensibly narrower taxonomies like diplomatic history and American foreign relations in textbooks and classrooms. For recent discussions on the utility of the British world framework, see Laidlaw, "Breaking Britannia's Bounds?"; Buckner and Francis, *Rediscovering the British World*. The efforts of the British Scholar Society and its journal, *Britain and the World*, pursue a similar but still distinct historiographical

turn toward globalizing British history. For discussions of the "United States in the world" paradigm and its competitors, see Zeiler et al., "Diplomatic History." Also see the essays in Costigliola and Hogan, *America in the World*.

3. For a critique of metaphors of movement, integration, and exchange, see Kramer, "Power and Connection," 1352–53; Sedgewick, "Against Flows"; Cooper, *Colonialism in Question*, 91–112.

4. See, for example, Chang, *Pacific Connections*; Takai, "Navigating Transpacific Passages."

5. For a broad survey of Chinese migration, see Kuhn, *Chinese among Others*. For a survey of Japanese migration, see Adachi, *Japanese Diasporas*. For an overview of the South Asian Diaspora's historical origins and experience, see Brown, *Global South Asians*.

6. On social Darwinism, see Bannister, *Social Darwinism*; Hawkins, *Social Darwinism in European and American Thought*; Hofstadter, *Social Darwinism in American Thought*. On the ideology of Anglo-Saxonism, see Kramer, "Empires, Exceptions, and Anglo-Saxons"; Martellone, "In the Name of Anglo-Saxondom, for Empire and for Democracy"; MacDougall, *Racial Myth in English History*; Horsman, *Race and Manifest Destiny*; Horsman, "Origins of Racial Anglo-Saxonism in Great Britain before 1850." On the yellow peril, see Hsu, *The Good Immigrants*; Kuo et al., *Yellow Peril!*; Walker and Sobocinska, *Australia's Asia*. For discussions of whiteness, see Painter, *The History of White People*; Carey and McLisky, *Creating White Australia*; Mohanram, *Imperial White*; Roediger, *Working toward Whiteness*; Jacobson, *Whiteness of a Different Color*; Roediger, *The Wages of Whiteness*.

7. Lee, *The Making of Asian America*; Young, *Alien Nation*; Sohi, *Echoes of Mutiny*; Chang, *Pacific Connections*; Delgado, *Making the Chinese Mexican*; Fujita-Rony, *American Workers, Colonial Power*; Lau, *Paper Families*; Azuma, *Between Two Empires*; Hsu, *Dreaming of Gold, Dreaming of Home*; Lee, *At America's Gates*; Hu-DeHart, *Across the Pacific*; McKeown, *Chinese Migration Networks and Cultural Change*; Geiger, *Subverting Exclusion*; Fitzgerald, *Big White Lie*; Mar, *Brokering Belonging*; Stanley, *Contesting White Supremacy*.

8. Sinn, "Highway to Gold Mountain," 221. See also Sinn, *Pacific Crossing*. The same kind of interpretive framework also characterizes recent studies of European migration. In the British and American context, with which this study is primarily concerned, see Fedorowich and Thompson, *Empire, Migration, and Identity in the British World*; Harper and Constantine, *Migration and Empire*; Gabbacia, *Foreign Relations*.

9. For Canada, see Roy, *The Oriental Question*; Roy, *A White Man's Province*; Ward, *White Canada Forever*; Adachi, *The Enemy That Never Was*. For the United States, see Takaki, *Strangers from a Different Shore*; Gyory, *Closing the Gate*; Saxton, *The Indispensable Enemy*; Daniels, *Asian America*. For Australia, see Markus, *Fear and Hatred*; Price, *The Great White Walls Are Built*; London, *Nonwhite Immigration and the "White Australia" Policy*. For New Zealand, see Moloughney and Stenhouse, "'Drug-Besotten, Sin-Besotten Fiends of Filth'"; Butler, *Opium and Gold*; Greif, *The Overseas Chinese in New Zealand*; O'Connor, "Keeping New Zealand White"; Fong, *The Chinese in New*

Zealand. For South Africa, see Desai and Vahed, *Inside Indenture*; Kynoch, "Controlling the Coolies"; Lloyd, " 'A Family Quarrel' "; Huttenback, *Gandhi in South Africa.* Two notable exceptions to the limited focus of these earlier studies are Brawley, *The White Peril,* and Huttenback, *Racism and Empire.*

10. Chang, *Pacific Connections*; McKeown, *Melancholy Order*; Bright, *Chinese Labour in South Africa.* See also Lee, "The 'Yellow Peril' and Asian Exclusion in the Americas."

11. Lake and Reynolds, *Drawing the Global Colour Line,* 4.

12. For Stoddard's spurious claim of a white settler "sacred union" against Asian migration, see *The Rising Tide of Color against White World Supremacy,* 281.

13. Ballantyne and Burton, *Empires and the Reach of the Global,* 19.

14. Rosenberg, *A World Connecting.*

15. Price, *The Great White Walls Are Built.*

16. See, for example, Geiger, *Subverting Exclusion*; Fitzgerald, *Big White Lie*; Lee, *At America's Gates*; Mar, *Brokering Belonging*; Stanley, *Contesting White Supremacy.*

17. The Anglo-Japanese Alliance committed each signatory to "support" the other in the event that either became involved in a war with more than one power. If either country became involved in a war with one other country by virtue of its interests in China and Korea, both Britain and Japan committed to remain neutral. For a discussion of this treaty's early history, see Nish, *The Anglo-Japanese Alliance.*

18. Gordon, *A Modern History of Japan*; Beasly, *Japanese Imperialism*; Myers and Peattie, *The Japanese Colonial Empire*; Iriye, *Pacific Estrangement,* 18–25. For an analysis of imperial interactions in Southeast Asia, see Foster, *Projections of Power.*

19. Uchida, *Brokers of Empire,* 35–62.

20. Chang, *Pacific Connections,* 53; Lee, "The 'Yellow Peril' and Asian Exclusion in the Americas," 550; Azuma, *Between Two Empires,* 19; Ichioka, *The Issei,* 4.

21. For a discussion of the unequal treaties and their subsequent revision, see Auslin, *Negotiating with Imperialism*; Hoare, "The Era of the Unequal Treaties"; Yuichi, "From Unequal Treaty to the Anglo-Japanese Alliance."

22. For the Anglo-Japanese Treaty of Commerce and Navigation, see "Treaty of Commerce and Navigation between Japan and Great Britain." For the Japanese-American agreement, see "Treaty of Commerce and Navigation between the United States and Japan."

23. Ernest Satow to the Marquis of Salisbury, April 10, 1896, TNA, FO 46/548, 1–4.

24. Lissington, *New Zealand and Japan,* 2. This continued recalcitrance may have derived in part from Japan's recent and dramatic victory over China in the Sino-Japanese War in 1895. The British minister in Japan, Power Henry Le Poer Trench, first raised the possibility of increased Japanese emigration to the British dominions following that war. Whatever the veracity of Le Poer Trench's analysis, the Japanese victory over China heralded a new era in East Asian politics. Power Henry Le Poer Trench to the Marquess of Ripon, December 20, 1894, LAC, RG 25, vol. 1430, 22–23.

25. This clause amended articles I and II of the treaty ("Treaty of Commerce and Navigation between the United States and Japan," 108). For the agreement between

the State Department and the Japanese legation in Washington, see Kurino to Gresham, October 20, 1894, in U.S. Department of State, *Japanese Emigration and Immigration to American Territory*, 14–15. This qualification enabled the Cleveland administration to placate opposition to the threat of Japanese mobility in the American West.

26. CPD, 4: 4633–34.

27. For discussions of imperial citizenship and subjecthood, see Banerjee, *Becoming Imperial Citizens*; Gorman, *Imperial Citizenship*.

28. The term *dominion* functions as shorthand throughout much of this book for Britain's predominantly white settler societies of Australia, New Zealand, Canada, and South Africa. It became a widely adopted and official designation with the establishment of the Dominions Department in the Colonial Office in 1907, although the term was officially applied to Canada in 1867 and to Australia in 1901 (Hyam, "Bureaucracy and 'Trusteeship' in the Colonial Empire," 256).

29. In his interpretation of nineteenth-century global history, Jürgen Osterhammel characterizes settler colonialism as a "special form of frontier colonization" that exercised a transformative influence over people and the environment. Epitomized by a market-inspired ethos of "voluntary settlement," the settler colonial project necessitated the seizure of land from indigenous peoples who were either displaced or exterminated (*The Transformation of the World*, 370–75). Though largely outside the scope of this study, the relationship between indigenous and settler populations is central to the settler colonial paradigm. See, for example, Coombes, *Rethinking Settler Colonialism*. See also Laidlaw and Lester, *Indigenous Communities and Settler Colonialism*.

30. Belich, *Replenishing the Earth*, 153–65. According to Belich, this ideology "converted emigration within the Anglo-world from an act of despair that lowered your standing to an act of hope that enhanced it" (164).

31. Veracini, *Settler Colonialism*, 3. For a discussion of settler sovereignty in Australia and the United States during an earlier period, see Ford, *Settler Sovereignty*.

32. In reality, of course, many Asian migrants were also participants—knowingly or not—in settler colonial projects of their own. This was especially true of Japanese migrants. See, for example, Uchida, *Brokers of Empire*; Fujikane and Okamura, *Asian Settler Colonialism*; Azuma, "Japanese Immigrant Settler Colonialism in the U.S.-Mexican Borderlands and the U.S. Racial-Imperialist Politics of the Hemispheric 'Yellow Peril,'" 257–58.

33. As Patricia Roy notes in her study of British Columbian restriction efforts during this period, Canadians (like their white compatriots throughout North America and the British Empire) frequently conflated color, biology, culture, politics, and economics in their rudimentary racial dialogues (*A White Man's Province*, viii). Warwick Anderson comes to the same conclusion in his study of Australian medicine and its intimate relation to whiteness: "The 'white race' and the 'white organism' were figures of speech that implied a wide range of physical and cultural signs of European difference" (*The Cultivation of Whiteness*, 2).

34. As these sentiments suggest, Asian immigration restriction was a deeply gendered project. The majority of Chinese, Japanese, and South Asian migrants were male,

and white campaigners often assumed that their detrimental influence would be felt most deleteriously among white working men.

35. Milner to Lyttleton, February 15, 1904, TNA, CO 879/80/4, 297–98.

36. "The American Fleet," *New Zealand Herald*, August 8, 1908.

37. VPD, 139: 1415. As David Day observes, "the almost universal support for 'white Australia' was an indication of the fears that surged beneath the surface of Australia's often confident exterior" (*Claiming a Continent*, 178).

38. Theodore Roosevelt, for example, often speculated on the propensity of the "higher races" to succumb to "race suicide." This fate could be remedied, he argued, by the application of strenuous, virile, "barbarian virtues." See Jacobson, *Barbarian Virtues*, 3–5; Bederman, *Manliness and Civilization*; Dyer, *Theodore Roosevelt and the Idea of Race*, 143–67.

Chapter One

1. For large-scale treatments of global migration patterns in this period, see Fisher, *Migration*; Hoerder, *Migrations and Belongings*; McKeown, "Global Migration."

2. See, for example, Lake and Reynolds, *Drawing the Global Colour Line*; McKeown, *Melancholy Order*; Huttenback, *Racism and Empire*; Martens, "A Transnational History of Immigration Restriction."

3. "Joseph Chamberlain's Scheme," *Bulletin*, May 15, 1897. The *Bulletin's* masthead stridently declared "Australia for the Australians" until May 1908, when it was changed to "Australia for the White Man." The *Bulletin* began publication in 1880 and was initially driven by a racist, anti-imperial, nationalist editorial policy (Ward, *A Nation for a Continent*, 24).

4. Daniels, "The Growth of Restrictive Immigration Policies in the Colonies of Settlement," 40.

5. CPD, 4: 4822.

6. Marquis of Salisbury, November 26, 1896, TNA, FO 46/548, 10.

7. The Under Secretary of State, Colonial Office, to the Undersecretary of State, Foreign Office, April 17, 1897, TNA, FO 46/548, 17.

8. TNA, CAB 18/9: Appendix No. 1, Restriction of Coloured Immigration, 170.

9. NSWPD, 88: 1744.

10. Belich, *Paradise Reforged*, 207.

11. Martens, "Richard Seddon and Popular Opposition in New Zealand to the Introduction of Chinese Labor into the Transvaal," 183. See also Huttenback, *Racism and Empire*, 81–82.

12. Greif, *The Overseas Chinese in New Zealand*, 26; Fong, *The Chinese in New Zealand*, 24.

13. Act to prevent the Influx into New Zealand of Persons of Alien Race who are likely to be hurtful to the Public Welfare, No. 64, 1896, TNA, FO 46/548, 20.

14. Fong, *The Chinese in New Zealand*, 24.

15. NZPD, 92: 252–53.

16. Ibid., 255. For a history of Seddon's Liberal Party and an overview of New Zealand politics during this period, see Hamer, *The New Zealand Liberals*.

17. NZPD, 92: 256.

18. Von Dadelszen, *Report on the Results of a Census of the Colony of New Zealand Taken for the Night of the 12th April, 1896*, 34.

19. NZPD, 92: 372.

20. Ibid., 472.

21. The original bill defined "Asiatic" as "any native of any part of Asia, or of the islands adjacent to Asia, or in Asiatic seas, and the descendants of such natives; but it does not include persons of European or Jewish extraction" (ibid., 253). "Native of any part" was later amended to read "persons of the coloured races," and the addendum exempting "persons of European or Jewish extraction" was also removed (258).

22. Ibid., 255, 450.

23. At one point in the debate Seddon wondered aloud whether the Legislative Council's intransigence on this issue was evidence that it ought to be abolished. "The Asiatic Restriction Bill," *Fielding Star*, July 2, 1896.

24. NZPD, 92: 373.

25. Ibid., 254–55.

26. Ibid., 376–79.

27. NZPD, 94: 310. The Legislative Council was characteristically more judicious in its assessment of the act, but it was nevertheless read for a second time, on August 18, 1896, receiving a vote of 19–10 (426–35).

28. NZPD, 95: 94.

29. NZPD, 100: 125.

30. Japanese Minister to the Marquis of Salisbury, November 25, 1896, TNA, FO 46/548, 8–9.

31. Chamberlain to Governors General, October 20, 1897, TNA, FO 46/548, 91–92.

32. Sir Ernest Satow to the Marquis of Salisbury, April 10, 1896, and November 24, 1896, TNA, FO 46/548, 1–4, 5–7. As the British minister in Japan, Satow used the actions of New Zealanders to convince the Japanese Foreign Ministry to finally offer this exemption to the British colonies.

33. G. W. Steevens, "Report of the Correspondent of the Daily Mail," in Walton, *A Centenary Celebration of the Diamond Jubilee of Queen Victoria*, 27; "The Colonies," *Times*, June 8, 1897; Morris, *Pax Britannica*, 31–34.

34. Extract from Queen's Journal, June 22, 1897, in *The Letters of Queen Victoria*, 174.

35. Garvin, *The Life of Joseph Chamberlain*, 185.

36. Proceedings of a Conference between the Secretary of State for the Colonies and the Premiers of the Self-Governing Colonies at the Colonial Office, TNA, CAB 18/9, 4–13. For a study of the "Greater Britain" concept, see Bell, *The Idea of Greater Britain*. For Chamberlain's contribution to that idea, see 56–58. For a discussion of the British Empire as a globalizing empire, see Ballantyne and Burton, *Empires and the Reach of the Global*, 18–20.

37. Proceedings of a Conference between the Secretary of State for the Colonies and the Premiers of the Self-Governing Colonies at the Colonial Office, TNA, CAB 18/9, 13–14.

38. The idea had its roots in the U.S. aborted literacy test of 1896 (Lake and Reynolds, *Drawing the Global Colour Line*, 131). See also Bright, *Chinese Labour in South Africa*, 19.

39. Appendix No. 1, "Natal," TNA, CAB 18/9, 170.

40. Ibid., 130–31.

41. Ibid., 131–35.

42. Ibid., 135. Moreover Kingston had no doubt "if England were similarly situated with reference to these other countries as we are the desire would be equally strong here as it is in Australia" (135).

43. Ibid., 136. Unlike Reid and Turner, Tasmanian premier Sir Edward Braddon was happy to accept the Natal formula since extant legislation in his colony did not already provide for the exclusion of British subjects, given that "the Indians are the coloured aliens who more than any other we should desire to exclude" (135).

44. Ibid., 13. Seddon did not attend the July 8 discussion due to a misunderstanding. He apparently believed the meeting was just for the Australian premiers.

45. Ibid., 137.

46. Colonial Office to Foreign Office, August 17, 1897, TNA, FO 46/548, 40.

47. Foreign Office to Colonial Office, October 7, 1897, TNA, CO 886/1/3; "Correspondence (1897–1908) Relating to the Treatment of Asiatics in the Dominions," June, 1909, 184.

48. "Undesirable Immigrants," *Sydney Morning Herald*, March 29, 1901.

49. "Coloured Labour," *Sydney Morning Herald*, June 11, 1901.

50. Alomes, *A Nation At Last?*, 39; Day, *Claiming a Continent*, 177.

51. Pearson, *National Life and Character*. For Barton's invocation of Pearson's ideas, see CPD, 3: 3497–503. For a deeper discussion of Pearson's thinking, see Lake and Reynolds, *Drawing the Global Colour Line*, 75–94.

52. CPD, 3: 3500, 3502–3.

53. CPD, 4: 4636, 4633–38.

54. Willard, *History of the White Australia Policy to 1920*; Yarwood, *Asian Migration to Australia*; London, *Nonwhite Immigration and the "White Australia" Policy*; Carey and McLisky, *Creating White Australia*; Windschuttle, *The White Australia Policy*. Even more internationally or transnationally oriented works tend to skip the content of the debates. See, for example, Huttenback, *Racism and Empire*, 279–85; Lake and Reynolds, *Drawing the Global Colour Line*, 147–50; McKeown, *Melancholy Order*, 194–96; Markus, *Fear and Hatred*. For an exception, see Atkinson, "The White Australia Policy, the British Empire, and the World." Much of the other recent scholarship on Asian immigration in Australia is concerned with recovering the agency, experiences, and communities of the migrants themselves. For an excellent overview of this work, see Reeves and Mountford, "Sojourning and Settling."

55. CPD, 4: 4626–29, 4633–34.

56. Ibid., 4634, 4649.

57. For a discussions of the region's commercial and labor networks, see Martinez and Vickers, *The Pearl Frontier*.

58. A thorough analysis of Australian conceptions of medicine, work, race, and the tropics can be found in Anderson, *The Cultivation of Whiteness*, 73–94. See also Harrison, *Medicine in an Age of Commerce and Empire*. For a broader discussion of climate, environment, and empire, see Beattie et al., *Eco-Cultural Networks and the British Empire*.

59. Parker, "'Australia for the White Man' Again," 830.

60. CPD, 4: 4654.

61. Ibid., 4666, 4659.

62. Price, *The Great White Walls Are Built*, 38–41.

63. Huttenback, *Racism and Empire*, 39–41. The majority of these workers came from the New Hebrides (Vanuatu) and the Solomon Islands.

64. Ward, *A Nation for a Continent*, 30. The term *Kanaka*, Ward relates, comes from the Melanesian word for "man."

65. Brown, "'A Most Irregular Traffic,'" 255–57.

66. CPD, 4: 4805, 5077.

67. Ibid., 4638–39, 4640–41, 4662.

68. Ibid., 4638, 4659.

69. Ibid., 4828.

70. Ibid., 4821, 4823, 5276.

71. Ibid., 5160.

72. Ibid., 4807, 4806.

73. Ibid., 4812.

74. Nish, "Australia and the Anglo-Japanese Alliance," 202–3.

75. Shigeru, "The Opening of the Twentieth Century and the Anglo-Japanese Alliance," 166–67.

76. Indeed Nish points out, "The Commonwealth government might congratulate itself on having passed the Immigration Restriction Act before, rather than after, the Anglo-Japanese Alliance, otherwise Britain might have found it even more delicate to give assent to the Australian legislation" ("Australia and the Anglo-Japanese Alliance," 204). Japan would, however, leverage the alliance in later years as it continued its struggle against colonial racism.

77. CPD, 4: 4653, 5250.

78. Ibid., 4845–46. Isaacs became the first Australian to occupy the post of governor-general in 1931.

79. See, for example, "The Immigration Restriction Bill 1901" Objection by Queensland Government to prepared test for admission of immigrants, August 22, 1901, NAA, A8, 1901/27/8, reel 1, 2; CPD, 4628, 4660, 4820, 5071.

80. Sir Charles Prestwood Lucas, "The Self-Governing Dominions and Coloured Immigration," July 1908, TNA, CO 886/1/1, 31.

81. Petition from Indian residents of Victoria to the Right Honourable J. Chamberlain, Secretary for the Colonies, October 25, 1901, NAA, A8, 1902/182/1.

82. [Cover memorandum] Chamberlain to the Earl of Hopetoun, December 24, 1901, NAA, A8, 1902/182/1.

83. Effect of Immigration Restriction Bill on Indian Community, November 19, 1901, NAA, A8, 1901/49/1.

84. Baron Hayashi to the Marquess of Lansdowne, July 4, 1901, NAA, A8, 1901/27/9.

85. Eitaki to Edmund Barton, September 16, 1901, 1–2, NAA, A8, 1901/203/1.

86. Eitaki to the Earl of Hopetoun, October 5, 1901, NAA, A8, 1901/203/1.

87. Baron Hayashi to the Marquess of Lansdowne, October 7, 1901, NAA, A8, 1901/203/1.

88. Hayashi to the Marquess of Lansdowne, December 16, 1901, TNA, FO 46/548, 444.

89. H. Bertram Cox to the Foreign Office, October 18, 1901, NAA, A8, 1901/203/1.

90. Cox to the Foreign Office, January 4, 1902, TNA, FO 46/670, 2.

91. Sir Charles Prestwood Lucas, "The Self-Governing Dominions and Coloured Immigration," July 1908, TNA, CO 886/1/1, 31.

92. Marquess of Lansdowne to Hayashi, February 8, 1902, NAA, CA 1, Governor-General, A11816, 2.

93. Sir Claude MacDonald to the Marquess of Landsdowne, June 11, 1902, TNA, FO 46/670, 79–80.

94. "The Immigration Restriction Bill," *Sydney Morning Herald*, September 11, 1901.

95. O'Connor, "Keeping New Zealand White," 43; Huttenback, "The British Empire as a 'White Man's Country,'" 108.

Chapter Two

1. Bright, *Chinese Labour in South Africa*; Kynoch, "Controlling the Coolies," 309–11.

2. Thompson, *A Wider Patriotism*, 82.

3. Pakenham, *The Boer War*, 493.

4. Mawby, *Gold Mining and Politics*, 352; Grant, *A Civilized Savagery*, 87.

5. Bright, *Chinese Labour in South Africa*; Lake and Reynolds, *Drawing the Global Colour Line*; McKeown, *Melancholy Order*.

6. Henning, *The Indentured Indian in Natal*; Desai and Vahed, *Inside Indenture*.

7. Lee, *African Women and Apartheid*; Dubow, *Apartheid*.

8. Smuts, *Selections from the Smuts Papers*, 1:82–83.

9. Proceedings of a Conference between the Secretary of State for the Colonies and the Premiers of the Self-Governing Colonies, TNA, CAB 18/9, 15.

10. For a global study of indentured labor and its demise, see Northrup, *Indentured Labor in the Age of Imperialism*.

11. For a detailed history of the South African War, see Pakenham, *The Boer War*. See also Judd and Surridge, *The Boer War*; Meredith, *Diamonds, Gold, and War*. Transvaal attained self-government in 1907, and Transvaal and the Orange Free State finally joined Britain's existing South African possessions, Natal and the Cape Colony, in the Union of South Africa in 1910.

12. Thompson, *A Wider Patriotism*, 82.

13. Thompson, *A History of South Africa*, 143–45. No great wave of British settlers ever immigrated to southern Africa under Milner's rule; fewer than three thousand British settlers eventually established homes there under his aegis. Most British emigrants preferred to make the short journey to Canada or North America.

14. "How Are We to Work the Mines on the Rand," *Times*, September 19, 1902.

15. Rachel Bright argues that Milner had likely settled on this course of action by March 1903 (*Chinese Labour in South Africa*, 32–33).

16. "Excerpt from the Rand Daily Mail," June 3, 1903, Cd. 1895, 40.

17. Ibid., 42.

18. According to Donald Denoon, there were approximately 12,039 white and approximately 72,011 African workers available on the Witwatersrand by the beginning of 1903 (*A Grand Illusion*, 135).

19. Minutes of Proceedings of the South African Customs Union Conference held at Bloemfontein, March 1903, Cd. 1640, 11–12. The original resolution, proposed by Sir Godfrey Lagden, read, "This Conference is of the opinion that South Africa is essentially a white man's country, and that the permanent settlement upon the land of Asiatic . . ." It was altered at the suggestion of Sir Gordon Sprigg (11).

20. As opponents of Chinese labor also noted, however, the widespread introduction of white workers would herald the introduction of trade unions on the Rand, something the Randlords dreaded with as much vigor as interracial labor (Milner, *The Milner Papers*, 458).

21. H. W. Just, "Proposal to import Asiatic, more particularly Chinese, Labour for the Transvaal Mines," January 1904, TNA, CO 879/82/3, 1–2.

22. Report of Mr. H. Ross Skinner furnished to the Witwatersrand Labour Association, September 22, 1903, Cd. 1895, 77–78.

23. Extract from the *Rand Daily Mail*, April 1, 1903, Cd. 1895, 14.

24. Mawby, "Capital, Government and Politics in the Transvaal," 395.

25. Milner to J. E. Moffat, April 1, 1903, in Milner, *The Milner Papers*, 460.

26. Milner to E. H. Walton, April 8, 1903, in Milner, *The Milner Papers*, 461. This was a key distinction in Milner's mind. He told Farrar, "The great and fatal confusion in people's minds is between Asiatic *Immigration* and Asiatic *importation*" (Milner to Sir George Farrar, April 21, 1903, in Milner, *The Milner Papers*, 461, emphasis in original).

27. Milner to Chamberlain, April 6, 1903, in Milner, *The Milner Papers*, 461.

28. Extract from Chamberlain's Speech at Johannesburg, January 17, 1903, TNA, CO 879/80/4, 357.

29. Denoon, *A Grand Illusion*, 143.

30. The Witwatersrand Trades and Labour Council to Colonial Office, August 8, 1903, Cd. 1895, 55.

31. Grant, *A Civilised Savagery*, 87; Mawby, *Gold Mining and Politics*, 422–23.

32. Labour Importation Association Manifesto, 1904, Cd. 1895, 58, 60–64.

33. Majority Report, February 1904, Cd. 1896, 1, 33, 39. In contrast the Commission's Minority Report, composed by two dissenting members, disputed that the labor

needs of the colony could not be met by African labor, and instead charged that "the policy of the Chamber of Mines is directed to the perpetuation of the Inferior Race Labour System by the importation of Asiatics" (Cd. 1896, 46).

34. Richardson, *Chinese Mine Labour in the Transvaal*, 22.

35. Ibid., 22; Grant, *A Civilised Savagery*, 88.

36. Yap and Leong Man, *Colour, Confusion and Concessions*, 112.

37. Extract from the *Transvaal Leader*, April 2, 1903, Cd. 1895, 15.

38. Mawby, *Gold Mining and Politics*, 397–99; Grant, *A Civilised Savagery*, 87.

39. Extract from the *Transvaal Leader*, April 2, 1903, Cd. 1895, 16.

40. Ibid., 15.

41. Ibid., 16, 18.

42. Mawby, *Gold Mining and Politics*, 399–400.

43. Extract from *Star*, July 1, 1903, Cd. 1895, 47–48.

44. The African Labour League to Colonial Office, August 4, 1903, Cd. 1895, 46–47.

45. Pretoria Trades' and Labour Council to High Commissioner, August 15, 1903, Cd. 1895, 69.

46. Resolution by the Citizens of Heidelberg, July 2, 1903, CUL, Smuts Private Letters, reel 667, vol. 2, no. 13.

47. Memorandum to Labour Commission, September 15, 1903, in Smuts, *Selections from the Smuts Papers*, 2:125–26, 132.

48. Ibid., 129–32.

49. Smuts to Emily Hobhouse, December 16, 1903, in Smuts, *Selections from the Smuts Papers*, 2:140.

50. Smuts to Hobhouse, February 21, 1904, CUL, Smuts Private Letters, reel 668, vol. 3, no. 122.

51. Milner to Lyttelton, January 11, 1904, Cd. 1899, 4, 5.

52. Milner to Lyttelton, January 29, 1904, Cd. 1899, 4.

53. Smuts to Hobhouse, March 13, 1904, in Smuts, *Selections from the Smuts Papers*, 2:154.

54. Governor Sir W. F. Hely-Hutchinson (Cape) to Chamberlain, July 3, 1903, Cd. 1895, 44.

55. Minute of Cape Government, August 17, 1903, TNA, CO 879/82/3, 24.

56. Lewsen, *John X. Merriman*, 1–42.

57. Extract from the *South African News*, December 8, 1903, Cd. 1895, 170, 171–72.

58. Hely-Hutchinson to Lyttelton, December 15, 1903, Cd. 1895, 181.

59. Extract from the *South African News*, November 27, 1903, Cd. 1895, 132.

60. Hely-Hutchinson to Lyttleton, January 21, 1904, TNA, CO 879/80/4, 288.

61. Milner to Lyttelton, February 6, 1904, Cd. 1899, 9, 10.

62. Lyttelton to Hely-Hutchinson, January 29, 1904, Cd. 1895, 329.

63. Sir George Fiddes, "Asiatic Labour for the Transvaal," November 9, 1903, TNA, CO 879/84/1, 1–2, 4, 6–7.

64. Seddon to Sir John Anderson, May 6, 1903, NLNZ, Seddon Family Papers, 1850–1971, MS-Papers-1619-013.

65. NZPD, 110: 468.

66. The Canadian Premier, Sir Wilfrid Laurier, declined an invitation from the Capetown Anti-Asiatic League to involve his dominion in the struggle to prevent Chinese importation. In his reply to that organization's entreaty he simply stated, "Not knowing local condition I do not think my interference advisable" (LAC, WLP, vol. 753, part 2, reel C1171, frame 215690).

67. Seddon to the colonial secretary, Pretoria, January 19, 1904, Cd. 1941, 28. An identical telegram was also sent by Deakin on the same day.

68. The Earl of Ranfurly to Lyttelton, January 20, 1904, Cd. 1895, 231; Lord Northcote to Lyttelton, March 28, 1904, Cd. 2104, 2.

69. Wellington Trades and Labour Council to Seddon, January 26, 1904, ANZ, Seddon, 2, box/item 17. Bright points out that many of the Transvaal's labor activists came from Australia, which helped facilitate these intercolonial connections (*Chinese Labour in South Africa*, 46).

70. Australasian Federated Seamen's Industrial Association, Dunedin Section, to Seddon, January 22, 1904, ANZ, Seddon, 2, box/item 17.

71. Carlton Trades Hall Council to Seddon, January 25, 1903, ANZ, Seddon, 2, box/item 17.

72. Mayor of Sydney to Seddon, March 30, 1904, ANZ, Seddon, 2, box/item 17.

73. [Illegible] to Seddon, February 11, 1904, ANZ, Seddon, 2, box/item 17.

74. F. R. McDonald to Seddon, January 21, 1904, ANZ, Seddon, 2, box/item 17.

75. Seddon to McDonald, March 15, 1904, ANZ, Seddon, 2, box/item 17.

76. Seddon to W. Hutchison, March 9, 1904, ANZ, Seddon, 2, box/item 17.

77. Grant, *A Civilised Savagery*, 80. As Grant points out, however, "it was Britain's trade unions that drove popular opposition to indentured Chinese labor in the Transvaal and raised the specter of slavery in British public debates" (89). English pamphlets tirelessly expounded these arguments during the debate. See, for example, Macnamara, *Chinese Labour*; Naylor, *Yellow Labour*. For a discussion of the broader debate in Britain, see Auerbach, *Race, Law, and "the Chinese Puzzle" in Imperial Britain*, 28–37.

78. UKPD, 129: 1533, 1504, 1516, 1523. Samuel's amendment ultimately failed, prompting the Liberal leader, Sir Henry Campbell-Bannerman, to introduce a censure motion: "This House disapproves the conduct of His Majesty's Government in advising the Crown not to disallow the Ordinance for the introduction of Chinese Labour into the Transvaal" (UKPD, 132: 271–72). This motion also narrowly failed in a 299–242 vote.

79. UKPD, 129: 1524–25, 1527.

80. UKPD, 130: 58.

81. UKPD, 132: 359.

82. UKPD, 129: 1589–90, 1592.

83. UKPD, 130: 29, 87.

84. UKPD, 132: 352–53, 354.

85. Colonial secretary, Pretoria, to Seddon and Deakin, January 20, 1904, Cd. 1941, 29.

86. Lyttelton to the Earl of Ranfurly (New Zealand), January 25, 1904, Cd. 1895, 327.
87. UKPD, 129: 1547–48.
88. Hely-Hutchinson to Lyttleton, January 21, 1904, TNA, CO 879/80/4, 289.
89. Kynoch, " 'Your Petitioners Are in Mortal Terror,' " 531.
90. Yap and Leong Man, *Colour, Confusion and Concessions*, 114.
91. Grant, *A Civilised Savagery*, 94–98, 104.

Chapter Three

1. Chang, *Pacific Connections*; Geiger, *Subverting Exclusion*; Lake and Reynolds, *Drawing the Global Color Line*; Sohi, *Echoes of Mutiny*; Lee, *The Making of Asian America*; Young, *Alien Nation*.
2. "The Curse of Colour," *Saturday Review*, September 14, 1907, 320.
3. Of course Asian migrants did settle east of the Rockies during this period. See, for example, Ling, *Chinese Chicago*; Ling, *Chinese St. Louis*; Jung, *Coolies and Cane*; Lui, *The Chinatown Trunk Mystery*; Marshall, *Cultivating Connections*; Marshall, *The Way of the Bachelor*.
4. As quoted in Johnson, *Discrimination against the Japanese in California*, 10. For a study of regional resentments in Canada, see Janigan, *Let the Eastern Bastards Freeze in the Dark*.
5. Jacobson, *Whiteness of a Different Color*; Tichenor, *Dividing Lines*, 114–49; Zolberg, *A Nation by Design*, 199–267.
6. Knowles, *Strangers at Our Gates*, 48–49; "The Chinaman before the Supreme Court," 260.
7. Daniels, *The Politics of Prejudice*, 111. The figures are deceptive, however, as Daniels observes. Many did not remain in the country, and the commissioner general of immigration did not begin tracking Japanese emigration from the United States until 1909.
8. Azuma, *Between Two Empires*, 30.
9. Price, *Orienting Canada*, 17.
10. The Australian figures come from Yarwood, *Asian Migration to Australia*, 163.
11. Yokota, "Transatlantic and Transpacific Connections in Early American History"; Armitage and Bashford, *Pacific Histories*; Chang, *Pacific Connections*; Sinn, *Pacific Crossing*; Belich, *Replenishing the Earth*; Cumings, *Dominion from Sea to Sea*.
12. Azuma, *Between Two Empires*, 29. See also Takai, "Bridging the Pacific."
13. LaFeber, *The Clash*.
14. Barman, *The West beyond the West*, 15–54; Gough, *The Northwest Coast*; Mackie, *Trading beyond the Mountains*.
15. Chang, *Pacific Connections*, 18.
16. Roy, *A White Man's Province*, 26–27; Anderson, *Vancouver's Chinatown*, 35; Knowles, *Strangers at Our Gates*, 50.
17. Roy, *A White Man's Province*, 54–61; Ward, *White Canada Forever*, 36–42; "An Act to Execute Certain Treaty Stipulations Relating to Chinese (a.k.a. Chinese Exclusion

Act), May 6, 1882," in Odo, *The Columbia Documentary History of the Asian American Experience*, 62–63.

18. *Report of the Royal Commission on Chinese and Japanese Immigration*, 327–35; Takai, "Navigating Transpacific Passages"; Geiger, *Subverting Exclusion*, 99–123; McLaren, "The Burdens of Empire and the Legalization of White Supremacy in Canada," 191.

19. Chang, *Pacific Connections*.

20. An act relating to the employment of Chinese or Japanese persons on Works carried on under franchises granted by Private Acts, *Statutes of the Province of British Columbia*, 3–4; Ward, *White Canada Forever*, 55.

21. For an exposition on the multiple layers of authority that overlay this region, see Atkinson, "Out of One Borderland, Many."

22. Japanese Consul General in Vancouver to the Governor-General, June 1, 1897, LAC, RG 25, vol. 1430, 26–27.

23. For a discussion of Japanese racial thought, which was just as fluid, contradictory, and complicated as Western racial thought, see Aydin, *The Politics of Anti-Westernism in Asia*; Weiner, "Discourses of Race, Nation and Empire in Pre-1945 Japan."

24. Report by the Minister of Justice, October 15, 1897, LAC, RG 25, vol. 1430, 28. Under the British North America Act, if the governor-general wished to disallow a reserved act he had to do so within two years of its passage. By withholding his assent during that time the reserved act could not become law.

25. Japanese Consul at Vancouver to the Governor-General, May 10, 1898, LAC, RG 25, vol. 1430, 29–30.

26. Japanese Consul at Vancouver to the Governor-General, May 28, 1898, LAC, RG 25, vol. 1430, 34–35. Each bill imposed specific prohibitions on Japanese employment in public works or public utility projects.

27. Secretary of State for the Colonies to the Governor-General, July 20, 1898, LAC, RG 25, vol. 1430, 36.

28. Ward, *White Canada Forever*, 55.

29. Japanese Minister to the Secretary of State for the Colonies, August 3, 1898, LAC, RG 25, vol. 1430, 40–41.

30. Japanese Consul at Vancouver to the Governor-General, February 16, 1899, LAC, RG 25, vol. 1430, 47.

31. Japanese Consul at Vancouver to the Governor-General, February 28, 1899, LAC, RG 25, vol. 1430, 48.

32. Minister of Finance and Agriculture to the Lieutenant Governor in Council, February 13, 1899, LAC, RG 25, vol. 1430, 51–53.

33. Secretary of State for the Colonies to the Governor-General, April 19, 1899, LAC, RG 25, vol. 1430, 55–56.

34. Governor-General to the Secretary of State for the Colonies, June 6, 1899, LAC, RG 25, vol. 1430, 59.

35. Roy, *A White Man's Province*, 103.

36. Ward, *White Canada Forever*, 55–56. Roy suggests a large number of these immigrants were also en route to the United States, where the Great Northern Railway awaited their services (*A White Man's Province*, 103).

37. Chargé d'affaires to the Secretary of State for Foreign Affairs, May 19, 1900, LAC, RG 25, vol. 1430, 72. See also Instructions issued by the Foreign Office to the Local Governors with regard to the restriction of emigration to Canada, May 17, 1900, LAC, RG 25, vol. 1430, 73; Roy, *A White Man's Province*, 104.

38. Chargé d'affaires to the Secretary of State for Foreign Affairs, August 12, 1900, LAC, RG 25, vol. 1430, 76. Japan's preparations for a possible war with Russia, rather than sensitivity toward British Columbia's claims to economic and racial hegemony, may actually have provided the more urgent context for this decision (Adachi, *The Enemy That Never Was*, 44).

39. Ward, *White Canada Forever*, 57.

40. Japanese Consul at Vancouver to the Governor-General, September 1, 1900, LAC, RG 25, vol. 1430, 73–74.

41. Secretary of State for the Colonies to the Governor-General, March 23, 1899, LAC, RG 25, vol. 1430, 79.

42. "As an election device," Patricia Roy notes, "the commission was remarkably successful." Laurier's Liberal Party held on to its four British Columbian constituencies (*A White Man's Province*, 112). For the report, see *Report of the Royal Commission on Chinese and Japanese Immigration*.

43. Interviews with British Columbia residents, laborers, and producers are scattered throughout the entire report.

44. Part 2, "Japanese Immigration," in *Report of the Royal Commission on Chinese and Japanese Immigration*, 397–98.

45. Newspaper clipping, June 11, 1903, LAC, RG 76, vol. 83, file 9309, vol. 1, 261779.

46. Memorandum showing Acts passed by the Provincial Legislature of British Columbia relating to Japanese Immigration, disallowed by His Excellency the Governor-General, n.d., LAC, RG 25, vol. 1430, 108. The province also continued its attempts to limit Japanese access to the franchise, with the same result.

47. Roy, *A White Man's Province*, 119.

48. For a detailed discussion of the issues surrounding this legislation, see Gyory, *Closing the Gate*; Lee, *At America's Gates*.

49. Chang, *Pacific Connections*, 54–88.

50. LaFeber, *The Clash*, 88. Daniels calculates that Japanese immigrants never composed more than .021 percent of the Californian population during this period (or .001 percent of the entire U.S. population; *The Politics of Prejudice*, 1).

51. Bailey, *Theodore Roosevelt and the Japanese-American Crises*, 11.

52. Ibid., 14; Hosokawa, *Nisei*, 85.

53. Neu, *An Uncertain Friendship*, 23; Esthus, *Theodore Roosevelt and Japan*, 130. The League changed its name to the Asiatic Exclusion League in 1907, once its members realized that South Asians were beginning to arrive in the United States in small but growing numbers (Jacoby, "U.S. Strategies of Asian Indian Immigration Restriction," 36).

54. The segregation order was never actually enforced (Daniels, *Guarding the Golden Door*, 43). Rather than attend the Oriental school many Japanese students were temporarily educated by private Japanese tutors at specially organized schools (Hosokawa, *Nisei*, 88).

55. See, for example, Neu, *An Uncertain Friendship*, 51; Takaki, Strangers from a Different Shore, 202–3.

56. Secretary of State Root, for example, later denied that any serious constitutional or international questions had been raised by the school board's actions ("War with Japan Never Near," *New York Times*, April 20, 1907).

57. Ambassador Luke E. Wright to Secretary Elihu Root, October 21, 1906, Case 1797/1, NA, RG 59, M862, reel 189.

58. Notes on the Boycotting of Japanese Restaurants and Assaults on Japanese Residents in San Francisco, October 25, 1906, Case 1797/4, NA, RG 59, M862, reel 189. This included two Japanese professors dispatched from Tokyo's Imperial University to conduct an investigation of the earthquake's effects (Esthus, *Theodore Roosevelt and Japan*, 132–33).

59. Root to Wright, October 23, 1906, Case 1797, NA, RG 59, M862, reel 189.

60. Wright to Root, October 22, 1906, Case 1797/47-48, NA, RG 59, M862, reel 189, 3–4.

61. Wright to Root, October 31, 1906, Case 1797/55-58, NA, RG 59, M862, reel 189, 1.

62. Scott, "The Japanese School Question," 151.

63. A Paraphrase of the Instructions Received from the Imperial Government, October 25, 1906, Case 1797/4, NA, RG 59, M862, reel 189.

64. Notes on the Exclusion of Japanese Children from the Public Schools of San Francisco, October 25, 1906, Case 1797/6, NA, RG 59, M862, reel 189.

65. Confidential Memorandum for Secretary Metcalf regarding the Exclusion of Japanese Children from the Public Schools and the Boycotting of Japanese Restaurants in San Francisco, October 27, 1906, Case 1797/13, NA, RG 59, M862, reel 189.

66. Bailey, *Theodore Roosevelt and the Japanese-American Crises*, 32.

67. Memorandum on the Discrimination against Japanese Subjects in California, November 27, 1906, Case 1797/61, NA, RG 59, M862, reel 189, 11–12, 12–13.

68. Secretary Victor Metcalf to President Theodore Roosevelt, November 2, 1906, Case 1797/37, NA, RG 59, M862, reel 189, 1, 2.

69. Robert T. Devlin to the Attorney General, November 2, 1906, Case 1797/53-54, NA, RG 59, M862, reel 189, 6.

70. Memorandum handed to secretary of state by Japanese ambassador, November 7, 1906, Case 1797/52, NA, RG 59, M862, reel 189, 1–3.

71. Root to the Attorney General, November 13, 1906, Case 1797/52, NA, RG 59, M862, reel 189, 2–3.

72. For Metcalf's report, see Final Report of Secretary Metcalf on the Situation Affecting the Japanese in the City of San Francisco, November 26, 1906, missing case number, NA, RG 59, M862, reel 191. For the response in California, see Bailey, *Theodore Roosevelt and the Japanese-American Crises*, 114–18.

73. Sixth Annual Message to Congress, December 3, 1906, in Richardson, *A Compilation of the Messages and Papers of the Presidents*, 7053–55.

74. Daniels, *The Politics of Prejudice*, 40. See also Huntington Wilson to Root, October 22, 1906, Case 1797/2, NA, RG 59, M862, reel 189. As Neu points out, the Japanese foreign minister also alluded to this possibility in December 1906 (*An Uncertain Friendship*, 52). See also Wright to Root, December 26, 1906, in U.S. Department of State, *Japanese Emigration and Immigration to American Territory*, 30.

75. H.R. 246, December 2, 1907, Case 12050, NA, RG 59, M862, reel 792.

76. Telegram from Root to Wright, November 19, 1906, Case 1797/58a, NA, RG 59, M862, reel 189.

77. Root to Aoki, December 28, 1906, in U.S. Department of State, *Japanese Emigration and Immigration to American Territory*, 32–33. His logic was contradictory, however, since it actually presupposed the existence of racist animosity. Root himself continued, "The difficulty which we are confronting is not the existence of any race feeling inconsistent with the strong and warm friendship which has existed between our countries, but it is that whenever there is a strong, interested motive to stir up race feeling among laborers of any two races as a means to prevent labor competition it is always easy to do so, and that motive exists on our Pacific coast" (32).

78. Root to Wright, February 2, 1907, Case 1797/58a, NA, RG 59, M862, reel 189.

79. Wright to Root, February 1, 1907, Case 1797/152-167, NA, RG 59, M862, reel 190; Paraphrase of a Telegram from Viscount Hayashi, Minister for Foreign Affairs, to Viscount Aoki, January 19, 1907, in U.S. Department of State, *Japanese Emigration and Immigration to American Territory*, 36.

80. U.S. Department of Commerce and Labor, Bureau of Immigration and Naturalization, *Immigration Laws and Regulations of July 1, 1907*, 5.

81. Daniels, *Guarding the Golden Door*, 44.

82. Root to Wright, February 20, 1907, Case 1797/152-167, NA, RG 59, M862, reel 190; Wilson and Hosokawa, *East to America*, 53.

83. Neu, *An Uncertain Friendship*, 70.

84. Executive Order, March 14, 1907, Case 2542/63, NA, RG 59, M862, reel 253.

85. Neu, *An Uncertain Friendship*, 71.

86. Wilson and Hosokawa, *East to America*, 54. Even this did not entirely resolve the issue, however, since the agreement did nothing to prevent the immigration of "picture brides," who married legal Japanese residents in absentia, often based on an exchange of photographs (54–55). This practice was so prevalent that the Japanese American population of the United States more than doubled in the next twenty years, and women soon outnumbered men in the Japanese American diaspora (Daniels, *Asian America*, 126).

87. Jensen, *Passage from India*, 15. See also Sohi, *Echoes of Mutiny*, 14–28.

88. L. Edwin Dudley to the Assistant Secretary of State, November 22, 1906, Case 2376, NA, RG 59, M862, reel 238. Canada had yet to impose restrictions on South Asian immigration.

89. Jensen, *Passage From India*, 45. See also Gilmour, *Trouble on Main Street*.

90. "Mob Drives Out Hindus," *New York Times*, September 6, 1907.

91. Report re Attack on Hindus at Bellingham, September 9, 1907, TNA, FO 371/360, no. 30029; "Mob Law Rules in City," *Bellingham Herald*, September 5, 1907.

92. "Scared Hindus in Hurry to Go," *Bellingham Herald*, September 5, 1907.

93. Jensen, *Passage From India*, 30.

94. Petition from the Indian residents of Everett, September 5, 1907, TNA, FO 371/360, no. 30029.

95. James Laidlaw to James Bryce, September 11, 1907, TNA, FO 371/360, no. 30029.

96. Laidlaw to Sir Edward Grey, September 16, 1907, TNA, FO 371/360, no. 30029. Those South Asians who actually made the journey to Alaska faced similar violence and intimidation. As Jensen notes, many were turned back at the Alaskan ports of Wrangell, Douglas Island, and Juneau, prevented from landing by angry whites (*Passage from India*, 53).

97. Laidlaw to Sir Edward Grey, October 3, 1907, TNA, FO 371/360, no. 35124.

98. Newton Jones to Laidlaw, September 14, 1907, TNA, FO 371/360, no. 35124.

99. "Mob Scares Everett Hindus," *Everett Daily Herald*, November 4, 1907, TNA, FO 371/360, no. 38792.

100. "Leader," *Everett Daily Herald*, November 4, 1907, TNA, FO 371/360, no. 38792. This feeling was apparently widespread. According to the British vice consul in Seattle, Everett's mayor was unable to deputize anybody in town since nobody was willing to defend the town's South Asian residents (Laidlaw to Sir Edward Grey, November 8, 1907, TNA, FO 371/360, no. 38882).

101. See TNA, FO 371/359, nos. 4089, 8359, 22924. See also Jensen, *Passage from India*, 19–21; Chang, *Pacific Connections*, 117–35; Sohi, *Echoes of Mutiny*.

102. "Bryce Sure to Act on Hindu Expulsion," *New York Times*, September 7, 1907.

103. Bryce to Sir Edward Grey, October 14, 1907, TNA, FO 371/274, no. 32090.

104. Under Secretary of State, India Office, to Under Secretary of State, Foreign Office, February 7, 1908, and Under Secretary of State, Foreign Office, to Under Secretary of State, India Office, February 25, 1908, TNA, FO 371/565, no. 4453.

105. Bryce to Sir Edward Grey, January 29, 1908, TNA, FO 371/565, no. 5201. The American government finally prohibited South Asian immigration in 1917, creating a "barred Asiatic zone" that stretched from Afghanistan to the Pacific, excepting Japan and the Philippines (Ngai, *Impossible Subjects*, 37).

106. Adachi, *The Enemy That Never Was*, 44–45.

107. Jensen, *Passage from India*, 63–65.

108. Adachi, *The Enemy That Never Was*, 72–73. Anticipating their arrival the British governor-general in Canada, Earl Grey, warned Laurier that preparations were necessary to accommodate these "refugees." Thankfully for Laurier and Grey, the 400 exiles from Bellingham reportedly crossed the border on September 15, after the violence in Vancouver had subsided (Earl Grey to the Earl of Elgin, September 24, 1907, TNA, FO 371/274, no. 34263).

109. Ward, *White Canada Forever*, 68.

110. Japanese Consul General to the Governor-General, September 8, 1907, LAC, RG 25, vol. 1003, 112–13; Mayor of Vancouver to Laurier, September 14, 1907, LAC, WLP, vol. 477, reel C852, frame 129142; Jensen, *Passage from India*, 67.

111. Japanese Consul General to the Governor-General, September 8, 1907, LAC, RG 25, vol. 1003, 109–10; From the Secretary of State for the Colonies to the Governor-General, September 11, 1907, LAC, RG 25, vol. 1003, 110.

112. Sir Wilfrid Laurier to Sir Claude MacDonald, October 11, 1907, TNA, FO 371/274, no. 35138.

113. Rossland Miners Union to Laurier, undated, LAC, WLP, vol. 441, reel C841, frame 117578.

114. Trades and Labour Congress of Canada to First Minister, September 17, 1907, LAC, RG 25, vol. 1003, 116.

115. Laurier to Francis J. Deane, September 11, 1907, LAC, WLP, vol. 476, reel C851, frame 128729. For its part, according to the British ambassador in Tokyo, Sir Claude MacDonald, the response of the Japanese press was actually "distinguished for its moderation" (Sir Claude MacDonald to Sir Edward Grey, October 2, 1907, TNA, FO 371/274, no. 35579).

116. MacDonald to Sir Edward Grey, November 15, 1907, TNA, FO 371/274, no. 37718. At the same time, the Canadian government also dispatched the deputy minister of labor (and future prime minister) William Lyon Mackenzie King to British Columbia in order to investigate the methods by which Asian immigrants were induced to make the journey to Canada (Extract from a Report of the Committee of the Privy Council, November 5, 1907, LAC, RG 25, vol. 1003, 126).

117. Report by the Honourable Rodolphe Lemieux, KC, Minister of Labor, of his Mission to Japan on the Subject of the Influx of Oriental Labourers into the Province of British Columbia, January 12, 1908, LAC, RG 25, vol. 727, file 83, part 1a, 11–12, 8–9.

118. Memorandum presented to Count Hayashi on the 25th November, 1907, by the Honourable Mr. Lemieux . . . , November 25, 1907, LAC, RG 25, vol. 1003, 133.

119. Lemieux Report, January 12, 1908, LAC, RG 25, vol. 727, file 83, part 1a, 13–14.

120. Ibid., 20.

121. Ibid., 21–22. Hayashi also imposed prohibitive registration fees on Japanese emigration companies.

122. First Minister to Postmaster General, December 10, 1907, LAC, RG 25, vol. 727, file 83, part 1a, 157; Governor-General to the Secretary of State for the Colonies, December 17, 1907, LAC, RG 25, Volume 1003. To complicate matters further the British Columbia legislature was once again debating outright anti-Asian restrictions and a new Natal Act (159–60).

123. Lemieux Report, January 12, 1908, LAC, RG 25, vol. 727, file 83, part 1a, 23–24. The agreement also received the approval of the British ambassador in Tokyo (His Majesty's Ambassador in Tokio to the Governor-General, December 5, 1907, LAC, RG 25, vol. 1003, 148).

124. Governor-General to His Majesty's Ambassador at Tokio, January 14, 1908, LAC, RG 25, vol. 1003, 201.

125. Governor-General to the Secretary of State for the Colonies, November 11, 1907, LAC, RG 25, vol. 1003, 127.

126. Governor-General to His Majesty's Consul, Honolulu, to Governor-General of Hong Kong, and to Viceroy of India, January 13, 1908, LAC, RG 25, vol. 1003, 200. The vast majority of South Asian immigrants arrived in Canada via Hong Kong (Buchignan et al., *Continuous Journey*, 23). For the Earl of Minto's response, see Viceroy of India to the Governor-General, January 25, 1908, LAC, RG 25, vol. 1003, 210–11.

127. Hawkins, *Critical Years in Immigration*, 17.

128. Roy, *A White Man's Province*, 202–7.

129. Report by W. L. King on Mission to England to Confer with the British Authorities on the Subject of Immigration to Canada from the Orient and Immigration from India in Particular, May 4, 1908, LAC, RG 25, vol. 1004, 7–10.

Chapter Four

1. "England Greatly Alarmed," *New York Times*, September 10, 1907; "The Vancouver Riots," *Times*, October 18, 1907; "Responsibility Disclaimed," *New York Times*, September 12, 1907; "The Vancouver Outrages," *Times*, September 11, 1907.

2. Chang, *Pacific Connections*; Lake and Reynolds, *Drawing the Global Colour Line*; Lee, *The Making of Asian America*; Lee, "The 'Yellow Peril' and Asian Exclusion in the Americas."

3. Roosevelt privately claimed that Laurier and Mackenzie King initiated this unorthodox diplomatic venture, and his only account of the meeting effectively constitutes a mirror image of that provided by Mackenzie King and Bryce. See Theodore Roosevelt to Arthur Hamilton Lee, 4578, February 2, 1908, in *The Letters of Theodore Roosevelt*, 918–20. John Price also describes this as Roosevelt's initiative in his brief treatment of the meetings, " 'Orienting' the Empire." Since the Canadian and British statesmen left the most detailed records of the substance of these meetings, however, this chapter accepts their interpretation. Regardless of who was responsible, the fact remains that this effort to enact Anglo-American-Canadian diplomatic collaboration against Japanese migration ultimately failed. See also Gordon, "Roosevelt's 'Smart Yankee Trick.' " For a deeper discussion of Mackenzie King's role, see Gilmour, *Trouble on Main Street*.

4. "News of the Week," *Spectator*, September 14, 1907, 345.

5. "Mob Law in Vancouver," *British Colonist*, September 10, 1907.

6. "The Anti-Asiatic Agitation," *Times*, September 13, 1907.

7. "Riots Not Caused by the Americans," *New York Times*, September 14, 1907. See also "The Vancouver Race Riot," *Independent*, September 19, 1907, 701.

8. James Bryce to Sir Edward Grey, September 14, 1907, TNA, FO 371/274, no. 32090.

9. James Bryce to Sir Edward Grey, September 21, 1907, TNA, FO 371/360, no. 30029.

10. T. R. E. McInnes to Wilfrid Laurier, September 11, 1907, LAC, WLP, vol. 478, reel C852, 129162. Patricia Roy suggests that W. W. B. McInnes may have been the League's de facto leader (*A White Man's Province*, 201). For a broader discussion of the

attitudes of the Canadian labor movement's leadership toward immigration, see Goutor, *Guarding the Gates.*

11. McInnes to Laurier, November 7, 1907, LAC, WLP, vol. 487, reel C854, 131593.

12. Mr. McInnes to Mr. Oliver, October 2, 1907, TNA, FO 371/274, no. 39250, 8.

13. McInnes to Governor Grey, February 7, 1908, TNA, FO 410/51, 378–79.

14. Resolution by the Asiatic Exclusion League of Vancouver, BC, February 21, 1908, LAC, WLP, vol. 506, reel C859, 136755.

15. Gordon M. Grant to Laurier, February 22, 1908, LAC, WLP, vol. 506, reel C859, 136740.

16. Extract from *The Week: A British Columbia Review,* January 25, 1908, LAC, WLP, vol. 506, reel C859, 135709.

17. Gordon M. Grant to Laurier, February 22, 1908, LAC, WLP, vol. 506, reel C859, 136740.

18. Huntington-Wilson to Root, October 12, 1907, Case 2542/170-174, NA, RG 59, reel 254.

19. Roosevelt to Root, November 19, 1907, Case 2542/175, NA, RG 59, reel 254.

20. Lemieux Report, January 12, 1908, LAC, RG 25, vol. 727, file 83, part 1a, 19.

21. Sir C. MacDonald to Foreign Office, March 11, 1908, TNA, FO 371/473, 386.

22. King report on Meeting with President Roosevelt, undated, TNA, FO 371/471, 2/217, 3/218.

23. Ibid., 3/218, 5/220, 7/222, 8/223, 9/224.

24. Memorandum, March 1908, TNA, FO 371/471, [no file number, p. 212].

25. Bryce to Sir Edward Grey, February 5, 1908, TNA, FO 410/51, 63–64.

26. Mackenzie King report on Meeting with President Roosevelt, undated, TNA, FO 371/471, 13/228-15/230, 19/234, 23/238.

27. Bryce to Sir Edward Grey, February 5, 1908, TNA, FO 410/51, 64–65.

28. Mackenzie King Report, undated, TNA, FO 371/471, 24/239.

29. Sir Edward Grey to Bryce, February 5, 1908, TNA, FO 371/471, 24/239, 58. The American Embassy in London did, however, transmit copies of British colonial immigration restriction acts for their "suggestive value" (Acting Secretary of State to the Secretary of Commerce and Labour, March 21, 1908, Case 12200, NA, RG 59, reel 803).

30. Bryce to Grey, February 7, 1908, TNA, FO 410/51, no. 5832.

31. King Report, undated, TNA, FO 371/471, 30/245, 38/253, 40/255-41/256.

32. Sir Charles Prestwood Lucas, "The Self-Governing Dominions and Coloured Immigration," July 1908, TNA, CO 886/1/1, 53–54.

33. Sir Charles Prestwood Lucas, "Suggestions as to Coloured immigration into the Self-Governing Dominions," July 1908, TNA, CO 886/1/2, 1–2, 3–4, 6–8.

34. Bryce to Sir Edward Grey, July 12, 1907, TNA, FO 371/360, no. 25775. Bryce and the Foreign Office dismissed their rumors.

35. Bryce to Sir Edward Grey, September 26, 1907, TNA, FO 371/360, no. 32092; C. W. Bennett to Bryce, December 5, 1907, TNA, FO 371/360, no. 41258. Bennett's suggestion was categorically rejected by the Foreign Office.

36. Bryce to Sir Edward Grey, January 22, 1908, TNA, FO 410/51, 53–54. The European press was seen as especially complicit in fostering a war scare between Japan and United States as the fleet progressed westward. The French newspaper *Le Matin* was considered particularly culpable by Bryce and the *New York Times*. See "War Talk in Paris," *New York Times*, January 3, 1908. In fact French opinion was considerably more nuanced than Bryce supposed. See, for example, Robinson, "The Debate over Japanese Immigration." Germany was similarly intrigued by the ongoing drama. See "War Talk Again Heard in Germany," *New York Times*, January 4, 1908; "War Talk Quieted by Diplomats," *New York Times*, January 9, 1908.

37. B. R. James to Bryce, January 21, 1908, TNA, FO 410/51, 54–55. Emperor Wilhelm II of Germany also attempted to complicate the situation. According to the British ambassador in Japan, it was well-known that Wilhelm offered to station the German fleet on America's East Coast for the duration of the American fleet's tour of the Pacific. He also offered Roosevelt a German army corps in case of war between Japan and the United States (McDonald to Grey, November 27, 1908, TNA, FO 371/477, no. 41475).

38. Reckner, *Teddy Roosevelt's Great White Fleet*, 11–13.

39. Memorandum respecting an Interview with President Roosevelt at Washington, February 10, 1908, TNA, FO 371/473, no. 7715.

40. Deakin to Lord Northcoate, January 24, 1908, NLA, Deakin Papers, MS 1540, series 15.5.7.6.1, box 48, folder 77, http://nla.gov.au/nla.ms-ms1540-15-3859-s1 (accessed November 17, 2008); Earl of Elgin to Lord Northcoate, March 22, 1908, NLA, Deakin Papers, MS 1540, series 15.5.7.6.1, box 48, folder 77, http://nla.gov.au/nla.ms-ms1540 -15-3867-s2 (accessed November 17, 2008).

41. Root to Roosevelt, February 21, 1908, Case 8258/145, NA, RG 59, reel 597.

42. Bryce to Root, March 21, 1908, Case 8258/254, NA, RG 59, reel 598; Root to Bryce, April 1, 1908, Case 8258/288, NA, RG 59, reel 598. On March 18, 1908, the Japanese government tendered an invitation to the State Department. According to the Japanese ambassador, Takahira Kogoro, the imperial government was "sincerely anxious to be afforded an opportunity to cordially welcome the magnificent fleet and to give an enthusiastic expression to the sentiment of friendship and admiration invariably entertained by the people of Japan toward the people of the United States." Takahira's government felt that the fleet's Pacific voyage would have a "reassuring effect" on Japanese-American relations. Takahira Kogoro to Root, March 18, 1908. Case 8258/252. NA, RG 59, reel 598. See also O'Brien to Root, October 25, 1908, Case 8258/575-579, NA, RG 59, M862, reel 599.

The Roosevelt administration quickly accepted the Japanese offer and arranged to visit Yokohama that October. An effort to invite the fleet to British Columbia, led by British Columbian politicians, local businessmen, and trade unions, failed due to time constraints, according to the Navy Department. This produced a collective sigh of relief from the British government. The secretary of state for the colonies, the Earl of Elgin, was particularly keen to prevent the fleet from visiting Vancouver since it "would probably be used as [an] opportunity for [an] anti-Japanese demonstration" (Secretary of State for the Colonies to the Governor-General of Canada, March 17, 1908, TNA, FO 371/475, no 9765). He was right. As one Vancouver councilor observed while proposing the invitation, "The visit of the fleet would be an object lesson to Asiatics and would show them that the Anglo-Saxons were united" (Dudley to the Assistant Secretary of State, March 12, 1908, Case 8258/248-250, NA, RG 59, reel 598).

43. NZPD, 143: 761.

44. Ibid., 590, 655, 555.

45. Ibid., 554, 555.

46. The previous year had witnessed an economic recession, and some of Wilford's Conservative colleagues, along with some trade union representatives and unemployed workers, opposed the elaborate preparations under way for the American visit. Taylor, "New Zealand, the Anglo-Japanese Alliance and the 1908 Visit of the American Fleet," 66.

47. NZPD, 143: 65. Successive members of Parliament insinuated that Wilford, as a representative from the Wellington area, was simply jealous that the fleet had time to visit only Auckland and would not be able to visit the capital.

48. Ibid., 658. Fraser did not address how the imperial government would explain to the majority nonwhite constituents of the empire its participation in an avowed Pacific race war.

49. Ibid., 199.

50. "The American Fleet," *New Zealand Herald*, August 8, 1908.

51. "America's Fleet," *Auckland Star*, August 8, 1908.

52. "The Lesson of the Fleet," *New Zealand Times*, August 7, 1908.

53. "More Binding than Treaties," *New Zealand Times*, August 17, 1908.

54. "White and Yellow," *New Zealand Times*, August 18, 1908.

55. "The American Fleet," *Dominion*, August 10, 1908.

56. "The Significance of the Fleet," *Dominion*, August 14, 1908.

57. "The Visit of the Fleet," *Dominion*, August 13, 1908; "A Timely Warning," *Dominion*, August 20, 1908.

58. "The Māori Welcome," *New Zealand Herald*, August 7, 1908.

59. NZPD, 143: 200, 201.

60. Ibid., 560–61.

61. "A Danger to Young Maoris?," *Evening Post*, July 20, 1908.

62. NZPD, 143: 201, 203, 562–63.

63. "The Maori Welcome," *New Zealand Herald*, August 7, 1908.

64. "Maoris and the United States Fleet," *Evening Post*, April 14, 1908.

65. "Speech by Prime Minister," *New Zealand Herald*, August 11, 1908.

66. Charles Sperry to his wife, August 16, 1908, LOC, Sperry Papers, box 5, Family Correspondence File, emphasis in original.

67. Roosevelt to Sperry, March 21, 1908, LOC, Sperry Papers, box 13, World Cruise Correspondence File.

68. The Earl of Dudley to the Earl of Crewe, September 18, 1908, TNA, FO 371/567, no. 32902.

69. The Earl of Crewe to the Earl of Dudley, October 12, 1908, TNA, FO 371/567, no. 35563.

70. Undated memorandum, NLA, Papers of Andrew Fisher, MS 2919, box 3, series 6, folder 20, 1–3. Such sentiments were by no means universal, however. Bruce Smith, a longtime opponent of the White Australia Policy and a staunch defender of Australia's imperial ties, warned Fisher in 1909, "The question of the unity of the British Empire transcends, at the present moment, every other national problem of the Anglo-Saxon race." Only by contributing to British naval power could the "unity and supremacy of our race as a whole . . . be guaranteed" (Bruce Smith to Andrew Fisher, May 20, 1909, Papers of Andrew Fisher, MS 2919, box 3, series 6, folder 20, 1–3.

Chapter Five

1. "Indians and the Empire," *New Statesman*, June 13, 1914, 294–95.

2. DCPD, 114: 1220.

3. Sir Conyngham Greene to Sir Edward Grey, May 22, 1914, TNA, FO 371/2011, no. 25785.

4. FO Minute, undated, TNA, FO 371/2011, no. 25785. Hamilton was personally hostile toward Japan. In a letter to renowned London *Times* correspondent Leopold Amery, written five years earlier, Hamilton revealed, "I detest them as a nation," and he decried Japanese interference in China. They were, he warned, "brave but thoroughly perfidious" (Ian Hamilton to L. S. Amery, August 7, 1909, CAC, GBR/0014/ AMEL 2/3/1).

5. Sir Conyngham Greene to Sir Edward Grey, May 22, 1914, TNA, FO 371/2011, no. 25785. "This note of racial distrust," wrote Greene, also undermined a recent effort by the First Lord of the Admiralty, Winston Churchill, to impress upon both the dominion governments and the Japanese that the Anglo-Japanese Alliance was vital to the defense of the Pacific dominions and ought to be preserved.

6. Grey to H. H. Asquith, June 14, 1914, TNA, FO 371/2011, no. 25785. Hamilton subsequently blamed erroneous press reports for the incident, and denied that his comments were aimed at the Japanese. His intended targets, he protested, were South Asian and Chinese coolies in South Africa (Sir Ian Hamilton to Asquith, June 26, 1914, TNA, FO 371/2011, no. 25785).

7. Lake and Reynolds, *Drawing the Global Colour Line*; Brawley, *The White Peril*; Shimazu, *Japan, Race, and Equality*.

8. Manela, *The Wilsonian Moment*; Aydin, *The Politics of Anti-Westernism in Asia*; Mishra, *From the Ruins of Empire*.

9. Although this chapter focuses on the tensions engendered by continued South Asian and Japanese restriction, it is important to note the vital role of Chinese migrant labor in Europe during the war. See Guoqi, *Strangers on the Western Front*.

10. Knowles, *Strangers at Our Gates*, 93.

11. Sohi, *Echoes of Mutiny*, 152–75.

12. The London Canadian-Indian Immigration Committee to the Colonial Office, May 30, 1913, LAC, RG 25, vol. 1003, 193; Report of the Committee of the Privy Council,

September 27, 1913, LAC, RG 25, vol. 1003, 199; From the India Office to the Colonial Office, December 9, 1913, LAC, RG 25, vol. 1003, 229.

13. Grandview Ratepayers Association to the First Minister, August 16, 1913, LAC, RG 25, vol. 1003, 195.

14. Report of the Committee of the Privy Council, August 25, 1913, LAC, RG 25, vol. 1003, 196.

15. Buchignani et al., *Continuous Journey*, 45.

16. Order in Council, December 8, 1913, LAC, RG 25, vol. 1003, 215; Ward, *White Canada Forever*, 185n28.

17. From the Secretary of State for the Colonies to the Governor-General, December 6, 1913, LAC, RG 25, vol. 1003, 236.

18. Buchignani et al., *Continuous Journey*, 54; Translation of Advertisement, undated, LAC, RG 25, vol. 1003, 303.

19. Governor of Hong Kong to Governor-General of Canada, March 30, 1914, LAC, RG 25, vol. 1003, 274–75; Undersecretary of State for External Affairs to the Governor-General's Secretary, April 6, 1914, LAC, RG 25, vol. 1003, 276–77.

20. Undersecretary of State for External Affairs to the Governor-General's Secretary, June 9, 1914, LAC, RG 25, vol. 1003, 317.

21. DCPD, 117: 5026.

22. Minutes of a Public Meeting Held in Dominion Hall, Vancouver, June 23, 1914, LAC, RBP, vol. 40, reel C4232, 17357–58.

23. Ibid., 17359–61, 17363–64, 17371.

24. Ibid., 17373.

25. Richard McBride to Robert Borden, June 24, 1914, LAC, RBP, vol. 40, reel C4232, 17356.

26. LOL Resolution, undated, LAC, RBP, vol. 40, reel C4232, 17394. For the resolution of Vancouver General Hospital's board of directors, see 17380.

27. Borden, "The Question of Oriental Immigration," in *Speeches*, 4, 9.

28. Secretary of State for the Colonies to the Governor-General, June 24, 1914, LAC, RG 25, vol. 1003, 324.

29. Gurdit Singh to the Governor-General, July 8, 1914, LAC, RBP, vol. 40, reel C4232, 17398.

30. Sir Charles Hibbert Tupper to Borden, July 10, 1914, LAC, RBP, vol. 40, reel C4232, 17404.

31. Borden to Sir Charles Hibbert, July 11, 1914, LAC, RBP, vol. 40, reel C4232, 17405.

32. Sir Charles Hibbert Tupper to Borden, July 13, 1914, LAC, RBP, vol. 40, reel C4232, 17409.

33. Report by E. B. Robertson, July 29, 1914, LAC, RG 25, vol. 1003, 351.

34. Buchignani et al., *Continuous Journey*, 57–58.

35. Ibid., 60–61. Singh finally surrendered in 1921.

36. "Says Japan Fights for Civilization," *New York Times*, December 13, 1914.

37. Grey to Japanese Ambassador, August 6, 1914, TNA, FO 371/2016, no. 35795.

38. Louis, "Australia and the German Colonies in the Pacific," 408. In addition to Japanese and Australian operations, New Zealand occupied German Samoa on August 30, 1914.

39. L. V. Harcourt to Ronald Crawford Munro Ferguson, December 6, 1914, NLA, RCMFP, box 2, folder 1295–1386.

40. Quoted in *Nichi Nichi*, Greene to Munro Ferguson, March 10, 1915, NAA, A981, JAP 181, part 1.

41. Quoted in *Mainichi Shimbun*, Greene to Munro Ferguson, April 30, 1916, NAA, A981, JAP 181, part 1.

42. Greene to Sir Edward Grey, March 15, 1915, NAA, A2219, vol. 1, part 2.

43. Translation of a Despatch from Baron Kato to Inouye, January 15, 1915, NAA, A2219, vol. 1, part 1.

44. Millar, *Australia in Peace and War*, 95. As Ian Nish puts it, the offer was simply "allowed to lapse" (*Alliance in Decline*, 172).

45. Munro Ferguson to King George V, January 3, 1915, NLA, RCMFP, box 1, folder 1–107.

46. Munro Ferguson to Harcourt, November 23, 1914, NLA, RCMFP, box 1, folder 524–653.

47. Sir John J. Jordan to Grey, August 9, 1914, TNA, FO 371/2016, no. 37436.

48. FO Minute by D. Alston, August 10, 1914, TNA, FO 371/2016, no. 37709.

49. Writing privately from his office in the South African Treasury that momentous August, Jan Smuts, who would play a crucial role in British planning for war and peace, was even less sanguine: "This war is a terrible business, which may put Europe and white civilization permanently back and hasten the day of the yellow peril" (Smuts to Sir B. Robertson, August 21, 1914, in *Selections from the Smuts Papers*, 3:190).

50. *CPD*, 75: 117.

51. Munro Ferguson to Harcourt, January 20, 1915, NLA, RCMFP, box 1, folder 1.

52. Munro Ferguson to Harcourt, March 17, 1915, NLA, RCMFP, box 1, folder 654–812.

53. Munro Ferguson to Harcourt, April 6, 1915, NLA, RCMFP, box 1, folder 654–812.

54. Munro Ferguson to Andrew Bonar Law, December 22, 1915, NLA, RCMFP, box 1, folder 654–812.

55. Munro Ferguson to Harcourt, May 13, 1915, NLA, RCMFP, box 1, folder 654–812.

56. Report on the Japanese Danger (1538/19/1-1538/19/14), October 21, 1915, NLA, WMHP, box 113, folder 1, 1, 5, 6–7.

57. Ibid., 7–8, 12, 9. They expected, fantastically, that Japan would most likely attack immediately after the present war, while Britain nursed its wounds.

58. Minute Paper: A Post-Bellum Naval Policy for the Pacific (1538/19/26-1538/19/42), December 21, 1915, NLA, WMHP, box 113, folder 1, 5–7. They were aware that this was not simply an Australian policy: "The policy of other British Dominions in the Pacific resembles that of Australia, although it is manifested in some cases in a milder form."

59. H. Norman to Munro Ferguson, March 1, 1916, NLA, WMHP, box 113, folder 1.

60. Memorandum from Atlee Arthur Hunt to Hugh Mahon, February 9, 1916, NAA, A981, JAP 101, part 1. Under the 1904 Passport Arrangement, Japanese merchants, students, and tourists could be admitted to Australia for a period of twelve months. They were not, however, allowed permanent residency under this agreement.

61. Unknown author to Hugh Mahon, February 17, 1916, NAA, A981, JAP 101, part 1.

62. Quoted in Memorandum from Geo. Steward to the Secretary, Prime Minister's Department, August 14, 1916, NAA, A981, JAP 181, part 1.

63. Quoted in H. May to Munro Ferguson, June 30, 1916, NAA, A2219, vol. 1, part 1.

64. Memorandum: Rentaro Kayahara (or "Kwazan")—Circulation in Australia of His Writings, August 29, 1918, NAA, A2219, vol. 1, part 2; J. H. Cann to the Prime Minister, September 14, 1915, NAA, A981, JAP 181, part 1.

65. Amended de-cypher of a cablegram received from the British ambassador, Tokio, April 12, 1916, NAA, A2219, vol. 1, part 2.

66. *Japan Weekly Chronicle*, February 10, 1916, 217, NAA, A2219, vol. 1, part 1.

67. Quoted in Memorandum from Conyngham Greene to Ronald Crauford Munro Ferguson, October 31, 1916, NAA, A981, JAP 181, part 1. Australian naval authorities bristled at this kind of insinuation. In November 1916, for example, the secretary of the Australian Naval Board, George Lionel Macandie, protested the laudatory tone of British newspaper references to Japan's contribution to the war effort in the Pacific. The British press, he implied, aimed to create the impression that "Australia must be very grateful to Japan and should show her gratitude appropriately" (Letter from George Lionel Macandie to the secretary, prime minister's department, November 22, 1916, NAA, A981, JAP 53).

68. Quoted in H. Norman to Munro Ferguson, July 31, 1916, TNA, FO 371/2694, 1916, no. 171598.

69. Press References to Japan and to Coloured Labor in Australia: Action by Censorship, undated, NAA, A2219, vol. 1, part 2.

70. Minute Paper: Lieutenant Colonel George G. McColl to The Chief of the General Staff, April 19, 1916, NAA, A2219, vol. 1, part 2.

71. "The Menace of Japan," November 20, 1917, NAA, A2219, vol. 1, part 2.

72. Amended de-cypher of a cablegram received from the British ambassador, Tokio, April 12, 1916, NAA, A2219, vol. 1, part 2.

73. Press References to Japan and to Coloured Labor in Australia: Action by Censorship, undated, NAA, A2219, vol. 1, part 2.

74. Day, *Claiming a Continent*, 208.

75. CPD, 80: 9643–44, 9645. Curiously these remarks escaped the censor's pen.

76. Munro Ferguson to Bonar Law, September 20, 1916, NLA, RCMFP, box 1, folder 813–898.

77. Captain Reginald Hayes to the Chief of the General Staff, June 24, 1918, NAA, A2219, vol. 1, part 2.

78. Munro Ferguson to Bonar Law, December 7, 1916, NLA, RCMFP, box 1, folder 813–898.

79. Munro Ferguson to King George V, December 8, 1916, NLA, RCMFP, box 1, folder 1–107.

80. Nish, *Alliance in Decline*, 207–8. Britain was especially keen to secure Japanese vessels for operations against German submarines in the Mediterranean in 1917 (Tate and Foy, "More Light on the Abrogation of the Anglo-Japanese Alliance," 533).

81. The Prime Minister's Official Secretary to the Governor-General, February 7, 1917, NLA, WMHP, box 103, folder 36.

82. Hughes to the Consul General for Japan, Sydney, February 12, 1917, NAA, A2219, vol. 2.

83. Hughes to the Consul General for Japan, Sydney, March 31, 1917, NAA, A2219, vol. 2.

84. Consul General for Japan, Sydney, to Hughes, July 23, 1917, NAA, A2219, vol. 2.

85. Munro Ferguson to King George V, March 22, 1917, NLA, RCMFP, box 1, folder 1–107.

86. Munro Ferguson to Walter Hume Long, October 25, 1917, NLA, RCMFP, box 2, folder 899–998. Munro Ferguson had earlier argued, "I am also afraid that Australian lack of sympathy with coloured races and the necessity any Australian Government would be under to govern in accordance with the fixed ideas of the Unions would render Government by Australia of Pacific Islands very unsatisfactory" (Munro Ferguson to Hume Long, December 24, 1916, NLA, RCMFP, box 1, folder 813–898).

87. Quoted in Memorandum from J. C. L. Fitzpatrick to W. M. Hughes, September 26, 1917, NAA, A981, JAP 181, part 1.

88. Keylor, *The Twentieth-Century World and Beyond*, 201–2.

89. Major Edmund L. Piesse, "The Far Eastern Question and Australia," 1918, NAA, A981, FAR 9, 9, 21. From Piesse's perspective, the implications of American resistance were compounded by Britain's willingness to appease Japanese expansionism: "There seems to be a blight over British policy in the East—some British representatives are not in sympathy with our interests." It was essential, therefore, for Australia to augment its own intelligence-gathering activities in East Asia in order to ascertain and monitor Japan's intentions (22).

90. Summary of Report on the Situation in China, June 25, 1918, NAA, A2219, vol. 2. Though unattributed, this memorandum was likely also produced by Piesse.

91. "Australia to Have a Monroe Doctrine," *New York Times*, June 1, 1918. This argument already had some currency in official British circles. In 1917, for example, Leopold Amery had vigorously defended the empire's claims to suzerainty over the former German colonies by invoking the U.S. experience in the western hemisphere. Here was a clear example, Amery contended, of the "application by the young Anglo-Saxon democracies of the British Commonwealth of the same principle which is the foundation of [the] Monroe Doctrine" (L. S. Amery, "The Future of the German Colonies,"

November 6, 1917, NAA, Garran Papers, CP 396, BUNDLE 2/7, Supreme War Council Pacific Islands 1918, W. M. Hughes).

92. Quoted in Greene to Munro Ferguson, July 8, 1918, NAA, A981, JAP 91.

93. Quoted in NSW Premier to the Acting Premier, July 5, 1918, NAA, A981, JAP 91.

94. Extract from *Japan Chronicle*, June 15, 1918, NAA, A2219, vol. 1, part 2.

95. Munro Ferguson to Long, June 5, 1918, NLA, RCMFP, box 2, folder 999–1124.

96. Munro Ferguson to Long, July 15, 1918, NLA, RCMFP, box 2, folder 999–1124.

97. British Foreign Policy, undated, NLA, Latham Papers, box 61, series 21, folder 22.

98. Munro Ferguson to Walter Hume Long, April 1, 1918, NLA, RCMFP, box 2, folder 999–1124.

99. Munro Ferguson to Lord Stamfordham, March 11, 1918, NLA, RCMFP, box 1, folder 211–324.

100. Greene to Munro Ferguson, November 5, 1918, NAA, A981, JAP 101, part 1.

Chapter Six

1. See, for example, Burkman, *Japan and the League of Nations*; Manela, *The Wilsonian Moment*; Aydin, *The Politics of Anti-Westernism in Asia*.

2. Darwin, "A Third British Empire?," 64. Hancock, *Smuts*, 496–97. The most important outcome of the 1917 deliberations was Resolution 9. It established the constitutional precedent for dominion representation in foreign affairs and subsequently the Paris Peace Conference. The resolution stated that Great Britain "should recognize the right of the Dominions and India to an adequate voice in foreign policy and in foreign relations" (Dawson, *The Development of Dominion Status*, 25). Yet it was evident that the dominions wished to retain an ambiguous dual status within the empire during the war, eschewing absolute autonomy in favor of a system of imperial organization that would allow them "to enjoy the benefits of Imperial partnership and yet increasingly to assert a measure of independence whenever it suited their interests" (Holland, "Empire and the Great War," 133).

3. Lloyd George, *War Memoirs*, 1738; Holland, "Empire and the Great War," 121–22; Spear, *The Oxford History of Modern India*, 335; Gandhi, *An Autobiography*, 447; Lloyd, "'A Family Quarrel'"; Huttenback, *Gandhi in South Africa*.

4. Resolution 22, Reciprocity of Treatment between India and the Self-governing Dominions, April 27, 1917, TNA, 1917, Cab 32/1/1, *Imperial War Conference*, xvi.

5. Ibid., 117–18.

6. Note on Immigration from India to the Self-Governing Dominions, March 22, 1917, TNA, 1917, Cab 32/1/1, *Imperial War Conference*, 161–62.

7. Ibid., 162.

8. Resolution 22, Reciprocity of Treatment between India and the Self-governing Dominions, TNA, 1917, Cab 32/1/1, *Imperial War Conference*, 118, 119.

9. German East Africa, Note by Representatives of India, undated memorandum, CAC, AMEL 1/3/36, part 2. There was no similar history of South Asian settlement

in that other British African conquest, German Cameroon, and the South African government was in control of German South-West Africa.

10. Note on Immigration from India to the Self-Governing Dominions, March 22, 1917, TNA, Cab 32/1/1, *Imperial War Conference*, 161–62.

11. Second Interim Report, Committee of Imperial Defence, Sub-Committee on Territorial Changes, March 22, 1917, CAC, AMEL 1/3/32, 4–5; Appendix B, Memorandum by the Colonial Office, CAC, AMEL 1/3/32, 13.

12. TNA, Cab 32/1/1, part 2, *Imperial War Conference, 1917: Extracts from Minutes*, July 24, 1918, 195.

13. Sir S. P. Sinha, "Reciprocity of Treatment between India and the Dominions," undated memorandum, TNA, Cab 32/1/1, part 2, *Imperial War Conference, 1917: Extracts from Minutes*, 245–48.

14. TNA, Cab 32/1/1, part 2, *Imperial War Conference, 1917: Extracts from Minutes*, July 24, 1918, 198.

15. Indian Desiderata for Peace Settlement, undated, TNA, FO 608/211/2, no. 3614.

16. "White Australia at Stake," *Melbourne Herald*, February 14, 1919, NAA, A2219, vol. 6.

17. Shimazu, *Japan, Race and Equality*, 6–9.

18. "Ishii Looks to End of Race Prejudice," *New York Times*, March 15, 1919.

19. "The League and Racial Discrimination—An Impediment to Permanent Peace," *Kokumin*, November 3, 1918, in Greene to Balfour, November 12, 1918, TNA, FO 608/211/2, no. 355.

20. Quoted in Greene to Balfour, December 2, 1918, TNA, FO 608/211/2, no. 475.

21. Extract from the *Asahi Shimbun*, December 23, 1918, in Greene to Munro Ferguson, January 8, 1919, NAA, A981, JAP 101, part 1.

22. Extract from an article by Toda Kaiichi, "Prejudice against the Immigration of the Colored Races," in Greene to Balfour, January 10, 1919, NAA, A981, JAP 101, part 1.

23. Greene to Curzon, February 6, 1919, NAA, A981, JAP 101, part 1.

24. Greene to Balfour, December 2, 1918, TNA, FO 608/211/2, no. 475.

25. Lionel Curtis, Memorandum on Asiatic Immigration, December 14, 1918, TNA, FO 608/211/2, no. 1914; T. W. Holderness to the Undersecretary of State, Foreign Office, January 11, 1919, TNA, FO 608/211/2, no. 315.

26. Max Muller to Ronald Macleay, February 10, 1919, TNA, FO 608/211/2, no. 2061.

27. Quoted in A. E. Collins to the Undersecretary of State, Public Department, India Office, January 25, 1919, TNA, FO 608/211/2, no. 2061.

28. Quoted in Lauren, "The Denial of Racial Equality," 245. See also Burkman, *Japan and the League of Nations*, 82–83. The Japanese delegation had informally submitted its amendment to Wilson's confidant Colonel House on February 4, 1919. The original proposal represented their highest aspiration for the Peace Conference: "The equality of nations being a basic principle of the League, the High Contracting Parties agree that concerning the treatment and rights to be accorded to aliens in their territories, they will not discriminate, either in law or in fact, against any person or

persons on account of his or their race or nationality." To their surprise President Wilson summarily rejected this opening gambit the next day.

29. Speech by Baron Makino to the League of Nations Commission, February 13, 1919, NAA, Garran Papers, CP351/1, bundle 2/1.

30. Burkman, *Japan and the League of Nations*, 83; Lake and Reynolds, *Drawing the Global Colour Line*, 291.

31. "Race Equality Is Now a Vital Issue," *Japan Advertiser*, February 23, 1919, NAA, A2219, vol. 6.

32. "Japan's Next Move," *Melbourne Herald*, February 22, 1919, NAA, A2219, vol. 6.

33. "Believe Question of Race Uppermost," *Japan Advertiser*, March 25, 1919; Editorial, *Hochi Shimbun*, quoted in *Japan Advertiser*, March 27, 1919, NAA, A2219, vol. 6.

34. Editorial, *Hochi Shimbun*, quoted in *Japan Advertiser*, March 27, 1919, NAA, A2219, vol. 6.

35. Extract from a Cable received by Acting Prime Minister from the Rt. Hon. W. M. Hughes, London, November 1, 1918, NLA, Latham Papers, box 61, series 21, folder 22.

36. Notes on the Draft Convention of the League of Nations, February 2, 1919, TNA, FO 608/243/1, no. 1289. With regard to the racial equality amendment, Hughes told Watt in a cable he had "declined [to] agree to any form of words . . . and stated plainly that Australia cannot agree to what [the Japanese] want" (Hughes to Watt, March 28, 1919, NAA, A981, JAP 101, part 1). One Foreign Office official wryly noted in a minute on Hughes's objections, "If the whole of his views were carried out the League would be reduced to the position of an International Debating Society and would die of anemia—which is perhaps what he desires" (TNA, FO 608/243/1).

37. Garran's notes on the Proposed Japanese Amendment, undated, NAA, Garran Papers, CP351/1, bundle 2/1. After his meeting with Baron Makino, Hughes claimed to have rushed to the Press Club, where he sought out American reporters from the West Coast, calling upon them to incite their readership to "rouse the country, overwhelm the President with messages imploring, demanding, that it be withdrawn. Send out cables breathing fire and slaughter—aye and worse still, defeat at the next elections" (Hughes, *Policies and Potentates*, 245–47). According to Garran, it appeared that on this subject "the terror of Hughes's tongue did seem to have an influence on Wilson" (*Prosper the Commonwealth*, 266).

38. Sir Robert Garran notes, April 10, 1919, NAA, Garran Papers, CP351/1, bundle 2/1.

39. Garran's notes on the Proposed Japanese Amendment, undated, NAA, Garran Papers, CP351/1, bundle 2/1.

40. Lauren, "The Denial of Racial Equality," 248.

41. Quoted in Burkman, *Japan and the League of Nations*, 83.

42. Shimazu, *Japan, Race and Equality*, 28.

43. Ibid., 29–30. As Shimazu points out, members of the Commission were required only to vote in favor of the measure; therefore no member was forced to actually vote against it. The Polish representative also rejected the amendment, albeit on purely technical grounds. Portugal, Romania, and Belgium too failed to vote for the proposal.

44. Ibid., 30–31. It is clear from State Department correspondence that the American delegation generally opposed the proposed Japanese amendment. In April 1919 the California State Legislature indicated to the State Department that it was preparing to begin debate on two bills. One was designed to prevent Japanese residents from leasing agricultural lands in the state; the other proposed to outlaw the immigration of Japanese "picture brides." Writing from Paris, Secretary of State Robert Lansing urged his subordinates back in Washington to somehow prevent the debate since Japan was preparing to reintroduce its racial equality amendment. "We are of course resisting anything that is of a binding nature," Lansing wrote, "but at [the] same time if these bills should be introduced it would cause very serious friction" (Lansing cable, April 6, 1919, NA, RG 256, M820, roll 49, vol. 23, 150.01/3).

45. Summary of Baron Makino Speech, April 30, 1919, TNA, FO 608/243/1, no. 8778.

46. The Australian Council of Defense believed that these new possessions could protect Australia from possible Japanese invasion (Watt to Hughes, December 9, 1918, NAA, A6006, 1919/2/18).

47. Hughes speech, July 24, 1918, NAA, Garran Papers, CP 396, bundle 2/7, Supreme War Council Pacific Islands, 1918, W. M. Hughes.

48. William M. Hughes, "Australia and the Pacific Islands," February 6, 1919, TNA, FO 608/175, no. 1810. As Sir Robert Garran contended in his postwar notes on the subject, the strategic position of New Guinea, the Bismarck Archipelago, and the German Solomon Islands around the continent's northern coastline made them "ramparts round the Australian coast, and their possession is vital to the defence of Australia" ("The Ex-German Colonies," undated notes, NAA, Garran Papers, CP 396, CP351/1, bundle 1/16, Sir Robert Garran Memoranda re Peace Conference 1919, 2).

49. Hughes to Munro Ferguson, January 17, 1919, NLA, RCMFP, box 4, folder 2754–2836. Hughes almost immediately dismissed Wilson as a dilettante and felt that it was "a thousand pities [that] Roosevelt died. *He* was a *Man*." Hughes told Munro Ferguson that "between ourselves he [Wilson] is rather a stick when it comes down to the facts of life. He is great on great principles. As to their application he is so much like Alice in Wonderland that I suspect him of being sat in a former incarnation for that dear little lady to Lewis Carroll." Munro Ferguson was similarly dismissive, replying, "It is somewhat of a puzzle why France and England should accept the lead from an individual with such a curious war record and who has just been handsomely defeated in his own country" (Munro Ferguson to Hughes, February 7, 1919, NLA, RCMFP, box 4, folder 2754–2836).

50. Pederson, *The Guardians*, 17–103; Callahan, *Mandates and Empire*, 8–46.

51. Hughes, "Memorandum Regarding the Pacific Islands," February 1919, TNA, FO 608/175, no. 2462. His public calls for annexation alarmed the Japanese delegation, who feared that he was attempting to assume jurisdiction over Germany's former colonies then under Japanese control. Cecil was forced to assuage Makino's concerns and reiterate Britain's earlier pledge to support Japan's claims (Cecil to Balfour, March 10, 1919, TNA, FO 608/211/2, no. 4719).

52. Hughes to Watt, January 31, 1919, NAA, CP360/8. This line of reasoning was further outlined by Sir John Latham, who concluded, "On the assumption that any restrictions upon Australia as a mandatory will also be applied to Japan as a mandatory, it is submitted that it is a wise policy for Australia to accept limitations upon the naval and military use of mandatory territories. The more strict such limitations are, the better for Australia" ("Mandatory System and the German Pacific Colonies," February 21, 1919, NLA, Latham Papers, box 55, series 21, folder 20).

53. Watt to Hughes, January 31, 1919, NAA, CP360/8.

54. Burkman, *Japan and the League of Nations*, 70, 130.

55. The British government was also keen to ensure that Australia and New Zealand respect South Asian sentiment when organizing their postwar administrations in the C mandates. L. S. Amery told the dominion governors-general in March 1920 that Lord Curzon was especially concerned that "Indian sentiment and Indian interests should not be overlooked when [Australia and New Zealand] approach the question of applying or modifying their own laws to the mandated territories, and he has accordingly asked that the share taken by India during the war may be borne in mind and that account should be taken of the bitter disappointment likely to be felt in India if the overthrow of German Colonial rule were to be followed by the imposition of legal disabilities which had not previously existed on Indian subjects" (Amery to Munro Ferguson, March 23, 1920, NAA, A2219, vol. 19).

56. Munro Ferguson to Milner, February 10, 1919, NLA, RCMFP, box 3, folder 2117–2202.

57. Munro Ferguson to Milner, May 29, 1919, NLA, RCMFP, box 2, folder 1125–1294.

58. Amery to Milner, February 12, 1919, CAC, AMEL 1/3/42, part 1.

59. Munro Ferguson to Milner, March 14, 1919, NLA, RCMFP, box 3, folder 2117–2202.

60. Munro Ferguson to King George V, February 2, 1919, NLA, RCMFP, box 1, folder 108–161.

61. Rupert W. Hornabrook, "Pacific Islands: Is Australian Control Justified?," *Mail*, June 28, 1919, NAA, A2219, vol. 8. Hornabrook later added his concerns about Australia's racial attitudes to the list of reasons why the dominion should relinquish its responsibilities to the British government. He told his brother in 1921, "The Australian is not the class of man to govern tropical Pacific Islands inhabited by colored races—there is far too much of the 'White Australia' twaddle in his veins" (quoted in Hiery, *The Neglected War*, 334n61).

62. Sir C. Hurst, "'B' and 'C' Mandates: Memorandum on the Present Position," July 20, 1920, TNA, CAB 27/98.

63. Paraphrase of a telegram received from Viscount Uchida, August 2, 1920, TNA, FO 371/6683, no. F1227.

64. Prime Minister's Office to Munro Ferguson, November 12, 1920, NAA, A2219, vol. 19.

65. Minister of Internal Affairs to the Prime Minister, November 29, 1920, ANZ, IT, 1, record EX 69/49.

66. Declaration by the Japanese Government, December 17, 1920, "Mandates: A Summary of the Proceedings of the League of Nations to December 1920," undated memorandum, NAA, A2219, vol. 18.

67. Quoted in Lake and Reynolds, *Drawing the Global Colour Line*, 308.

68. "Hughes, Paris and Peace," *Bulletin*, October 2, 1919.

69. Hughes to Watt, April 13, 1919, NAA, A981, JAP 101, part 1.

70. From the Diary of Colonel House, February 13, 1919, in Link et al., *The Papers of Woodrow Wilson*, 55: 155.

71. From the Diary of Dr. Grayson, March 22, 1919, in Link et al., *The Papers of Woodrow Wilson*, 56: 164.

72. Extract from *Nichi Nichi*, in Greene to Munro Ferguson, January 20, 1919, NAA, A981, JAP 53.

73. "Irresponsible Utterances of the Australian Premier," *Nichi Nichi*, January 27, 1919, in Greene to Munro Ferguson, January 29, 1919, TNA, FO 608/211/2, no. 4971.

74. "Racial Bar Angers," *Melbourne Herald*, April 10, 1919, in Greene to Munro Ferguson, January 29, 1919, TNA, FO 608/211/2, no. 4971.

75. Sir Beilby Alston to Curzon, April 10, 1919, TNA, FO 608/211/2, no. 4971.

76. Watt to Hughes, April 15, 1919, TNA, FO 608/211/2, no. 4971.

77. Hughes to Watt, April 17, 1919, NAA, A981, JAP 101, part 1.

78. "Hughes Discusses Racial Amendment," *Japan Advertiser*, April 25, 1919, NAA, A981, JAP 101, part 1.

79. E. L. Piesse to Commander Bertram Home Ramsay, June 12, 1919, NAA, A2219, vol. 8.

80. Summary of Baron Makino Speech, April 30, 1919, TNA, FO 608/243/1, no. 8778.

81. Munro Ferguson to Baron Stamfordham, April 30, 1919, NLA, RCMFP, box 1, folder 325–449.

82. Munro Ferguson to Hughes, April 29, 1919, NLA, RCMFP, box 4, folder 2754–2836. Invoking the name of the French minstrel who allegedly rescued King Richard I from his Austrian captors in 1192, Munro Ferguson joked to Hughes, "I assume your return journey will not be via Tokio or Washington—otherwise I should anticipate having to send Sir John Higgins, like another Blondel, to trace you to some dungeon."

83. Hughes to Long, October 7, 1919; Long to Hughes, October 10, 1919; Hughes to Long, October 15, 1919; Long to Hughes, October 17, 1919, all in TNA, CAB 27/71, 52–53.

84. Henry Lawson to Hughes, December 10, 1919, and George Pearce to Hughes, December 29, 1919, NAA, A981, JAP 101, part 1.

85. Prime Minister's Office to the Governor-General's Office, January 24, 1920, NAA, A981, JAP 101, part 1.

86. Milner to Munro Ferguson, February 3, 1920, NAA, A981, JAP 101, part 1.

87. Alston to Curzon, February 14, 1920, NAA, A981, JAP 101, part 1.

88. Longfield Lloyd to Director of Military Intelligence, August 20, 1920, NAA, A2219, vol. 8.

89. Piesse to Hughes, November 11, 1920, NAA, A981, JAP 53.

90. Department of the Navy to the Prime Minister's Secretary, January 28, 1921, NAA, A981, JAP 53. The Department of the Navy remained vigilant throughout 1920 to any apparently unwarranted praise in the British, Australian, or Japanese press for Japan's contribution to the Australian war effort.

91. As Robert Gowen puts it, "the union flouted the color consciousness of an age obsessed with yellow peril visions and was particularly unholy in the eyes of Britain's own Pacific offspring" ("British Legerdemain at the 1911 Imperial Conference," 385).

92. T. Iyenaga, "Japan's Position as a Participant in the World War," *New York Times*, January 24, 1915. The war had challenged the alliance, even as it facilitated Japanese participation in the war. By early 1916 increasingly vociferous attacks on the Anglo-Japanese Alliance appeared in the Japanese press, apparently emanating from a concerted campaign directed by the Imperial University in Tokyo ("Japanese Assailing Pact with England," *New York Times*, February 6, 1916). Later, in paraphrasing one Japanese newspaper, the *Nichi Nichi*, the *New York Times* reported, "It is declared that in Canada, Australia, and other British colonies Japanese are refused treatment on an equal footing" and that the Japanese minister for foreign affairs had announced that his country was "negotiating with Great Britain concerning the anti-Japanese agitation in British colonies" ("New British Treaty Demanded in Japan," *New York Times*, March 19, 1916).

93. Tate and Foy, "More Light on the Abrogation of the Anglo-Japanese Alliance," 533–35; Nish, "Echoes of Alliance," 255–56. For Canada's position, see also Brebner, "Canada, the Anglo-Japanese Alliance and the Washington Conference," 48–49.

94. In some ways this could be seen as a ruse, reflecting the reality that both sides sought a diplomatic exit from the alliance. After all, France concluded an alliance with Belgium in 1920 and would continue to construct a European alliance system outside the League throughout the 1920s. At the same time, however, it also reflected a genuine hope among some British diplomats that the League of Nations would succeed in its mission. Sir Beilby Alston, for example, hoped the alliance would be rendered unnecessary by the League, and the British Foreign Office apparently believed that it was genuinely necessary to alter the alliance in the context of the new League (Fry, "The North Atlantic Triangle and the Abrogation of the Anglo-Japanese Alliance," 48).

95. Foreign Office Memorandum on the Effect of the Anglo-Japanese Alliance upon Foreign Relationships, February 28, 1920, NAA, A981, JAP 96, Anglo-Japanese Alliance, 2–3.

96. "Mr. Watt Entertained Abroad," *Sydney Morning Herald*, May 13, 1920, NAA, A981, JAP 96, Anglo-Japanese Alliance, 2–3.

97. Extract from *Argus*, June 3, 1920, in NAA, A981, JAP 96, Anglo-Japanese Alliance, 2–3.

98. Extract from *Sydney Morning Herald*, June 3, 1920, in NAA, A981, JAP 96, Anglo-Japanese Alliance, 2–3.

99. "Australia and Japan," *Melbourne Herald*, March 29, 1920, NAA, A981, JAP 96, Anglo-Japanese Alliance, 2–3.

100. "The Anglo-Japanese Alliance," *Sydney Telegraph*, March 27, 1920, NAA, A981, JAP 96, Anglo-Japanese Alliance, 2–3. In July 1920 Piesse warned Hughes that, based on Australian press reports, the Japanese press had largely concluded that Australia opposed renewal of the Anglo-Japanese Alliance. He urged the prime minister to make a statement clarifying his government's position, lest Australian-Japanese relations suffer (Piesse to the Prime Minister's Secretary, July 24, 1920, NAA, A981, JAP 96, Anglo-Japanese Alliance, 2–3).

101. Piesse, "Notes for Use in Preparing Reply," May 12, 1920, NAA, A981, JAP 96, Anglo-Japanese Alliance, 2–3.

102. Charles Eliot to Earl Curzon, June 17, 1920, NAA, A981, JAP 96, Anglo-Japanese Alliance, 2–3.

103. "The Anglo-Japanese Alliance," extract from *Japan Chronicle*, April 9, 1921, NAA, A981, JAP 96, Anglo-Japanese Alliance, 2–3.

104. Edmund L. Piesse, "The Anglo-Japanese Alliance: Review of Newspaper Opinions," March–May 1920, June 3, 1920, NAA, A981, JAP 96, Anglo-Japanese Alliance, 2–3.

105. "Speech by the Rt. Hon. W. M. Hughes," April 7, 1921, NAA, A981, JAP 96, Anglo-Japanese Alliance, 2–3.

106. Piesse memorandum, Massey's and Hughes's speeches of March and April 1921 on the Anglo-Japanese Alliance—Japanese comments, July 7, 1921, NAA, A981, JAP 96, Anglo-Japanese Alliance, 2–3.

107. Quoted in ibid.

108. Opening Speech by David Lloyd George, June 20, 1921, in *Conference of Prime Ministers and Representatives of the United Kingdom, the Dominions, and India*, 13.

109. Opening Speech by Mr. Hughes, June 21, 1921, in *Conference of Prime Ministers and Representatives of the United Kingdom, the Dominions, and India*, 19–20.

110. Opening Speech by Mr. Massey, June 21, 1921, in *Conference of Prime Ministers and Representatives of the United Kingdom, the Dominions, and India*, 30–31.

111. Nish, "Echoes of Alliance," 256.

112. Fry, "The Pacific Dominions and the Washington Conference," 77–78, 90–94. William Hughes wrote approvingly of the conference in 1929, which he thought had at least temporarily solved the problems associated with the Anglo-Japanese Alliance and American resentment (Millar, *Australia in Peace and War*, 98).

113. See Goldstein and Maurer, *The Washington Conference*; Buckley, *The United States and the Washington Conference*; Dingman, *Power in the Pacific*.

114. Secretary of State to the Ambassador in Great Britain, July 13, 1921, in U.S. Department of State, *Papers relating to the Foreign Relations of the United States*, 31–32; Ambassador in Great Britain to the Secretary of State, July 19, 1921, in U.S. Department of State, *Papers relating to the Foreign Relations of the United States*, 36–37.

115. The Charge in Japan to the Secretary of State, July 26, 1921, in U.S. Department of State, *Papers relating to the Foreign Relations of the United States*, 45.

116. H. G. Parlett, "Memorandum Respecting the Tone of the Japanese Press with regard to the Washington Conference," August 25, 1921, TNA, FO 371/6705, no. F3585; Extract from the *Japan Chronicle*, September 2, 1921, TNA, FO 371/6705, no. F3763.

117. Eliot to Curzon, August 7, 1921, TNA, FO 371/6704, no. 2960.

118. Curzon to Eliot, August 4, 1921, TNA, FO 371/6683, no. F2859.

119. See, for example, "Discriminatory Disabilities of Foreigners in Japan," August 15, 1921, TNA, FO 371/6683, no. F3484. Curzon also sought specifics regarding Japanese population growth. After questioning the Japanese foreign minister on the subject, Ambassador Eliot replied that Japan did not intend to raise the issue of territorial expansion at the conference. In fact, Eliot noted, the Japanese Foreign Ministry was well aware that it "would strike a snag" if it claimed a "sphere of expansion" at the upcoming Washington conference (Eliot to Curzon, November 4, 1921, TNA, FO 371/6683, no. F4086).

120. Frank Ashton-Gwatkin, "A Conference of Pacific Powers," August 1, 1921, TNA, FO 371/6704, no. 2996.

121. Frank Ashton-Gwatkin, "Racial Discrimination and Immigration," October 10, 1921, TNA, FO 371/6684, no. F4212, 21.

122. Ibid., 22–23, 1, 23.

Chapter Seven

1. Stoddard, *The Rising Tide of Color against White World Supremacy*, 236, 9, 281.

2. "Hindus and Chinese," *Auckland Star*, April 20, 1920.

3. O'Connor, "Keeping New Zealand White," 51–59.

4. NZPD, 187: 905.

5. The Governor-General to the Secretary of State for the Colonies, October 27, 1920, TNA, CO 886/9/1, 50; Lake and Reynolds, *Drawing the Global Colour Line*, 316.

6. NZPD, 187: 905–6. Apirana Ngata, a longtime member of Parliament for the Eastern Maori District, expressed concern that New Zealand's indigenous population might fall under the act's purview. Massey assured him, "The Maori is a European for our purposes.... The Maori has the same rights and privileges as the European, in every sense of the word" (907).

7. Ibid., 926.

8. Ibid., 921–23, 931.

9. Ibid., 928, 916–18, 920–21.

10. Ibid., 912–13. Holland's speech highlights the internal divisions within the New Zealand Labour Party. As P. S. O'Connor reveals, some Labour Party members were caught between Holland's ideological internationalism and the clamorous anti-Asian attitudes of their working-class constituents ("Keeping New Zealand White," 57–58).

11. NZPD, 187: 918–19.

12. Ibid., 911–12. When the Chinese government learned that New Zealand was amending its immigration legislation, the Chinese legation in London unsuccessfully lobbied the imperial government for the poll tax's removal (Alfred Sao-ke Sze to the Earl of Kedleston, August 30, 1920, and the Administrator to the Secretary of State, September 21, 1920, TNA, CO 886/9/1, 43–44).

13. Governor-General to the Secretary of State for the Colonies, October 27, 1920, TNA, CO 886/9/1, 49, 50.

14. Government of India to the Secretary of State for India, May 12, 1921, TNA, CO 886/9/1, 54–56.

15. Sir Francis Bell to the Government of India, September 5, 1921, TNA, CO 886/9/1, 57–58.

16. *Conference of Prime Ministers and Representatives of the United Kingdom, the Dominions, and India: Summary of Proceedings and Documents,* 8.

17. Secretary of State for the Colonies to the Governor-General, January 19, 1922, LAC, RG 25, vol. 1003, 199.

18. Report by the Right Honorable V. S. Srinivasa Sastri, PC, Regarding his Deputation to the Dominions of Australia, New Zealand, and Canada, 1923, NAA, A2219, vol. 23, 2–3, 4, 6–7, 8–9.

19. Ibid., 10–12.

20. Ibid., 13.

21. Ward, *White Canada Forever,* 123–28, 130–34.

22. DCPD, 157: 2317.

23. Anderson, *Vancouver's Chinatown,* 137.

24. Hawkins, *Critical Years in Immigration,* 19–20.

25. DCPD, 157: 2309–10.

26. Ibid., 2312–13.

27. Ibid., 2316, 2317, 2322, 2326–27.

28. Ibid., 2486–87. In fact the Chinese consul general, Dr. Chilien Tsur, had tried to open negotiations for a Chinese-Canadian gentleman's agreement in 1922 and 1923. His proposals foundered before the swell of anti-Chinese animus that emanated from British Columbia (Con et al., *From China to Canada,* 139–41).

29. Knowles, *Strangers at Our Gates,* 107.

30. External Affairs to the Governor-General's Secretary, July 23, 1923, LAC, RG 25, vol. 1003, 225–26.

31. Japanese Consul General at Ottawa to the Minister of Immigration, August 22, 1923, LAC, RG 25, vol. 1003, 241.

32. Buchignani et al., *Continuous Journey,* 71–72.

33. Circular from Secretary to the Government of India to all Local Governments and Administrations, February 8, 1923, LAC, RG 25, vol. 1003, 250–51.

34. Buchignani et al., *Continuous Journey,* 73–74.

35. Daniels, *Coming to America,* 278–80; Zolberg, *A Nation by Design,* 262. The Australian government and press, it should be noted, took a keen interest in the *Ozawa* decision. See, for example, "Japanese not 'White,'" *Age,* November 15, 1922, NAA, A1, 1922/19928, Japanese Naturalised in America—Status of.

36. Takaki, *A Different Mirror,* 257–58.

37. U.S. House of Representatives, Committee on Immigration and Naturalization, "Admission of Certain Refugees from Near Eastern Countries and Restriction of

Immigration into the United States, Including Revision of Quota Act," in U.S. Congress, *Restriction of Immigration*, 25.

38. U.S. House of Representatives, Committee on Immigration and Naturalization, *Report: Restriction of Immigration*, March 24, 1924, 711.945/1043, NA, RG 59, M423, reel 7, 8, 9.

39. Masanao Hanihara to Charles Evans Hughes, January 15, 1924, 711.945/1063, NA, RG 59, M423, reel 7, 1–8.

40. Ringer, *"We the People" and Others*, 794–96.

41. Ngai, *Impossible Subjects*, 48. Indeed, as Ronald Takaki notes, if Japan had been apportioned a regular quota under the new system, their immigrants would have been restricted to the minimum 100 per year, since the Japanese population in 1890 numbered only 2,039 (*Strangers from a Different Shore*, 209).

42. "Racial Discrimination," *New York Times*, February 15, 1924.

43. George Cary to Rep. Albert Johnson, February 20, 1924; David Starr Jordan to Rep. Albert Johnson, February 21, 1924; Franklin D. Arnold to Rep. Albert Johnson, March 4, 1924, all in NARA, RG233, HR 68A-F18.3, box 268.

44. See, for example, Ringer, *"We the People" and Others*, 811.

45. Memorandum of Interview with the Ambassador of Japan, Mr. Hanihara, March 27, 1924, 711.945/1042, 1/2, NA, RG 59, M423, reel 7, 1–4.

46. Hanihara to Hughes, April 10, 1924, 711.945/1043, NA, RG 59, M423, reel 7, 1–13.

47. Ibid., 12–13.

48. Charles Evans Hughes to Cyrus Woods (American ambassador in Japan), April 11, 1924, 711.945/1043, NA, RG 59, M423, reel 7, 12–13.

49. Hughes to Woods, April 15, 1924, 711.945/1043, NA, RG 59, M423, reel 7, 4.

50. Hanihara to Hughes, April 17, 1924, 711.945/1051, NA, RG 59, M423, reel 7, 4.

51. Ringer, *"We the People" and Others*, 822.

52. Woods to Hughes, April 19, 1924, 711.945/1054, NA, RG 59, M423, reel 7.

53. Charles Eliot to Ramsay MacDonald, April 25, 1924, TNA, FO 371/9585, file A3129. As Matsui deduced, Hanihara's poor choice of words merely provided a smokescreen for some American legislators. According to Izumi Hirobe, for example, southern senators had initially resisted the Shortridge amendment because the California senator was also attempting to pass antilynching legislation. Their concerns had little to do with Japanese pride and dignity. Thanks to California's senior senator, Hiram Johnson, Shortridge agreed to drop his support for the antilynching measure in return for southern support for Japanese exclusion. Hanihara's supposed threat merely represented an opportune pretext upon which to justify their sudden change of heart (Hirobe, *Japanese Pride, American Prejudice*, 9).

54. Woods to Hughes, April 15, 1924, 711.945/1045; Woods to Hughes, April 17, 1924, 711.945/1050; Woods to Hughes, April 17, 1924, 711.945/1078; Woods to Hughes, April 18, 1924, 711.945/1052, all in NA, RG 59, M423, reel 7. The American ambassador in China reported a similarly resentful response from Peking (Jacob Gould Schurman to Hughes, April 17, 1924, 711.945/1049, NA, RG 59, M423, reel 7). For a discussion of Japanese politics during this period, see Duus, *Party Rivalry and Political Change in Taishō Japan*, 162–87.

55. Woods to Hughes, April 22, 1924, 711.945/1059, and Woods to Hughes, May 5, 1924, 711.945/1081, NA, RG 59, M423, reel 7.

56. H. F. Hawley (American consul in Nagoya) to Hughes, April 28, 1924, 711.945/1099, NA, RG 59, M423, reel 7.

57. Schurman to Hughes, April 30, 1924, 711.945/1071, NA, RG 59, M423, reel 7.

58. Quoted in Schurman to Hughes, May 6, 1924, 711.945/1079, NA, RG 59, M423, reel 7.

59. Quoted in Exclusion of Japanese Immigrants from the United States, May 6, 1924, 711.945/1106, NA, RG 59, M423, reel 7; J. Webb Benton to Hughes, June 19, 1924, 711.945/1179, NA, RG 59, M423, reel 7. According to Nobuko Adachi, Japanese immigration to Brazil did indeed significantly increase after the new U.S. restrictions began ("Brazil," 24–25). For a detailed discussion of the Japanese diaspora in Brazil, see Lesser, *Searching for Home Abroad*. For Japanese experiences in Peru, see Takenaka, "The Japanese in Peru." For a broader study of Japanese immigrants across the western hemisphere, see Hirabayashi et al., *New Worlds, New Lives*; Lee, *The Making of Asian America*.

60. Quoted in American Legation in Bogota to Hughes, July 13, 1924, 711.945/1209, NA, RG 59, M423, reel 8.

61. Esme Howard to MacDonald, April 18, 1924, TNA, FO 371/9585, file A2644.

62. Eliot to MacDonald, May 16, 1924, TNA, FO 371/9585, file A3016.

63. Eliot to MacDonald, June 5, 1924, TNA, FO 371/9585, file A3987.

64. See, for example, Memorandum from the Prime Minister's Office to the New Zealand Governor-General, June 9, 1924, ANZ, Confidential Inwards Despatches from the Secretary of State, box/item 60.

65. Robert Ian Campbell Minute, May 19, 1924, TNA, FO 371/9586, file A3016.

66. "War and Peace," undated speech delivered in the United States, NLA, WMHP, box 128, series 26, folder 3, items 152–238.

67. "The Evolution of the White Australia Policy," undated speech delivered in the United States, NLA, WMHP, box 128, series 26, folder 4, items 239–310.

68. Hughes to Calvin Coolidge, April 25, 1924, 711.945/1065a, NA, RG 59, M423, reel 7.

69. Memorandum of Interview with the Japanese Ambassador, May 23, 1924, 711.945/1103, 1/2, NA, RG 59, M423, reel 7.

70. Ibid.

71. Memorandum of Conversation with the Japanese Ambassador, May 15, 1924, 711.945/1112, NA, RG 59, M423, reel 7.

72. Quoted in Ringer, *"We the People" and Others*, 829.

73. Woods to Hughes, May 28, 1924, 711.945/1113; Woods to Hughes, June 4, 1924, 711.945/1127; Jefferson Caffery (interim American chargé d'affaires in Tokyo) to Hughes, June 6, 1924, 711.945/1129, all in NA, RG 59, M423, reel 7; "What Ails Japan," *Current Opinion* 77 (July–December 1924): 19.

74. Hanihara to Hughes, May 31, 1924, 711.945/1124, NA, RG 59, M423, reel 7.

75. Hughes to Hanihara, June 16, 1924, 711.945/1124, NA, RG 59, M423, reel 7.

76. Quoted in Caffery to Hughes, June 20, 1924, 711.945/1147, NA, RG 59, M423, reel 7.

77. Caffery to Hughes, July 1, 1924, 711.945/1165, and H. F. Hawley to Hughes, June 10, 1924, 711.945/1172, NA, RG 59, M423, reel 7. A short-lived boycott against Hollywood faded after only two weeks when Japanese moviegoers pressured theaters to once again show American movies (Itatsu, "Japan's Hollywood Boycott Movement of 1924").

78. Caffery to Hughes, June 16, 1924, 711.945/1173, NA, RG 59, M423, reel 7.

79. Henry B. Hitchcock (American consul in Nagasaki) to Hughes, July 17, 1924, 711.945/1207, NA, RG 59, M423, reel 8.

80. Edgar Bancroft to Hughes, January 5, 1925, 711.945/1258, NA, RG 59, M423, reel 8. For a discussion that situates the 1924 protests in the context of Japanese political culture, see Stalker, "Suicide, Boycotts and Embracing Tagore."

Conclusion

1. For an in-depth interrogation of the reception of Kipling's poem in the United States, see Murphy, *Shadowing the White Man's Burden*.

2. Imperial War Cabinet Minute, June 11, 1918, TNA, Cab 23/43.

3. "President Demands Hard Hitting Navy," *New York Times*, July 23, 1908.

4. "The Immigration Restriction Bill," *Sydney Morning Herald*, September 11, 1901.

5. Garner, "The Geneva Protocol for the Pacific Settlement of International Disputes"; Williams, "The Geneva Protocol of 1924 for the Pacific Settlement of International Disputes."

6. Miller, *The Geneva Protocol*, 66. See also Burkman, *Japan and the League of Nations*, 120–22.

7. "Japan and the League," *Sydney Morning Herald*, October 2, 1924.

8. "The Protocol," *Sydney Morning Herald*, October 24, 1924.

9. Burks, "The United States and the Geneva Protocol of 1924"; "Japanese Imperil League Peace Plan by New Demands," *New York Times*, September 29, 1924. New Zealanders expressed similar reservations. See "Deadlock Ended," *Evening Post*, October 1, 1924; "A Dangerous Compromise," *Auckland Star*, November 19, 1924.

10. Iriye, *Across the Pacific*, 151–53; Iriye, *After Imperialism*, 35–36. Iriye is even more forceful on this issue in a 1972 bibliographical essay on American–East Asian relations: "Had America taken a more conciliatory stand on the immigration question, scores of prominent Japanese would have found sufficient courage and intellectual honesty to speak out against the exponents of forceful expansionism [in East Asia]" ("1922–1931," 240).

11. For a discussion of Pan-Asian currents in Japanese (and Turkish) thought, see Aydin, *The Politics of Anti-Westernism in Asia*, especially 151–54. For a discussion of Japanese colonial expansion, see Myers and Peattie, *The Japanese Colonial Empire*; Duus et al., *The Japanese Wartime Empire*.

12. For discussions of sovereignty's intellectual and political development, see Bartelson, *A Genealogy of Sovereignty*; Hinsely, *Sovereignty*; Jackson, *Sovereignty*; Krasner, *Sovereignty*.

13. Ngai, *Impossible Subjects*, 9–10.

14. Jackson, *Sovereignty*, 107–8; Manela, *The Wilsonian Moment*, 61.

15. Daniels, *Guarding the Golden Door*, 91–93; Takaki, *Strangers from a Different Shore*, 376–78. According to Takaki, between 1943 and 1953 an average of only fifty-nine new Chinese immigrants entered the United States annually. Naturalization was similarly limited; only 1,428 Chinese were granted American citizenship between 1944 and 1952. Roger Daniels perceptively points out, "China, and not Chinese Americans, was the focal point" (*Guarding the Golden Door*, 94). Also see Ma, "The Sino-American Alliance during World War II and the Lifting of the Chinese Exclusion Acts"; Leong, "Foreign Policy, National Identity, and Citizenship"; Riggs, *Pressure on Congress*.

16. Daniels, *Guarding the Golden Door*, 95 Similar bills designed to extend these courtesies to Korean, Thai, and of course Japanese immigrants each failed that year (95).

17. For a nuanced discussion of the relationship between migration and diplomacy during the cold war, see Oyen, *The Diplomacy of Migration*.

18. See, for example, Hsu, *The Good Immigrants*; Wu, *The Color of Success*; Wu, " 'America's Chinese' "; Dudziak, *Cold War Civil Rights*; Borstelmann, *The Cold War and the Color Line*.

19. Ngai, *Impossible Subjects*, 238. The act also granted broad deportation powers, which allowed the government to deport suspected subversives. The 1965 Immigration and Nationality Act removed the discriminatory national origins quotas, that other stigma of 1924. The new legislation instead placed hemispheric limits on immigration, with caps of 20,000 per year on individual countries (Daniels, *Coming to America*, 340–44).

20. Adachi, *The Enemy That Never Was*, 344–51; Knowles, *Strangers at Our Gates*, 131.

21. Hawkins, *Critical Years in Immigration*, 38–39; Knowles, *Strangers at Our Gates*, 158–60.

22. Day, *Claiming a Continent*, 300. As Frank Welsh asserts, Calwell "was an unabashed racist" (*Great Southern Land*, 442).

23. Day, *Claiming a Continent*, 318–19.

24. Although, as Lake and Reynolds point out, many of these gradual changes in policy were not widely publicized by the Australian government (*Drawing the Global Color Line*, 353).

25. See Brawley, *The White Peril*, 301–2; Walter and MacLeod, *The Citizens' Bargain*, 186–89.

26. Day, *Claiming a Continent*, 356.

27. Brawley, *The White Peril*, 319–20; Dutton, *One of Us?*, 79–83.

28. Mein Smith, *A Concise History of New Zealand*, 171–72; Belich, *Paradise Reforged*, 531.

29. Belich, *Paradise Reforged*, 532.

30. Denoon et al., *A History of Australia, New Zealand, and the Pacific*, 351.

31. Quoted in Brawley, *The White Peril*, 270.

32. Belich, *Paradise Reforged*, 533–34.

33. Denoon et al., *A History of Australia, New Zealand, and the Pacific*, 351.

34. Brawley, *The White Peril*, 321–22. As Belich argues, however, elements of New Zealand's discriminatory immigration policy remained until at least 1986 (*Paradise Reforged*, 523).

35. Thompson, *A History of South Africa*, 187–88.

36. Quoted in Van den Berghe, *South Africa*, 152.

37. Goodman, *Fault Lines*, 42–43.

38. White House, "Building a 21st Century Immigration System," May 2011, 2, http://www.whitehouse.gov/sites/default/files/rss_viewer/immigration_blueprint .pdf (accessed February 18, 2014).

39. For an outline of Donald Trump's plan to build a 1,000 mile long barrier between the United States and Mexico, see "Trump Reveals How he Would Force Mexico to Pay for Border Wall," *Washington Post*, April 5, 2015.

Bibliography

Archival Sources

Australia

National Archives of Australia, Canberra

CA 1, Governor-General; A11816, Despatches and Correspondence from Secretary of State for the Colonies to the Governor-General; Despatches and other papers from Secretary of State to Governor-General. Imposed numbers 53–84.

CA 6, Department of Defence [I]—Director of Military Intelligence; A2219, Volumes of Papers on "External Relations."

Volume 1 Part 1, Relations of Australia and Japan and Far Eastern and Pacific Questions May–December 1918.

Volume 1 Part 2, Relations of Australia and Japan and Far Eastern and Pacific Questions May–December 1918.

Volume 2, B–N, Far Eastern Affairs Brazil, China, India, Japan.

Volume 6, J–W, Cuttings Compiled October 1918–April 1919.

Volume 8, A, Documents April 1919–September 1920.

Volume 18, L–M, Documents September 1920–October 1921.

Volume 19, N, Documents September 1920–October 1921.

Volume 23, E–L, Documents October 1921–June 1923.

CA 7, Department of External Affairs [I] Melbourne; A1, Correspondence Files, annual single number series. 1922/19928, Japanese Naturalised in America—Status of.

CA 7, Department of External Affairs [I]; A8, Correspondence Files [External Affairs], 1895–1905.

CA 12, Prime Minister's Department; A457, Correspondence Files, multiple number series, first system.

CA 12, Prime Minister's Department; A458, Correspondence Files, multiple number series, second system.

CA 12, Prime Minister's Department; A461, Correspondence Files, multiple number series, third system.

CA 12, Prime Minister's Department; CP360/8, Cables exchanged between Acting Prime Minister and Prime Minister.

CA 18, Department of External Affairs [II] Central Office; A981, Correspondence Files, alphabetical series.

A981, Correspondence Files, alphabetical series; FAR 9, Far East; Reports. Major Piesse.

A981, Correspondence Files, alphabetical series; JAP 53, Japan—Services in the War Naval & Military.

A981, Correspondence Files, alphabetical series; JAP 91, Japan: Press General.

A981, Correspondence Files, alphabetical series; JAP 96, Anglo-Japanese Alliance.

A981, Correspondence Files, alphabetical series; JAP 101 Part 1. "Japan Relations with Australia."

A981, Correspondence Files, alphabetical series; JAP 181 Part 1; "Japan—Foreign Policy—Gen. Part I."

CA 241, Australian High Commission, United Kingdom [London]; A2910, Correspondence Files, multiple number series (Class 400); 417/4/4 Part 2, Amendment to Empire Settlement Act.

CA 8550, A6006, Folders of Copies of Cabinet Papers, January 1, 1901–January 11, 1956.

CP 396, Sir Robert Randolph GARRAN KG, GCMG; CP351/1, Papers of Sir Robert Garran relating to the Peace Conference of 1918, to the Imperial Economic Conference of 1923, and to the Commonwealth Oil Refineries Ltd.

National Library of Australia, Canberra

Papers of Alfred Deakin

Ronald Crawford Munro Ferguson (Lord Novar) Papers

Andrew Fisher Papers

William Morris Hughes Papers

MS 1538, Series 19, Items 1–439, Box 113, Folder Series 19, Items 1–149, December 21, 1915–August 1919, 1.

Sir John Latham Papers

Edmund Leolin Piesse Papers

Canada

Library and Archives Canada, Ottawa

RG 25, Department of External Affairs, Volume 727, File 83, Part 1a.

RG 25, Department of External Affairs, Volume 1003.

RG 25, Department of External Affairs, Volume 1004.

RG 25, Department of External Affairs, Volume 1430, File 1925-799 FP, "Asiatic Immigration—No. 1."

RG 76, Department of Labour, Volume 83, File 9309 Volume 1, 1891–1908.

Sir Robert L. Borden Papers

C (Correspondence OC Series, 196 (2)—OC 196 (6), MG 26 H 1 (a), Volume 40 [pages 17286–947]. Microfilm reel C4232.

Sir Wilfrid Laurier Papers

MG 26 G, Volume 477, reel C852; Volume 441, reel C841; Volume 476, reel C851; Volume 478, reel C852; Volume 487, reel C854; Volume 506, reel C859.

New Zealand

National Archives of New Zealand, Wellington

Confidential Inwards Despatches from the Secretary of State—March 28–
April 4, 1924; G, 2, Box/Item 60.

Japanese in the Pacific, 1918–21; IT, 1, Record EX 69/49.

Labour—Maltese; IT, 1, Record EX 17/5.

Newspaper Cuttings—Queen's Diamond Jubilee, 1897, Volume I, Seddon, 3,
Box/Item 15.

South African War—Papers re Protest at Introduction of Chinese Labour into
the Transvaal, 1904; Seddon, 2, Box/Item 17.

Alexander Turnbull Library, National Library of New Zealand, Wellington

Seddon Family Papers, 1850–1971

MS-Group-0170. South African War—Miscellaneous Outward Letters to Sir
John Anderson, Colonial Office, in Seddon Family Papers, 1850–1971.
MS-Papers-1619-013.

United Kingdom

Cambridge University Library, Cambridge

Jan Christiaan Smuts Private Letters, Volume 2, 1900–1903; Volume 3, 1904–5.

Churchill Archives Center, Churchill College, Cambridge University

Leopold Amery Papers

The National Archives, London

CAB 18, Records of the Cabinet Office: Records of Committee of Imperial
Defence, Miscellaneous Reports and Papers.

Appendix No. 1, "Natal" in Report of a Conference between the Right Hon.
Joseph Chamberlain, MP (Her Majesty's Secretary of State for the
Colonies) and the Premiers of the Self-Governing Colonies of the
Empire at the Colonial Office, Downing Street, London, SW, in June
and July 1897; with Appendices.

Appendix No. 1, Restriction of Coloured Immigration: Abstract of
Australian Acts; with Remarks in Report of a Conference between the
Right Hon. Joseph Chamberlain, MP (Her Majesty's Secretary of State
for the Colonies) and the Premiers of the Self-Governing Colonies of the
Empire at the Colonial Office, Downing Street, London, SW, in June
and July 1897; with Appendices.

Records of the Cabinet Office: Records of the Committee of Imperial
Defence, Committee of Imperial Defence: Miscellaneous Reports and
Papers, Proceedings of a Conference between the Secretary of State for
the Colonies and the Premiers of the Self-Governing Colonies at the
Colonial Office, London, June and July 1897.

CAB 23, Records of the Cabinet Office; War Cabinet and Cabinet: Minutes;
Minutes of Meetings.

CAB 27, Records of the Cabinet Office: Records of Cabinet Committees,
1916–39; War Cabinet and Cabinet: Miscellaneous Committees: Records
(General Series).

CAB 27/71 Records of the Cabinet Office: Records of Cabinet Committees, 1916–39: War Cabinet and Cabinet: Miscellaneous Committees: Records (General Series): Finance: Minutes, 1919–22.

CAB 27/98, Records of the Cabinet Office: Records of Cabinet Committees, 1916–39: War Cabinet and Cabinet: Miscellaneous Committees: Records (General Series): League of Nations, 1920–21.

CAB 31, Records of the Cabinet Office: Records of Imperial, Commonwealth and International Conferences, etc.

CAB 32, Cabinet Office: Imperial and Imperial War Conferences: Minutes and Memoranda.

Cab 32/1/1, *Imperial War Conference, 1917: Minutes of Proceedings and Papers Laid before the Conference*, [Dominions No. 62].

Cab 32/1/1 part 2, *Imperial War Conference, 1917: Extracts from Minutes of Proceedings and Papers Laid before the Conference*, [Cd. 9177].

CO 879, War and Colonial Department and Colonial Office: Africa.

CO 879/80/4, War and Colonial Department and Colonial Office: Africa, Confidential Print, "Correspondence [January 15, 1902–March 31, 1904] Respecting the Labour Question."

CO 879/82/3, War and Colonial Department and Colonial Office: Africa, Confidential Print, "Proposal to import Asiatic, more particularly Chinese, Labour for the Transvaal Mines."

CO 879/84/1, War and Colonial Department and Colonial Office: Africa, Confidential Print, "Memorandum, Asiatic Labour for the Transvaal."

CO 886, Colonial Office: Dominions, Confidential Print. Dominions Nos. 1 to 7.

CO 886/1/1, Colonial Office: Dominions, Confidential Print. Dominions Nos. 1 to 7, "Self-Governing Dominions and Coloured Immigration," Memorandum by Sir Charles Prestwood Lucas, Head of the Dominions Department of the Colonial Office, 1907–11.

CO 886/1/3, Colonial Office: Dominions, Confidential Print. Dominions Nos. 1 to 7, Dominions No. 3, "Correspondence (1897–1908) Relating to the Treatment of Asiatics in the Dominions," June 1909.

CO 886/9/1, Confidential Print: Dominions No. 74, Further Correspondence [1919 (Nos. 1, 2, 50), 1920, 1921] relating to the treatment of Asiatics in the Dominions.

FO 46/548, Foreign Office: Political and Other Departments: General Correspondence before 1906, Japan.

FO 46/670, Foreign Office: Political and Other Departments: General Correspondence before 1906, Japan, Immigration of Japanese into British Colonies, 1902–5.

FO 371, Foreign Office: Political Departments: General Correspondence 1906–66, Japan.

FO 371/274, Foreign Office: Political Departments: General Correspondence 1906–66, Japan, 1907.

FO 371/471, Foreign Office: Political Departments: General
Correspondence 1906–66, Japan, 1908.

FO 371/473, Foreign Office: Political Departments: General
Correspondence 1906–66, Japan, 1908.

FO 371/475, Foreign Office: Political Departments: General
Correspondence 1906–66, Japan, 1908.

FO 371/2011, Foreign Office: Political Departments: General
Correspondence 1906–66, Japan, 1914.

FO 371/2016, Foreign Office: Political Departments: General
Correspondence 1906–66, Japan, 1914.

FO 371/6683, Foreign Office: Political Departments: General
Correspondence 1906–66, Japan, 1921.

FO 371/6684, Foreign Office: Political Departments: General
Correspondence 1906–66, Japan, 1921.

FO 371/6704, Foreign Office: Political Departments: General
Correspondence 1906–66, Japan, 1921.

FO 371/6705, Foreign Office: Political Departments: General
Correspondence 1906–66, Japan, 1921.

FO 371, Foreign Office: Political Departments: General Correspondence
1906–66, United States.

FO 371/359, Foreign Office: Political Departments: General
Correspondence 1906–66, United States, 1907.

FO 371/360, Foreign Office: Political Departments: General
Correspondence 1906–66, United States, 1907.

FO 371/565, Foreign Office: Political Departments: General
Correspondence 1906–66, United States, 1908.

FO 371/567, Foreign Office: Political Departments: General
Correspondence 1906–66, United States, 1908.

FO 371/9585, Foreign Office: Political Departments: General
Correspondence 1906–66, United States, 1924.

FO 371/9586, Foreign Office: Political Departments: General
Correspondence 1906–66, United States, 1924.

FO 410, Foreign Office: Confidential Prints: Japan, Further Correspondence.

FO 410/51, Foreign Office: Confidential Prints: Japan, Further
Correspondence Part IV, January–June 1908.

FO 608, Foreign Office: Records of Conferences, Committees, and Councils,
Peace Conference: British Delegation, correspondence and papers.

FO 608/175, Peace Conference: British Delegation, correspondence and
papers.

FO 608/211/2, British Delegation, correspondence and papers relating to
the Far East (Political): Convention; Emigration-immigration; India;
Japan; Korea; Labour; Portugal; Peace Congress; and Post/Telephones.
No. 3614.

FO 608/243/1, Peace Conference: British Delegation, correspondence and papers. British delegation, correspondence and papers relating to the League of Nations: Programmes; Procedure at Peace Conference; Propaganda; Representation; Races; Russia; Scandinavia; Secretariat of the League of Nations; Spain.

United States

Library of Congress, Washington, D.C.

Charles S. Sperry Papers

Box 13, Subject File, World Cruise Correspondence.

Box 5, Family Correspondence.

National Archives and Records Administration, College Park, Maryland

Department of State, Numerical and minor files of the Department of State, 1906–10, RG 59, M862.

General Records of the American Commission to Negotiate Peace, 1918–31, RG 256, M820.

Records of the Department of State Relating to Political Relations between the United States and Japan, 1910–29, RG 59, M423.

National Archives and Records Administration, Washington, D.C.

Records of the U.S. House of Representatives, 68th Congress, Correspondence, Committee on Immigration and Naturalization.

RG233, Correspondence, Committee on Immigration and Naturalization, Japanese Exclusion, HR 68A-F18.3.

Published Primary Sources

AUSTRALIA

Commonwealth of Australia, *Parliamentary Debates*. Victoria: J. Kemp, 1902–1945.

Garran, Robert Randolph. *Prosper the Commonwealth*. Sydney: Angus and Robertson, 1958.

Hughes, William Morris. *The Day and After: Speeches by the Right Honorable W. M. Hughes*. New York: Cassell, 1916.

———. *Policies and Potentates*. Sydney: Angus and Robertson, 1950.

New South Wales, *Parliamentary Debates*. Sydney: Government Printer, 1880–.

Victoria, *Parliamentary Debates*. Melbourne: John Ferris, 1866–1958.

CANADA

Borden, Robert L. *Speeches*. Publishing information unknown, 1907–8.

Dominion of Canada, *Parliamentary Debates*. Ottawa, ON: Queen's Printer, 1875–1951.

Report of the Royal Commission on Chinese and Japanese Immigration. New York: Arno Press, 1978.

Statutes of the Province of British Columbia. Victoria, BC: Richard Wolfenden, 1897.

NEW ZEALAND

New Zealand, *Parliamentary Debates*. Wellington: Government Printer, 1855–

von Dadelszen, E. J. *Report on the Results of a Census of the Colony of New Zealand Taken for the Night of the 12th April, 1896*. Wellington: Government Printer, 1897.

SOUTH AFRICA

Smuts, Jan. *Selections from the Smuts Papers*. Volume 1: *June 1886–May 1902*. Edited by W. K. Hancock and Jean van der Poel. Cambridge, UK: Cambridge University Press, 1966.

———. *Selections from the Smuts Papers*. Volume 2: *June 1902–May 1910*. Edited by W. K. Hancock and Jean van der Poel. Cambridge, UK: Cambridge University Press, 1966.

———. *Selections from the Smuts Papers*. Volume 3: *June 1910–November 1918*. Edited by W. K. Hancock and Jean van der Poel. Cambridge, UK: Cambridge University Press, 1966.

UNITED KINGDOM

Conference of Prime Ministers and Representatives of the United Kingdom, the Dominions, and India: Summary of Proceedings and Documents. London: His Majesty's Stationery Office, 1921.

Conference of Prime Ministers: Summary of Proceedings and Documents. London: His Majesty's Stationery Office, 1923.

Correspondence (Containing the Chinese Labour Ordinance) relating to Affairs in the Transvaal and Orange River Colony (Africa, South: Transvaal and Orange River Colonies: Transvaal and Orange River Colonies: Mines, Chinese Labour), 1904. Cd. 1895, LXI.213. National Archives, London, http://parlipapers.chadwyck.com/home.do.

Reports of the Transvaal Labour Commission (Africa, South: Transvaal Labour Commission), 1904. Cd. 1896, XXXIX.137. National Archives, London, http://parlipapers.chadwyck.com/home.do.

Correspondence (Containing the Chinese Labour Ordinance) relating to Affairs in the Transvaal and Orange River Colony (Africa, South: Transvaal and Orange River Colonies: Transvaal and Orange River Colonies: Mines, Chinese Labour), 1904. Cd. 2104, LXI.875. National Archives, London, http://parlipapers.chadwyck.com/home.do.

The Letters of Queen Victoria: Third Series. A Selection from Her Majesty's Correspondence and Journal between the Years 1886 and 1901. Volume 3: *1896–1901*. Edited by George Earle Buckle. New York: Longmans, Green, 1932.

Lloyd George, David. *War Memoirs of David Lloyd George*. Volume 4. Boston: Little, Brown, 1934.

Macnamara, Dr. *Chinese Labour*. London: New Age Press, 1904.

Milner, Alfred. *The Milner Papers: South Africa, 1899–1905*. Volume 2. Edited by Cecil Headlam. London: Cassell, 1933.

Minutes of Proceedings of the South African Customs Union Conference Held at Bloemfontein, March 1903 (Africa, South: Customs Union Convention), 1903. Cd. 1640, XLV.103. National Archives, London, http://parlipapers.chadwyck.com /home.do.

Naylor, Thomas. *Yellow Labour: The Truth about the Chinese in the Transvaal.* London: Daily Chronicle, n.d.

Parliamentary Debates. London: H.M. Stationary Office, 1904

Telegraphic Correspondence relating to the Transvaal Labour Ordinance, with Appendix the Ordinance Amended in Accordance with Telegrams of 1904 (Africa, South: Transvaal and Orange River Colonies: Mines, Chinese Labour), 1904. Cd. 1899, LXI.609. National Archives, London, http://parlipapers.chadwyck.com/home .do.

Telegraphic Correspondence relating to the Transvaal Labour Ordinance, with Appendix the Ordinance Amended in Accordance with Telegrams (Africa, South: Transvaal and Orange River Colonies: Mines, Chinese Labour), 1904. Cd. 1941, LXI.633. National Archives, London, http://parlipapers.chadwyck.com/home.do.

UNITED STATES

"The Chinaman before the Supreme Court." *Albany Law Journal: A Weekly Record of the Law and the Lawyers* 67, no. 9 (1905): 258–67.

Johnson, Herbert B. *Discrimination against the Japanese in California: A Review of the Real Situation.* Berkeley, CA: Press of the Courier Publishing Company, 1907.

Link, Arthur, et al., eds. *The Papers of Woodrow Wilson.* 69 vols. Princeton, NJ: Princeton University Press, 1966–94.

Richardson, James D. *A Compilation of the Messages and Papers of the Presidents.* Volume 15. New York: Bureau of National Literature, n.d.

Roosevelt, Theodore. *The Letters of Theodore Roosevelt.* Edited by Elting E. Morison. Cambridge, MA: Harvard University Press, 1952.

Scott, James Brown. "The Japanese School Question." *American Journal of International Law* 1, no. 1 (1907): 150–53.

"Treaty of Commerce and Navigation between Japan and Great Britain." *Journal of International Law* 5, no. 3, Supplement: Official (1911): 187–99.

"Treaty of Commerce and Navigation between the United States and Japan." *Journal of International Law* 5, no. 2, Supplement: Official (1911): 106–16.

U.S. Congress. *Restriction of Immigration. Hearings before the Committee on Immigration and Naturalization, House of Representatives.* Sixty-eighth Congress, first session, on HR 5, HR 101, HR 561 [HR 6540]. Washington, DC: Government Printing Office, 1924.

U.S. Department of Commerce and Labor, Bureau of Immigration and Naturalization. *Immigration Laws and Regulations of July 1, 1907.* Washington, DC: Government Printing Office, 1908.

U.S. Department of State. *Japanese Emigration and Immigration to American Territory, Part 1.* Washington, DC, 1909.

————. *Papers relating to the Foreign Relations of the United States, 1921*. Volume 1. Washington, DC: Government Printing Office, 1936.

NEWSPAPERS AND PERIODICALS

Argus (Australia)
Auckland Star (New Zealand)
Bellingham Herald (United States)
Bulletin (Australia)
Dominion (New Zealand)
Evening Post (New Zealand)
Fielding Star (New Zealand)
Journal of International Law (United States)
New Statesman (Great Britain)
New York Times (United States)

New Zealand Herald (New Zealand)
New Zealand Times (New Zealand)
New Zealand Truth (New Zealand)
Nineteenth Century and After: A Monthly Review (Great Britain)
North & South (New Zealand)
Review of Reviews (Great Britain)
Saturday Review (Great Britain)
Sydney Morning Herald (Australia)
Times (Great Britain)
Victoria Daily Colonist (Canada)

Secondary Sources

Adachi, Ken. *The Enemy That Never Was*. Toronto: McClelland and Stewart, 1976.

Adachi, Nobuko. "Brazil: A Historical and Contemporary View of Brazilian Migration." In Maura Isabel Toro-Morn and Marixsa Alicea, eds., *Migration and Immigration: A Global View*. Westport, CT: Greenwood Press, 2004: 19–34.

————, ed. *Japanese Diasporas: Unsung Pasts, Conflicting Presents, and Uncertain Futures*. New York: Routledge, 2006.

Albertson, Mark. *They'll Have to Follow You! The Triumph of the Great White Fleet*. Mustang, OK: Tate, 2007.

Allen, Theodore W. *The Invention of the White Race*. Volume 1: *Oppression and Social Control*. New York: Verso, 1994.

————. *The Invention of the White Race*. Volume 2: *The Origins of Racial Oppression in Anglo-America*. New York: Verso, 1997.

Alomes, Stephen. *A Nation At Last? The Changing Character of Australian Nationalism, 1880–1988*. North Ryde, NSW: Angus and Robertson, 1988.

Anderson, Benedict. *Imagined Communities: Reflections on the Origins and Spread of Nationalism*. New York: Verso, 1991.

Anderson, Kay J. *Vancouver's Chinatown: Racial Discourse in Canada, 1875–1980*. Montreal: McGill-Queen's University Press, 1991.

Anderson, Stuart. *Race and Rapprochement: Anglo-Saxonism and Anglo-American Relations, 1895–1904*. Rutherford, NJ: Associated University Presses, 1981.

Anderson, Warwick. *The Cultivation of Whiteness: Science, Health and Racial Destiny in Australia*. New York: Basic Books, 2003.

Armitage, David, and Alison Bashford, eds. *Pacific Histories: Ocean, Land, People*. New York: Palgrave Macmillan, 2014.

Arnesen, Eric. "Whiteness and the Historians' Imagination." *International Labor and Working-Class History*, 60 (Fall 2001): 3–32.

Atkinson, David C. "Out of One Borderland, Many: The 1907 Anti-Asian Riots and the Spatial Dimensions of Race and Migration in the Canadian-U.S. Pacific Borderlands." In Benjamin Bryce and Alexander Freund, eds., *Entangling Migration History: Borderlands and Transnationalism in the United States and Canada*. Gainesville: University Press of Florida, 2015: 120–40.

———. "The White Australia Policy, the British Empire, and the World." *Britain and the World* 8, no. 2 (2015): 204–24.

Auerbach, Sascha. *Race, Law, and "the Chinese Puzzle" in Imperial Britain*. New York: Palgrave Macmillan, 2009.

Auslin, Michael R. *Negotiating with Imperialism: The Unequal Treaties and the Culture of Japanese Diplomacy*. Cambridge, MA: Harvard University Press, 2004.

Austin, Douglas. *Malta and British Strategic Policy, 1925–43*. New York: Frank Cass, 2004.

Aydin, Cemil. *The Politics of Anti-Westernism in Asia: Visions of World Order in Pan-Islamic and Pan-Asian Thought*. New York: Columbia University Press, 2007.

Azuma, Eiichiro. *Between Two Empires: Race, History, and Transnationalism in Japanese America*. New York: Oxford University Press, 2005.

———. "Japanese Immigrant Settler Colonialism in the U.S.-Mexican Borderlands and the U.S. Racial-Imperialist Politics of the Hemispheric 'Yellow Peril.'" In "Conversations on Transpacific History." Special issue, *Pacific Historical Review* 83, no. 2 (2014): 255–76.

Bacevich, Andrew. *American Empire: The Realities and Consequences of American Diplomacy*. Cambridge, MA: Harvard University Press, 2004.

Bailey, Thomas A. *Theodore Roosevelt and the Japanese-American Crises: An Account of the International Complications Arising from the Race Problem on the Pacific Coast*. Stanford, CA: Stanford University Press, 1934.

Ballantyne, Tony. "Mobility, Empire, Colonisation." *History Australia* 11, no. 2 (2014): 7–37.

———. *Orientalism and Race: Aryanism in the British Empire*. New York: Palgrave Macmillan, 2002.

Ballantyne, Tony, and Antoinette Burton. *Empires and the Reach of the Global, 1870–1945*. Cambridge, MA: Belknap Press of Harvard University Press, 2012.

Ballara, Angela. *Proud to Be White? A Survey of Pakeha Prejudice in New Zealand*. Auckland: Heinemann, 1986.

Banerjee, Sukanye. *Becoming Imperial Citizens: Indians in the Late-Victorian Empire*. Durham, NC: Duke University Press, 2010.

Bannister, Robert. *Social Darwinism: Science and Myth in Anglo-American Social Thought*. Philadelphia: Temple University Press, 2010.

Barber, James. *South Africa in the Twentieth Century: A Political History. In Search of a Nation State*. Malden, MA: Blackwell, 1999.

Barman, Jean. *The West beyond the West: A History of British Columbia*. Toronto: University of Toronto Press, 1991.

Bartelson, Jens. *A Genealogy of Sovereignty*. New York: Cambridge University Press, 1995.

Bayly, C. A. *The Birth of the Modern World, 1780–1914*. Malden, MA: Blackwell, 2004.

Beasly, W. G. *Japanese Imperialism, 1894–1945*. New York: Oxford University Press, 1987.

Beattie, James, Edward Melillo, and Emily O'Gorman, eds. *Eco-Cultural Networks and the British Empire: New Views on Environmental History*. New York: Bloomsbury Academic, 2015.

Beck, Roger B. *The History of South Africa*. Westport, CT: Greenwood Press, 2000.

Bederman, Gail. *Manliness and Civilization: A Cultural History of Gender and Race in the United States, 1880–1917*. Chicago: University of Chicago Press, 1995.

Belich, James. *Paradise Reforged: A History of the New Zealanders from the 1880s to the Year 2000*. Honolulu: University of Hawai'i Press, 2001.

———. *Replenishing the Earth: The Settler Revolution and the Rise of the Anglo-World, 1783–1939*. New York: Oxford University Press, 2009.

Bell, Duncan. *The Idea of Greater Britain: Empire and the Future of World Order, 1860–1900*. Princeton, NJ: Princeton University Press, 2007.

Bender, Thomas. "Commentary: Widening the Lens and Rethinking Asian American History." *Pacific Historical Review* 76, no. 4 (2007): 605–10.

———. *A Nation among Nations: America's Place in World History*. New York: Hill & Wang, 2006.

Bennett, James. "Maori as Honorary Members of the White Tribe." *Journal of Imperial and Commonwealth History* 29, no. 3 (2001): 33–54.

Bennett, Neville. "White Discrimination against Japan: Britain, the Dominions and the United States, 1908–1928." *New Zealand Journal of Asian Studies* 3, no. 2 (2001): 91–105.

Bolt, Christine. *Victorian Attitudes to Race*. Toronto: University of Toronto Press, 1971.

Borstelmann, Thomas. *The Cold War and the Color Line: American Race Relations in the Global Arena*. Cambridge, MA: Harvard University Press, 2001.

Bothwell, Robert. *The Penguin History of Canada*. Toronto: Penguin Canada, 2006.

Bradley, Mark. *Imagining Vietnam and America: The Making of Postcolonial Vietnam, 1919–1950*. Chapel Hill: University of North Carolina Press, 2000.

Brawley, Sean. *The White Peril: Foreign Relations and Asian Immigration to Australasia and North America, 1919–1978*. Sydney: University of New South Wales Press, 1995.

Brebner, J. Bartlet. "Canada, the Anglo-Japanese Alliance and the Washington Conference." *Political Science Quarterly* 50, no. 1 (1935): 48–49.

Bright, Rachel K. *Chinese Labour in South Africa, 1902–10: Race, Violence, and Global Spectacle*. New York: Palgrave Macmillan, 2013.

Brown, Judith M. *Global South Asians: Introducing the Modern Diaspora*. New York: Cambridge University Press, 2006.

Brown, Laurence. " 'A Most Irregular Traffic': The Oceanic Passages of the Melanesian Labor Trade." In Emma Christopher, Cassandra Pybus, and Marcus Rediker, eds., *Many Middle Passages: Forced Migration and the Making of the Modern World*. Berkeley: University of California Press, 2007: 184–203.

Buchignani, Norman, and Doreen M. Indra, with Ram Srivastava. *Continuous Journey: A Social History of South Asians in Canada*. Toronto: McClelland and Stewart, 1985.

Buckley, Thomas H. *The United States and the Washington Conference, 1921–1922*. Knoxville: University of Tennessee Press, 1970.

Buckner, Phillip, and R. Douglas Francis, eds. *Rediscovering the British World*. Calgary: University of Calgary Press, 2005.

Burkman, Thomas W. *Japan and the League of Nations: Empire and World Order, 1914–1938*. Honolulu: University of Hawai'i Press, 2008.

Burks, David D. "The United States and the Geneva Protocol of 1924: 'A New Holy Alliance'?" *American Historical Review* 64, no. 4 (1959): 891–905.

Butler, Peter. *Opium and Gold: A History of the Chinese Goldminers in New Zealand*. Martinborough, NZ: Alister Taylor, 1977.

Cain, P. J., and A. G. Hopkins. *British Imperialism, 1688–2000*. London: Longman, 2002.

Callahan, Michael D. *Mandates and Empire: The League of Nations and Africa, 1914–1931*. Portland, OR: Sussex Academic Press, 1999.

Cammack, Diana. *The Rand at War: The Witwatersrand and the Anglo-Boer War, 1899–1902*. London: James Currey, 1990.

Cannadine, David. *Ornamentalism: How the British Saw Their Empire*. New York: Oxford University Press, 2001.

Carey, Jane, and Claire McLisky, eds. *Creating White Australia*. Sydney: Sydney University Press, 2009.

Carrothers, W. A. *Emigration from the British Isles: With Special Reference to the Development of Overseas Dominions*. 2nd ed. New York: Frank Cass, 1966.

Castles, Stephen, et al., eds. *Australia's Italians: Culture and Community in a Changing Society*. Sydney: Allen & Unwin, 1992.

Chang, Kornel. "Circulating Race and Empire: Transnational Labor Activism and the Politics of Anti-Asian Agitation in the Anglo-American-Pacific World, 1880–1910." *Journal of American History* 96, no. 3 (2009): 678–701.

———. *Pacific Connections: The Making of the U.S.-Canadian Borderlands*. Berkeley: University of California Press, 2012.

Clark, C. M. H. *A History of Australia*. Volume 4: *The Earth Abideth for Ever, 1851–1888*. Melbourne: Melbourne University Press, 1980.

Cohen, Robin, ed. *The Cambridge Survey of World Migration*. New York: Cambridge University Press, 1995.

Con, Harry, et al. *From China to Canada: A History of the Chinese Communities in Canada*. Edited by Edgar Wickberg. Toronto: McClelland and Stewart, 1982.

Connelly, Matthew. *A Diplomatic Revolution: Algeria's Fight for Independence and the Origins of the Post–Cold War Era*. New York: Oxford University Press, 2002.

Constantine, Stephen, ed. *Emigrants and Empire: British Settlement in the Dominions between the Wars*. Manchester, UK: Manchester University Press, 1990.

Coombes, Annie E., ed. *Rethinking Settler Colonialism: History and Memory in Australia, Canada, Aotearoa New Zealand, and South Africa*. Manchester, UK: Manchester University Press, 2006.

Cooper, Frederick. *Colonialism in Question: Theory, Knowledge, History*. Berkeley: University of California Press, 2005.

Costigliola, Frank, and Michael J. Hogan, eds. *America in the World: The Historiography of American Foreign Relations since 1941*. 2nd ed. New York: Cambridge University Press, 2014.

Cowan, James. *The Maoris of New Zealand*. Christchurch, NZ: Whitcombe and Tombs, 1910.

Cumings, *Dominion from Sea to Sea: Pacific Ascendency and American Power*. New Haven, CT: Yale University Press, 2009.

Daniels, Roger. *Asian America: Chinese and Japanese in the United States since 1850*. Seattle: University of Washington Press, 1988.

———. *Coming to America: A History of Immigration and Ethnicity in American Life*. 2nd ed. New York: Harper Perennial, 2002.

———. "The Growth of Restrictive Immigration Policies in the Colonies of Settlement." In Robin Cohen, ed., *The Cambridge Survey of World Migration*. New York: Cambridge University Press, 1995: 39–44.

———. *Guarding the Golden Door: American Immigration Policy and Immigrants since 1882*. New York: Hill and Wang, 2004.

———. *The Politics of Prejudice*. New York: Atheneum, 1973.

Darwin, John. "A Third British Empire? The Dominion Idea in Imperial Politics." In Judith Brown and Wm. Roger Louis, eds., *The Oxford History of the British Empire*. Volume 4. New York: Oxford University Press, 1999: 64–87.

Davenport, T. R. H. *South Africa: A Modern History*. 2nd ed. Toronto: University of Toronto Press, 1980.

Dawson, Robert MacGregor. *The Development of Dominion Status, 1900–1936*. London: Oxford University Press, 1937.

Day, David. *Claiming a Continent: A New History of Australia*. 4th ed. Sydney: Harper Perennial, 2005.

Delgado, Grace. *Making the Chinese Mexican: Global Migration, Localism, and Exclusion in the U.S.-Mexico Borderlands*. Palo Alto, CA: Stanford University Press, 2012.

Denoon, Donald. *A Grand Illusion: The Failure of Imperial Policy in the Transvaal Colony during the Period of Reconstruction, 1900–1905*. London: Longman, 1973.

Denoon, Donald, and Philippa Mein-Smith, with Marivic Wyndham. *A History of Australia, New Zealand, and the Pacific*. Malden, MA: Blackwell, 2000.

Desai, Ashwin, and Goolam H. Vahed. *Inside Indenture: A South African Story, 1860–1914*. Durban: Madiba, 2007.

Dingman, Roger. *Power in the Pacific: The Origins of Naval Arms Limitation, 1914–1922*. Chicago: University of Chicago Press, 1976.

Dirlik, Arif, ed. *Chinese on the American Frontier*. Lanham, MA: Rowan & Littlefield, 2001.

Donaghy, Greg, and Patricia E. Roy, eds. *Contradictory Impulses: Canada and Japan in the Twentieth Century*. Vancouver: University of British Columbia Press, 2008.

Douglas, R. M. "Anglo-Saxons and Attacotti: The Racialization of Irishness in Britain between the World Wars." *Ethnic and Racial Studies* 25, no. 1 (2002): 40–63.

Dubow, Saul. *Apartheid, 1948–1994*. New York: Oxford University Press, 2014.

Dudziak, Mary. *Cold War Civil Rights: Race and the Image of American Democracy*. Princeton, NJ: Princeton University Press, 2000.

Dutton, David. *One of Us? A Century of Australian Citizenship*. Sydney: University of New South Wales Press, 2002.

Duus, Peter. *Party Rivalry and Political Change in Taishō Japan*. Cambridge, MA: Harvard University Press, 1968.

Duus, Peter, Ramon H. Myers, and Mark R. Peattie, eds. *The Japanese Wartime Empire, 1931–1945*. Princeton, NJ: Princeton University Press, 1996.

Dyer, Thomas G. *Theodore Roosevelt and the Idea of Race*. Baton Rouge: Louisiana State University Press, 1980.

Elkins, Caroline. *Imperial Reckoning: The Untold Story of Britain's Gulag in Kenya*. New York: Henry Holt, 2005.

Esthus, Raymond. *Theodore Roosevelt and Japan*. Seattle: University of Washington Press, 1967.

Fedorowich, Kent, and Andrew S. Thompson, eds. *Empire, Migration, and Identity in the British World*. Manchester, UK: Manchester University Press, 2013.

Fisher, Michael H. *Migration: A World History*. New York: Oxford University Press, 2014.

Fitzgerald, John. *Big White Lie: Chinese Australians in White Australia*. Sydney: University of New South Wales Press, 2007.

Fojas, Camilla, and Rudy P. Guevarra Jr., eds. *Transnational Crossroads: Remapping the Americas and the Pacific*. Lincoln: University of Nebraska Press, 2012.

Foley, Neil. *The White Scourge: Mexicans, Blacks, and Poor Whites in Texas Cotton Culture*. Berkeley: University of California Press, 1997.

Foner, Philip S., and Daniel Rosenberg, eds. *Racism, Dissent, and Asian Americans from 1850 to the Present*. Westport, CT: Greenwood Press, 1993.

Fong, Ng Bickleen. *The Chinese in New Zealand: A Study in Assimilation*. Hong Kong: Hong Kong University Press, 1959.

Ford, Lisa. *Settler Sovereignty: Jurisdiction and Indigenous People in America and Australia, 1788–1836.* Cambridge, MA: Harvard University Press, 2010.

Foster, Anne L. *Projections of Power: The United States and Europe in Colonial Southeast Asia, 1919–1941.* Durham, NC: Duke University Press, 2010.

Fredrickson, George M. *White Supremacy: A Comparative Study in American and South African History.* New York: Oxford University Press, 1981.

Frost, Linda. *Never One Nation: Freaks, Savages, and Whiteness in U.S. Popular Culture, 1850–1877.* Minneapolis: University of Minnesota Press, 2005.

Fry, Michael Graham. "The North Atlantic Triangle and the Abrogation of the 'Anglo-Japanese Alliance." *Journal of Modern History* 39, no. 1 (1967): 46–64.

———. "The Pacific Dominions and the Washington Conference, 1921–1922." In Erik Goldstein and John Maurer, eds., *The Washington Conference, 1921–22: Naval Rivalry, East Asian Stability and the Road to Pearl Harbor.* Portland, OR: Frank Cass, 1994: 60–101.

Fujikane, Candace, and Jonathan Y. Okamura, eds. *Asian Settler Colonialism: From Local Governance to the Habits of Everyday Life in Hawaiʻi.* Honolulu: University of Hawaiʻi Press, 2008.

Fujita-Rony, Dorothy B. *American Workers, Colonial Power: Philippine Seattle and the Transpacific West, 1919–1941.* Berkeley: University of California Press, 2002.

Gabbacia, Donna. *Foreign Relations: American Immigration in Global Perspective.* Princeton, NJ: Princeton University Press, 2012.

Gabbacia, Donna, and Dirk Hoerder. *Connecting Seas and Connected Ocean Rims: Indian, Atlantic, and Pacific Oceans and China Seas Migrations from the 1830s to the 1930s.* Boston: Brill, 2011.

Gainer, Bernard. *The Alien Invasion: The Origins of the Aliens Act of 1905.* New York: Crane, Russak, 1972.

Gandhi, Mohandas K. *An Autobiography: The Story of My Experiments with Truth.* Boston: Beacon Press, 1957.

Garner, James W. "The Geneva Protocol for the Pacific Settlement of International Disputes." *American Journal of International Law* 19, no. 1 (1925): 123–32.

Garvin, J. L. *The Life of Joseph Chamberlain: Empire and World Policy.* Volume 3: *1895–1900.* London: MacMillan, 1934.

Geiger, Andrea. *Subverting Exclusion: Transpacific Encounters with Race, Caste, and Borders, 1885–1928.* New Haven, CT: Yale University Press, 2011.

Gerstle, Gary. *American Crucible: Race and Nation in the Twentieth Century.* Princeton, NJ: Princeton University Press, 2001.

Gilmour, Julie F. *Trouble on Main Street: Mackenzie King, Reason, Race, and the 1907 Vancouver Riots.* Toronto: Allan Lane, 2014.

Goldstein, Erik, and John Maurer, eds. *The Washington Conference, 1921–22: Naval Rivalry, East Asian Stability and the Road to Pearl Harbor.* Portland, OR: Frank Cass, 1994.

Goodman, David. *Fault Lines: Journeys into the New South Africa.* Berkeley: University of California Press, 1999.

Gordon, Andrew. *A Modern History of Japan: From Tokugawa Times to the Present.* New York: Oxford University Press, 2003.

Gordon, Donald C. "Roosevelt's 'Smart Yankee Trick.'" *Pacific Historical Review* 30, no. 4 (1961): 351–58.

Gorman, Daniel. *Imperial Citizenship: Empire and the Question of Belonging.* New York: Manchester University Press, 2006.

Gough, Barry M. *The Northwest Coast: British Navigation, Trade, and Discoveries to 1812.* Vancouver: University of British Columbia Press, 1992.

Goutor, David. *Guarding the Gates: The Canadian Labour Movement and Immigration, 1872–1934.* Vancouver: University of British Columbia Press, 2007.

Gowen, Robert Joseph. "British Legerdemain at the 1911 Imperial Conference: The Dominions, Defense Planning, and the Renewal of the Anglo-Japanese Alliance." *Journal of Modern History* 52, no. 3 (1980): 385–413.

Grant, Kevin. *A Civilised Savagery: Britain and the New Slaveries in Africa, 1884–1926.* New York: Routledge, 2005.

Greif, Stuart William, ed. *Immigration and National Identity in New Zealand: One People, Two Peoples, Many Peoples?* Palmerston North, NZ: Dunmore Press, 1995.

———. *The Overseas Chinese in New Zealand.* Singapore: Asia Pacific Press, 1974.

Guoqi, Xu. *Strangers on the Western Front: Chinese Workers in the Great War.* Cambridge, MA: Harvard University Press, 2011.

Guterl, Matthew Pratt. *The Color of Race in America, 1900–1940.* Cambridge, MA: Harvard University Press, 2001.

Gyory, Andrew. *Closing the Gate: Race, Politics, and the Chinese Exclusion Act.* Chapel Hill: University of North Carolina Press, 1998.

Hale, Grace Elizabeth. *Making Whiteness: The Culture of Segregation in the South, 1890–1940.* New York: Vintage Books, 1999.

Hall, H. Duncan. *Commonwealth: A History of the British Commonwealth of Nations.* New York: Van Nostrand Reinhold, 1971.

Hamer, D.A. *The New Zealand Liberals: The Years of Power, 1891–1912.* New York: Oxford University Press, 1988.

Hancock, Keith W. *Smuts: The Sanguine Years, 1870–1919.* Cambridge, UK: Cambridge University Press, 1962.

Harper, Marjory, and Stephen Constantine. *Migration and Empire.* New York: Oxford University Press, 2010.

Harrison, Mark. *Medicine in an Age of Commerce and Empire: Britain and Its Tropical Colonies 1660–1830.* Oxford: Oxford University Press, 2010.

Hawkins, Freda. *Critical Years in Immigration: Canada and Australia Compared.* 2nd ed. Montreal: McGill-Queen's University Press, 1991.

Hawkins, Mike. *Social Darwinism in European and American Thought, 1860–1945: Nature as Model and Nature as Threat.* New York, Cambridge University Press, 1997.

Henning, C. G. *The Indentured Indian in Natal, 1860–1917.* New Delhi: Promilla, 1993.

Hiery, Hermann. *The Neglected War: The German South Pacific and the Influence of World War I*. Honolulu: University of Hawai'i Press, 1995.

Higham, John. *Strangers in the Land: Patterns of American Nativism, 1860–1925*. 2nd ed. New York: Atheneum, 1972.

Hinsely, F. H. *Sovereignty*. 2nd ed. Cambridge, UK: Cambridge University Press, 1986.

Hirabayashi, Lane Ryo, Akemi Kikumura-Yano, and James A. Hirabayashi, eds. *New Worlds, New Lives: Globalization and People of Japanese Descent in the Americas and from Latin America in Japan*. Stanford, CA: Stanford University Press, 2002.

Hirobe, Izumi. *Japanese Pride, American Prejudice: Modifying the Exclusion Clause of the 1924 Immigration Act*. Stanford, CA: Stanford University Press, 2001.

Hoare, James, "The Era of the Unequal Treaties, 1858–99." In Ian Nish and Yoichi Kibata, eds., *The History of Anglo-Japanese Relations*. Volume 1: *The Political-Diplomatic Dimension, 1600–1930*. New York: St. Martin's Press, 2000: 107–30.

Hobsbawm, Eric. *Nations and Nationalism since 1780*. New York: Cambridge University Press, 1992.

Hoerder, Dirk. *Migrations and Belongings, 1870–1945*. Cambridge, MA: Harvard University Press, 2012.

Hofstadter, Richard. *Social Darwinism in American Thought*. Boston: Beacon Press, 1992.

Holland, Robert F. "Empire and the Great War, 1914–1918." In Judith M. Brown and Wm. Roger Louis, eds., *The Oxford History of the British Empire*. Volume 4: *The Twentieth Century*. Oxford: Oxford University Press, 1999: 114–37.

Horne, Gerald. "Race from Power: U.S. Foreign Policy and the General Crisis of 'White Supremacy.'" In Michael Hogan, ed., *The Ambiguous Legacy: U.S. Foreign Relations in the "American Century."* New York: Cambridge University Press, 1999: 302–36.

———. *Race War! White Supremacy and the Japanese Attack on the British Empire*. New York: New York University Press, 2004.

Horsman, Reginald. "Origins of Racial Anglo-Saxonism in Great Britain before 1850." *Journal of the History of Ideas* 37, no. 3 (1976): 387–410.

———. *Race and Manifest Destiny: The Origins of American Racial Anglo-Saxonism*. Cambridge, MA: Harvard University Press, 1981.

Hosokawa, Bill. *Nisei: The Quiet Americans*. Niwot: University Press of Colorado, 1992.

Hsu, Madeline. *Dreaming of Gold, Dreaming of Home: Transnationalism and Migration between the United States and South China, 1882–1943*. Stanford, CA: Stanford University Press, 2000.

———. *The Good Immigrants: How the Yellow Peril Became the Model Minority*. Princeton, NJ: Princeton University Press, 2015.

Hu-DeHart, Evelyn, ed. *Across the Pacific: Asian Americans and Globalization*. Philadelphia: Temple University Press, 1999.

Hudson, W. J. *Billy Hughes in Paris: The Birth of Australian Diplomacy*. Melbourne: Nelson, 1978.

Hughes, Aneurin. *Billy Hughes: Prime Minister and Controversial Founding Father of the Australian Labor Party.* Milton, QLD: John Wiley & Sons, 2005.

Hunt, Michael. *Ideology and U.S. Foreign Policy.* New Haven, CT: Yale University Press, 1987.

Huntington, Samuel P. *Who Are We? America's National Identity and the Challenges It Faces.* New York: Simon and Schuster, 2004.

Huttenback, Robert A. "The British Empire as a 'White Man's Country'—Racial Attitudes and Immigration Legislation in the Colonies of White Settlement." *Journal of British Studies* 13, no. 1 (1973): 108–37.

———. *Gandhi in South Africa: British Imperialism and the Indian Question, 1860–1914.* Ithaca, NY: Cornell University Press, 1971.

———. *Racism and Empire: White Settlers and Colored Immigrants in the British Self-Governing Colonies, 1830–1910.* Ithaca, NY: Cornell University Press, 1976.

Hyam, Ronald. "Bureaucracy and 'Trusteeship' in the Colonial Empire." in Judith M. Brown and Wm. Roger Louis, eds., *The Oxford History of the British Empire.* Volume 4: *The Twentieth Century.* Oxford: Oxford University Press, 1999: 255–79.

Ichioka, Yuji. *The Issei: The World of the First Generation Japanese Immigrants, 1885–1924.* New York: Free Press, 1988.

Igler, David. *The Great Ocean: Pacific Worlds from Captain Cook to the Gold Rush.* New York: Oxford University Press, 2013.

Ingham, Kenneth. *Jan Christian Smuts: The Conscience of a South African.* New York: St. Martin's Press, 1986.

Iriye, Akira. *Across the Pacific: An Inner History of American–East Asian Relations.* New York: Harcourt, Brace & World, 1967.

———. *After Imperialism: The Search for a New Order in the Far East, 1921–1931.* Cambridge, MA: Harvard University Press, 1965.

———. *The Cambridge History of American Foreign Relations.* Volume 3: *The Globalizing of America, 1913–1945.* New York: Cambridge University Press, 1997.

———. *Global and Transnational History: The Past, Present, and Future.* New York: Palgrave Macmillan, 2013.

———. "The Internationalization of History." *American Historical Review* 94, no. 1 (1989): 1–10

———. "1922–1931." In Ernest R. May and James C. Thomson Jr., eds., *American–East Asian Relations: A Survey.* Cambridge, MA: Harvard University Press, 1972: 221–42.

———. *Pacific Estrangement: Japanese and Amercian Expansion, 1897–1911.* Cambridge, MA: Harvard University Press, 1972.

Itatsu, Yuko. "Japan's Hollywood Boycott Movement of 1924." *Historical Journal of Film, Radio and Television* 28, no. 3 (2008): 353–69.

Jackson, Robert. *Sovereignty: Evolution of an Idea.* Malden, MA: Polity Press, 2007.

Jacobson, Matthew Frye. *Barbarian Virtues: The United States Encounters Foreign Peoples at Home and Abroad.* New York: Hill and Wang, 2000.

———. *Whiteness of a Different Color: European Immigrants and the Alchemy of Race.* Cambridge, MA: Harvard University Press, 1998.

Jacoby, Harold S. "U.S. Strategies of Asian Indian Immigration Restriction, 1882–1917." In Sripati Chandrasekhar, ed., *From India to America: A Brief History of Immigration; Problems of Discrimination, Admission and Assimilation.* La Jolla, CA: Population Review, 1982: 35–40.

Janigan, Mary. *Let the Eastern Bastards Freeze in the Dark: The West versus the Rest Since Confederation.* Toronto: Vintage Canada, 2013.

Jasanoff, Maya. *Edge of Empire: Lives Culture, and Conquest in the East, 1750–1850.* New York: Knopf, 2005.

Jensen, Joan M. *Passage from India: Asian Indian Immigrants in North America.* New Haven, CT: Yale University Press, 1988.

Johnston, Hugh. *The Voyage of the Komagata Maru: The Sikh Challenge to Canada's Colour Bar.* Delhi: Oxford University Press, 1979.

Judd, Denis. *Empire: The British Imperial Experience from 1765 to the Present.* New York: Basic Books, 1996.

Judd, Denis, and Keith Surridge. *The Boer War: A History.* New York: I. B. Tauris, 2013.

Jung, Moon-Ho. *Coolies and Cane: Race, Labor, and Sugar in the Age of Emancipation.* Baltimore: Johns Hopkins University Press, 2008.

Kaplan, Amy, and Donald E. Pease. *Cultures of United States Imperialism.* Durham, NC: Duke University Press, 1993.

Keith, Arthur Berriedale. *Speeches and Documents of the British Dominions, 1918–1931: From Self-Government to National Sovereignty.* London: Oxford University Press, 1932.

Kennedy, Dane. "Empire Migration in Post-War Reconstruction: The Role of the Overseas Settlement Committee, 1919–1922." *Albion* 20, no. 3 (1988): 403–19.

Keylor, William R. *The Twentieth-Century World and Beyond.* 5th ed. New York: Oxford University Press, 2006.

King, Michael. *The Penguin History of New Zealand.* Auckland, NZ: Penguin Books, 2003.

Knock, Thomas J. *To End All Wars: Woodrow Wilson and the Quest for a New World Order.* Princeton, NJ: Princeton University Press, 1992.

Knowles, Valerie. *Strangers at Our Gates: Canadian Immigration and Immigration Policy, 1540–1997.* Toronto: Dundurn Press, 1997.

Kolchin, Peter. "Whiteness Studies: The New History of Race in America." *Journal of American History* 89, no. 1 (2002): 154–73.

Kramer, Paul A. *The Blood of Government: Race, Empire, the United States, and the Philippines.* Chapel Hill: University of North Carolina Press, 2006.

———. "Empires, Exceptions, and Anglo-Saxons: Race and Rule between the British and U.S. Empires, 1880–1910." In Julian Go and Anne L. Foster, eds., *The American Colonial State in the Philippines: Global Perspectives.* Durham, NC: Duke University Press, 2003: 43–91.

———. "Power and Connection: Imperial Histories of the United States in the World." *American Historical Review* 116, no. 5 (2011): 1348–91.

Krasner, Stephen D. *Sovereignty: Organized Hypocrisy.* Princeton, NJ: Princeton University Press, 1999.

Kuhn, Philip. *Chinese among Others: Emigration in Modern Times.* Lanham, MD: Rowman & Littlefield, 2009.

Kuo, John, Wei Tchen, and Dylan Yeats, eds. *Yellow Peril! An Archive of Anti-Asian Fear.* New York: Verso, 2014

Kurashige, Lon, Madeline Y. Hsu, and Yujin Yaguchi, eds. "Introduction: Conversations on Transpacific History." In "Conversations on Transpacific History." Special issue, *Pacific Historical Review* 83, no. 2 (2014): 183–88.

Kynoch, Gary. "Controlling the Coolies: Chinese Mineworkers and the Struggle for Labour in South Africa, 1904–1910." *International Journal of African Historical Studies* 36, no. 2 (2003): 309–29.

———. "'Your Petitioners Are in Mortal Terror': The Violent World of Chinese Mineworkers in South Africa, 1904–1910." *Journal of Southern African Studies* 31, no. 3 (2005): 531–46.

LaFeber, Walter. *The Clash: A History of U.S.-Japan Relations.* New York: Norton, 1997.

Laidlaw, Zoë. "Breaking Britannia's Bounds? Law, Settlers, and Space in Britain's Imperial Historiography." *Historical Journal* 55, no. 3 (2012): 807–30.

Laidlaw, Zoë, and Alan Lester, eds. *Indigenous Communities and Settler Colonialism: Land Holding, Loss and Survival in an Interconnected World.* New York: Palgrave Macmillan, 2015.

Lake, Marilyn, and Henry Reynolds. *Drawing the Global Colour Line: White Men's Countries and the International Challenge of Racial Equality.* New York: Cambridge University Press, 2008.

Langfield, Michele. "Attitudes to European Immigration to Australia in the Early Twentieth Century." *Journal of Intercultural Studies* 12, no. 1 (1991): 1–15.

———. "'White Aliens': The Control of European Immigration to Australia, 1920–1930." *Journal of Intercultural Studies* 12, no. 2 (1991): 1–14.

Lau, Estelle T. *Paper Families: Identity, Immigration Administration, and Chinese Exclusion.* Durham, NC: Duke University Press, 2006.

Lauren, Paul Gordon. "The Denial of Racial Equality." In William R. Keylor, ed., *The Legacy of the Great War: Peacemaking, 1919.* Boston: Houghton Mifflin, 1998: 238–54.

———. *Power and Prejudice: The Politics and Diplomacy of Racial Discrimination.* Boulder, CO: Westview Press, 1988.

Leach, Michael, Geoff Stokes, and Ian Ward. *The Rise and Fall of One Nation.* St. Lucia: University of Queensland Press, 2000.

Lee, Erika. *At America's Gates: Chinese Immigration during the Exclusion Era, 1882–1943.* Chapel Hill: University of North Carolina Press, 2003.

———. "Enforcing the Borders: Chinese Exclusion at the Borders with Canada and Mexico, 1882–1924." *Journal of American History* 89, no. 1 (2000): 54–86.

———. *The Making of Asian America: A History.* New York: Simon & Schuster, 2015.

———. "The 'Yellow Peril' and Asian Exclusion in the Americas." *Pacific Historical Review* 76, no. 4 (2007): 537–62.

Lee, Rebekah. *African Women and Apartheid: Migration and Settlement in Urban South Africa.* London: I. B. Tauris, 2009.

Leong, Karen J. "Foreign Policy, National Identity, and Citizenship: The Roosevelt White House and the Expediency of Repeal." *Journal of American Ethnic History* 22, no. 4 (2003): 3–30.

Lesser, Jeffrey, ed. *Searching for Home Abroad: Japanese Brazilians and Transnationalism.* Durham, NC: Duke University Press, 2003.

Lewsen, Phyllis. *John X. Merriman: Paradoxical South African Statesman.* New Haven, CT: Yale University Press, 1982.

Ling, Huping. *Chinese Chicago: Race, Transnational Migration, and Community since 1870.* Palo Alto, CA: Stanford, CA University Press, 2012.

———. *Chinese St. Louis: From Enclave to Cultural Community.* Philadelphia: Temple University Press, 2004.

Lissington, M. P. *New Zealand and Japan, 1900–1941.* Wellington, NZ: A. R. Shearer, Government Printer, 1972.

Lloyd, Lorna. "'A Family Quarrel': The Development of the Dispute over Indians in South Africa." *Historical Journal* 34, no. 3 (1991): 703–25.

Logevall, Fredrik. *Embers of War: The Fall of an Empire and the Making of America's Vietnam.* New York: Random House, 2014.

London, H. I. *Nonwhite Immigration and the "White Australia" Policy.* Sydney: Sydney University Press, 1970.

Louis, Wm. Roger. "Australia and the German Colonies in the Pacific, 1914–1919." *Journal of Modern History* 38, no. 4 (1966): 407–21.

Lui, Mary Ting Yi. *The Chinatown Trunk Mystery: Murder, Miscegenation, and Other Dangerous Encounters in Turn-of-the-Century New York.* Princeton, NJ: Princeton University Press, 2005.

Ma, Xiaohua. "The Sino-American Alliance during World War II and the Lifting of the Chinese Exclusion Acts." *American Studies International* 38, no. 2 (2000): 39–61.

MacDougall, Hugh. *Racial Myth in English History: Trojans, Teutons, and Anglo-Saxons.* Hanover, NH: University Press of New England, 1982.

Macintyre, Stuart. *A Concise History of Australia.* 2nd ed. Cambridge, UK: Cambridge University Press, 2004.

Mackie, Richard Somerset. *Trading beyond the Mountains: The British Fur Trade on the Pacific, 1793–1843.* Vancouver: University of British Columbia Press, 1997.

MacMillan, Margaret. *Paris 1919: Six Months That Changed the World.* New York: Random House, 2003.

Magee, Gary B., and Andrew S. Thompson. *Empire and Globalisation: Networks of People, Goods, and Capital in the British World*. New York: Cambridge University Press, 2010.

Manchow, Howard L. *Population Pressures: Emigration and Government in Late Nineteenth-Century Britain*. Palo Alto, CA: SPOSS, 1979.

Mandler, Peter. *The English National Character: The History of an Idea from Edmund Burke to Tony Blair*. New Haven, CT: Yale University Press, 2006.

Manela, Erez. *The Wilsonian Moment: Self-Determination and the International Origins of Anticolonial Nationalism*. New York: Oxford University Press, 2007.

Mar, Lisa Rose. *Brokering Belonging: Chinese in Canada's Exclusion Era, 1885–1945*. New York: Oxford University Press, 2010.

Marais, J. S. *The Fall of Kruger's Republic*. Oxford: Clarendon Press, 1961.

Markus, Andrew. *Australian Race Relations, 1788–1993*. St. Leonards, NSW: Allen & Unwin, 1994.

———. *Fear and Hatred: Purifying Australia and California, 1850–1901*. Sydney: Hale and Iremonger, 1979.

Marshall, Alison. *Cultivating Connections: The Making of Chinese Prairie Canada*. Seattle: University of Washington Press, 2014.

———. *The Way of the Bachelor: Early Chinese Settlement in Manitoba*. Seattle: University of Washington Press, 2011.

Martellone, Anna Maria. "In the Name of Anglo-Saxondom, for Empire and for Democracy: The Anglo-American Discourse, 1880–1920." In David K. Adams and Cornelis A. van Minnen, eds., *Reflections on American Exceptionalism*. Keele, UK: Ryburn, Keele University Press, 1994: 83–97.

Martens, Jeremy. "Richard Seddon and Popular Opposition in New Zealand to the Introduction of Chinese Labor into the Transvaal, 1903–1904." *New Zealand Journal of History* 42, no. 2 (2008): 176–95.

———. "A Transnational History of Immigration Restriction: Natal and New South Wales, 1896–97." *Journal of Imperial and Commonwealth History* 34, no. 3 (2006): 323–44.

Martinez, Julia, and Adrian Vickers. *The Pearl Frontier: Indonesian Labor and Indigenous Encounters in Australia's Northern Trading Network*. Honolulu: University of Hawai'i Press, 2015.

Matsuda, Matt K. *Pacific Worlds: A History of Seas, Peoples, and Cultures*. New York: Cambridge University Press, 2012.

Mawby, Arthur Andrew. "Capital, Government and Politics in the Transvaal, 1900–1907: A Revision and a Reversion." *Historical Journal* 17, no. 2 (June 1974): 387–415.

———. *Gold Mining and Politics—Johannesburg 1900–1907*. Volume 1: *The Origins of Old South Africa?* Lewiston, NY: Edwin Mellen Press, 2000.

McCoy, Alfred W., and Francisco Scarano. *Colonial Crucible: Empire and the Making of the Modern American State*. Madison: University of Wisconsin Press, 2009.

McGuiness, Aims. *Path of Empire: Panama and the California Gold Rush*. Ithaca, NY: Cornell University Press, 2008.

McIntyre, W. David. *The Commonwealth of Nations: Origins and Impact, 1869–1971*. Minneapolis: University of Minnesota Press, 1977.

McKeown, Adam. *Chinese Migration Networks and Cultural Change: Peru, Chicago, Hawaii, 1900–1936*. Chicago: University of Chicago Press, 2001.

———. "Global Migration, 1846–1940." *Journal of World History* 15, no. 2 (2004): 155–89.

———. *Melancholy Order: Asian Migration and the Globalization of Borders*. New York: Columbia University Press, 2008.

McKinnon, Malcolm. *Immigrants and Citizens: New Zealanders and Asian Immigration in Historical Context*. Wellington, NZ: Institute of Policy Studies, 1996.

McLaren, John P. S. "The Burdens of Empire and the Legalization of White Supremacy in Canada, 1860–1910." In W. M. Gordon and T. D. Fergus, eds., *Legal History in the Making: Proceedings of the Ninth British Legal History Conference*. 1989; London: Hambledon Press, 1991: 187–200.

McMinn, W. G. *Nationalism and Federalism in Australia*. Oxford: Oxford University Press, 1994.

Mein Smith, Philippa. *A Concise History of New Zealand*. New York: Cambridge University Press, 2012.

Meredith, Martin. *Diamonds, Gold, and War: The British, the Boers, and the Making of South Africa*. New York: Public Affairs, 2008.

Miles, David. *The Tribes of Britain: Who Are We? And Where Do We Come From?* London: Phoenix, 2006.

Millar, Thomas B. *Australia in Peace and War: External Relations, 1788–1977*. New York: St. Martin's Press, 1978.

Miller, David Hunter. *The Geneva Protocol*. New York: Macmillan, 1925.

Mishra, Pankaj. *From the Ruins of Empire: The Intellectuals Who Remade Asia*. New York: Farrar, Straus and Giroux, 2012.

Mohanram, Radhika. *Imperial White: Race, Diaspora, and the British Empire*. Minneapolis: University of Minnesota Press, 2007.

Moloughney, Brian, and John Stenhouse. "'Drug-Besotten, Sin-Besotten Fiends of Filth': New Zealanders and the Oriental Other, 1850–1920." *New Zealand Journal of History* 33, no. 1 (1999): 43–64.

Morrell, W. P. *The Gold Rushes*. London: Adam and Charles Black, 1940.

Morris, Jan. *Pax Britannica: The Climax of an Empire*. London: Faber and Faber, 1998.

Morrison, Toni. *Playing in the Dark: Whiteness and the Literary Imagination*. Cambridge, MA: Harvard University Press, 1992.

Morton, James. *In the Sea of Sterile Mountains: The Chinese in British Columbia*. Vancouver: J. J. Douglas, 1974.

Murphy, Gretchen. *Shadowing the White Man's Burden: U.S. Imperialism and the Problem of the Color Line*. New York: New York University Press, 2010.

Myers, Ramon H., and Mark R. Peattie, eds. *The Japanese Colonial Empire, 1895–1945*. Princeton, NJ: Princeton University Press, 1984.

Neu, Charles E. *An Uncertain Friendship: Theodore Roosevelt and Japan, 1906–1909.* Cambridge, MA: Harvard University Press, 1967.

Ngai, Mae M. *Impossible Subjects: Illegal Aliens and the Making of Modern America.* Princeton, NJ: Princeton University Press, 2004.

———. *The Lucky Ones: One Family and the Extraordinary Invention of Chinese America.* New York: Houghton Mifflin Harcourt, 2010.

Nish, Ian. *Alliance in Decline: A Study in Anglo-Japanese Relations, 1908–1923.* London: Athlone Press, 1972.

———. *The Anglo-Japanese Alliance: The Diplomacy of Two Island Empires, 1894–1907.* London: Athlone Press, 1968.

———. "Australia and the Anglo-Japanese Alliance, 1901–1911." *Australian Journal of Politics and History* 9, no. 2 (1963): 201–12.

———. "Echoes of Alliance, 1920–30." In Ian Nish and Yoichi Kibata, eds., *The History of Anglo-Japanese Relations.* Volume 1: *The Political-Diplomatic Dimension, 1600–1930.* New York: St. Martin's Press, 2000: 255–78.

———. *Japanese Foreign Policy in the Interwar Period.* Westport, CT: Praeger, 2002.

Northrup, David. *Indentured Labor in the Age of Imperialism, 1834–1922.* New York: Cambridge University Press, 1995.

O'Connor, P. S. "Keeping New Zealand White, 1908–1920." *New Zealand Journal of History* 2, no. 1 (1968): 41–65.

Odo, Franklin, ed. *The Columbia Documentary History of the Asian American Experience.* New York: Columbia University Press, 2002.

Osterhammel, Jürgen. *The Transformation of the World: A Global History of the Nineteenth Century.* Translated by Patrick Camiller. Princeton, NJ: Princeton University Press, 2014.

Oyen, Meredith. *The Diplomacy of Migration: Transnational Lives and the Making of U.S.-Chinese Relations in the Cold War.* Ithaca, NY: Cornell University Press, 2015.

Painter, Nell Irvin. *The History of White People.* New York: Norton, 2010.

Pakenham, Thomas. *The Boer War.* London: Abacus, 2004.

Palmer, Mabel. *The History of the Indians in Natal.* Westport, CT: Greenwood Press, 1977.

Parker, Gilbert. "'Australia for the White Man' Again." *Nineteenth Century and After: A Monthly Review* 49, no. 291 (1901).

Pearson, Charles. *National Life and Character: A Forecast.* London: Macmillan, 1893.

Pederson, Susan. *The Guardians: The League of Nations and the Crisis of Empire.* New York: Oxford University Press, 2015.

Perkins, Bradford. *The Great Rapprochement: England and the United States 1895–1914.* New York: Atheneum, 1968.

Price, Charles A. *The Great White Walls Are Built: Restrictive Immigration to North America and Australasia, 1836–1888.* Canberra: Australian National University Press, 1974.

Price, John. *Orienting Canada: Race, Empire, and the Transpacific.* Vancouver: University of British Columbia Press, 2011.

———. " 'Orienting' the Empire: Mackenzie King and the Aftermath of the 1907 Race Riots." *B.C. Studies* 156 (Winter 2007–8): 53–81.

Reckner, James R. *Teddy Roosevelt's Great White Fleet.* Annapolis, MD: Naval Institute Press, 1988.

Reeves, Keir, and Benjamin Mountford. "Sojourning and Settling: Locating Chinese Australian History." *Australian Historical Studies* 42, no. 1 (2011): 111–25.

Reynolds, Susan. "What Do We Mean by 'Anglo-Saxon' and 'Anglo-Saxons'?" *Journal of British Studies* 24, no. 4 (1985): 395–414.

Rich, Paul B. *Race and Empire in British Politics.* Cambridge, UK: Cambridge University Press, 1986.

Richardson, Peter. *Chinese Mine Labour in the Transvaal.* London: MacMillan, 1982.

Riggs, Fred W. *Pressure on Congress: A Study of the Repeal of Chinese Exclusion.* New York: King's Crown Press, 1950.

Ringer, Benjamin B. *"We the People" and Others: Duality and America's Treatment of Its Racial Minorities.* New York: Tavistock, 1983.

Robinson, Greg. "The Debate over Japanese Immigration: The View from France." *Prospects* 30 (2005): 539–80.

Roediger, David R. *The Wages of Whiteness: Race and the Making of the American Working Class.* New York: Verso, 1991.

———. *Working toward Whiteness: How America's Immigrants Became White. The Strange Journey from Ellis Island to the Suburbs.* New York: Basic Books, 2005.

Rosenberg, Emily, ed. *A World Connecting, 1870–1945.* Cambridge, MA: Belknap Press of Harvard University Press, 2012.

Roy, Patricia. *The Oriental Question: Consolidating a White Man's Province, 1914–41.* Vancouver: University of British Columbia Press, 2003.

———. *A White Man's Province: British Columbia Politicians and Chinese and Japanese Immigrations, 1858–1914.* Vancouver: University of British Columbia Press, 1989.

Sacks, Benjamin. *South Africa, an Imperial Dilemma: Non-Europeans and the British Nation, 1902–1914.* Albuquerque: University of New Mexico Press, 1967.

Saxton, Alexander. *The Indispensable Enemy: Labor and the Anti-Chinese Movement in California.* Berkeley: University of California Press, 1995.

———. *The Rise and Fall of the White Republic: Class Politics and Mass Culture in Nineteenth-Century America.* New York: Verso, 1990.

Sedgewick, Augustine. "Against Flows." *History of the Present* 4, no. 2 (2014): 143–70.

Shanks, Cheryl. *Immigration and the Politics of American Sovereignty, 1890–1990.* Ann Arbor: University of Michigan Press, 2001.

Shigeru, Murashima. "The Opening of the Twentieth Century and the Anglo-Japanese Alliance, 1895–1923." In Ian Nish and Yoichi Kibata, eds., *The History of Anglo-Japanese Relations.* Volume 1: *The Political-Diplomatic Dimension, 1600–1930.* New York: St. Martin's Press, 2000: 159–96.

Shimazu, Naoko. *Japan, Race and Equality: The Racial Equality Proposal of 1919.* London: Routledge, 1998.

Siak, Steven W. "'The Blood That Is in Our Veins Comes from German Ancestors': British Historians and the Coming of the First World War." *Albion* 30, no. 2 (1998): 221–52.

Sinn, Elizabeth. "Highway to Gold Mountain, 1850–1900." In "Conversations on Transpacific History." Special issue, *Pacific Historical Review* 83, no. 2 (2014): 220–37.

———. *Pacific Crossing: California Gold, Chinese Migration, and the Making of Hong Kong.* Hong Kong: Hong Kong University Press, 2013.

Smedley, Audrey. *Race in North America: Origin and Evolution of a Worldview.* 2nd ed. Boulder, CO: Westview Press, 1999.

Smith, Iain R. *The Origins of the South African War, 1899–1902.* New York: Longman, 1996.

Sohi, Seema. *Echoes of Mutiny: Race, Surveillance, and Indian Anticolonialism in North America.* New York: Oxford University Press, 2014.

Sorrenson, M. P. K. "Maori and Pakeha." In W. H. Oliver with B. R. Williams, eds., *The Oxford History of New Zealand.* Oxford: Clarendon Press, 1981: 168–93.

Spartalis, Peter. *The Diplomatic Battles of Billy Hughes.* Sydney: Hale and Iremonger, 1983.

Spear, Percival. *The Oxford History of Modern India, 1740–1975.* 2nd ed. Delhi: Oxford University Press, 1978.

Spickard, Paul. *Japanese Americans: The Formation and Transformation of an Ethnic Group.* Rev. ed. New Brunswick, NJ: Rutgers University Press, 2009.

Stalker, Nancy. "Suicide, Boycotts and Embracing Tagore: The Japanese Popular Response to the 1924 U.S. Immigration Exclusion Law." *Japanese Studies* 26, no. 2 (2006): 153–70.

Stanley, Timothy. *Contesting White Supremacy: School Segregation, Anti-Racism, and the Making of Chinese Canadians.* Vancouver: University of British Columbia, 2011.

Stephanson, Anders. *Manifest Destiny: American Expansionism and the Empire of Right.* New York: Hill and Wang, 1995.

Stevens, Christine. *Tin Mosques and Ghantowns: A History of Afghan Cameldrivers in Australia.* Alice Springs, NT: Paul Fitzsimmons, 2002.

Stoddard, Lothrop. *The Rising Tide of Color against White World Supremacy.* New York: Scribner's Sons, 1920.

Takai, Yukari. "Bridging the Pacific: Diplomacy and the Control of Japanese Transmigration via Hawaii, 1890–1910." In Benjamin Bryce and Alexander Freund, eds., *Entangling Migration History: Borderlands and Transnationalism in the United States and Canada.* Gainesville: University Press of Florida, 2015: 141–61.

———. "Navigating Transpacific Passages: Steamship Companies, State Regulators, and Transshipment of Japanese in the Early-Twentieth-Century Pacific Northwest." *Journal of American Ethnic History* 30, no. 3 (2011): 7–34.

Takaki, Ronald. *A Different Mirror: A History of Multicultural America*. Rev. ed. New York: Back Bay Books, 2008.

———. *Strangers from a Different Shore: A History of Asian Americans*. Rev. ed. Boston: Little, Brown, 1998.

Takenaka, Ayumi. "The Japanese in Peru: History of Immigration, Settlement, and Racialization." *Latin American Perspectives* 31, no. 3 (2004): 77–98.

Tamis, Anastasios Myrodis. *The Greeks in Australia*. New York: Cambridge University Press, 2005.

Tate, Merze, and Fidele Foy. "More Light on the Abrogation of the Anglo-Japanese Alliance." *Political Science Quarterly* 74, no. 4 (1959): 532–554.

Tavan, Gwenda. *The Long Slow Death of White Australia*. Melbourne: Scribe Publications, 2005.

Taylor, G. P. "New Zealand, the Anglo-Japanese Alliance and the 1908 Visit of the American Fleet." *Australian Journal of Politics and History* 15, no. 1 (1969): 55–76.

Thompson, J. Lee. *A Wider Patriotism: Alfred Milner and the British Empire*. London: Pickering & Chatto, 2007.

Thompson, Leonard. *A History of South Africa*. New Haven, CT: Yale University Press, 2001.

Tichenor, Daniel J. *Dividing Lines: The Politics of Immigration Control in America*. Princeton, NJ: Princeton University Press, 2002.

Tiwari, Kapil N., ed. *Indians in New Zealand: Studies in a Subculture*. Wellington, NZ: Price Milburn, 1980.

Totman, Conrad. *A History of Japan*. Malden, MA: Blackwell, 2000.

Tozer, Horace. "A White Australia." In "A Plea for a White Australia." *Review of Reviews*, November 1901.

Tsai, Shih-shan Henry. *China and the Overseas Chinese in the United States, 1868–1911*. Fayetteville: University of Arkansas Press, 1983.

Uchida, Jun. *Brokers of Empire: Japanese Settler Colonialism in Korea, 1876–1945*. Cambridge, MA: Harvard University Asia Center, 2014.

Van den Berghe, Pierre L. *South Africa: A Study in Conflict*. Berkeley: University of California Press, 1967.

Veracini, Lorenzo. *Settler Colonialism: A Theoretical Overview*. New York: Palgrave Macmillan, 2010.

Walker, David, and Agnieszka Sobocinska, eds. *Australia's Asia: From Yellow Peril to Asian Century*. Crawley: University of Western Australia, 2012.

Walter, James, and Margaret MacLeod. *The Citizens' Bargain: A Documentary History of Australian Views since 1890*. Sydney: University of New South Wales Press, 2002.

Walton, Peter. *A Centenary Celebration of the Diamond Jubilee of Queen Victoria, 1837–1897*. London: Spellmount, 1997.

Walworth, Arthur. *Wilson and His Peacemakers: American Diplomacy at the Paris Peace Conference, 1919*. New York: Norton, 1986.

Ward, Russel. *A Nation for a Continent: The History of Australia, 1901–1975.* Richmond, Victoria: Heinemann Educational Australia, 1977.

Ward, W. Peter. *White Canada Forever: Popular Attitudes and Public Policy toward Orientals in British Columbia.* Montreal: McGill-Queen's University Press, 1978.

Weiner, Michael. "Discourses of Race, Nation and Empire in Pre-1945 Japan." In Michael Weiner, ed., *Race, Ethnicity, and Migration in Modern Japan.* New York: Routledge Curzon, 2004: 217–39.

Welsh, Frank. *Great Southern Land: A New History of Australia.* London: Penguin Books, 2005.

———. *A History of South Africa.* Rev. ed. London: HarperCollins, 2000.

White, George, Jr. *Holding the Line: Race, Racism, and American Foreign Policy toward Africa, 1953–1961.* Lanham, MD: Rowan & Littlefield, 2005.

Willard, Myra. *History of the White Australia Policy to 1920.* New York: Augustus M. Kelley, 1968.

Williams, John F. "The Geneva Protocol of 1924 for the Pacific Settlement of International Disputes." *Journal of the British Institute for International Affairs* 3, no. 6 (1924): 288–304.

Wilson, Robert A., and Bill Hosokawa. *East to America: A History of the Japanese in the United States.* New York: William Morrow, 1980.

Winder, Robert. *Bloody Foreigners: The Story of Immigration to Britain.* London: Abacus, 2005.

Windschuttle, Keith. *The White Australia Policy.* Sydney: Macleay Press, 2004.

Wray, Matt. *Not Quite White: White Trash and the Boundaries of Whiteness.* Durham, NC: Duke University Press, 2006.

Wu, Ellen D. "'America's Chinese': Anti-Communism, Citizenship, and Cultural Diplomacy during the Cold War." *Pacific Historical Review* 77, no. 3 (2008): 391–422.

———. *The Color of Success: Asian Americans and the Origins of the Model Minority.* Princeton, NJ: Princeton University Press, 2013.

Wu, Ellen D., et al. "Ethnic History and the Cold War, Part II: Refashioning Asian Immigration during the Cold War." *Journal of American Ethnic History* 31, no. 4 (2012): 7–80.

Yap, Melanie, and Dianne Leong Man. *Colour, Confusion and Concessions: The History of the Chinese in South Africa.* Hong Kong: Hong Kong University Press, 1996.

Yarwood, A. T. *Asian Migration to Australia: The Background to Exclusion.* London: Cambridge University Press, 1967.

Yokota, Kariann Akemi. "Transatlantic and Transpacific Connections in Early American History." In "Conversations on Transpacific History." Special issue, *Pacific Historical Review* 83, no. 2 (2014): 204–19.

Young, Elliott. *Alien Nation: Chinese Migration in the Americas from the Coolie Era through World War II.* Chapel Hill: The University of North Carolina Press, 2014.

Yuichi, Inouye. "From Unequal Treaty to the Anglo-Japanese Alliance, 1897–1902." In Ian Nish and Yoichi Kibata, eds., *The History of Anglo-Japanese Relations.* Volume 1: *The Political-Diplomatic Dimension, 1600–1930.* New York: St. Martin's Press, 2000: 131–58.

Zeiler, Thomas et al. "Diplomatic History: A Roundtable on U.S. Foreign Relations History." *Journal of American History* 95, no. 4 (2009): 1053–91.

Zolberg, Aristide R. *A Nation by Design: Immigration Policy in the Fashioning of America.* Cambridge, MA: Harvard University Press, 2006.

Index